How Your Government Really Works

HOW YOUR GOVERNMENT REALLY WORKS

A Topical Encyclopedia of the Federal Government

Glenn L. Starks and F. Erik Brooks

GREENWOOD PRESS

Westport, Connecticut • London

Library of Congress Cataloging-in-Publication Data

Starks, Glenn L., 1966–
   How your government really works : a topical encyclopedia of the federal government /
Glenn L. Starks and F. Erik Brooks.
       p.   cm.
   Includes bibliographical references and index.
   ISBN 978–0–313–34761–0 (alk. paper)
 1. Federal government—United States—Encyclopedias.   I. Brooks, F. Erik.   II. Title.
   JK311.S723 2008
   320.473—dc22   2008024134

British Library Cataloguing in Publication Data is available.

Library of Congress Catalog Card Number: 2008024134
ISBN: 978–0–313–34761–0

First published in 2008

Greenwood Press, 88 Post Road West, Westport, CT 06881
An imprint of Greenwood Publishing Group, Inc.
www.greenwood.com

Printed in the United States of America

The paper used in this book complies with the
Permanent Paper Standard issued by the National
Information Standards Organization (Z39.48–1984).

10 9 8 7 6 5 4 3 2 1

CONTENTS

ALPHABETICAL LIST
OF ENTRIES

PREFACE

The purpose of this book is to provide a concise but clear explanation of how the U.S. federal government operates. This is accomplished by first providing the reader with a historical outline of how the government was founded and why it was structured as it was. The reader is then given an account of the government's contemporary structure, specifically outlining and defining the roles of its three branches. This account includes detailed descriptions of the roles of the president, the Congress, and the Supreme Court, as well as of the many employees of the three branches. Throughout the book, the relationship of the federal government to the state governments is discussed, providing a holistic view of the governing process.

The reader is also provided with detailed descriptions of processes critical to maintaining the U.S. government. These include the presidential and congressional election processes, the appointment process for selecting federal judges, and the process the government employs to establish and maintain the federal budget. Foreign and domestic policy also receive sustained attention: these areas are addressed to explain how the U.S. government maintains its infrastructure while acting as a leading member of the international community. Among the topics discussed in these areas are immigration, equal rights, foreign aid, humanitarian assistance, and treaties.

This book also provides supporting materials to foster the reader's understanding of the aforementioned areas. The book's historical perspective is enhanced by a timeline of events that have shaped the U.S. government in terms of its structure, laws, and policies; the entries presented were carefully chosen to cover areas critical to explaining the various functions and roles of the government. In addition to the timeline the reader may consult a glossary of key definitions critical to understanding government operations, an explanation of how to read government laws and court cases, and numerous other appendixes that supplement the book's chapters with such research resources as an annotated list of helpful Web sites; organizational charts; and the texts of the U.S. Constitution and the Declaration of Independence. Also among the appendixes are lists of presidents; Supreme Court justices; independent government agencies, commissions, boards, and corporations; and U.S. embassies abroad. Charts, figures, graphs, photographs, and tables throughout the book provide visual aids to enhance the information contained in the text.

ACKNOWLEDGMENTS

Dr. Glenn L. Starks wishes to thank his mother, Mrs. Rosa D. Starks, and niece, Ms. Erica S. Starks, for their support during the writing of this book. Their patience and dedication were unwavering. I also wish to thank a group of special friends and colleagues who were equally supportive: Mr. Teddy DuPree, Mrs. Bernadette L. Whitehead, Mrs. Charleen R. Trotter, and Mr. Miguel Zayas. I could never have gained the motivation to complete such an endeavor without the mentorship and guidance of my professional mentors Mrs. Verona McLeod, Mrs. Brenda Longest, and Ms. Claudia Scottie Knott, and my academic mentors at the L. Douglas Wilder School of Public Policy at Virginia Commonwealth University. These include Dr. Robert S. Holsworth and Dr. Blue Wooldridge.

F. Erik Brooks wishes to thank Mr. Frank Brooks Jr., Mrs. Theresa Brooks, and the rest of his family for their support. I also thank Dr. Tara Johnson and Ms. Savannah Brooks. I thank my colleagues at Auburn University Montgomery, in particular Dr. Tom Vocino and Dr. Brad Moody. I also thank my friends and colleagues at the Public Policy Center and the L. Douglas Wilder School of Public Policy at Virginia Commonwealth University, in particular the late Dr. Amin Alimard, Dr. Blue Wooldridge, Dr. Michael Pratt, Dr. Melvin Urofsky, Dr. Robert Holsworth, and Mrs. Betty Moran. Lastly, I thank my friends and colleagues at Georgia Southern University, Dr. Nicholas Henry, Dr. Richard Pacelle, Dr. Saba Jallow, Dr. Ted Brimeyer, Mrs. Mandy Brimeyer, Mrs. Jo Hoch, and Ms. Juanita Grant.

Both authors would like to give a special thanks to Mr. Michael P. Austin of St. Louis, Michigan. Mr. Austin provided tremendous personal and professional assistance to the authors in writing this book. His dedication and hard work were invaluable to the authors, as were his professional insights and academic assistance. This book is dedicated to his exemplary commitment to advancement of the field of public administration.

INTRODUCTION

The United States government is the largest, most complex, and most dynamic organization in the world. Its basic structure has remained the same since it was founded, with three branches of government that operate a democratic, Constitution-based federal republic. In short, it is a system of government under which the people choose their representatives. The duties of these representatives are granted by the Constitution, and the representatives make decisions on issues of national interest and importance to ensure that the basic needs of the people of the United States are met. These interests today predominantly fall into the categories of agriculture, commerce, defense, education, energy, health and human services, homeland security, housing and urban development, the interior, justice, labor, state, transportation, treasury, and veterans affairs. These are the areas around which the president's cabinet-level departments are organized.

As the population of the United States has grown, so has the size of the government. In 2007 federal agencies employed almost three million workers. These numbers do not take into account the thousands of contractors working for government agencies or the members of the armed services. These workers reported to hundreds (if not thousands) of agencies, boards, commissions, and committees. All of these agencies and other entities serve the needs of America's three hundred million citizens, along with the 50 state governments, 6 territorial governments, and thousands of local governments. The federal government also works closely with hundreds of allied nations in the interest of democracy and in support of issues that have an impact on the nation. To accomplish all of this, the reach of the government has expanded around the world and into outer space.

As the government has grown in size, it has also grown in complexity. Labyrinthine regulations and an accretion of customs determine how laws are passed, offices are filled, and money is raised and spent. An intricate system of checks and balances exists to ensure each federal branch adheres to its constitutionally defined missions. For example, some citizens believe the president of the United States runs the entire government. In actuality, that office is only the head of the executive branch. Congress heads the legislative branch, and the Supreme Court heads the judicial branch. Each branch has distinct responsibilities, but they all must work in concert for the government to effectively operate.

The government is also dynamic. The government must adapt to changes in the demographics of its citizens. It must also adapt to changes in technology and the environment, and to changes that occur in other parts of the world. Each year new laws are passed due to these changes, and old laws are revised. Agencies change their missions and adapt their personnel levels and budgets accordingly.

As citizens, we need to understand how our government operates. The government can only serve our needs if we take the proper steps to ensure we are actively engaged in the governmental process. These steps include voting and communicating with our representatives. The task of being an informed and responsible citizen, however, is very difficult because of the size, complexity, and dynamics of our government. Thus, this book unravels the complexities of the federal government and provides a clear understanding of how it operates.

What factors actually drive the passage of laws? How can a president be elected even if he or she does not receive the most votes from citizens? How can the United States be the richest nation in the world and still have such a tremendous national deficit? Why does the government sometimes establish policies that the majority of the populace opposes? These questions, asked by citizens, students, and even researchers, are difficult to answer—and they are just some of the questions that are answered in this book.

A historical framework is provided as a point of reference to foster an understanding of how our government has evolved. The remainder of the book focuses on the inner workings of the government, including such subjects as elections, appointments, legislation, foreign policy, domestic policy, and the national budget, in order to provide a clear explanation of government systems and processes. The goal of this book is to help the reader to become a better citizen by becoming a better student of the government.

1

HOW THE UNITED STATES GOVERNMENT BEGAN

The founding of the United States occurred after many attempts to establish a permanent settlement in the New World and then turbulent years of conflict with Great Britain. The eventual independence of the original thirteen colonies was immediately preceded by years of war after all other attempts for solidarity were unsuccessful. Once the war ended, the founding fathers faced the daunting task of crafting a governing document to both establish a national government structure and legally ensure each citizen the right to life, liberty, and the individual pursuit of happiness. This was accomplished within the lines of the Constitution, which remains the supreme law of the United States.

FOUNDING OF A NEW NATION

Settlers in a New World.   Several unsuccessful endeavors to establish colonies in North America occurred before the founding of Jamestown in 1607. The first attempt by the British was at Roanoke Island by Sir Walter Raleigh in the late sixteenth century. In 1587 the first attempt at a colonizing expedition, consisting entirely of men, returned to England, even as a second group of some 100 men, women, and children, arrived to settle on the island (in what is now part of North Carolina). By 1590 they had mysteriously disappeared. The Roanoke settlement became known as the Lost Colony.

Settlers came to North America in 1607 to establish a new English settlement in what is present-day Virginia, settling in what they named Jamestown. The river along the encampment was named the James River. Later, many came to seek the new opportunities offered by a new land, including financial riches. Others came to escape intolerance and persecution in Britain. For example, the Puritans (called Pilgrims since they were pilgrims, or journeymen, to the new land) arrived in Massachusetts in 1620 on the Mayflower after facing religious persecution and exile in Europe. The Mayflower Compact was established before they set foot on land. The document would serve as the constitution for the Plymouth Colony for many years.

By the mid 1700s, there were thirteen flourishing colonies in the "new world" (see Table 1.1). The colonies were mostly free to run their own affairs, and began developing systems of democracy based on the will of the people. Local representatives were

Embarkation of the Pilgrims (1844, Rotunda of the U.S. Capitol), by Robert W. Weir. The painting depicts Protestant pilgrims on the deck of the *Speedwell* before their departure in July 1620 from Delft Haven, Holland, for the New World. Weir (1803–1890) taught art at the U.S. Military Academy at West Point, New York. *Photograph by the Architect of the Capitol. Reprinted by permission.*

elected, local governments passed laws, and the colonies developed governing documents. But there were two major problems. First, the colonies operated as separate entities. They argued over religious issues, had trade disputes, and there were several forms of currency. The colonies even had separate governing documents. These included The Fundamental Orders of Connecticut and the Massachusetts Body of

Table 1.1.   The First Thirteen Colonies, Year Established, and Year of Statehood

Colony	Year established	Year of statehood
Virginia	1607	1788
New Jersey	1618	1787
Massachusetts	1620	1788
New Hampshire	1622	1788
Pennsylvania	1623	1787
New York	1624	1788
Maryland	1634	1788
Connecticut	1635	1788
Rhode Island	1636	1790
Delaware	1638	1787
North Carolina	1653	1789
South Carolina	1670	1788
Georgia	1733	1788

Liberties. Second, and most important, the colonies were still under the rule of Britain. The British government began exercising more control over its colonies through excessive taxation and oppressive legislation during the second half of the eighteenth century.

In addition to being oppressive, Britain passed legislation ruling the colonies without allowing them representation in the British parliament. The colonies boycotted British goods on the basis of this "taxation without representation." Tensions led to military occupation by British soldiers and greater acts of rebellion by the colonists. One of the most famous acts of rebellion occurred in 1773 when the Sons of Liberty dumped over three hundred chests of tea from British ships into Boston Harbor. Britain responded with a series of laws the colonists called the Intolerable Acts. These included closing the harbor and taking control of the local government in response to what became known as the Boston Tea Party. These and other events eventually led to the Revolutionary War in 1775.

First and Second Continental Congresses.   The colonies convened the First Continental Congress at Carpenter's Hall in Philadelphia from September 5 until October 26 in 1774. With delegates from each colony (except Georgia), the purpose was to speak with one voice against Britain's taxation and oppression. This was a secret meeting in which the colonists sought autonomy from Great Britain to run their own affairs, rather than complete independence as a separate nation. The Second Continental Congress was held in 1775 and evolved into the nation's central government. Under this new governing body, the Declaration of Independence was adopted on July 4, 1776 (see the complete Declaration of Independence in Appendix E). The purpose of the document was just as its name suggests: It declared that the colonies were free from British rule and that all of its citizens were guaranteed equal rights by virtue that all men are created equal. Thomas Jefferson drafted the document, but approximately twenty-five percent of his original text was deleted in congressional review and debate. For example, Thomas Jefferson's original draft included a condemnation of the slave trade, but the clause was removed. Slaves made up twenty percent of the total colonies' population by the time the Revolutionary War began. Most who argued for slavery's continued existence did so on economic grounds. The southern states were the primary proponents. Most of those opposed to slavery believed it to be immoral. The Quakers, for example, founded the first antislavery society in 1775 because they believed it to be against their religious doctrines. The delegates of the Second Continental Congress reached a compromise to table the slavery debate until 1808. Most believed slavery would end by then. In 1787, Congress barred slavery in any of the new western states.

The Articles of Confederation were introduced on July 6, 1775, but not approved by the Congress until November 15, 1777. This document formally established the United States of America, a legislative branch in which each state would have representation, and also provided each state with sovereignty over its own individual affairs. The Articles were not ratified until March 1, 1781, but even after ratification, the document was never effective. The states argued over such issues as boundaries, western territory ownership, trade, slavery, and the form of currency.

The Articles of Confederation were also ineffective because the states retained their individual powers, sometimes treating each other as foreign nations, especially regarding trade. All legislation required a unanimous vote, so any one state could halt a new national law. The new Congress of the Confederation did not even have the power to tax to raise steady revenue, and could not establish a national army.

Surrender of Lord Cornwallis (1820, Rotunda of the U.S. Capitol), by John Trumbull. Trumbull (1756–1843) positions General Benjamin Lincoln at the center, with General George Washington mounted at the right rear. British General Charles Cornwallis is not shown. Like Trumbull's other Revolutionary War paintings displayed in the Capitol Rotunda, this painting is Trumbull's own enlargement of his 20″ × 30″ original painting to the 12′ × 18′ dimensions required by its Rotunda setting. *Photograph by the Architect of the Capitol. Reprinted by permission.*

The British surrendered on October 19, 1781, after George Washington defeated British General Charles Cornwallis at Yorktown, Virginia. The formal treaty to end the war, the Treaty of Paris, was signed in 1783. The settlers emerged from the war victorious, but then faced the daunting task of structuring a government based on the liberties they had fought so hard to obtain.

ROAD TO THE CONSTITUTION

The Constitutional Convention.   State representatives met in Philadelphia from May through September in 1787 for a Constitutional Convention to revise the Articles of Confederation. The delegates were among the most prominent leaders of the time and included the most educated colonists, with nearly half being college educated and wealthy. Collectively known today as the Founding Fathers, these delegates included Robert Morris, Benjamin Franklin, George Mason, James Madison, and Alexander Hamilton. Two notable leaders who were absent were Thomas Jefferson and John Adams, who were serving as ambassadors at the time of the convention.

Many disagreements existed among the delegates, particularly by those from smaller states, who feared any plan where national representation would be based on population because the larger states would have more control. Another area of concern was what powers were to be given to the national government. Because the colonies did not want to return to a monarchial government, there was fear by many that too much power was being given to the president and to the central government in the Articles of Confederation. Rhode Island did not send delegates to the convention because its representatives opposed the establishment of a strong national government.

Prior to attending the convention, James Madison reviewed European political theory and on the first day of the convention he and his delegation began crafting fifteen resolutions that became a blueprint for the Virginia Plan. The Virginia Plan proposed an entirely new national government comprised of a bicameral legislature. The lower house would be chosen by the people and the smaller upper house by elected members of the lower house. The number of representatives would be in proportion to each state's population. The larger states would thus have more representatives. The proposal also called for a national executive branch that would be elected by the legislature, and a court system created by the legislature.

In rebuttal, the smaller states offered various alternative plans. William Paterson offered the New Jersey Plan, which would give each state equal power under the Articles of Confederation. Under this plan, the acts of Congress would be the supreme law of the land, each state would have one congressional vote, and Congress would regulate trade and impose taxes. There would be an executive office with several people serving in a committee rather than just a single individual running the branch. This executive office would appoint a national supreme court. The Connecticut Plan, also known as the Great Compromise, was presented by Roger Sherman and called for a legislature with two houses. According to this plan, the lower house, the House of Representatives, would be comprised of members from each state chosen by the votes of its citizens. The number of people in each state would determine their number of representatives in the legislature. The upper house, the Senate, would have two members from each state elected by the state legislatures. This plan offered compromises to each side of the debate. The larger states would have more representatives in the House of Representatives while each state would have an equal number of representatives in the Senate.

A second compromise dealt with the issue of slavery and how many representatives each state would have in the House of Representatives based on its population of slaves. Forty percent of the slaves lived in the South. Basing the number of representatives on this population would have given the southern states a population advantage in the number of representatives sent to the House of Representatives. The delegates from the South thus wanted slaves to be counted as people but the northern delegations disagreed. After much debate, it was decided that a slave would be counted as three-fifths of a person in determining Congressional representation. This became known as the Three-Fifths Compromise. It was eventually overturned in 1868 by the passage of the Fourteenth Amendment, which provides each state with Congressional representation based on its total number of people (i.e., not a fraction of a person).

The Final Constitution.   The result of the Constitutional Convention was a completely new document, mostly based on a compromise between the delegates. The new document was written by Roger Sherman of Connecticut and named the Constitution of the United States.

The British Magna Carta was used as one of the primary founding documents of the Constitution. Adopted in 1215 under King John, the Magna Carta granted civil rights to noblemen and ordinary citizens, while placing the rule of the monarchy under law. It originated from those English barons who did not join Britain's campaign against the French and who seized London, subsequently forcing the King to listen to their concerns. The King had attempted to levy fees on the barons for not joining his military forces. They demanded that their traditional rights be documented, confirmed with the royal seal, and issued to all the counties. The document was never executed because it was believed the King approved it under duress.

Federalists supported the Constitution's strong central government with shared state powers. Led by Alexander Hamilton, James Madison, and John Jay, they published *The Federalist Papers* outlining their support for the Constitution. They believed the checks and balances among the three branches would maintain a balanced central government. Antifederalists supported strong state governments and a weaker central government. Their members included John Hancock, George Mason, Patrick Henry, and James Monroe. They did not support the Constitution as written because it did not contain a bill of rights outlining the basic freedoms of all citizens. They also published writings outlining their points of opposition. It took several years for each state to individually ratify the Constitution due to the differences in opinion over how the national government should be structured. Special conventions were held in each state by the document's framers to explain it in detail. The Constitution was officially ratified on June 21, 1788, when New Hampshire became the ninth state out of the original thirteen colonies to approve it. Rhode Island was the last to ratify it in May 1790.

The basic foundation of the new government was one based on democracy, where people choose those who represent their interests. Note that the Constitution begins with the words "We the People," which stipulates the people both establish and control the government. Any actions taken by the government are done so under the consent of its citizens. The words contained in the preamble outline the Constitution's basic purpose:

> We the People of the United States, in Order to form a more perfect Union, establish Justice, insure domestic Tranquility, provide for the common defence, promote the general Welfare, and secure the Blessings of Liberty to ourselves and our Posterity, do ordain and establish this Constitution for the United States of America.

The basic tenets of the Constitution are that all U.S. citizens have an inherent right to basic freedoms, namely, life, liberty, and the pursuit of happiness. Citizens control the government by selecting the representatives that speak for them, in essence, delegating their voices to their representatives. The government's purpose is to represent the people, protect their right to liberty and justice, and provide for their defense. If citizens feel their needs are not being met, they can make changes to the government through voting and communicating their needs to their representatives.

The new Constitution established three branches of government versus just the legislative branch that existed before the Constitution was written. Congress was reestablished as the Congress of the United States with an upper chamber composed of two senators from each state and a lower chamber with the number of state representatives determined by the population of each state. The office of the president was established as the chief executive in the executive branch. The president was to be elected by an electoral college whose members would be selected by each state's legislature. It was decided that the general public was not educated or informed enough to choose the holder of such an important office. The judicial branch was formed with a Supreme Court of judges nominated by the president and ratified by the Senate for lifelong terms, and lower courts.

The government was established under the concept of federalism (i.e., a federal republic). *Federalism* is the principle that the national government shares sovereign power with the state governments. Establishing the government according to this principle was a compromise that solved the debate over sovereignty and whether more power should be under the national or state governments. Both federal and state governments hold concurrent powers under federalism. Examples of concurrent powers include the power to levy and collect taxes, charter banks, establish courts, borrow money, and to make and enforce laws. Other countries today using a form of federalism include Argentina, Australia, Brazil, Canada, Germany, Mexico, and Switzerland.

The Constitution gave the federal government powers that it did not have under the Articles of Confederation. For example, the Constitution declares that all laws created by the federal government take precedence over conflicting state laws (per Article VI, known as the Supremacy Clause). The federal government also has the power to collect taxes, coin money, and regulate commerce (per Article I, Section 8, of the Constitution, known as the Commerce Clause). James Madison devised the model of government in which the powers of the government are separated into three branches of government, which is the principle of separations of powers outlined in Articles I, II, and III of the Constitution. The separation of powers principle specifically divides the government into three sectors or branches: the executive, the judicial, and legislative.

The government was established with a system of checks and balances to balance the actions of each branch and ensure each does not exert control not granted to it under the Constitution, but most important to ensure that the president does not dominate the government. In basic terms, the legislative branch makes the laws, the executive branch executes the established laws, and the judicial branch ensures the laws are being written and executed according to the Constitution. The executive branch (led by the president) can recommend laws, veto laws passed by Congress, nominate Supreme Court judges, and make treaties with foreign nations. The legislative branch (led by the two houses of Congress) passes laws, can amend the Constitution, confirms federal judges nominated by the president, approves foreign treaties set forth by the president, and can impeach the president and judges. Congress controls the types of cases the federal courts can hear, and approves the budget of the judicial and executive branches. The judicial branch (led by the Supreme Court) hears court cases on executive and legislative issues. However, the judicial branch relies on the other two branches to enforce court decisions.

The Constitution grants three specific types of powers to the federal government while prohibiting it from exercising other powers: expressed powers, implied powers, and inherent powers. Expressed powers are those that are provided by the Constitution or congressional laws. Article I, Section 8, enumerates the twenty-seven powers that Congress may exercise. A notable expressed power is Congress' ability to coin money and to regulate interstate commerce. An example of an expressed power that was created through a congressional amendment is the ability of Congress to impose an income tax, which was added in 1913 (the Sixteenth Amendment). Article II, Section 2 gives the president the power to make treaties and appoint certain federal office holders. Implied powers, are those powers of the federal government that are implied by the expressed powers in the Constitution. The implied powers are granted in Article I, Section 8, Clause 18, also called the Necessary and Proper Clause. The clause

The Declaration of Independence (1819; Rotunda of the U.S. Capitol), by John Trumbull. John Adams, Roger Sherman, Robert Livingston, Thomas Jefferson, and Benjamin Franklin are shown presenting the document to John Hancock, president of the Second Continental Congress. Adopted in final form at Independence Hall in Philadelphia on July 4, 1776, the Declaration was not actually committed to parchment and signed until August; Trumbull's painting memorializes the actors rather than depicts a historical event. Over a period of years, Trumbull captured the likenesses of thirty-seven of the figures from life, for a 20″ × 30″ painting first sketched in 1786. When the Capitol (burned by the British in August 1814) was rebuilt, Trumbull was commissioned to enlarge his small original for display in the Rotunda. *Photograph by the Architect of the Capitol. Reprinted by permission.*

specifically states that Congress has the power to make "all Laws which shall be necessary and proper for carrying into Execution the foregoing Powers, and all Powers vested by this Constitution in the Government of the United States, or in any Department or Officer thereof." Inherent powers, the third type of powers, are those created to ensure the nation's integrity and survival as a political entity. These include, for example, the powers to make treaties and wage war. These powers are not expressly granted by the Constitution.

CONSTITUTIONAL ARTICLES AND AMENDMENTS

The original Constitution contained seven articles. The articles consist of sections and clauses that discuss the operation of three branches of government, and the relationship of the federal government to the state governments. Ten amendments (out of the original twelve that were introduced) were added in 1791. These amendments, called the Bill of Rights, outline the civil rights and liberties of citizens. They guarantee such rights as freedom of speech, assembly, and religion. Citizens are protected against infringement of these rights and liberties by the government and other citizens. The spirit of the Bill of Rights was first expressed in the Pennsylvania Frame of Government in 1682 and the Pennsylvania Charter of Privileges in 1701.

As the needs of citizens have changed over the centuries, other amendments have been added to the Constitution by Congress. Constitutional amendments are never altered once ratified. Rather, additional amendments are added as changes are needed that nullify the amendments they are meant to replace. The Constitution is thus a "living document." For example, the Eighteenth Amendment prohibited the manufacture and distribution of alcohol. When alcohol became legal again, the Eighteenth Amendment was not altered, but rather repealed by the Twenty-first Amendment.

There are two methods of proposing an amendment to the Constitution. The first is a two-thirds vote in both the Senate and House of Representatives. The second method is when two-thirds of the state legislatures request that Congress call a national amendment convention to vote on a proposed amendment. This second method has been used only once, which was to ratify the Twenty-first Amendment (that ended prohibition). Since the Constitution was authored, there have been over eleven thousand amendments proposed in Congress. Some of the most notable proposals have been to abolish the Electoral College, a prohibition against the burning of the U.S. flag, a proposal to establish English as the nation's official language, and a proposal to set term limits for members of Congress. A total of only twenty-seven amendments have actually been approved. The last, the Twenty-seventh Amendment, was passed in 1992 to prohibit changes to the salaries of members of Congress until after an election. The Constitution remains the oldest written constitution in the world still in use. The following sections briefly discuss each article and amendment (see the complete United States Constitution in Appendix F).

The Seven Articles of the Constitution.

- Article I (the longest article in the Constitution) gives legislative powers to Congress (head of the legislative branch) and establishes its two houses or chambers, the Senate and House of Representatives. It outlines the requirements for citizens to hold congressional offices. The powers of Congress are outlined, including the power to regulate interstate commerce and foreign trade, collect taxes to fund the government's operation, create a military, declare war, create lower courts in the judicial branch (i.e., beneath the Supreme Court), create currency, and impeach members of the executive and judicial branches (including the president and Supreme Court justices). Most importantly, Congress is granted the authority to make "necessary and proper" laws required to execute the powers outlined in Article I. Actions Congress cannot take are also outlined, including granting titles of nobility and passing laws that inflict punishment without a trial.

- Article II gives executive powers to the president of the United States (head of the executive branch), and describes the qualifications, selection process, oath of office, and duties of this office. Those eligible to run for president must be a natural born United States citizen, at least thirty-five years old, and a resident of the United States for at least fourteen years. The president is designated as commander-in-chief of the armed forces, and is given the power to grant reprieves and pardons for federal offenses, make treaties with foreign countries, receive foreign ambassadors, appoint Supreme Court judges and ambassadors, and make temporary appointments when the Senate is not in session. The president can also call special congressional sessions, and is required to provide Congress information on the State of the Union. The vice president is established as the president's successor in case of involuntary or voluntary removal. The president and vice president can both be impeached for treason, bribery, or other high crimes and misdemeanors. The article establishes the Electoral College, which consists of members or "electors" from each state equal to their number of congressional representatives in both chambers of Congress. In a presidential election, the general public does not vote directly for presidential candidates. They vote for electors from the political party of their presidential choice in their state, who in turn vote for the president and vice president.

- Article III gives judicial powers to the Supreme Court and lower federal courts (the judicial branch). Lower courts can only be established by Congress. As the highest court in the nation, the Supreme Court hears cases on legislative and executive issues and can overturn cases decided in lower courts. These cases include disputes between the United States and an opposing party, a state and the federal government, or a dispute between two states. The judges of the Supreme Court (called justices) serve for life terms so they cannot be subjected to the political pressures that arise when politicians run for or hold offices, particularly political compromising when deciding court cases. Additionally, the article explicitly defines the crime of treason as waging war against the United States or "giving aid and comfort" to enemies of the United States. Congress decides the punishment for treason.

- Article IV outlines the relationship between the federal and state governments, and the relationship of the state governments to one another. Under the federalist system, both the state and federal governments have the ability to make laws through a sharing of authority. However, no state laws can contradict a federal law. Under the Full Faith and Credit Clause, the states are required to abide by public acts, records, and rulings in judicial proceedings of other states. States are forbidden from discriminating against citizens of other states in favor of their residents, and must return (i.e., extradite) criminals back to the state where a crime was committed. New states may be created by Congress, and the federal government must protect the states from invasion, as well as from foreign and domestic violence.

- Article V requires a two-thirds vote by each house of Congress or two-thirds approval by the states in an application to Congress to hold a national convention to amend the Constitution. Under the first approach, an amendment must then be ratified by three-fourths of all state legislatures for it to be adopted. The article also guarantees each state equal representation in the Senate.

- Article VI (known as the Supremacy Clause) establishes the Constitution and associated laws and treaties as the supreme law of the land, to be upheld by all legislative, executive and judicial officers. These federal documents take precedence over those established by the states. It also forbids religious tests from being used as a qualification to hold a federal or state office or public trust.

- Article VII establishes requirements to ratify the Constitution. When developed, there were thirteen states. At least nine had to approve the Constitution.

Constitutional Amendments.

Amendments 1–10: The Bill of Rights

- First Amendment guarantees citizens the freedoms of speech, the press, peaceful assembly, and the right to petition the government for grievances (i.e., make complaints to government officials or request legislative changes). It forbids the government from prohibiting the free exercise of religion (called the Free Exercise Clause) and from establishing religions (called the Establishment Clause).

- Second Amendment provides for the right of individuals to keep and bear arms, that is, own weapons. It declares a well-regulated militia is necessary to maintain a free state.

- Third Amendment prohibits the government from seizing private homes to house, or "quarter," soldiers without the consent of homeowners.
- Fourth Amendment protects individuals from unreasonable search and seizure, and from arrest warrants being issued without probable cause. Law enforcement and military officers must take an oath to affirm the reason a warrant is needed, and the place to be searched and persons or things to be seized must be described.
- Fifth Amendment provides individuals the right to a grand jury when being tried for major crimes. Individuals are protected from being tried for the same crime twice (called *double jeopardy*), deprived or punished without due process of law, and from having to testify against themselves. The government may also not seize private property without paying the owner just compensation.
- Sixth Amendment guarantees a speedy public trial for individuals convicted of a crime before an impartial jury in the state or district where the crime was committed. Persons accused must be made aware of what and why they are being accused. They then have the right to be represented by legal counsel and to have accusing and supporting witnesses present during the trial.
- Seventh Amendment provides individuals the right to a trial by jury in civil cases involving more than twenty dollars. (Twenty dollars was a large amount of money at the time of the writing of the Constitution.)
- Eighth Amendment prohibits individuals from being charged excessive bails or fines for crimes, and from cruel and unusual punishments if accused or convicted.
- Ninth Amendment stipulates that the individual rights specifically stated in the Constitution are not meant to deny those held by the people. (For example, the Constitution does not specifically grant a right to privacy, but it is an implicit right of each citizen.)
- Tenth Amendment stipulates that those powers not delegated to the federal government in the Constitution and not forbidden to the states are reserved by the states or the people.

Amendments Ratified After the Bill of Rights (with year ratified)

- Eleventh Amendment (1795) limits the ability of citizens to sue states.
- Twelfth Amendment (1804) allows members of the Electoral College to cast separate ballots for the president and vice president.
- Thirteenth Amendment (1865) abolishes slavery and gives former slaves the same rights as other citizens.
- Fourteenth Amendment (1868) stipulates that all persons born or naturalized in the United States are citizens of the United States and the state in which they reside. The states cannot pass laws that infringe on the rights of citizens or deprive citizens of their rights without due process. Provides each state with congressional representation based on the number of each resident male at least twenty-one years of age (essentially invalidating earlier practices of counting slaves as three-fifths of a person).
- Fifteenth Amendment (1870) prohibits the use of a citizen's race, color, or previous status as a slave as a qualification to vote.
- Sixteenth Amendment (1913) provides for a federal income tax.
- Seventeenth Amendment (1913) establishes direct elections of senators by the people rather than by votes cast by state legislatures.
- Eighteenth Amendment (1919) prohibits the production, distribution, and transportation of alcohol. (Repealed by the Twenty-first Amendment.)

- Nineteenth Amendment (1920) prohibits the use of a citizen's sex as a qualification to vote, that is, gives women the right to vote.
- Twentieth Amendment (1933) ends the incumbent president's term of office at noon on January 20th following a presidential election, and ends the term for an incumbent congressman at noon on January 3rd following a congressional election. Also establishes a line of presidential succession if the president dies before being sworn into office.
- Twenty-first Amendment (1933) repeals the Eighteenth Amendment, making alcohol legal again. However, the states can pass individual laws to regulate the manufacture, distribution, and transportation of alcohol within their borders.
- Twenty-second Amendment (1951) limits the president to two elected terms in office.
- Twenty-third Amendment (1961) gives the District of Columbia presidential electors in the Electoral College.
- Twenty-fourth Amendment (1964) prohibits the use of a voting tax (i.e., poll tax) as a qualification to vote.
- Twenty-fifth Amendment (1967) updates the line of presidential succession, steps to remove the president, and steps to replace the vice president.
- Twenty-sixth Amendment (1971) grants the right to vote to any U.S. citizen at least eighteen years of age.
- Twenty-seventh Amendment (1992) limits congressional pay raises.

THE FIRST PRESIDENT OF THE UNITED STATES

George Washington was not only the first president of the United States, but one of the most dedicated and influential politicians in the nation's history. He was elected commander-in-chief of the Continental Army when the Continental Congress met in Philadelphia in 1775. When state representatives met in Philadelphia in 1787 for the Constitutional Convention, Washington was chosen to chair the convention. After the Constitution was ratified, Washington was unanimously elected as president by the Electoral College and served from 1789 until 1797. John Adams was selected as vice president because he received the second highest number of Electoral College votes, and later became the nation's second president in 1797.

On April 30, 1789, Washington took the oath of office on the balcony of Federal Hall on Wall Street in New York City (the capital of the United States at the time). The formal ceremony used during his swearing in as president has been used by all later presidents, and included many of the traditions still observed today, such as placing his left hand on the Bible when being sworn in, saying "So help me God" at the end of the oath, and attending an inaugural ball. Washington moved the seat of government from New York to Philadelphia in 1790. In 1800 the capitol was moved to Washington, DC.

Washington's first major action in office was working with Congress and the states to have the Bill of Rights added to the Constitution, a task that was completed in 1791 by ratification of three-fourths of the states. This was a difficult undertaking given the political divisions that existed within the young government. Washington's secretary of the treasury (Alexander Hamilton) and secretary of state (Thomas Jefferson) were great rivals, leading to the establishment of the nation's first political parties. Hamilton and his supporters called themselves Federalists. They supported a stronger central government over the states, the government's protection of industry, high tariffs on imports, and strong trade ties with Great Britain, in opposition to France. Jefferson and his supporters were antifederalists and called themselves the Democratic-Republicans. They favored a smaller central government with more powers going to the states and thus the people; specifically, they favored low tariffs to keep prices of foreign goods low, and supported France over Great Britain. Washington's views were more in line with the Federalists but refused to officially align himself with either party.

Washington ran unopposed during his reelection campaign in 1792. He wanted to retire to his home in Mount Vernon, but knew his reputation was needed to keep the government progressing. He made several bold moves that solidified the power of the federal government. First, he took a neutral stance on the war between Great Britain and France that erupted in 1793, keeping the United States out of the war. There were many who wanted the United States to support Britain because they still considered it the homeland. In opposition to them were supporters of France, because the French had supported the United States during the Revolutionary War. Washington maintained his stance of neutrality and successfully kept the United States out of the conflict. He also commanded the military forces that ended the Whiskey Rebellion, led by whiskey distillers in Pennsylvania who were upset over a 1794 tax on liquor.

During his farewell address, Washington warned the nation against the factions being created by political parties and against forming alliances with foreign nations. He felt both would serve to separate the nation. His first warning was not heeded. The second president of the United States, John Adams, was a Federalist. His vice president, Thomas Jefferson, was a Democratic-Republican. Their two political parties were the impetus for the political divisions within the U.S. political system today that are based on the party affiliation of elected officials. The nation did, however, heed his second warning until the presidency of Theodore Roosevelt, when the federal government began expanding its foreign policy. After retiring, Washington agreed to command the military when President Adams feared a conflict with France. The conflict never occurred. Before he died, Washington freed almost half of his slaves in his will.

2

STRUCTURE OF THE UNITED STATES GOVERNMENT TODAY

The contemporary structure of the U.S. government consists of the three branches established under the Constitution: the executive, legislative and judicial. However, the government has grown so large that the branches have expanded to consist of departments, agencies, offices, boards, and commissions that execute the various missions and functions of each branch. The system of checks and balances originally established under the Constitution is still in place to ensure the branches do not violate their constitutionally defined separation of powers. Due to the government's size and complexity, checks and balances are also in place within the branches to regulate their individual components. A graphical representation of the government's structure is shown in Figure 2.1.

The executive branch, headed by the president, is the largest of the three branches in terms of number of employees and number of agencies. It includes the vice president, executive office of the president, the president's cabinet, executive branch departments, independent agencies, government corporations, government sponsored enterprises, and many boards, commissions, and committees. Its primary function is to execute laws.

The legislative branch is led by the two houses or chambers of Congress, and is thus called a bicameral legislature. The House of Representatives is the lower house and the Senate is the upper house. The legislative branch also consists of various offices that support Congress, and independent agencies. Congress also establishes regulatory agencies that exist outside of the three branches to execute specific laws and oversee specific sectors of the government, industry, or U.S. population. The primary functions of Congress are passing laws, approving budgets and authorizing funding for agencies, and conducting hearings and investigations. While Congress provides checks and balances to the executive and judicial branches, it has an internal system of checks and balances between the two chambers. Laws introduced and approved in one chamber must also be reviewed and approved in the other.

Article III of the Constitution established the judicial branch. The Judiciary Act of 1789 established the federal judicial system as a three-tier hierarchical system. At the lowest level are district courts. At the second level are appellate courts that hear

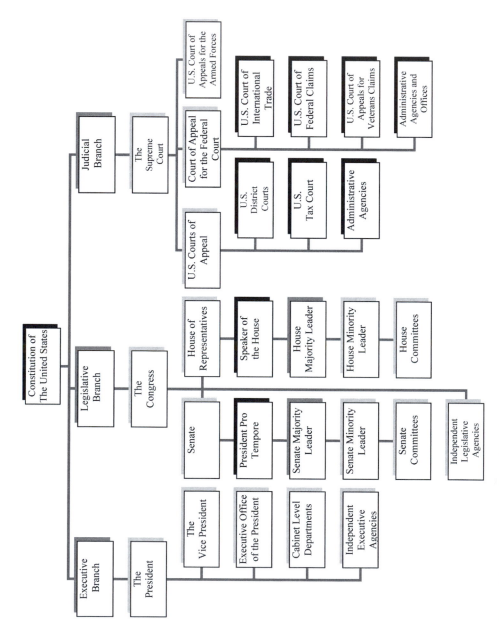

Figure 2.1. Organization of the U.S. federal government.

appeals from district courts and administrative agencies. At the highest level is the U.S. Supreme Court.

THE EXECUTIVE BRANCH

The President of the United States.   The requirements to become president of the United States are delineated in Article II, Section 1 of the Constitution. It specifically states:

> No person except a natural born Citizen, or a Citizen of the United States, at the time of the Adoption of this Constitution, shall be eligible to the Office of the President; neither shall any Person be eligible to that office who shall not have attained the Age of thirty-five Years, and been fourteen Years a Resident within the United States.

Most presidents have had backgrounds in the legal profession, but there have been exceptions. President Ronald W. Reagan was an actor, President Jimmy Carter was a peanut farmer, and President Harry S. Truman was a men's clothing salesman. To date, twenty-six presidents were lawyers, and most were wealthy. President John F. Kennedy was the youngest president elected to office at forty-three in 1961. President Ronald W. Reagan was the oldest elected at sixty-nine in 1981.

The framers of the Constitution grappled over the issue of how much power and authority should be granted to the president. They did not want to give too much power to the position for fear of creating a powerful king. However, they wanted the president to have the necessary powers required to successfully lead the nation. They outlined the specific powers of the president in Sections 2 and 3 of Article II:

- To serve as commander-in-chief of the armed forces and the state militias
- To appoint, with the Senate's consent, the heads of executive departments, ambassadors, justices of the Supreme Court, and other top federal officials
- To grant reprieves and pardons
- To make treaties with the advice and consent of Congress
- To deliver the annual State of the Union address to Congress and the nation
- To call either house or both houses of Congress into special session
- To receive ambassadors and other representatives from foreign countries
- To commission all federal officers of the United States
- To ensure that the laws passed by Congress are faithfully executed

The president's official roles granted by the Constitution can be categorized as follows: chief of state, chief of the executive branch (or chief executive), and commander-in-chief of the military forces. The president has the difficult task of balancing the responsibilities of all these roles on a daily basis. In many instances, unforeseen events dictate which role is required. For example, while traveling abroad on a diplomatic visit (as chief of state) the president may be called back to the United States because of a natural disaster in one of the states to act as chief of the executive branch. While directing actions of the military forces overseas, the president has to also ensure domestic policies are being executed. In some other countries, the roles of chief of state

The north facade of the White House.

and chief executive are split. For example, in Great Britain the queen serves as chief of state and the prime minister performs the duties of chief executive.

As chief of state, the president is the official public representative of the nation and represents the United States to the rest of the world. In this role, the president is considered chief diplomat. The Constitution did not explicitly create this role, but presidents have assumed this role under the explicit power to recognize foreign governments, appoint ambassadors, and make treaties. Unlike presidents prior to the twentieth century, those today spend a great deal of time visiting other nations. The numerous wars and conflicts of the twentieth century, including the Cold War, and the increasing number of nations developing weapons of mass destruction have made foreign policy a major part of the president's agenda. The president visits and receives foreign leaders and dignitaries, and establishes treaties and executive agreements with other countries. Treaties, which bind future presidents to the agreement, require congressional approval while executive agreements do not. Executive agreements are only in effect during the administration of the signing president, unless each future president agrees to their continuation.

The president also performs various ceremonial roles as chief of state, such as sending holiday greetings, lighting the nation's Christmas tree, dedicating parks and post offices, bestowing awards and medals, giving public speeches, addressing the country in times of national mourning, and commemorating special events.

As chief of the executive branch, the president oversees the development of executive policy, appointment of high-ranking officials, and the operations of the departments, agencies, offices, boards, and commissions that fall under the branch. The president has considerable appointment authority, appointing all executive branch department heads, heads of all independent agencies, Supreme Court justices, federal judges, and U.S. ambassadors. The president issues executive orders that direct the

Photograph of Dr. Martin Luther King, Jr., whose birthday was established as a national holiday during the second administration of President Ronald W. Reagan. *Courtesy of the National Archives.*

actions of agencies and officials in executing and complying with laws and regulations. Executive orders are not laws, and therefore do not require congressional approval. However, each must be issued in connection with a law passed by Congress, and cannot alter the terms and conditions of that law. For this reason, executive orders carry the same weight as laws and the president can punish violators. For example, government officials can be removed from office, agencies can lose their funding, and individuals can be fined or face legal action. Executive orders cannot overstep the executive powers granted to the president by the Constitution, even if passed pursuant to a congressional law. If one does, Congress or the Supreme Court can challenge its constitutionality. Executive orders are predominantly used in two instances: when agencies, organizations, or officials fail to carry out laws passed by Congress, or when laws are vague and there is a need for more clarification for the law to be effectively executed. Executive orders are numbered consecutively and published in the *Federal Register* by the Office of the Federal Register.

The president influences and executes laws passed by Congress. He or she influences which laws Congress passes by proposing new legislation and through the ability to veto unfavorable legislation. The word *veto* is derived from the Latin word meaning "I forbid." A veto allows the president to influence law by refusing to sign a bill into law. However, that veto can be overridden by a majority vote of at least two-thirds of the House of Representatives and the Senate. The president has the ability to veto a bill without sending it back to Congress for reconsideration if Congress has adjourned. This is called a *pocket veto*. Presidents used the power of the veto sparingly until Andrew Johnson became president. President Johnson vetoed twenty-one bills and President Ulysses S. Grant later vetoed forty-five. President Franklin D. Roosevelt used more vetoes than any of his predecessors. By the end of his presidency, he had vetoed 372 bills, with Congress overriding 9. The majority of President Roosevelt's vetoes were pocket vetoes.

The president can also introduce new legislation to Congress, including new laws the president promised voters during presidential campaigning or during State of the

Union addresses to Congress. The president develops an annual budget submission to Congress for the entire government and submits an annual economic report. He or she can also call a special session of Congress to discuss new legislation. One of the most difficult tasks the president faces is gaining support for policies and proposed legislation from all members of Congress as a consequence of partisanship issues. Partisanship involves political actions or decisions that are influenced by political party ideologies. Due to partisanship, a Republican president may not gain the support of Democratic senators simply because they are not members of the same party. For example, President George W. Bush, a member of the Republican Party, faced continued opposition from congressional Democrats on most of his policies, particularly the war in Iraq.

As commander-in-chief of the U.S. military, the president develops the nation's defense and military policies. The president appoints the secretary of defense and senior ranking military commanders of each of the armed services. The chiefs of the armed services collectively form the Joint Chiefs of Staff and advise the president and secretary of defense on all military matters. The president can deploy troops but cannot officially declare war without congressional approval. However, the president can commit troops up to ninety days in response to a military threat under the War Powers Resolution. The armed forces may also be deployed in cases of emergency, such as during natural disasters or civil disputes. For example, President George Washington used troops to end the Whiskey Rebellion in Pennsylvania in 1791. President Dwight D. Eisenhower sent troops from the 101st Airborne from Fort Campbell, Kentucky, to Little Rock, Arkansas, in September 1957 to ensure that nine African American students were admitted to the newly integrated Central High School as a result of the Supreme Court ruling to end segregation in *Brown v. Board of Education of Topeka*, 347 U.S. 483 (1954). He also took control of the Arkansas National Guard by federalizing them (i.e., bringing them under federal control rather than the state's control) after the governor of Arkansas had ordered its troops to block the students' entry into the school. The president can call for a cease fire to end military fighting, make secret agreements with other countries, and set up governments in conquered lands.

As commander-in-chief, the president outranks any military officer and has the authority to take command of military troops on the battlefield. It is, however, unlikely that a president will actually be on the battlefield of an active war or conflict. However, the definition of *battlefield* has changed as a result of the attack on the United States on September 11, 2001. President George W. Bush justified the passage of several surveillance and interrogation acts without congressional approval on the grounds that he had authority to do so since the war on terrorism was a global conflict. Debate continues on whether President Bush overstepped his Constitutional authority.

One role presidents have assumed over the years that is not tied to their officially elected duties is leader of their political party. In this role, the president takes the lead in developing and executing the party's political agenda. Each party develops a *political party platform* that outlines the goals and principles for major programs and policies it deems necessary to serve the people. The president incorporates these programs and policies into his or her official agenda. The president also plays a major role in raising funds for the party, often appearing at fund-raising events for candidates running for Congress and state governor. The president also supports fellow party members running for office by publicly endorsing them and appearing with them at campaign functions to attract voters.

Over the years, the office of president has been reshaped based upon the president in office. Presidents such as Theodore Roosevelt, Franklin D. Roosevelt, John F. Kennedy, and Ronald W. Reagan have turned the office into the most powerful in the world because of their personal influence as strong leaders. These presidents have extended their influence globally by establishing policies and alliances that have had lasting impacts on nations around the world. The president is now seen as the holder of the most powerful office in the world for this and several other reasons. The United States is the wealthiest nation in the world. Many nations depend on trade with the United States for their economic survival. Thus, presidents have used the United States' economic power as leverage in both allied and adversarial negotiations with other nations.

The United States also has the greatest military strength in the world. The president can deploy military forces wherever threats to the United States or democracy arise. Starting in the late twentieth century, the United States became known as the world's policeman. American forces have been deployed around the world to assist other nations being threatened by both internal dangers and external hostile forces. Last, the president has considerable influence with other nations as a result of U.S. alliances with other powerful nations such as Great Britain.

Several legislative actions have led to the current presidential line of succession in the event the president or vice president are unable to complete their terms in office. The first Presidential Succession Act was passed in 1792, and the second in 1886. These two did not provide a line of succession that was extensive enough to ensure lower critical government positions were not left vacant. For example, Vice President Theodore Roosevelt was sworn in as president after the death of President William McKinley, but the office of the vice president remained vacant. The Presidential Succession Act of 1947 (3 U.S.C 19) included steps to include executive and legislative branch members in the line of presidential succession. According to the 1947 act, the following is the line of succession (or replacement) for the president if he or she can no longer complete the duties of the office:

vice president
Speaker of the House
president pro tempore of the Senate
secretary of state
secretary of the treasury
secretary of defense
attorney general
secretary of the interior
secretary of agriculture
secretary of commerce
secretary of labor
secretary of health and human services
secretary of housing and urban development
secretary of transportation
secretary of energy
secretary of education
secretary of veterans affairs
secretary of homeland security

The successor must meet the qualifications of presidency (i.e., be a natural born citizen, at least thirty-five years old, and a U.S. resident for at least fourteen years). Careful steps are taken to protect the line of succession. For example, during the president's State of Union address to Congress one member of the cabinet is taken to an undisclosed location in case of an unexpected catastrophe. (See a complete list of the presidents of the United States in Appendix G.)

The Vice President of the United States.   Under the original Constitution, separate Electoral College votes were not cast for the president and vice president as they are today. Whichever presidential candidate received the second highest number of votes from the Electoral College became vice president. The problem with this system was quickly realized when Thomas Jefferson and Aaron Burr both received the same number of electoral votes even though they were running mates. Jefferson was running for president against John Adams, and Burr was actually running as Jefferson's vice president. Each candidate received seventy-three electoral votes and the election had to be decided by the House of Representatives in 1801 (which voted in favor of Jefferson as president and Burr as vice president). The Twelfth Amendment to the U.S. Constitution was subsequently passed in 1804, allowing members of the Electoral College to cast separate ballots for the president and vice president.

Today the presidential candidate selects his or her running mate, usually with the assistance of an advisory group or selection committee. Normally, the vice presidential candidate possesses some politically competitive advantage the presidential candidate does not possess, such as popularity in a key state, a more liberal or conservative ideology, or active duty military experience.

The primary responsibility of the vice president is to assume the presidency if the president is unable to serve or is removed from office. To date, fourteen vice presidents have become presidents. Nine assumed the office in succession to the president and five were elected in their own presidential bids for office.

- John Tyler succeeded the natural death of William H. Harrison in 1841
- Millard Fillmore succeeded the natural death of Zachary Taylor in 1850
- Andrew Johnson became president after the assassination of Abraham Lincoln in 1865
- Chester A. Arthur became president after the assassination of James A. Garfield in 1881
- Theodore Roosevelt became president after the assassination of William McKinley in 1901
- Calvin Coolidge succeeded the natural death of Warren G. Harding in 1923
- Harry S. Truman succeeded the natural death of Franklin D. Roosevelt in 1945
- Lyndon B. Johnson became president after the assassination of John F. Kennedy in 1963
- Gerald R. Ford became president after Richard M. Nixon resigned in 1974 (Ford became Nixon's vice president in 1973 after the resignation of Spiro T. Agnew)
- John Adams was elected as president in 1797; he served two terms as vice president under George Washington from 1789 through 1797
- Thomas Jefferson was elected as president in 1801; he served as vice president under John Adams from 1797 through 1801
- Martin Van Buren was elected as president in 1837; he served as vice president under Andrew Jackson from 1833 through 1837
- Richard M. Nixon was elected as president in 1969; he served as vice president under Dwight D. Eisenhower from 1953 through 1961
- George H. W. Bush was elected as president in 1989; he served two terms as vice president under Ronald W. Reagan from 1981 through 1989

As the demands on the presidency have grown due to growing national demands and U.S. involvement in international affairs, so have the demands of the vice presidency and the prestige of the office. The vice presidency was a relatively ineffectual position until Richard M. Nixon held the office under President Dwight D. Eisenhower. Before him, those who held the position had few if any significant duties. Henry Wilson, vice president under President Ulysses S. Grant, for example, had so much free time that he spent most of his time writing a three-volume book on the history of slavery. Theodore Roosevelt was chosen for the office under William McKinley in part because the Republican leaders in New York wanted to remove him from office as governor and into the almost invisible role as vice president. Nixon, on the other hand, traveled to other nations, served the nation while Eisenhower was ill, and successfully debated with then–Soviet Premier Nikita Khrushchev in a televised debate. Walter F. Mondale, who served under President Jimmy Carter, was the first vice president to have an office in the West Wing. President Carter referred to Mondale as his "equal partner."

According to Article I, Section 3, of the Constitution, the vice president is also president of the Senate but can only vote when there is a tie among members. Today, the vice president only presides over the Senate during ceremonial functions or when there is a need for a tie-breaking vote. During normal sessions, the senior member of the political party with the most members presides as the president pro tempore (also called the president pro tem). Under Title 3 of the *United States Code*, Section 15 (3 U.S.C. 15), the vice president also announces the results of votes by the Electoral College for presidential elections before both houses of Congress. As a result of federal statutes, the vice president serves as an ex officio member of the National Security Council and as an ex officio member of the Board of Regents of the Smithsonian Institution (ex officio means simply by virtue of one's office).

Executive Office of the President.   The executive office of the president was established under President Theodore Roosevelt in 1939 as the White House office to deal with the increased government responsibilities and challenges resulting from the Great Depression. The office is comprised of a group of staff agencies that assist the president in carrying out major executive branch duties. The office keeps the president informed, assists in the development and implementation of the president's policies, acts as a liaison to the press and public, and coordinates with department and agency heads. Members of the office also complete such administrative functions as preparing the president's speeches, setting up meetings, and maintaining the White House. The agencies and offices that report to the president change over time, and are established and disbanded depending upon their usefulness to the executive branch. The following are the components of the executive office under President George W. Bush, the year they were established, and their primary duties (The White House, 2008):

- Council of Economic Advisers (1946) provides the president with objective economic analysis and advice on the development and implementation of a wide range of domestic and international economic policy issues.
- Council on Environmental Quality (1969) coordinates federal environmental efforts and works closely with agencies and other White House offices in the development of environmental policies and initiatives.
- National Security Council (1947) advises the president on issues of national security and foreign policy. The council includes the vice president, secretary of state, secretary of defense, and director of the Office of Emergency Planning.

- Office of Administration (1977) provides administrative services to the president and the entire executive office of the president, including financial management, information technology support, human resources management, library and research assistance, facilities management, procurement, printing and graphics support, security, and mail and messenger operations.
- Office of Management and Budget (1970) assists the president in developing the annual budget, setting fiscal policy, and evaluating spending across the executive branch.
- Office of National Drug Control Policy (1989) seeks to reduce drug use and drug-related crimes.
- Office of Science and Technology Policy (1976) advises the president and others within the executive office of the president on the effects of science and technology on domestic and international affairs, and develops policies and budgets.
- President's Foreign Intelligence Advisory Board (1956) advises the president on the quality and adequacy of intelligence collection, of analysis and estimates, of counterintelligence, and of other intelligence activities, and the legality of foreign intelligence activities.
- Office of the United States Trade Representative (1963) promotes international trade opportunities.
- White House Office (1939) includes the president's direct staff, which provides direct support and advice, and handles the president's meetings and schedule. The office includes the White House chief of staff, senior advisor to the president, personal secretary, press secretary, communications director, and legal counsel.

The White House Office has the most direct contact with the president. The early presidents completed many of their own administrative functions. For example, the early presidents answered their own mail until Congress authorized the president to have a secretary in 1857. When President Franklin D. Roosevelt was elected, his entire staff consisted of only thirty-seven employees. The staff grew after President Roosevelt began implementing his New Deal policies and the demands of World War II increased. By the time President George W. Bush assumed office, the White House Office employed more than four hundred people.

The duties of the staff are numerous. They investigate and analyze problems that require the president's attention. They screen questions, issues, and problems presented to the president and provide recommended solutions. They also ensure that the president's initiatives are transmitted to the appropriate government personnel for action, and provide public relations support to the president. This office is headed by the chief of staff who advises the president and directs the operations of the presidential staff. The chief of staff advises the president on national security issues, the economy, and political affairs. Another member of the White House Office is the press secretary. This person holds news conferences and makes public statements on behalf of the president. The counsel to the president serves as the White House lawyer and handles all legal matters. The White House staff also consists of speech writers, researchers, the president's physician, the director of the staff for the First Lady, and a correspondence secretary. The following are the offices of the White House Office under President George W. Bush:

- Domestic Policy Council advises the president on domestic policy in such areas as education, health, housing, welfare, justice, federalism, transportation, environment, labor, and veteran's affairs; coordinates and monitors the policy-making process throughout federal agencies; and represents the president's priorities to other branches of government.

- Homeland Security Council, created as a result of the events of September 11, 2001, ensures coordination of all homeland security–related activities among executive departments and agencies, and promotes the effective development and implementation of all homeland security policies.
- National Economic Council coordinates policy making for domestic and international economic issues, coordinates economic policy advice for the president, ensures policy decisions and programs are consistent with the president's economic goals, and monitors implementation of the president's economic policy agenda.
- Office of Faith-Based and Community Initiatives coordinates with faith-based (i.e., religious) and community organizations in providing federally funded services to communities.
- Office of the First Lady executes initiatives as directed by the First Lady.
- Office of National AIDS Policy provides funds and oversees services to internationally support those living with HIV and AIDS.
- Privacy and Civil Liberties Oversight Board advises the president and other senior executive branch officials to ensure that concerns with respect to privacy and civil liberties are appropriately considered in the implementation of laws, regulations, and executive branch policies related to efforts protecting the nation against terrorism.
- USA Freedom Corps created by President George W. Bush, builds and recognizes acts of service, sacrifice, and generosity that followed the events of September 11, 2001, and builds a culture of service, citizenship, and responsibility in America by partnering with national service programs, strengthening the nonprofit sector, recognizing volunteers, and helping to connect individuals with volunteer opportunities.
- White House Fellows Office offers exceptional young men and women first-hand experience working at the highest levels of the federal government through one-year, paid assistantships with senior White House staff, the vice president, cabinet secretaries, and other top-ranking government officials.
- White House Military Office provides a wide variety of functions from critical military command-and-control missions to ceremonial duties at presidential events. This office maintains the president's primary modes of air transportation (Air Force One and Marine One), Camp David, the White House Communications Agency, the White House Transportation Agency, the White House Medical Unit, and the Presidential Food Service.

The President's Cabinet and Executive Branch Departments.   The president's advisory board is called the president's cabinet. Although the Constitution did not specifically provide for assistants or advisors for the president, every president since George Washington has had some type of advisory group. The president's advisors consisted of only four positions in 1789: the secretary of state, secretary of treasury, secretary of war, and the attorney general. The term *president's cabinet* originated from the name Kitchen Cabinet given to Andrew Jackson's advisors because he met with them in the kitchen of the White House.

Today the presidential cabinet includes the vice president, White House chief of staff, and secretaries of each cabinet-level department. Each secretary (including the attorney general of the Department of Justice) heads an executive department that is designed to serve a specific need of the citizenry, and each advises the president on any subject relating to the duty of that department. Each department consists of agencies that execute the policies of that department. These agencies are responsible for the day-to-day administration of department operations and execution of associated laws and policies.

While the president chooses each executive department's secretary, each must be approved by a majority vote in the Senate. None of these cabinet heads can hold any other office and, as political appointees, they must resign when a new president takes office. The incoming president can, but rarely does, reappoint a secretary. Today there are fifteen executive branch departments. The following is a list of the cabinet-level departments, showing the year each department was established and providing a brief description of its functions and a short list of some of the agencies under each.

- Department of Agriculture (1862) promotes programs directly and indirectly related to food; sets standards for food quality; supports farmers and ranchers; provides support to low-income families with such programs as WIC (Women, Infants, and Children Special Supplemental Nutrition Program) and food stamps. Agencies include the Forest Service, Farm Service Agency, and Food Safety and Inspection Service.
- Department of Commerce (1903) promotes the growth of the United States economy through jobs, trade, development, technology, and U.S. travel and tourism; compiles and issues data on all facets of the U.S. economy; issues weather reports; regulates patents and trademarks; and collects census data. Agencies include the Census Bureau, Bureau of Economic Analysis, the Patent and Trademark Office, and the National Weather Service.
- Department of Defense (1947) defends the United States and its interests around the world, and manages the military forces; includes support agencies and activities that perform functions for the rest of the department such as payroll and travel. Agencies include the Departments of the Army, Navy (the Marine Corps is part of the Navy), and Air Force.
- Department of Education (1979) improves the quality of education for all citizens; provides financial aid to schools; and provides financial aid to students, including student loans and

A U.S. Air Force jet flying over NASA's Cape Canaveral. *Courtesy of the United States Northern Command.*

scholarships. Agencies include the Offices of Elementary and Secondary Education, Federal Student Aid, and Safe and Drug-Free Schools.

- Department of Energy (1977) plans for current and future energy use, oversees the national and international safe production and use of nuclear energy and weapons, and promotes environmentally safe energy uses. Agencies include the Office of Environmental Management, Office of Science, National Nuclear Security Administration, and Federal Energy Regulatory Commission.
- Department of Health and Human Services (1953) promotes the health of U.S. citizens; approves new drugs; administers Medicare; sponsors health-related programs and research; and maintains medical statistics on the U.S. population. Agencies include the Food and Drug Administration, Centers for Disease Control and Prevention, Centers for Medicare and Medicaid Services, and National Institutes of Health.
- Department of Homeland Security (2003) is responsible for preventing terrorist threats and attacks against the United States, and minimizing the damage from attacks and natural disasters. This department was established as a result of the terrorist attacks against the United States on September 11, 2001. Several agencies from other departments related to the mission of homeland security were moved under this department, such as parts of the Immigration and Naturalization Service and the U.S. Customs Service. Agencies include the U.S. Secret Service, U.S. Customs and Border Protection, U.S. Coast Guard, and Federal Emergency Management Agency (FEMA).
- Department of Housing and Urban Development (1965) creates opportunities for home ownership and affordable housing, provides services to the homeless, funds public housing projects, and enforces fair housing laws. Agencies include the Office of Fair Housing and Equal Opportunity, Office of Public and Indian Housing, and the Government National Mortgage Association (Ginnie Mae).
- Department of the Interior (1849) manages federal lands (including national parks and forests), oversees the affairs of Native Americans, and promotes conservation of wildlife and natural resources. Agencies include the Bureau of Indian Affairs, Fish and Wildlife Service, National Park Service, and Bureau of Land Management.
- Department of Justice (1870) enforces federal laws, provides the president legal advice, represents the United States in legal issues, investigates misconduct by Executive Branch officials, prosecutes cases in federal courts, and runs the federal prison system. Agencies include the Federal Bureau of Investigation (FBI), Drug Enforcement Administration (DEA), Federal Bureau of Prisons, and U.S. Marshals Service.
- Department of Labor (1913) executes policies for fair pay, fair working hours, workplace safety, and nondiscriminatory employment practices; administers unemployment insurance; monitors negotiations between unions and labor management; and collects extensive data related to these topics. Agencies include the Bureau of Labor Statistics, Occupational Safety and Health Administration (OSHA), Women's Bureau, and the Employment and Training Administration.
- Department of State (1789) assists the president in developing foreign policy, handles U.S. diplomatic ties and coalitions with other countries, mediates foreign conflicts, oversees U.S. embassies and consulates, issues passports and visas, and has custody of the Great Seal of the United States of America. Agencies include the Office of Arms Control and International Security, Office of Global Affairs, and the U.S. Mission to the United Nations.
- Department of Transportation (1966) has oversight for every form of national transportation. The department plans, funds, and regulates new systems for land, maritime, aviation, rail, and metro transportation. Agencies include the Federal Aviation Administration (FAA), the Federal Highway Administration, and the Pipeline and Hazardous Materials Safety Administration.

- Department of the Treasury (1789) oversees the nation's fiscal policy, regulates banks and other financial institutions, administers the public debt, and prints currency through the Bureau of Engraving and Printing (paper money) and the U.S. Mint (coins). Agencies include the Internal Revenue Service, and the Alcohol and Tobacco Tax and Trade Bureau.
- Department of Veterans Affairs (1988) administers benefits and programs to support military veterans and their families, operates the veterans affairs' hospitals, and operates the national cemeteries. Agencies include the National Cemetery Administration, Veterans Benefits Administration, and the Veterans Health Administration.

Beyond the heads of the fifteen cabinet-level departments listed above, the president may also grant cabinet-level rank to the head of any major agency. President George W. Bush granted such status to the heads of the Environmental Protection Agency, Office of Management and Budget, Office of National Drug Control Policy, and the Office of the United States Trade Representative.

Independent Executive Branch Agencies.   Independent executive branch agencies report directly to the president, but are not part of the cabinet-level departments. Each is established by a *statute* (a federal law passed by Congress and signed by the president stipulating a policy) to handle complex issues or an issue of such importance that a stand-alone organization is needed to oversee its administration. These agencies establish rules or regulations pursuant to their statutory granted authority, so these rules and regulation have the power of federal law. The heads of these agencies are political appointees, that is, they are chosen by the president to serve during his or her term in office. The following are among the largest and most prominent of these agencies (see Appendix I for a complete list):

Central Intelligence Agency (CIA)
Environmental Protection Agency (EPA)
General Services Administration (GSA)
National Aeronautics and Space Administration (NASA)
National Archives and Records Administration (NARA)
National Endowment for the Arts (NEA)
National Science Foundation (NSF)
Office of Personnel Management (OPM)
Peace Corps
Small Business Administration (SBA)
Social Security Administration (SSA)

Government Corporations.   Government corporations are chartered by an act of Congress to conduct government activities and have similarities to commercial businesses. However, most provide a public service that would be unprofitable for a private company to provide. The U.S. Postal Service is the largest of these corporations. Congress charters government corporations and the president selects a board of directors to oversee each. A chief executive officer manages its day-to-day operation. Government corporations raise all or a portion of their own finances, can borrow money, sue and be sued, and some issue stock. Some are exempt from civil service rules regulating pay and employee tenure. Wholly owned corporations are those whose equity is fully held by the government (such as the Commodity Credit Corporation and the Federal Prison Industries, Inc.). The equity of mixed-ownership federal corporations is partly owned

The U.S. Postal Service's 2007 Christmas stamp, reproducing *The Madonna of the Carnation* (ca. 1515, National Gallery of Art), by the Milanese painter Bernardino Luini. *Courtesy of the United States Post Office.*

by the government and partly by private owners (e.g., Amtrak). The government holds no equity in private federal corporations (e.g., the Communications Satellite Corporate, or COMSAT).

Government corporations are nonpartisan entities, that is, they are not subject to pressures or allegiances to political parties. Once a corporation is no longer needed, it may be dissolved. For example, the Federal Savings and Loan Insurance Corporation was dissolved in 1989 because it could not maintain its solvency. Some may also become private companies. Once a corporation has reached the point at which it is financially self-sustaining, it may relinquish ties to and support from the federal government and become a private entity. Conrail, for example, became a private, for-profit corporation when the federal government sold all of its stock in the company in 1987 because it was financially self-sustaining.

The following are some of the largest and most prominent government corporations (see Appendix I for a full list):

Amtrak (National Railroad Passenger Corporation)
Commodity Credit Corporation
Corporation for Public Broadcasting
Export-Import Bank of the United States
Federal Deposit Insurance Corporation (FDIC)
Legal Services Corporation
National Endowment for Democracy
Overseas Private Investment Corporation
Pension Benefit Guaranty Corporation
Tennessee Valley Authority
United States Postal Service

Government-Sponsored Enterprises.   Government-Sponsored Enterprises (GSEs) are types of government corporations Congress creates to offer affordable lending programs and other financial services to specific sectors of the economy, such as farmers, students, homeowners, and insolvent savings and loan institutions. The first GSE created by Congress was the Farm Credit System in 1916. Its authority to improve the income and well-being of American farmers and ranchers through credit and other services is granted under the Farm Credit Act of 1971. It provides billions of dollars in grants and loans to farmers, ranchers, rural homeowners, rural utility systems, and agricultural cooperatives.

Although Congress creates them, GSEs are privately owned. However, they may be granted special privileges because of the services they provide to the public. For example, Federal National Mortgage Association (Fannie Mae) and Federal Home Loan Mortgage Corporation (Freddie Mac) provide stability and liquidity in the mortgage market by assisting low- and moderate-income families, and promoting access to mortgage credit nationwide, including underserved areas. In carrying out these public purposes, they are each exempt from paying state and local taxes (excluding property taxes), and have conditional access to a $2.25 billion line of credit from the U.S. Treasury Department. Because they have the implicit backing of the U.S. Treasury, they are able to raise funds at lower interest rates than other private companies.

GSEs are subject to regulation by regulatory government agencies according to the type of service each provides. For example, the U.S. Department of Housing and Urban Development (HUD) regulates Fannie Mae and Freddie Mac. GSEs may also be audited by the U.S. Government Accountability Office (GAO). The government may also appoint a minority of the members on their Boards of Directors. GSEs may also become fully owned private companies. For example, Sallie Mae was formed as a GSE in 1972. It is the largest provider of educational loans in the United States. In 2004 it became a completely independent publicly traded company. The following are examples of other GSEs:

Central and Regional Banks for Cooperatives
Farm Credit Banks
Farm Credit System Financial Assistance Corporation
Federal Agricultural Mortgage Corporation (Farmer Mac)
Federal Farm Credit Bank
Federal Home Loan Bank
Financial Assistance Corporation
Government National Mortgage Association (Ginnie Mae)
Resolution Funding Corporation

Boards, Commissions, and Committees.   The president can establish and appoint members to boards, commissions, and committees that focus on special issues or problems. Some are permanent and others are temporary. Some present and past examples include the Advisory Commission on Electronic Commerce, Advisory Council on Historic Preservation, Attorney General's Commission on Pornography, and the National Commission on Terrorist Attacks Upon the United States (also called the 9/11 Commission).

THE LEGISLATIVE BRANCH

House of Representatives.   The House of Representatives, also called the People's House, represents the greatest number of people in the United States. Today there are 435 members of the House. The determination of how many representatives or seats each state has depends on the results of the U.S. Census, with states with larger populations having more representatives. The states create districts to determine which parts of the state will be represented by each of its representatives. The District of Columbia, the U.S. Virgin Islands, Guam, and American Samoa each have one delegate in the House, and Puerto Rico has a resident commissioner. These representatives have no voting power on the floor of Congress but may participate in debates. They can, however, vote in committees and sponsor legislation.

Each congressman or congresswoman in the House is elected for a two-year term (with the exception of Puerto Rico's resident commissioner, who is elected for a four-year term), and there is no limit on how many times they can be reelected. Eligibility for office includes being at least twenty-five years old at the time of inauguration (i.e., when sworn into office), a resident of the state the member represents, and a U.S. citizen for at least seven years prior to being inaugurated.

The House has one special authority outlined in the Constitution. All bills dealing with federal revenues (i.e., appropriations and raising funds) must originate in the House, according to Article I of the U.S. Constitution. This includes bills dealing with raising funds through taxes, tariffs, and loans. The only position of House leadership specifically stated in the Constitution is the Speaker of the House, who oversees sessions. The person in this position is first nominated by his or her political party members, so generally the party with the most representatives in the House selects the Speaker with their majority voting power. Speakers have considerable political power because they appoint House members to committees, assign legislation to committees, determine the agenda for the House, recognize those who wish to speak on the

The west front of the U.S. Capitol. *Courtesy of the Architect of the Capitol.*

House floor, and coordinate with the Senate. The Speaker can thus accelerate or block legislation from being considered in the House.

The House also has a majority leader who is selected as the deputy to the Speaker, and is also a member of the party with the most House members. The House majority leader is generally more vocal on party philosophy, since the Speaker should attempt to serve the needs of the entire House and not just the agenda of a single political party. The political party with the next most representatives selects a minority leader. Each party also elects House whips, who serve as deputies to the House majority and minority leaders, and coordinate within their respective parties to ensure its members are supporting issues being pushed by party leaders.

The House has committees that deal with specific issues. They develop legislation and resolutions, have oversight over laws and agencies dealing with their respective committee subject matters, and conduct investigations. Some are permanent in nature (standing committees), and others are temporarily established to handle special or emergency issues (special committees). Standing committees meet at least once a month. There are also joint committees that include members from the Senate, which can be permanent or temporary. Some House committees are more powerful than others by virtue of the types of issues they handle. For example, the Appropriations, Rules, and Ways and Means Committees are considered the three most powerful. The House Appropriations Committee writes the annual federal appropriation bills. The House Committee on Rules has jurisdiction over the rules and order of business of the House. The House Committee on Ways and Means has jurisdiction over the following areas:

- Customs, collection districts, and ports of entry and delivery
- Reciprocal trade agreements
- Revenue measures (generally)
- Revenue measures relating to insular possessions
- Bonded debt of the United States
- Deposit of public monies
- Transportation of dutiable goods (goods on which customs must be paid)
- Tax-exempt foundations and charitable trusts
- National Social Security (except health care and facilities programs that are supported from general revenues as opposed to payroll deductions and except work incentive programs)

Usually, House members with the greatest seniority are assigned to the most sought-after committees. Other considerations applied are each member's experience, expertise, and availability. Each committee has a chairperson. The following were the standing committees in place during the 110th session of Congress (2007–2008):

- Committee on Agriculture
- Committee on Appropriations
- Committee on Armed Services
- Committee on the Budget
- Committee on Education and Labor
- Committee on Energy and Commerce
- Committee on Financial Services
- Committee on Foreign Affairs
- Committee on Homeland Security

- Committee on House Administration
- Committee on the Judiciary
- Committee on Natural Resources
- Committee on Oversight and Government Reform
- Committee on Rules
- Committee on Science and Technology
- Committee on Small Business
- Committee on Standards of Official Conduct
- Committee on Transportation and Infrastructure
- Committee on Veterans' Affairs
- Committee on Ways and Means
- House Permanent Select Committee on Intelligence

The following were joint committees consisting of members from both the House and the Senate:

- Joint Economic Committee
- Joint Committee on Printing
- Joint Committee on Taxation
- Joint Committee on the Library

Congressional representatives also join together and form caucuses. These are informal or unofficial groups that form because their members share common concerns, interests, or ideologies. Caucus members cross party lines and are often comprised of members from both the House of Representatives and the Senate. For example, the congressional Black Caucus's members strive to influence the passing of laws that support minorities and block legislation and the appointment of individuals who they believe are in opposition to minorities. Others include the Women's Caucus, congressional Hispanic Caucus, and the congressional Children's Caucus.

Various officers in the House have specific administrative duties. Each is elected at the commencement of each congressional session and remains in office until successors are chosen. They may be removed by the full House or by the Speaker of the House for misconduct. These officers are each allowed to appoint members of their staff. The clerk of the House maintains the official records of House proceedings in the official *House Journal*. The clerk also signs all bills and resolutions that are passed, certifies all votes, maintains and distributes the House calendars, and provides documents to House members and the public. The clerk calls the House to order and records the presence of members. The clerk is in charge of the House if the Speaker of the House has not yet been selected. He or she also manages the office of any member, delegate, or the resident commissioner who has died, resigned, or has been expelled until a successor is elected. The sergeant at arms maintains order on the floor during House sessions, under the direction of the Speaker or other presiding officer. This person may also compel absent members to attend sessions. The chaplain offers a prayer at the commencement of each day's sitting of the House. The chief administrative officer has the responsibility of completing functions as assigned by the Committee on House Administration. This includes providing operational and financial support such as information technology, budget management, human resource management, payroll support, childcare, food and vending, procurement, logistics, and administrative counseling.

Two other important offices are the Office of the Inspector General and the Office of the General Counsel. The Speaker of the House, the House majority leader, and the House minority leader appoint the Inspector General (IG). The IG conducts audits of House financial and administrative functions, and reports findings and violations to the Committee on Standards of Official Conduct. This includes information involving congressional members, delegates, the resident commissioners' officers, or employees of the House. The Office of General Counsel also provides legal assistance and legal representation to House members.

United States Senate.   The Senate was established as the upper house of Congress. As such, it has more constitutionally granted powers than the House, including approving presidential appointments and approving treaties. This first power is extensive because it covers the president's selections and appointments of his or her cabinet members, other top executive branch officials, Supreme Court justices, federal judges, and U.S. ambassadors. If the need for a presidential impeachment arises, the Senate actually holds the trial and decides whether a conviction is warranted. A conviction by the Senate cannot be appealed.

There are 100 senators (two per state). Of the two senators in a state, the one elected first or the one elected for a full term versus a partial term is referred to as the senior senator and the other is the junior senator. The requirements for being elected to a seat in the Senate are more stringent than for those in the House. Because they have broader roles than House members and represent more people, senators are elected for a term of six years. There is no limit to how many times they may be reelected. One-third of the Senate runs for reelection every two years. Senators must be at least thirty years old, have been U.S. residents for nine years prior to being sworn in, and be residents of the state they represent.

The vice president rarely presides over the Senate although it is a constitutionally granted authority. Normally, the president pro tempore presides. This position is filled through a majority vote, so normally the political party with the most members controls the majority of votes in the Senate and therefore selects the president pro tempore. The Senate also has a majority leader who represents the political party with the most members, and a minority leader representing the minority party. The two leaders schedule floor debates, assist in determining committee assignments, and assist in setting legislative priorities. Each political party also elects Senate whips to serve as deputies to the Senate majority and minority leaders, and coordinate within their respective parties to ensure its members are supporting issues being pushed by party leaders.

As in the House of Representatives, the Senate has standing committees, special committees, and joint committees. However, in the Senate each is ranked by importance, from Class A (most important) to Class B and then Class C. The most coveted committee chairmanships are over the Judiciary, Budget, and Foreign Relations Committees because of the power and prestige of these committees. The Judiciary Committee has one of the broadest jurisdictions in the Senate, ranging from criminal justice to intellectual property law. The Budget Committee drafts the federal budget. The Senate Committee on Foreign Relations dates back to 1816 and has a major role in shaping U.S. policy around the world. The following were the standing committees in place during the 110th session of Congress (2007–2008):

- Agriculture, Nutrition, and Forestry
- Appropriations
- Armed Services

- Banking, Housing, and Urban Affairs
- Budget
- Commerce, Science, and Transportation
- Energy and Natural Resources
- Environment and Public Works
- Finance
- Foreign Relations
- Health, Education, Labor, and Pensions
- Homeland Security and Governmental Affairs
- Judiciary
- Rules and Administration
- Small Business and Entrepreneurship
- Veterans Affairs

The following were special, select, and other committees in the Senate:

- Indian Affairs
- Select Committee on Ethics
- Select Committee on Intelligence
- Special Committee on Aging

The Senate Caucus on International Narcotics Control, established by law in 1985, is the only officially recognized caucus in the Senate. It was created to monitor and encourage the federal government and private entities seeking to expand international cooperation against drug abuse and narcotics trafficking, and to promote international compliance with narcotics control treaties, including eradication. This caucus is unlike those in the House, which are unofficial groups comprised of members that share ideologies. The Senate caucus was established on August 16, 1985, by the Foreign Relations Authorization Act. It has the status of a standing committee.

Just as in the House, there are various officers in the Senate who have specific administrative duties. The secretary of the Senate is elected by the Senators to complete an array of administrative functions and to oversee the day-to-day operations of the Senate. The sergeant at arms and doorkeeper serves as the protocol and chief law enforcement officer, and is the principal administrative manager for most support services in the Senate. The Office of the Senate legislative counsel provides legislative drafting services for Senators and Committees. The legislative counsel is appointed by the Senate president pro tempore and is responsible for the management and administration of the office. The chaplain opens each day's session with a prayer, and also provides spiritual counseling services to Senators, their families, and their staff. Each party has a party secretary. The secretary for the majority and the secretary for the minority sit on either side of the Senate chamber, and each ensures Senate pages are at their posts and Republican and Democratic staff members are on hand as needed. (See Appendix H for an Organizational Chart of the United States Senate for the 110th Congress.)

Legislative Branch Agencies and Offices.   Just as in the executive branch, the legislative branch also has agencies and offices that support Congress and its members. The following is a list of these agencies:

- Architect of the Capitol
- Congressional Budget Office

- Congressional Office of Compliance
- Congressional Research Service (located within the Library of Congress)
- Government Accountability Office (formerly called the General Accounting Office)
- Government Printing Office
- House Information Resources
- House Chief Administrative Officer
- House Office of the Clerk
- House Office of Inspector General
- House Office of the Legislative Counsel
- House Sergeant at Arms
- Library of Congress
- Medicare Payment Advisory Commission
- Office of Attending Physician
- Office of the Law Revision Counsel
- Senate Office of the Legislative Counsel
- Stennis Center for Public Service
- U.S. Botanic Garden
- U.S. Capitol Police

THE JUDICIAL BRANCH

Article III of the Constitution established the judicial branch. The Judiciary Act of 1789 established the federal judicial system as a three-tier hierarchical system. At the lowest level are district courts. At the second level are appellate courts that hear appeals from district courts and administrative agencies. At the highest level is the U.S. Supreme Court.

District courts are the trial courts of the federal judicial system. They try civil and criminal federal cases, and juries hear trials. There are currently a total of ninety-four district courts, with at least one in each state, Washington, DC, Puerto Rico, Guam, the U.S. Virgin Islands, and the Northern Mariana Islands. Larger states such as California and New York have more than one. Within each district court system is a bankruptcy court that hears all bankruptcy cases. Magistrate judges are appointed by district court judges and perform four basic functions. They conduct the initial proceedings in federal criminal cases such as issuing search warrants and appointing attorneys. They try certain misdemeanor criminal cases. They may try civil cases if both parties consent. Finally, they conduct other proceedings as directed by district court judges such as conducting settlement conferences.

In addition to district courts, there are other lower courts and special courts in the federal judiciary system. The U.S. Court of International Trade hears all cases involving trade and customs. The U.S. Court of Federal Claims hears claims against the U.S. government, including disputes over federal contracts and unlawful seizure of personal property by the government. The U.S. Tax Court hears cases brought by citizens disputing tax deficiencies determined by the Commissioner of the Internal Revenue (head of the Internal Revenue Service) prior to payment of the disputed amounts.

Citizens who are not satisfied with the outcomes in district courts can appeal to the next level, appellate courts. These twelve Courts of Appeals hear cases appealed from the

The Supreme Court Building. *Courtesy of the U.S. Supreme Court.*

district courts in their jurisdictions or circuits (see Table 2.1). They also hear appeals to decisions made by federal administrative agencies. Courts of Appeal cannot refuse to hear any appealed cases.

There are two special appeals courts. The U.S. Court of Appeals for the Armed Forces has international appellate jurisdiction over members of the armed forces on active duty and other persons subject to the *Uniform Code of Military Justice*, which outlines the military law of the United States. For example, members of the armed forces who have been discharged due to a court martial appeal their cases here. Appeals to cases heard in this court are taken directly to the Supreme Court. The U.S. Court of Appeals for Veterans Claims provides judicial review of decisions by the Department of Veterans Affairs' Boards of Veterans' Appeals. These cases involve claims by veterans or their families for disability benefits, survivor benefits, education payments, and waivers of indebtedness.

The U.S. Court of Appeals for the Federal Circuit hears appeals from all federal district courts, the U.S. Court of International Trade, the U.S. Court of Federal Claims, the U.S. Court of Appeals for Veterans Claims, and certain administrative agencies and offices. These agencies and offices include the U.S. Merit Systems Protection Board, the Boards of Contract Appeals, the Board of Patent Appeals and Interferences, the Trademark Trial and Appeals Board, the U.S. International Trade Commission, the Office of Compliance of the U.S. Congress, and the Government Accountability Office Personnel Appeals Board.

The Supreme Court is the highest court in the land. It hears appeals from lower federal courts and from state courts, and all lower courts must abide by whatever decisions it hands down. Unlike the district and appeals court, the Supreme Court can choose which cases it wants to hear. At least four Supreme Court judges must agree to hear a case before it is accepted. This is called the Rule of Four.

The Supreme Court is currently comprised of nine justices: the Chief Justice of the United States and eight associate justices. Congress can change the number of justices if needed. The chief justice oversees the business of the Court, controls which cases are heard, and assigns tasks to the associate justices such as writing court opinions on cases. However, the chief justice's vote or opinion on a case carries the same weight as the other justices. The chief justice sits in the middle of the bench during cases.

Table 2.1.   The Twelve Circuits of the United States Courts of Appeals

Circuit	Location	Jurisdiction
1st	Boston	Maine, Massachusetts, New Hampshire, Rhode Island, Puerto Rico
2nd	New York City	Connecticut, New York, Vermont
3rd	Philadelphia	Delaware, New Jersey, Pennsylvania, U.S. Virgin Islands
4th	Richmond	Maryland, North Carolina, South Carolina, Virginia, West Virginia
5th	New Orleans	Louisiana, Mississippi, Texas
6th	Cincinnati	Kentucky, Michigan, Ohio, Tennessee
7th	Chicago	Illinois, Indiana, Wisconsin
8th	St. Louis	Arkansas, Iowa, Minnesota, Missouri, Nebraska, North Dakota, South Dakota
9th	San Francisco	Alaska, Arizona, California, Hawaii, Idaho, Montana, Nevada, Oregon, Washington, Guam, Northern Mariana Islands
10th	Denver	Colorado, Kansas, New Mexico, Oklahoma, Utah, Wyoming
11th	Atlanta	Alabama, Florida, Georgia
12th	Washington, DC	District of Columbia

The other justices are seated according their seniority, with the most senior nearest the chief justice. Each of the justices is also assigned to at least one of the federal appeals courts. In this capacity, they have the authority to take such actions as issuing injunctions, staying executions, and granting bail.

Each federal court has a clerk of the court who acts as the primary administrative officer. The clerk maintains all court records and the court dockets, provides courtroom support services such as interpreters, and issues notices and summons. The Supreme Court has additional officers to assist in the performance of its duties. These officers include the administrative assistant to the chief justice, the clerk, the reporter of decisions, the librarian, the marshal, the court counsel, the curator, the director of data systems, and the public information officer. Federal courts rely on assistance from the executive department. For example, the Department of Justice represents the government in civil cases. The U.S. Marshals Service provides security for federal courthouses and judges. The General Services Administration builds and maintains federal courthouses.

The Judicial Conference of the United States sets policy for federal courts. The chief justice of the Supreme Court presides over it. It also includes twenty-six other members, including the chief judge of each court of appeals, one district court judge from each circuit, and the chief judge of the U.S. Court of International Trade. The administrative office of the U.S. courts carries out the policies of the conference. This office was created in 1939 and also provides many support functions including reporting judicial branch statistics, recommending policies and programs, conducting studies, providing technical support, and providing training.

The president appoints federal judges for life terms, with the advice and consent of the Senate. There are three exceptions. Bankruptcy judges are appointed by Courts of Appeals for fourteen-year terms. The judges of the district courts appoint magistrate judges for eight-year terms. The president and Senate play no role in selecting these judges. The third exception involves judges of the U.S. Court of Federal Claims. While these judges are appointed by the president and confirmed by the Senate, they are only appointed for fifteen-year terms.

There are no specific qualifications to become a federal judge. Those nominated are generally successful private or public attorneys, judges in lower courts, or law professors. Once appointed, federal judges are expected to abide by the *Code of Conduct for United States Judges*. Among its rules are that judges should exhibit integrity, avoid any appearance of impropriety, report their sources of income, and not engage in political campaign activities. Judges are also encouraged to engage in activities to improve the legal system, such as writing and teaching.

ENTITIES OUTSIDE OF THE THREE BRANCHES

Independent Regulatory Commissions.   Independent regulatory commissions are established to operate outside the three branches. The Interstate Commerce Commission was the first, established in 1887. Its function was to regulate carriers between states, such as bus lines and railroads. It was disbanded in 1995 and most of its functions were transferred to the Surface Transportation Board (STB) by the Interstate Commerce Commission Termination Act of 1995. The STB is an independent regulatory commission whose mission is to resolve railroad rate and service disputes and review proposed railroad mergers.

Congress issues laws to establish independent regulatory commissions. Each is established to set policy, and regulate public and private activities that fall under the delegated authority of each commission. The president appoints a board of commissioners to run each commission rather than a single individual, and the Senate confirms these appointments. However, the president has no authority over commission operations. The following are examples:

Equal Employment Opportunity Commission
Federal Communications Commission
Federal Election Commission
Federal Reserve Board of Governors
Federal Trade Commission
National Labor Relations Board
National Transportation Safety Board
Nuclear Regulatory Commission
Securities and Exchange Commission

Patriotic and Charitable Nonprofit Organizations.   Congress charters, or licenses, patriotic and charitable nonprofit organizations but does not provide them any funding or federal powers. A congressional charter is a law passed by Congress that states the mission and authority of an organization. For example, the National Academy of Sciences was chartered by Congress and approved by President Abraham Lincoln in 1863 to investigate, examine, and report upon any subject of science or art as requested by the government. Federal, state, and local governments all utilize the

National Academy of Public Administration (NAPA) for assistance in budgeting, human resource management, and strategic planning. It received its charter under Public Law 98-257 on April 10, 1984. The charter outlines the NAPA's objectives and purposes of corporation as follows:

1. Evaluating the structure administration, operation, and program performance of federal and other governments and government agencies, anticipating, identifying, and analyzing significant problems and suggesting timely corrective action;
2. Foreseeing and examining critical emerging issues in governance, formulating practical approaches to their resolution;
3. Assessing the effectiveness, structure, administration, and implications for governance of present or proposed public programs, policies, and processes, recommending specific changes;
4. Advising on the relationship of federal, state, regional, and local governments; increasing public officials', citizens', and scholars' understanding of requirements and opportunities for sound governance and how these can be effectively met; and
5. Demonstrating by the conduct of its affairs a commitment to the highest professional standards of ethics and scholarship.

The Boys & Girls Clubs of America received a congressional charter in 1956 and provides educational and recreational support to almost five million children in over four thousand locations in all the fifty states, Puerto Rico, and the U.S. Virgin Islands.

These organizations completely manage their own affairs but provide invaluable support to the U.S. government and citizens. The following are other examples (see Appendix J for a complete list):

The American Legion
Big Brothers–Big Sisters of America
Frederick Douglas Memorial and Historical Association
Future Farmers of America
Girl Scouts of America
The National Society of the Daughters of the American Revolution
United States Olympic Committee
Vietnam Veterans of America, Inc.

CHECKS AND BALANCES AMONG THE THREE BRANCHES

The U.S. government operates under a system of checks and balances. The nation's founders developed this system to balance the need for a strong central government with protections against any one person or group gaining control of the government. These checks and balances are achieved by the separation of powers among the three branches. The primary duty of the legislative branch is to make laws, of the executive branch is to execute laws, and of the judicial branch is to ensure laws are being made and executed according to the Constitution. Leaders in each branch take actions that affect the structure and membership of the other two branches, take actions to ensure members of the other branches do not overstep their authority, and take actions when they do not agree with decisions being made in the other branches.

The executive branch (led by the president) recommends laws, nominates federal judges, and makes treaties with foreign nations. The president can veto laws passed by Congress if he or she does not agree with them. The vice president has influence over Congress as the official president of the Senate. The president nominates Supreme Court judges and can therefore nominate someone with similar ideologies. The president can pardon officials found guilty by the courts, or refuse to enforce a Supreme Court ruling since the Supreme Court has no power to enforce the rulings it makes. However, the president can face drastic political repercussions if Supreme Court rulings are ignored.

The legislative branch (led by two chambers of Congress) has ultimate approval of foreign treaties established by the president, can investigate actions taken by the executive branch, and can impeach the president. Congress can require the executive branch to submit reports on programs and policies, and can also conduct investigations and audits. The president is required to provide Congress an annual State of the Union address. Congress can overturn presidential vetoes with approval by two-thirds of its members. It must approve presidential nominations before they can take effect, including nominations for the president's cabinet and the president's nomination of Supreme Court justices. The president cannot declare war without congressional approval. Congress controls the budget of the entire federal government. It can pass or amend laws in favor of or against court cases, alter the size of the Supreme Court, establish lower courts, and impeach Supreme Court justices and other federal judges. Congress can pass legislation when it does not agree with a Supreme Court decision. For example, Congress passed the Civil Rights Act of 1991 in response to Supreme Court rulings it found too conservative against discrimination.

The judicial branch (led by the Supreme Court) hears court cases on executive and legislative issues. It can declare presidential actions unconstitutional. It can also declare laws passed by Congress unconstitutional. The Court conducts judicial reviews as part of their checks and balances of the other two branches. These reviews are conducted to ensure laws passed and actions taken are constitutional. The Supreme Court also reviews the acts and laws of state legislatures. The Chief Justice sits as president of the Senate during presidential impeachment hearings. Judges are appointed for life and their salaries cannot be reduced, so are not influenced by political bias.

RELATIONSHIP OF THE FEDERAL GOVERNMENT TO STATE GOVERNMENTS

The sovereignty of the states to run their internal affairs without federal government interference was originally established under the Articles of Confederation in 1775. After much debate and compromise, the U.S. Constitution established the United States as a federal republic wherein the federal and state governments share powers. The states delegate certain powers to the national government. These enumerated powers were delegated by the states ratifying the Constitution, as outlined in Article I, Section 8, of the U.S. Constitution. Examples include Congress' sole power to raise a navy, establish lower federal courts, and regulate commerce with foreign nations. Those powers that are therefore not specifically delegated to the federal government in the Constitution are reserved for the states.

Implementing the government under federalism was a compromise that solved the debate over sovereignty and whether more power should be vested in the national or state governments. Both federal and state governments hold concurrent powers under federalism. Examples of concurrent powers include the power to levy and collect taxes, charter banks, and to make and enforce laws. Other countries using a form of federalism include Argentina, Australia, Germany, Switzerland, Mexico, Canada, and Brazil.

The Constitution declares that all laws created by the federal government take precedence over conflicting state laws. There have therefore been instances in which the federal government has acted to render a state law ineffective. For example, President George W. Bush made several attempts to pass federal legislation banning same-sex marriages in response to a growing number of states passing laws allowing these marriages. The goal of this new legislation was not to stop individual states from passing laws, but rather to invalidate the federal government's legal recognition of such marriages or the requirement that other states must recognize them.

The states can influence federal laws. Two-thirds of the state legislatures can request that Congress call for a national convention to vote on a proposed Constitutional amendment. This has only been done once and led to the ratification of the Twenty-first Amendment that ended prohibition. Two or more states can also join and pass laws to attempt to influence the federal government to act. For example, Governor Arnold Schwarzenegger attempted to pass stricter emission laws in California in an attempt to be a catalyst for stricter federal laws. As of December 2007, however, his efforts were being blocked by the executive branch. This action has brought more controversy to the issue and prompted other states to side with California.

The states' government structure are similar to that of the federal government. The states also operate under a system of checks and balances with three branches. The governor is their chief executive officer, each state's legislature makes laws, and their state courts interpret laws and provide judicial oversight over the other two branches. Each state passes a state Constitution, similar to the U.S. Constitution. Laws, rules, and regulations are not only passed at the state level, but also by counties, districts, school districts, and other municipalities. Municipal laws are called ordinances. Local governments also have chief executive officers, such as a mayor or county administrator. Just as federal agencies execute and enforce federal laws, the states have state administrative agencies that execute and enforce state laws.

3

FEDERAL GOVERNMENT EMPLOYEES

Civil servants are the foundation of the federal government. These career employees provide continuity to the government and complete the daily tasks of agency operations. Working within a system of bureaucracy, civil servants are provided an array of protections against employment discrimination through various acts and agencies charged with ensuring federal employees are recruited and retained per merit principles. Civil servants are also held to high standards of ethical conduct in their positions.

CIVIL SERVANTS

Civil servants carry out the daily work of the federal government. According to *United States Code* Title 5, Section 2101 (5 U.S.C. 2101), the civil service consists of all appointive positions in the executive, judicial, and legislative branches of the government of the United States, except positions in the uniformed services. *Uniformed services* are made up of the armed forces, the commissioned corps of the Public Health Service, and the commissioned corps of the National Oceanic and Atmospheric Administration. *Armed forces* are made up of the Army, Navy, Air Force, Marine Corps, and Coast Guard. The civil service consists of civilian employees who have chosen a career in the public sector. In other words, these employees are not political appointees, members of the armed services, or elected officials. They have applied for their jobs and were selected (i.e., appointed) based on their qualifications and are therefore not affected by partisanship. Since they competed for their jobs, they are considered competitive workers.

The existence of these permanent, nonelected, nonpartisan employees is critical to the success of the U.S. system of government. Civil service employees ensure laws and policies are executed without bias. Their existence in agencies ensures that a continuity of expertise remains in place within organizations.

PROFILE OF CIVILIAN WORKERS IN THE FEDERAL GOVERNMENT

Table 3.1 shows the total number of employees in the federal civilian workforce in 2007. The federal workforce consisted of 2.67 million people, or approximately 2 percent of the total U.S. workforce. By far, the executive branch has the largest workforce of the three branches, employing 97.7 percent of the federal workforce in 2007. The legislative branch employed 1.1 percent of the federal workforce and the judicial branch 1.2 percent. The Department of Defense employed 25.1 percent of all workers.

The Office of Personnel Management provides an annual profile of the federal civilian workforce. Its 2006 profile was conducted on 1.8 million federal workers. As of September 30, 2006, 93.5 percent were permanent full-time employees, with the remainder split among part-time (3.5 percent), and intermittent (2.8 percent) employees. The average age of full-time federal workers was 46.9 years, their average length of government service was 16.3 years, and the average worldwide base salary

Table 3.1.   Total Civilian Employment of the Federal Government by Branch in January 2007

Branch	Total civilian employment	Percent of employees
Total, all agencies*	2,670,857	
Legislative branch	29,364	1.1%
Judicial branch	31,928	1.2%
Executive branch	2,609,565	97.7%
Executive Office of the President	1,719	0.1%
Executive departments	1,674,713	62.7%
Department of State	34,446	1.3%
Department of the Treasury	110,078	4.1%
Department of Defense	670,686	25.1%
Department of Justice	106,745	4.0%
Department of the Interior	65,854	2.5%
Department of Agriculture	93,484	3.5%
Department of Commerce	39,381	1.5%
Department of Labor	16,126	0.6%
Department of Health and Human Services	60,512	2.3%
Department of Housing and Urban Development	9,720	0.4%
Department of Transportation	53,221	2.0%
Department of Energy	14,608	0.5%
Department of Education	4,157	0.2%
Department of Veterans Affairs	242,641	9.1%
Department of Homeland Security	153,054	5.7%
Independent agencies	93,133	3.5%

*Excludes Central Intelligence Agency, National Security Agency, Defense Intelligence Agency, and National Imagery and Mapping Agency.

Aerial photograph of the Pentagon. *Courtesy of the U.S. Department of Defense.*

was $66,371. The average salary was higher in the Washington, DC area at $86,444. Men comprised 55.9 percent of the workforce, 32.1 percent were minorities, and 6.8 percent had disabilities. Approximately 43 percent of workers had at least a bachelor's degree, and white-collar workers were 88.9 percent of the workforce (U.S. Office of Personnel Management, 2006).

HOW FEDERAL EMPLOYEES PERFORM THEIR JOBS

Federal employees perform their jobs within a system based on bureaucracy. Generally Max Weber identified seven principles or characteristics of bureaucracies, which hold true for the U.S. federal government (Weber, 1946):

1. There is a hierarchical division of labor.
2. There are clear and documented rules for conducting business.
3. Work is accomplished by full-time permanent professionals who are specialists in their fields.
4. Professionals do not have personal ownership of their jobs (i.e., their professional and private lives are completely separate).
5. Professionals are accountable for their assigned duties.
6. Rules and duties are executed impersonally.
7. Employees advance based on merit.

There first exists a formal hierarchical chain of organizations reporting to a central administration. For example, the Department of State reports to the president. Numerous under secretaries report to the secretary of state. Each under secretary is in charge of subordinate agencies (or offices) that in turn have their own chain of command. Next, there is a formal, hierarchical line of authority within each agency. Authority and responsibilities are delegated to specific individuals within agencies by departments. Standardized procedures for accomplishing duties and formal divisions of labor based on assigned employee duties exist. These duties are assigned based on job specialties.

Professional jobs (i.e., white-collar jobs) in the federal government are designated as part of the general schedule (GS). Blue-collar positions are designated as wage grade (WG) jobs. Positions in the government are further designated by an occupational group and then a numerical Series. An occupational group consists of jobs that are similar. Examples of occupational groups are accounting and budget, human resource management, engineering and architecture, information and arts, and information technology management. A series is a subdivision of an occupational group further consisting of positions similar in specialized line of work and qualification requirements. It identifies specific positions and qualification standards that outline the skills required to accomplish duties. The following are examples of GS series positions under the occupational group accounting and budget:

GS-501	Financial Administration and Program Series
GS-510	Accounting Series
GS-511	Auditing Series
GS-512	Internal Revenue Agent Series
GS-525	Accounting Technician Series
GS-526	Tax Specialist Series
GS-560	Budget Analysis Series
GS-570	Financial Institution Examining Series
GS-592	Tax Examining Series

Here, the GS-592 series consists of senior managers, supervisors, nonsupervisory employees, and trainees, all of whom perform tasks related to tax examining. Managerial and supervisory positions have additional requirements above the technical expertise required of tax examiners, such as the ability to plan work and the ability to communicate effectively.

The duties, responsibilities, and areas of accountability for each civil servant job are outlined in a position description. This document is issued to employees at the time of their official appointment and maintained for each position at each grade level. Based on the information contained in their position descriptions, employees are rated according to performance standards, which outline threshold levels of an employee's performance required to be rated as unsuccessful, successful or exceptional in completing the duties outlined in their position description. Normally, these standards are established on several critical elements of the job. In some agencies, employees are rated on a range. For example, there may be various ranges of what is considered being qualified as successful depending upon an employee's level of performance compared to several rating factors. Employees' ratings may affect their salary levels and may be used as the basis for monetary or nonmonetary awards. Employees are held accountable to their position descriptions and performance standards as part of their performance plans, and supervisors cannot require employees to perform duties not outlined in these documents.

Federal employees maintain professional and impersonal relationships. They interact with employees in other departments and agencies, in their own and other branches, and in private sector organizations. They interact with the media, regulators, educators, and citizens. The levels, frequencies, and reasons for contact constantly change due to changing customer needs, new laws and regulations, and changes in the global environment.

LAWS PROTECTING THE RIGHTS OF FEDERAL EMPLOYEES

Federal employees have several laws that protect their professional rights. According to the Equal Employment Opportunity Commission (EEOC), employees are protected from discrimination based on race, color, religion, sex, national origin, disability, or age. They cannot be discriminated against in hiring or firing; compensation, assignment, or classification; transfer, promotion, layoff, or recall; job advertisements; recruitment; testing; use of company facilities; training and apprenticeship programs; fringe benefits; pay, retirement plans, and disability leave; or other terms and conditions of employment (U.S. Equal Employment Opportunity Commission, 2004). Other prohibited actions are pregnancy discrimination, sexual harassment, and retaliation. Retaliation is an adverse action being taken against a person because he or she submitted a complaint, participated in a case, or opposed discrimination or harassment in any other manner. Laws protecting the rights of employees in all of these cases are enforced by agency-level equal employment offices as well as the EEOC. The EEOC provides oversight and coordination over all federal equal employment opportunity laws and policies. The following are summaries of some of the acts they enforce:

- The Equal Pay Act of 1963 (EPA) prohibits sex-based wage discrimination and requires employees of different sexes who perform substantially the same work to be provided equal pay.
- Title VII of the Civil Rights Act of 1964 prohibits employment discrimination based on race, color, religion, sex, or national origin. It also prohibits reprisal or retaliation against employees participating in the complaint process or for opposing any unlawful employment practice covered by Title VII. The Supreme Court ruled in *Oncale v. Sundowner Offshore Services, Incorporated*, 523 U.S. 75 (1998) that Title VII covers same-sex discrimination and harassment.
- The Age Discrimination in Employment Act of 1967 (ADEA) protects individuals who are forty years of age or older from employment discrimination.
- The Rehabilitation Act of 1973 prohibits discrimination against qualified individuals with disabilities who work in the federal government. Agencies must also provide qualified individuals with reasonable accommodations.
- The Americans with Disabilities Act of 1990 (ADA) prohibits state and local governments, employment agencies, and labor unions from discriminating against qualified individuals with disabilities (physical or mental) in employment, transportation, public accommodation, communications, and governmental activities.
- The Civil Rights Act of 1991 provides monetary damages for employees who have been subjected to employment discrimination.

These laws collectively prohibit actions falling under various categories of discrimination (U.S. Equal Employment Opportunity Commission, 2003, pp. 4–5):

1. Harassment on the basis of race, color, religion, sex, national origin, disability, or age;
2. Retaliation against an individual for filing a charge of discrimination, participating in an investigation, or opposing discriminatory practices;

3. Employment decisions based on stereotypes or nonwork-related assumptions about the abilities, traits, or performance of individuals of a certain sex, race, age, religion, or ethnic group, or individuals with disabilities;
4. Denying employment opportunities to a person because of marriage to, or association with, an individual of a particular race, religion, national origin, or an individual with a disability; and
5. Neutral practices and neutral policies that adversely affect individuals because of their race, color, religion, sex, or national origin when the neutral practices and policies cannot be shown to be justified by business necessity.

Discrimination charges can be filed with the EEOC by any individuals who believe they have been harmed. They may also be filed by an organization, agency, or other individual on behalf of an individual in order to protect that individual's identity. A charge must be filed within 180 of the date of the alleged discriminatory action. This deadline is extended to 300 days if state or local discrimination laws have also been violated. Charges under the Equal Pay Act do not have to be filed with the EEOC before a suit is filed in court, so these time limits do not apply.

After a charge is filed with the EEOC, the employer is notified of the filing and charges. The case is investigated to determine if a violation of law actually took place. If evidence supports the claim of discrimination, the EEOC will attempt to reach an informal settlement between the parties (i.e., outside of a formal court hearing). EEOC offers mediation as a possible means of resolving the case, but all parties in the case (employer and employee) must agree to mediation. Mediation involves a neutral third party meeting with and relaying information from one party to the other in an attempt to reach a mutual agreement on a settlement. The mediator cannot make a decision or enforce any actions. If mediation is not used or is unsuccessful, the agency or the employer can take the case to federal court. If the court rules in favor of the employee, the employer may be required to provide several types of relief (i.e., remedies) to the employee. Monetary relief may include financial compensation to the employee for any lost gains in wages (if the charge was based on the employee not being given a job or promotion), or monetary damages (liquidated, compensatory, or punitive). Monetary relief may also include paying the plaintiff's attorney fees, fees for expert witnesses, and court costs. Nonmonetary relief may include hiring the claimant, granting them a noncompetitive promotion, reinstating them into a position, or allowing them to take specific training they desire.

The aim of the relief is make the claimant "whole," which means to put the claimant in the position or condition they would have been in if the discriminatory act had not taken place. The employer may also be required to take corrective or preventive actions to ensure the source of the discrimination does not occur again. For example, a discriminating supervisor may be penalized, moved to another position, or removed. A new position may be established to provide oversight over employees and enforce actions taken to eliminate the source of the discrimination. The harmed employee and discriminating supervisor may sign a binding agreement on specific corrective courses of action. Additionally, the employee who suffered discrimination may be offered a position in another area or position of their choice.

A law that protects both federal employees and citizens is the Privacy Act of 1974, which prohibits agencies from obtaining, maintaining, or disclosing information about individuals that is not necessary and pertinent. Individuals have a right to gain access to any information maintained about them and to make corrections to the information if needed. Agencies are required to have administrative procedures for releasing information, and security systems and processes to safeguard the security of information. There are exceptions or stipulations as to when personal information can be disclosed:

- to those officers and employees of the agency that maintains the record who have a need for the record in the performance of their duties
- for a routine use (i.e., for the purpose the data was collected)
- to the Bureau of the Census for purposes of planning or carrying out a census or survey or related activity
- to a recipient who has provided the agency with advance adequate written assurance that the record will be used solely as a statistical research or reporting record, and that the record is to be transferred in a form that is not individually identifiable
- to the National Archives and Records Administration as a record that has sufficient historical or other value to warrant its continued preservation by the United States government, or for evaluation by the archivist of the United States or the designee of the archivist to determine whether the record has such value
- to another agency or to an instrumentality of any governmental jurisdiction within or under the control of the United States for a civil or criminal law enforcement activity if the activity is authorized by law, and if the head of the agency or instrumentality has made a written request to the agency that maintains the record specifying the particular portion desired and the law enforcement activity for which the record is sought
- to a person pursuant to a showing of compelling circumstances affecting the health or safety of an individual if upon such disclosure notification is transmitted to the last known address of such individual
- to either chamber of Congress, or, to the extent of the matter within its jurisdiction, any committee or subcommittee thereof, any joint committee of Congress or subcommittee of a joint committee
- to the comptroller general, or authorized representatives, in the course of the performance of the duties of the government accountability office
- pursuant to the order of a court of competent jurisdiction
- to a consumer reporting agency in accordance with established rules

The Computer Matching and Privacy Protection Act of 1988 amended the Privacy Act to establish requirements for the exchange of information across agencies. It requires that information collected must only be used for the purpose it was originally intended, even if allowed to be shared with another agency. Data matching is regulated by this act and involves two or more agencies using specific information about an individual in order to conduct computer matches to identify him or her. An example would be an individual's social security number being used to match his or her records from two computer systems.

AGENCIES OVERSEEING THE CIVIL SERVICE SYSTEM

Unlike private sector employees, public sector employees are prohibited by law from taking certain actions. For example, they cannot endorse private organizations in connection with their positions, or accept payment for speaking engagements associated with their positions. Under the Hatch Act Reform Amendments of 1993 (latest amendment to the Hatch Act of 1939), public employees are prohibited from running for political offices and from engaging in political activities in connection with their jobs.

Restrictions on government employees have not always been so stringent. Reforms to the civil service system are the result of actions to end years of corruption in federal employment. Under what was termed the *spoils system*, prior to 1883 political candidates who were elected to office would appoint their loyal supporters to coveted public offices. They also gave jobs to family members and close friends. The final event that led to effective reforms was the assassination of President James A. Garfield in 1881 by a disappointed attorney whose application to be the U.S. ambassador to France was denied. In 1883, the Pendleton Civil Service Reform Act was passed and established the U.S. Civil Service Commission. This placed most federal employees under a merit system in which they competed for job vacancies and promotions based upon their individual qualifications (i.e., skills, training and experience). The commission was reorganized under the Civil Service Reform Act of 1978 (also known as the Federal Service Labor-Management Relations Statute) and replaced by three separate agencies: the Office of Personnel Management, the Federal Labor Relations Authority, and the U.S. Merit Systems Protection Board.

The Office of Personnel Management (OPM) oversees the recruiting, hiring, and evaluating of civil servants. Based on the principle of merit promotion, civil servants compete for promotions based on their professional experience, seniority, on-the-job training, and professional training. In some agencies, written exams are also administered. Under the Civil Service Reform Act of 1978 (5 U.S.C. 2301):

- recruitment should be from qualified individuals from appropriate sources in an endeavor to achieve a work force from all segments of society, and selection and advancement should be determined solely on the basis of relative ability, knowledge, and skills, after fair and open competition, which assures that all receive equal opportunity;
- all employees and applicants for employment should receive fair and equitable treatment in all aspects of personnel management without regard to political affiliation, race, color, religion, national origin, sex, marital status, age, or handicapping condition, and with proper regard for their privacy and constitutional rights;
- equal pay should be provided for work of equal value, with appropriate consideration of both national and local rates paid by employers in the private sector, and appropriate incentives and recognition should be provided for excellence in performance.

The Federal Labor Relations Authority (FLRA) is an independent administrative agency responsible for administrating the labor–management relations programs for federal employees. Its primary responsibilities include the following:

- resolving complaints of unfair labor practices
- determining the appropriateness of units for labor organization representation
- adjudicating exceptions to arbitrator's awards
- adjudicating legal issues relating to duty to bargain/negotiability
- resolving impasses during negotiations

The U.S. Merit Systems Protection Board (MSPB) ensures federal employees are protected from management abuse, that executive branch agencies execute employment decisions and programs according to the principles of the merit system, and that prohibited practices that negatively affect merit system principles are not used. The board hears numerous types of cases by federal employees, including appeals of personnel actions such as suspensions, removal, or demotions; appeals under the civil service retirement programs; requests to review OPM regulations that may result in prohibited personnel practices; and studies of the civil service system to ensure it is free from prohibited personnel practices.

The EEOC promotes equal opportunity in employment by enforcing the federal civil rights employment laws through administrative and judicial actions. It also educates agencies and other components of the federal government on applicable laws, agency regulations, and acceptable employment practices. The EEOC is an independent agency originally created by Congress in 1964 to enforce Title VII of the Civil Rights Act of 1964. It now enforces numerous federal laws affecting federal employment. These laws protect employees in hiring, training, pay, promotions, maintaining their employment, and separation from federal service. The EEOC is composed of five commissioners appointed by the president for five-year staggered terms. Their appointments are subject to approval by the Senate. The commissioners establish equal employment policy and approve litigations. The EEOC is also composed of a general counsel appointed by the president for four years, who conducts litigations. The president also designates a chair and vice-chair of the commission. The commission has district offices, field offices, area offices, and local offices across the United States.

Nonsupervisory employees may also submit complaints to the local unions. The American Federation of Government Employees is the largest federal employee union. It represents approximately six hundred thousand federal employees and provides federal employees legal representation, legislative advocacy, technical expertise, and informational services.

ETHICS IN FEDERAL EMPLOYMENT

Federal employees are required to follow statutory and moral codes of ethics. Part 2635 of Title 5 of the *Code of Federal Regulations* (5 C.F.R. Part 2635) contains the *Standards of Ethical Conduct for Executive Branch Employees* that extensively provides ethical regulations for employees. The following are the subparts or sections of the Standards and examples of rules in each:

> Subpart A outlines the basic obligation of employees in public service. A basic principle stated is that "*Public service is a public trust*" requiring employees to place "loyalty to the Constitution, the laws and ethical principles above private gain."
>
> Subpart B provides guidelines for accepting gifts from outside sources and provides examples of gifts that are acceptable and prohibited. For example, it states
>
> an employee shall not: (1) Accept a gift in return for being influenced in the performance of an official act; (2) Solicit or coerce the offering of a gift; (3) Accept gifts from the same or different sources on a basis so frequent that a reasonable person would be led to believe the employee is using his public office for private gain; . . . (4) Accept a gift in violation of any statute . . . (5) Accept vendor promotional training contrary to applicable regulations, policies or guidance relating to the procurement of supplies and services for the Government.
>
> Subpart C provides guidelines for gifts between employees. For example, "an employee may not: (1) Directly or indirectly, give a gift to or make a donation toward a gift for an official superior; or (2) Solicit a contribution from another employee for a gift to either his own or the other employee's official superior."

Subpart D defines financial interests (such as investments) that conflict with federal service. For example,

An agency may prohibit or restrict an individual employee from acquiring or holding a financial interest or a class of financial interests based upon the agency designee's determination that the holding of such interest or interests will: (1) Require the employee's disqualification from matters so central or critical to the performance of his official duties that the employee's ability to perform the duties of his position would be materially impaired; or (2) Adversely affect the efficient accomplishment of the agency's mission because another employee cannot be readily assigned to perform work from which the employee would be disqualified by reason of the financial interest.

Subpart E contains two basic provisions for employees to maintain an appearance of impartiality in performing their duties:

Unless he receives prior authorization, an employee should not participate in a particular matter involving specific parties which he knows is likely to affect the financial interests of a member of his household, or in which he knows a person with whom he has a covered relationship is or represents a party, if he determines that a reasonable person with knowledge of the relevant facts would question his impartiality in the matter . . . [and] an employee who has received an extraordinary severance or other payment from a former employer prior to entering Government service is subject, in the absence of a waiver, to a two-year period of disqualification from participation in particular matters in which that former employer is or represents a party.

Subpart F outlines rules for seeking employment outside and after federal service. In summary, "it addresses the requirement of 18 U.S.C. 208(a) that an employee disqualify himself from participation in any particular matter that will have a direct and predictable effect on the financial interests of a person 'with whom he is negotiating or has any arrangement concerning prospective employment.'"

Subpart G defines four situations where an employee can misuse his or her position: use of public office for private gain, use of nonpublic information, misuse of government property, and misuse of official time. For example, "An employee shall not engage in a financial transaction using nonpublic information, nor allow the improper use of nonpublic information to further his own private interest or that of another, whether through advice or recommendation, or by knowing unauthorized disclosure. . . . For purposes of this section, nonpublic information is information that the employee gains by reason of Federal employment and that he knows or reasonably should know has not been made available to the general public."

Subpart H discusses allowed and prohibited activities outside of work, including outside employment, serving as an expert witness, participating in professional associations, teaching, speaking, writing, and fund-raising. For example, a government employee "shall not receive compensation from any source other than the Government for teaching, speaking or writing that relates to the employee's official duties."

Subpart I lists related statutes affecting employment. Just a few include

(a) The prohibition against solicitation or receipt of bribes (18 U.S.C. 201(b)). (b) The prohibition against solicitation or receipt of Illegal gratuities (18 U.S.C. 201(c)). . . . (d) The prohibition against assisting in the prosecution of Claims against the Government or acting as agent or attorney before the Government (18 U.S.C. 205). . . . (f) The prohibition on certain former agency officials' acceptance of compensation from a contractor (41 U.S.C. 423(d)). . . . (s) The prohibition against Employment of an individual who habitually uses intoxicating beverages to excess (5 U.S.C. 7352). . . . (z) The prohibitions against disclosure of classified information (18 U.S.C. 798 and 50 U.S.C. 783(b)). . . . (gg) The prohibition against participation in the Appointment or promotion of relatives (5 U.S.C. 3110). . . . (kk) The prohibition against failing to account for public money (18 U.S.C. 643).

Employees of the legislative branch have guidelines for employment in the House of Representatives and the Senate. Some of the stipulations outlined in the *Ethics Manual for Members, Officers, and Employees of the U.S. House of Representatives* (House Committee on Standards of Ethical Conduct, 1992) include the following sections:

1. A Member, officer, or employee of the House of Representatives shall conduct himself at all times in a manner which shall reflect creditably on the House of Representatives. . . .
3. A Member, officer, or employee of the House of Representatives shall receive no compensation nor shall he permit any compensation to accrue to his beneficial interest from any source, the receipt of which would occur by virtue of influence improperly exerted from his position in the Congress. . . .
5. A Member, officer, or employee of the House of Representatives shall accept no honorarium for a speech, writing for publication, or other similar activity. . . .
6. A Member of the House of Representatives shall keep his campaign funds separate from his personal funds. A Member shall convert no campaign funds to personal use in excess of reimbursement for legitimate and verifiable campaign expenditures and shall expend no funds from his campaign account not attributable to bona fide campaign or political purposes. . . .
9. A Member, officer, or employee of the House of Representatives shall not discharge or refuse to hire any individual, or otherwise discriminate against any individual with respect to compensation, terms, conditions, or privileges of employment, because of such individual's race, color, religion, sex (including marital or parental status), age, or national origin, but may take into consideration the domicile or political affiliation of such individual.

The Senate has a *Senate Ethics Manual* (U.S. Senate Select Committee on Ethics, 2003) that outlines rules for gifts, conflicts of interest, income earned outside of the Senate, prohibition on unofficial office accounts, financial disclosure, political activity, use of rank, use of stationary, use of Senate facilities, constituent service, and employment practices. For example, the manual stipulates the following regulation for gifts:

A Member, officer, or employee may accept a gift (other than cash or cash equivalent) which the Member, officer, or employee reasonably and in good faith believes to have a value of less than $50, and a cumulative value from one source during a calendar year of less than $100. No gift with a value below $10 shall count toward the $100 annual limit. No formal recordkeeping is required by this paragraph, but a Member, officer, or employee shall make a good faith effort to comply with this paragraph.

The manual requires members of the Senate to complete financial disclosures because "Public disclosure of a public official's personal financial interests is often considered the key component to an effective code of conduct for legislative ethics." Senators must respond to all constituent requests and complaints, regardless of the constituent's political affiliation.

The Senate developed its ethical code of conduct in large part because of the misconduct of one of its own members. The following section from the *Senate Ethics Manual* describes the impetus for Senate reforms:

> Momentum for reform grew after Robert G. (Bobby) Baker, Secretary to the Democratic Majority, resigned from his job in October 1963 following allegations that he had misused his official position for personal, financial gain. For the next year and a half, the Senate Rules and Administration Committee held hearings to investigate the business interests and activities of Senate officials and employees (focused on Bobby Baker) in order to ascertain what, if any, conflicts of interest or other improprieties existed and whether any additional laws or regulations were needed. The Senate recognized that serious allegations had been made against a former employee and that it had no specific rules or regulations governing the duties and scope of activities of Members, officers, and employees.
>
> In its first report, the Rules Committee characterized many of Baker's outside activities as being in conflict with his official duties and made several recommendations, including adoption of public financial disclosure rules and other guidelines for senatorial employees.
>
> Subsequently, as part of its conclusion of the Baker case, the Rules Committee held additional hearings on proposals advocating a code of ethics in conjunction with a pending pay raise, the creation of a joint congressional ethics committee to write an ethics code, and the adoption of various rules requiring public disclosure of personal finances by Senators and staff and the disclosure of ex-parte communications. Additions to the Senate rules—calling for public financial disclosure reports and more controls on staff involvement in Senate campaign funds—were then introduced to implement the Committee's Baker investigation recommendations.

Numerous ethical laws and regulations, particularly in connection with their licenses to practice law, bind judges and lawyers in the judicial branch. New federal judges are issued a pamphlet entitled *Ethics Essentials: A Primer for New Judges on Conflicts, Outside Activities, and Other Potential Pitfalls* (Judicial Conference of the United States, 2006). It provides rules and guidelines for conflicts of interest and recusal, gifts from outside sources, use of official positions, outside activities, fund-raising activities, political activities, and former employment. It summarizes standards of conduct, and provides examples of situations new judges may encounter. It also includes checklists for determining allowed and prohibited financial and other interests. The document provides the following canons of the Principles of Ethical Conduct:

- A judge should uphold the integrity and independence of the judiciary.
- A judge should avoid impropriety and the appearance of impropriety in all activities.
- A judge should perform the duties of the office impartially and diligently.
- A judge may engage in extra-judicial activities to improve the law, the legal system, and the administration of justice.
- A judge should regulate extra-judicial activities to minimize the risk of conflict with judicial duties.
- A judge should regularly file reports of compensation received for law-related and extra-judicial activities.
- A judge should refrain from political activity.

There are many other laws, regulations, and guidance governing the entire federal government. The Ethics in Government Act of 1978 requires government officials to disclose their financial holdings by filing financial disclosure statements within specific periods of time. The act covers employees in all three branches of government, including the president, vice president, and candidates running for office in the executive and legislative branches. The Lobbying Disclosure Act of 1995 requires executive branch officials to disclose contacts with lobbyists. Guidance from the National Archives and Records Administration (NARA) reminds heads of federal agencies that official records must remain in the custody of the agency. Additionally, most agencies issue their own internal codes of ethics to employees.

GOVERNMENT OUTSOURCING (PRIVATIZATION)

Private sector contractors are now performing many functions that were once performed by government employees. Called *outsourcing* or *privatization*, agencies hire contractors to provide temporary or permanent services. Agencies are faced with the dual challenge of reducing the size of the federal workforce while ensuring vital services are still being provided. Outsourcing allows them to meet their personnel level goals because contractors are not counted as government employees. Contractors are held to contractual performance standards, and sometimes provided financial incentives if they exceed threshold levels of performance.

There are many benefits to agencies when jobs are outsourced. Utilizing contractors gives agencies access to best commercial practices in providing support to customers. It also gives them access to the latest innovations in technology being developed by the commercial market. Agencies are able to reduce their costs and expenditures by not having to hire full-time permanent workers who require continual training and benefits. Agencies no longer have to deal with human resource responsibilities such as hiring, training, and maintaining personnel records for work that is outsourced. They also do not have to deal with problem employees. Contractors who do not perform well are quickly dismissed.

There are some issues that must be addressed when a government agency is considering outsourcing. Certain government jobs are considered "core" and cannot be outsourced. Core positions are those that are considered critical or sensitive and thus can only be performed by a government employee. Another concern is ensuring that outsourcing does not violate federal laws mandating a certain percentage of work remaining with the government. For example, under Title 10 of the U.S. Code, "Not more than 50 percent of the funds made available in a fiscal year to a military department or a Defense Agency for depot-level maintenance and repair workload may be used to contract for the performance by non-Federal Government personnel of such workload for the military department or the Defense Agency." In layman's terms, this means that a military department or agency cannot spend more than fifty percent of its funding on contracts awarded to private contractors in support of work being done by their government repair facilities. Also, even though positions or tasks are outsourced, the government still maintains all responsibility and accountability. Lastly, agencies must develop contingency plans in case an outsourcing contract is canceled or not renewed.

4

FEDERAL ELECTIONS

The electoral process that occurs every four years in the United States to select the president is very complex. Beginning up to two years before the general election, the election process begins with potential candidates seeking the nomination of their respective political parties. Candidates travel the nation, and sometimes the world, striving to gain financial and political support with the ultimate goal of making it to their party conventions. Throughout the process, they abide by both their political party rules and federal campaign laws. The process culminates with the Electoral College selecting the president and vice president, primarily based upon the votes of the general population.

POLITICAL PARTIES

Most candidates running for presidential, congressional, gubernatorial, and state congressional positions are members of political parties. Members of federal and state executive and legislative branches make decisions, set policies, and support legislation in large part based on their party affiliation. Political parties evolved from individuals with common ideas and ideologies joining together to use their collective power and influence to sway the government to make decisions in their favor. There have been political parties ever since the presidency of George Washington. Alexander Hamilton and John Adams led the Federalists, who favored a strong central government. Thomas Jefferson and James Madison led the Democratic-Republicans (or the Anti-Federalists), who favored a weaker central government, with more power being given to the states. Today, political parties have become the foundation of our political system.

Political parties are structured entities with clear purposes and clear lines of responsibility and authority. They have clear and structured political agendas, and have organized support in Congress, the states, and in local governments. They help candidates raise campaign funds and they develop future leaders for the party by grooming young members in the political process. Each party has a national organization that oversees its affairs, led by an elected national chairman. The Democratic National Convention (DNC) "plans the Party's quadrennial Presidential nominating convention; promotes the election of Party candidates with both technical and financial support; and works

President Gerald R. Ford and former California governor Ronald W. Reagan, rivals for the Republican Party's 1976 presidential nomination. The two shared the podium in a show of party solidarity on the closing night of the Republican National Convention, August 19, 1976. *William Fitzpatrick/Gerald R. Ford Library.*

with national, State, and local party organizations, elected officials, candidates, and constituencies to respond to the needs and views of the Democratic electorate and the nation" (Democratic National Committee, 2008). The Republican National Committee (RNC) performs basically the same functions for the Republican party.

Individuals usually choose a political party based on which one they believe most represents their views on a majority of issues. Each party has a party platform (also called a *national platform* or *political agenda*) that outlines the party's official position on a variety of issues. The issues are organized into categories called *planks*. These issues may include support for abortion, a strong military, or government involvement in the affairs of private businesses. Others choose a party due to their admiration or feeling of commonality with individuals in the party. Over time, some people change parties for such reasons as a change in their personal views, disagreement with the position of party leaders on pertinent issues, or a gaining of respect for political leaders of another party.

There are two dominant political parties in the United States: Democratic and Republican. The Republican party is also called the GOP (Grand Old Party). Over the years the basic ideologies of these parties have changed. Changing party platforms and apathy toward the two leading parties has given rise to some citizens declaring themselves Independents. During elections, these voters are more prone to vote for the candidate that is running as an Independent (i.e., not associated with an organized political party), or for other individual candidates rather than for all the candidates from the same party.

The donkey is the official symbol of the Democratic party. The elephant is the official symbol of the Republican party. The origins of each party are best described from the histories on each of their official websites:

Thomas Jefferson founded the Democratic Party in 1792 as a Congressional caucus to fight for the Bill of Rights and against the elitist Federalist Party. In 1798, the "party of the common" was officially named the Democratic-Republican Party and in 1800 elected Jefferson as the first Democratic President of the United States. . . . In 1848, the National Convention established the Democratic National Committee, now the longest running political organization in the world. The Convention charged the DNC with the responsibility of promoting "the Democratic cause" between the conventions and preparing for the next convention. ("Party History," 2008)

The Republican Party was born in the early 1850s by anti-slavery activists and individuals who believed that government should grant western lands to settlers free of charge. The first informal meeting of the party took place in Ripon, Wisconsin, a small town northwest of Milwaukee. The first official Republican meeting took place on July 6th, 1854 in Jackson, Michigan. The name "Republican" was chosen because it alluded to equality and reminded individuals of Thomas Jefferson's Democratic-Republican Party. At the Jackson convention, the new party adopted a platform and nominated candidates for office in Michigan. In 1856, the Republicans became a national party when John C. Fremont was nominated for President under the slogan: "Free soil, free labor, free speech, free men, Fremont." Even though they were considered a "third party" because the Democrats and Whigs represented the two-party system at the time, Fremont received 33% of the vote. Four years later, Abraham Lincoln became the first Republican to win the White House. ("The Republican Party—GOP History," 2008)

Members of political parties qualify their views along a spectrum based on being liberal or conservative. Being *liberal* is defined as being in favor of citizens being free to act on their personal views with little or no infringement on those rights by the government. For example, a person who is liberal on the issue of crime would support more lenient laws to punish a convicted criminal. Being *conservative* is defined as being in favor of stricter government control over the actions of citizens. On the issue of abortion, for example, a conservative person would support stricter laws to control or end abortion rights. Democratic and Republican members range from very liberal (called far left or left-wing) to very conservative (called far right or right-wing). Therefore, their members' views will vary on many issues. For example, while Democrats generally favor abortion rights, there are some moderate Democrats who do not.

Table 4.1 lists the general differences in ideologies between Democrats and Republicans. Generally, Democrats today are more liberal on social issues (such as support for gay rights) and in support of government policies supporting the average citizen (such as free health care). Republicans are generally more conservative on social issues (such as opposition to abortion) and in favor of free enterprise, that is, in favor of citizens helping themselves rather than relying on government support.

Many other political parties exist in the United States besides the Democratic and Republican parties, but few have any significant political power. Most originated as a collective means for a group of people to share their common views or beliefs. The only two that are truly organized with political candidates that have actually held any major political offices are the Libertarian party and the Green party. Members of the Libertarian party are generally conservative on the issue of government control and believe the government should not be involved in the decisions that affect citizens. They believe citizens' personal freedoms should not be infringed upon. Libertarians believe in a free market controlling the economy, free trade, no income tax, U.S. nonintervention in international affairs, they are pro-choice on abortion, in favor of same-sex marriages, the legalization of drugs, and no gun control. (See their official Web site, http://www.lp.org, for more information.)

Table 4.1.   Basic Ideological Differences Between the Democratic and Republican Parties, as of January 2008

On these issues . . .	Democrats are generally . . .	Republicans are generally . . .
Basic ideology	Liberal	Conservative
Legalized abortion	For (pro-choice)	Against (pro-life)
Tax cuts	In favor of cuts for lower income Americans	In favor of cuts for everyone
Role of the government in supporting citizens	In favor of a more authoritative government	In favor of a less authoritative government
Government regulation of business	In favor of more regulation	In favor of less regulation
Government spending for social programs	Supportive of more assistance to the poor and middle class	In favor of citizens supporting themselves
Environmentalism	In favor of stricter laws	Opposed to stricter laws
Affirmative action	In favor of laws supporting	Opposed to laws supporting
Gun control	In favor of more laws controlling	Opposed to laws controlling as violating the Second Amendment
Health care	In favor of universal care supported by the government	In favor of Health Maintenance Organizations (HMOs)
Education	In favor or more federal spending	In favor of less federal spending
Foreign policy	In favor of U.S. involvement through the United Nations	In favor of direct U.S. involvement
The death penalty	Against, feeling it is not a deterrent to crime	Favor as a deterrent to crime
Same-sex unions	In favor	Opposed
Minimum wage increases	In favor because it helps workers prosper	Opposed because it puts a burden on businesses

Members of the Green party are generally liberal and believe U.S. power should rest in the hands of the people. They believe big business and the wealthy have too much power, and thus the United States is in need of social and economic reforms. Green party members are considered even more liberal than left-wing Democrats. The party operates under ten key values: grassroots democracy, social justice and equal opportunity, ecological wisdom, nonviolence, decentralization, community-based economics, feminism and gender equality, respect for diversity, personal and global responsibility, and future focus and sustainability. (See their official Web site, http://www.gp.org, for more information.)

In the United States, one member of a political party running in an election wins, based on gaining a majority of votes. In other nations elections are not decided based on a single party winner in an election. Great Britain, for example, has several parties and winners in Parliament receive seats based on the percentage of votes received.

CAMPAIGN SPENDING

Today, it takes millions of dollars for a candidate to fund an effective national campaign. Funds are needed for travel, television and radio time, and printed material. Candidates receive funding from their political parties, individuals, corporations, and federal funding. They also use their personal funds. The data on campaign funding in the following sections is available from campaign and finance reports from the Federal Election Commission (Federal Election Commission, 2007a, 2007b).

During the 2004 general election, presidential candidates garnered net receipts of $860.5 million, the highest ever reported up until that time. In 2000, the candidates reported total receipts of $709.5 million. These figures do not include the millions of dollars in transfers among committees within the same campaign. Candidates made net disbursements of $834.5 million in the 2004 election, compared to $687 million in 2000. Table 4.2 provides the net receipts and disbursements for the leading candidates for the 2004 presidential general election. As shown, Republican presidential incumbent George W. Bush led in receipts and disbursements. Running for reelection, President Bush had receipts of $367.2 million and disbursements of $351.7 million. John F. Kerry, the Democrat candidate, had $300.9 million in receipts and $285.2 million in disbursements. The top candidate not from the two main parties was Ralph Nader, a member of the Green Party. He had net receipts of $4.6 million and disbursements of $4.5 million. Both Bush and Kerry received $74.6 million for the general election from the Presidential Election Campaign Fund (see "General Election PublicFunding" below for more information). The last two columns show the amount of cash on hand and debt owed by each candidate at a point in time.

CAMPAIGN FUNDING

Campaign Finance Reform. Numerous attempts have been made to regulate campaign financing over the years. Two historic concerns have been (1) individuals or groups exerting too much control over the political process by making large financial contributions and (2) certain candidates being able to raise very large amounts of money from various sources in comparison to other candidates. The first act that tried to establish campaign finance regulations was the Tillman Act of 1907, which attempted to

Table 4.2. Campaign Funds, Receipts, and Disbursements Through December 31, 2004, by Candidate for the 2004 Presidential General Election, as Reported to the Federal Election Commission

Candidate	Net receipts	Net disbursements	Cash	Debt
George W. Bush	$367,228,801	$351,759,170	$20,660,222	$1,704,871
John F. Kerry	$300,931,559	$285,221,280	$18,794,154	$4,175,901
Ralph Nader	$4,567,299	$4,549,032	$23,872	$298,561
Michael Badnarik	$1,093,013	$1,073,940	$19,602	$0
Michael A. Peroutka	$729,087	$728,221	$864	$453,055
David K. Cobb	$493,723	$385,707	$108,014	$4,926

Source: Federal Election Commission (2007a). *Campaign Finance Reports and Data.* Federal Election Commission, Washington, DC. Retrieved April 15, 2007, from http://www.fec.gov/disclosure.shtml

regulate corporate contributions to candidates by prohibiting direct donations. Later acts included the Federal Corrupt Practices Acts of 1910 and 1925, which set campaign spending limits and financial disclosure requirements for congressional campaigns, and the Smith-Connally Act of 1943 and the Taft-Hartley Act of 1947, which both prohibited labor unions from making contributions to political campaigns. None of these Acts was effective. They were not comprehensive laws, and allowed candidates and contributors to still make donations based upon limitations in the legislation.

The first effective law reforming campaign finance was the Federal Election Campaign Act passed in 1971. This law set clear and stringent requirements on federal campaign financing. The act set requirements for candidates to disclose both their sources and uses of campaign funds. National party committees and political action committees (PACs) were also required to disclose contributions. It also set limits on who could donate funds and how much could be given to candidates. The act was amended several times: in 1974, 1976, and 1979. In 1974, requirements were made even more stringent, and the Federal Election Commission (FEC) was established in 1975 to enforce campaign finance regulations. As an independent regulatory agency, it discloses campaign finance information, enforces contribution limits and prohibitions, and oversees public funding used for presidential elections. Public funding for candidates through matching funds was also added. The Supreme Court ruled that parts of the act were unconstitutional in 1976 (*Buckley v. Valeo*, 424 U.S. 1, 1976). As a result of amendments and the Supreme Court ruling, this act also provided numerous loopholes for campaign funding.

Bipartisan Campaign Reform Act of 2002.   The most recent campaign reform legislation passed was the Bipartisan Campaign Reform Act of 2002. It essentially replaced the requirements in the Federal Election Campaign Act of 1971. The 2002 Act prohibits federal officeholders, candidates, and political parties from accepting *soft money*. Soft money includes donations from individuals, corporations, and unions that are not donated directly to a candidate but have an impact on elections. Funds go to a candidate's political party, and thus indirectly support the candidate. Because funds do not go directly to candidates, in the past, soft money did not have to be reported to the Federal Election Commission (FEC). State and local candidates and political parties can still accept soft money, within limits, as long as the use of the funds is in no way associated with federal elections. In 1996, the Democratic and Republican parties raised more than $260 million in soft money. Almost half of the money was used to fund advertisements supporting party positions on specific issues, that is, issue ads.

The act also regulates political advertising. It requires candidates to verbally approve any authorized ad that champions their campaign in the ad itself. If a candidate did not authorize the ad, the name of the individual or organization who did authorize it must be disclosed. Ads not endorsed directly by a candidate are called *electioneering communications* and are made by corporations or labor unions via radio or television. These ads support or oppose a specific candidate and are targeted at a relevant electorate or population of people. Corporations and labor unions are prohibited from advertising for or against candidates thirty days prior to a political party primary or sixty days prior to the general election. Electioneering communications that cost $10,000 or more to produce and air must be reported to the FEC.

The act also specifies campaign contribution limits: individuals can contribute no more than $2,000 to a candidate per election; no more than $10,000 to state and local party committees combined per year; no more than $25,000 to national party committees per year; and no more than a total of $95,000 every two years. This last limit includes a maximum of $37,500 to candidates and $37,500 to committees that are not national parties. National party committees can contribute up to $35,000 per six-year campaign to Senate candidates.

Political Action Committees (PACs).   Political action committees (PACs) are private groups that organize to support or oppose a candidate or legislation. PACs are the largest contributors to political campaigns in the United States. They are formed because certain entities, including corporations and trade unions, are not allowed to provide funds to federal candidates directly but can do so through PACs. The organizations that contribute to PACs are interest groups. Interest groups donate funds and provide organizational influence to gain support for their individual causes or issues. Members of Congress establish PACs called Leadership PACs to raise and distribute money to members of their party. The FEC defines a PAC as an organization that receives or makes contributions of over $1,000 during a calendar year for the purpose of influencing a federal election. A single PAC can give no more than $15,000 a year to a national party. The definition of a PAC varies for state and local elections, and some impose no limits on the amount of funds PACs can provide state and local candidates. PAC records must be filed with the FEC, and are made available to the public.

The FEC distinguishes between two types of PACs:

- Separate segregated funds (SSFs) committees: political committees established and administered by corporations, labor unions, membership organizations, or trade associations. These committees can only solicit contributions from individuals associated with or sponsoring an organization.
- Nonconnected committees: political committees not sponsored by or connected to any of the aforementioned entities, which are free to solicit contributions from the general public.

There were 4,168 PACs in existence as of July 1, 2007 (as compared to 608 in 1974). Corporate PACs (SSFs) were the largest number of PACs in 2007 with 1,586 committees. The remaining were nonconnected (1,247), trade/membership/health (926), labor (273), corporations without stock (99), and cooperatives (37).

Table 4.3 shows PAC financial activity from January 1, 2005, through June 30, 2006. As shown, PACs received $773.5 million in contributions and made disbursements of $656.2 million. Approximately $248.3 million went to political candidates, mostly from corporate PACs.

General Election Public Funding.   Federal campaign contributions must be reported to the FEC. The FEC administers and enforces federal campaign finance laws including the Presidential Election Campaign Fund Act of 1966 and Presidential Primary Matching Payment Account Act of 1974 (also called the Matching Payment Act). Candidates receive matching funds for their primary race from the Presidential Primary Matching Payment Account, and matching funds for the general election campaign from the Presidential Election Campaign Fund. Funds raised by presidential candidates of political parties after January 1 of the year before the election year are eligible for federal matching through general election public funding. Independent candidates do not qualify. Funds are also not provided to congressional candidates. These funds originate from the contributions income tax filers may elect to give on their federal tax returns ($3 for individuals or $6 for married couples, as of 2007).

Table 4.3.   Political Action Committee (PAC) Financial Activity, January 1, 2005, through June 30, 2006 (in millions of dollars)

Type of PAC	Number of committees	Receipts	Disbursements	Cash on hand	Contributions to candidates
Corporate	1,712	$205.5	$188.5	$95.6	$93.7
Labor	299	$153.6	$118.6	$93.8	$38.1
Nonconnected	1,492	$241.1	$212.0	$70.7	$44.2
Trade/member/ health	950	$158.8	$124.4	$86.6	$66.1
Cooperative	40	$4.3	$3.2	$3.5	$2.4
Corporations without stock	108	$10.2	$9.5	$4.9	$3.8
Total	4,601	$773.5	$656.2	$355.1	$248.3

Source: Biersack, B., et al. (2006). *PAC Financial Activity Increases.* Federal Election Commission, Washington, DC. Retrieved September 1, 2007, from http://www.fec.gov/press/press2006/20060828pac/20060830pac.html

To qualify for matching primary funds, candidates must first raise at least $5,000 in at least twenty different states (a total of $100,000). Only contributions from individuals qualify for matching. While individuals can contribute up to $2,000 to a candidate, only $250 from each individual's donation is matched and used to calculate the $100,000 minimum. Candidates must then abide by FEC regulations on spending limits, record keeping, and reporting. For example, a candidate can only spend $50,000 of his or her personal funds once federal matching funds are accepted and they cannot accept private contributions. There are spending limits for each state based on the total voting age population, capped at $200,000 (adjusted for inflation during each election). Additionally, each candidate can only spend $10 million on primary elections (adjusted for inflation during each election), an additional 20 percent on fund-raising expenses, and an amount on legal and accounting fees. Adjusted for inflation, this allowed each candidate in 2004 to spend between $40 and $50 million on his or her presidential nomination campaigns.

Matching funds are paid to candidates monthly, starting January 1 of the election year. If a candidate does not receive 10 percent of votes in two consecutive state primaries, he or she becomes ineligible for additional funds unless 20 percent of votes in the next state primary are won. Eligible candidates can continue to request funds to pay off their campaign debts until late February or March of the year following the general election. Using these funds is voluntary. For their presidential primary races, Steve Forbes did not use matching funds in 1996, John F. Kerry and Howard Dean did not in 2004, and George W. Bush did not in 2000 or 2004.

For the general election campaign, the nominee for each party is eligible for matching federal funds of up to $20 million based on 1974 dollars. This amount is adjusted for inflation during each general election. For 2004, the amount was $74.6 million and was accepted by both John F. Kerry and George W. Bush. Every Democratic and Republican candidate since 1976 has accepted general election funds. They therefore were not allowed to use any other funds for general election campaigning.

Table 4.4 shows the primary, party convention, and general election funds paid to candidates for each presidential election from 1976 through 2004. In 1976, Republican

Table 4.4. Presidential Public Funding Fact Sheet During 1976–2004 Presidential General Elections

	1976	1980	1984	1988	1992	1996	2000	2004
Primary Matching Funds Paid to Candidates								
Republicans	$9,745,917	$20,760,484	$10,100,000	$35,495,823	$15,858,507	$43,996,632	$29,961,585	
Democrats	$15,203,584	$10,671,171	$26,225,665	$31,114,979	$24,628,595	$14,036,889	$29,366,518	$27,175,310
Other parties			$193,734	$938,798	$2,366,482	$504,830	$5,933,266	$865,425
Total	$24,949,501	$31,431,655	$36,519,399	$67,549,600	$42,853,584	$58,538,351	$62,261,369	$28,040,735
General Election Grants								
Republicans	$21,820,000	$29,440,000	$40,400,000	$46,100,000	$55,240,000	$61,820,000	$67,560,000	$74,620,000
Democrats	$21,820,000	$29,440,000	$40,400,000	$46,100,000	$55,240,000	$61,820,000	$67,560,000	$74,620,000
Other Parties		$4,242,304				$29,055,400	$12,613,452	
Total	$43,640,000	$63,122,304	$80,800,000	$92,200,000	$110,480,000	$152,695,400	$147,733,452	$149,240,000
Party Convention Grants								
Republicans	$1,963,800	$4,416,000	$8,080,000	$9,220,000	$11,048,000	$12,364,000	$13,512,000	$14,924,000
Democrats	$2,185,829	$4,416,000	$8,080,000	$9,220,000	$11,048,000	$12,364,000	$13,512,000	$14,924,000
Other Parties							$2,522,690	
Total	$4,149,629	$8,832,000	$16,160,000	$18,440,000	$22,096,000	$24,728,000	$29,546,690	$29,848,000
Total Public Funding Payouts	$72,739,130	$103,385,959	$133,479,399	$178,189,600	$175,429,584	$235,961,511	$239,541,511	$207,128,735

Source: Federal Election Commission (2007b). *Presidential Election Campaign Fund (PECF)*. Federal Election Commission, Washington, DC. Retrieved September 21, 2007, from http://www.fec.gov/press/bkgnd/fund.shtml

and Democratic candidates received $24.9 million in matching funds for their primaries, $43.6 million for the general election, and $4.1 million for their political party conventions. No candidates from any other party received funds. In total, $72.7 million were paid. Matching funds have grown substantially ever since. In 2004, candidates received $28 million for primaries, $149.2 million for the general election, and $29.8 million for party conventions. In total, $207.1 million was paid in 2007.

PRESIDENTIAL CAMPAIGNING

Presidential Candidates.   Presidential elections take place every four years during even-numbered years. Potential candidates begin planning their campaigns years in advance of an election, but may wait to publicly announce their intentions. With the help of political consultants, they determine if they have a serious chance of being nominated by their political party, weigh the pros and cons of such extreme public attention and scrutiny by the media, and consider the effect of winning or losing on their future aspirations.

The presidential race begins when candidates officially announce their intentions to run for office and their party affiliation. This usually occurs at least a year before the first party primary or caucus (see section "Caucuses and Primaries" below). Next, they seek the nomination of their political party to run as its presidential candidate. The president in office must still gain the nomination from his party to run for reelection. Candidates not wishing to run for an organized political party can run as an Independent candidate. Each candidate develops a campaign based on positions on major issues he or she believes are in line with the position of their political party platform and will win the support of its members. In rare cases, these two may differ. If a candidate is running for an office previously held by a member of his or her own party and that member's actions were viewed as unpopular by a large percentage of potential voters, the candidate may run with different views on issues.

Candidates obtain a host of campaign support. Most hire campaign managers, professional consultants, and an entire personal campaign staff whose size depends on the candidate's financial resources. The campaign manager oversees the consultants and campaign staff and is a carefully chosen professional. The campaign staff is divided into functioning departments, such as fund-raising and communication. Volunteers, interns, and organizers also help candidates throughout their campaigns. Candidates then travel extensively to gain support from voters in their party, develop alliances with interest groups and corporations, and raise funds for their campaigns.

Political parties often have internal debates when candidates strive to gain support for their party's nomination to run in the general election. Eight Democratic candidates met for the first Democratic debate of the 2008 presidential campaign on April 26, 2007, at South Carolina State University in Orangeburg, South Carolina. The candidates mostly debated U.S. involvement in the war in Iraq. Other issues included gun control, abortion, and health care. The eight candidates included Senator Hillary Rodham Clinton (NY), Senator Barack Obama (IL), former Senator John Edwards (NC), former Representative Dennis Kucinich (OH), former Senator Mike Gravel (AL), New Mexico Governor Bill Richardson, Senator Joseph Biden (DE), and Senator Christopher Dodd (CT). Ten Republican candidates met at the Ronald Reagan Presidential Library in Simi Valley, California, on May 3, 2007, for the first Republican debate of the 2008 campaign. They debated on such issues as the U.S. war in Iraq, abortion, and same sex-marriage. The ten candidates included Senator John McCain (AZ), Arkansas Governor Mike Huckabee, former New York City Mayor Rudy Giuliani, former Massachusetts Governor Mitt Romney, Senator Sam Brownback (KS), former Virginia Governor Jim Gilmore, Representative Duncan Hunter (CA), Representative Ron Paul (TX), Representative Tom Tancredo (CO), and former Governor of Wisconsin Tommy Thompson.

Media attention is critical for candidates. Candidates strive to gain the attention of major news organizations to gain increased exposure to the public. This free publicity reaches millions of Americans daily and garners exposure the candidates could never obtain on their own. Media attention is also very important because many citizens use media reports in their election decision-making process. They rely on reports of candidate activities, their historical stance on pertinent issues, and pay attention to the opinions of leading commentators.

Caucuses and Primaries.   The official process of choosing candidates for each party begins with *political caucuses* (also called *conventions*) or *primaries* in each state. A few states have *straw polls* that occur before caucuses and primaries. These are generally surveys of randomly selected people in the population. Responses are unofficial and used to indicate general voter support for candidates. During caucuses, voters select delegates who then choose the candidates that will run for the party. During primaries, voters directly choose their favorite candidate. There are two general types of primaries. In an open primary, registered voters can choose which primary to vote in regardless of which political party is holding the primary. Voters do not actually change party affiliation. If a Democrat decides to vote in the Republican primary, he or she can still remain a member of the Democratic Party. However, voters can only participate in one primary. In a closed primary, only voters who are registered party members can vote. Republicans can only vote in a Republican primary, Democrats only vote in a Democratic primary, and members of other parties or who are Independents cannot vote in a Republican or Democratic primary.

Blanket primaries were once used by a few states and allowed voters to participate in all party primaries. However, the Supreme Court struck down their use (*California Democratic Party v. Jones*, 530 U.S. 567, 2000). According to Justice Antonin Scalia, a blanket primary was "forcing political parties to associate with those who do not share their beliefs. And it has done this at the crucial juncture at which party members traditionally find their collective voice and select their spokesman."

States begin holding caucuses or primaries in the winter before the general election. The candidates that generally win in each state's primary or caucus are those that can obtain the support of the state governor, congressmen, other political leaders, and other prominent figures. These individuals officially endorse candidates and thus influence the decisions of voters in their states. Iowa has the first national caucus in January or February and New Hampshire has a primary next. Candidates who gain majority votes in the Iowa caucus and New Hampshire primary are considered serious candidates. Those who do not achieve at least a significant number of votes generally end their campaigns. Candidates who continue next compete in the South Carolina, Arizona, and then Michigan primaries. The other states follow.

The next major event after the Iowa and New Hampshire conventions is Super Tuesday, which normally occurs on the first Tuesday in March. For the 2008 presidential election, Super Tuesday was held earlier than normal and occurred on February 5,

2008. On this day, ten states have primaries on the same day: California, Connecticut, Georgia, Maryland, Massachusetts, Minnesota, New York, Ohio, Rhode Island, and Vermont. After Super Tuesday, the top candidate for each party has usually been determined. Other states continue to have primaries and caucuses, but these are often more ceremonial than required. Table 4.5 lists the dates on which states held primaries and caucuses during the 2000 general election. It also shows whether each primary held was closed or open.

In recent years, there have been several instances of states attempting to change the order of their causes and primaries, resulting in controversy. The main reason a state attempts this is to increase the notoriety of its event and influence on the candidate selection process. Since Iowa and New Hampshire hold their conventions first, they

Table 4.5.   Presidential Election State Primaries and Caucuses Held in the 2000 Presidential Election

State	Democratic primary or caucus in 2000	Republican primary or caucus in 2000	Month held	Closed primary	Open primary
Alabama	Primary	Primary	June		x
Alaska	Caucus	Caucus	February (R) March (D)	x	
American Samoa	Caucus	Caucus	February (R) March (D)		
Arizona	Caucus	Primary	February (R) March (D)	x	
Arkansas	Primary	Primary	May		x
California	Primary	Primary	March	x	
Colorado	Primary	Primary	March		x
Connecticut	Primary	Primary	March	x	
Delaware	Caucus	Primary	February (R) March (D)	x	
District of Columbia	Primary	Primary	May	x	
Florida	Primary	Primary	March	x	
Georgia	Primary	Primary	March		x
Guam	Caucus	Caucus	February (R) May (D)		
Hawaii	Caucus	Caucus	February (R) March (D)		
Idaho	Caucus	Primary	March (D) May (R)		x
Illinois	Primary	Primary	March		x
Indiana	Primary	Primary	May		x
Iowa	Caucus	Caucus	January		
Kansas	Primary	Primary	April	x	
Kentucky	Primary	Primary	May	x	
Louisiana	Primary	Primary	March	x	

(Continued)

Table 4.5.   (Continued)

State	Democratic primary or caucus in 2000	Republican primary or caucus in 2000	Month held	Closed primary	Open primary
Maine	Primary	Primary	March		x
Maryland	Primary	Primary	March	x	
Massachusetts	Primary	Primary	March	x	
Michigan	Caucus	Primary	February (R) March (D)		x
Minnesota	Caucus	Caucus	March (R)		
Mississippi	Primary	Primary	March		x
Missouri	Primary	Primary	March		x
Montana	Primary	Primary	June		x
Nebraska	Primary	Primary	May	x	
Nevada	Caucus	Caucus	March		
New Hampshire	Primary	Primary	February	x	
New Jersey	Primary	Primary	June	x	
New Mexico	Primary	Primary	June	x	
New York	Primary	Primary	March	x	
North Carolina	Primary	Primary	May	x	
North Dakota	Caucus	Caucus	February (R) March (D)		
Ohio	Primary	Primary	March		x
Oklahoma	Primary	Primary	March	x	
Oregon	Primary	Primary	May	x	
Pennsylvania	Primary	Primary	April	x	
Puerto Rico	Primary	Primary	February (R) March (D)		x
Rhode Island	Primary	Primary	March	x	
South Carolina	Caucus	Primary	February (R) March (D)		x
South Dakota	Primary	Primary	June	x	
Tennessee	Primary	Primary	March		x
Texas	Primary	Primary	March		x
Utah	Primary	Primary	March		x
Vermont	Primary	Primary	March		x
Virgin Islands	Caucus	Caucus	April		
Virginia	Caucus	Primary	February (R) April (D)		x
Washington	Caucus	Primary & Caucus	February (R) March (D)		x
West Virginia	Primary	Primary	May	x	
Wisconsin	Primary	Primary	April		x
Wyoming	Caucus	Primary	March	x	

garner a great deal of media and political attention. Other states have thus attempted to move their conventions earlier. This has met with mixed reactions from voters and concern from political parties. For example, Michigan did change the date of its Democratic primary for the 2008 presidential election to January 15, 2008. The Democratic National Convention rules restricted all states from holding nominating contests (i.e., caucuses or primaries) before February 5 except for Iowa, New Hampshire, Nevada, and South Carolina. As a result of Michigan's actions, the Democratic National Committee did not allow Michigan to send any delegates to the national convention. The Democratic candidates for president refused to campaign in Michigan during the week of Michigan's scheduled January 15, 2008 primary.

National Conventions.   Each political party holds a national convention to select a final presidential candidate from the top contenders in the primaries and caucuses, and to confirm the vice presidential candidate. Each state sends delegates to the national convention. Most Republican conventions use a "winner-take-all" process of selecting delegates to their national convention. The candidate that receives the most votes in a state is the primary or caucus winner, and thus "wins" all of the delegate votes for that state. Most Democratic conventions use a proportional process, where candidates receive a proportion of the delegate votes based on primary or caucus results.

Since the actual candidates are most often determined after Super Tuesday, the national conventions are usually ceremonial occasions where each party's candidate is officially celebrated with political fanfare. During the proceedings, each state or territory announces its tally of votes for each candidate. National conventions are also used to vote on issues, including changes to the party platform.

National conventions generally take place in August. City governments submit proposals to each political party outlining the benefits of holding its convention in their city. Political parties choose a city based on its social offerings, ability to support large groups, and importance in gaining political support from voters. For example, one party may choose a city because it has historically lacked votes from a majority of that state's registered voters. The Republican Party held its 2000 presidential election national convention in Philadelphia, Pennsylvania, from July 31 to August 3, 2000. Its 2004 presidential election national convention was held in New York City August 30 to September 2, 2004. Its 2008 election national convention was held in Minneapolis, Minnesota, from September 1 to September 4, 2008. For the 2008 convention, proposals were submitted to the party from Cleveland (Ohio), Minneapolis-St. Paul (Minnesota), New York City (New York), and Tampa-St. Petersburg (Florida). Minneapolis was chosen because the Republicans had not gained a majority of the votes for president in Minnesota since the election of President Richard M. Nixon.

The Democratic Party held its 2000 presidential election national convention in Los Angeles, California, from August 14 to August 17, 2000. For the 2004 presidential election, the party held its convention in Boston, Massachusetts, from July 26 to June 29, 2004. Its 2008 convention was held in Denver, Colorado, from August 25 to August 28, 2008. Three cities submitted proposals to the party for their 2008 convention: Denver (Colorado), Minneapolis-Saint Paul (Minnesota), and New York City (New York). The Republicans had already chosen Minneapolis and New York City was financially unable to support the convention. Hosting a convention can cost a city between $50 million and $100 million, although the city can recoup up to three times as much by the time the convention ends.

Other parties also hold national conventions. The Green Party's national convention was held in Denver, Colorado, in June 2000 and the Reform Party held their national convention in Los Angeles, California, in August 2000.

Presidential and Vice Presidential Debates.   Once selected by their political parties, presidential candidates attempt to solidify voter support from their own party and sway voters of other parties to vote for them. Candidates develop their campaigns based on their stance on major issues, their personal and professional strengths, and their opponent's weaknesses. They campaign daily up until election day, spending extra time in states where they feel they may not have support from a clear majority of voters. The presidential candidates have public debates, as do the vice presidential candidates. In recent years, there have been at least two televised debates between the main presidential candidates and at least one separate debate between the main vice presidential candidates. A mediator asks questions from a list of the most pressing political issues. Each candidate is allowed a specific amount of time to respond, and then to rebut his or her opponent. During the 2004 election, George W. Bush and John F. Kerry participated in two ninety-minute debates. They were allowed two minutes to respond to questions and given ninety seconds for rebuttals. The mediator could grant one-minute extensions at his discretion. Issues discussed during their debates included the war in Iraq, the economy, tax cuts, the No Child Left Behind Act of 2002 (which increased the accountability of schools in educating children), health care, and welfare reform.

The 1960s brought a new dimension to presidential campaigning with televised debates. Candidates were being exposed to audiences of millions of people, placed under increased scrutiny by being asked questions they were required to respond to,

President Gerald R. Ford and his Democratic opponent, Jimmy Carter, meet at the Walnut Street Theater in Philadelphia to debate domestic policy in the first of three Ford-Carter debates, September 23, 1976. *David Hume Kennerly/Courtesy of the Gerald R. Ford Library.*

and their words and actions were being permanently recorded. The first televised general election presidential debate took place on September 26, 1960, in Chicago, Illinois, between Democratic Senator John F. Kennedy (from Massachusetts) and Republican Vice President Richard M. Nixon. Over 66 million Americans watched the debate from 9:30 until 10:30 P.M. There were a moderator and three panelists representing all the major television networks. The format of the debate gave each candidate eight-minute opening statements, two-and-a-half minutes to respond to questions, the option for rebuttals, and three minutes for closing statements. During the first debate, Nixon refused to use television makeup. He wore a gray suit that blended into the background of the stage set. Compared to the tanned and relaxed Kennedy who wore a blue suit (that did not blend into the background), Nixon appeared tired and agitated. This negatively affected his appeal to many viewers. Televised debates were not held again until the 1976 presidential election campaign between Democratic candidate Jimmy Carter and the Republican incumbent, President Gerald R. Ford. During that election, the first televised vice presidential debate was held on October 15, 1976, between Democratic Senator Walter F. Mondale (from Minnesota) and Republican Senator Robert Dole (from Kansas).

The Commission on Presidential Debates (CPD) was established in 1987 to ensure debates provide the best possible information to the public. According to the Commission's official Web site (http://www.debates.org), "Its primary purpose is to sponsor and produce debates for the United States presidential and vice presidential candidates and to undertake research and educational activities relating to the debates. The organization, which is a nonprofit, nonpartisan corporation, sponsored all the presidential debates in 1988, 1992, 1996, 2000 and 2004." Transcripts from past debates can also be found on its Web site.

Electoral College.   The general election for the president is held the first Tuesday after the first Monday in November every four even-numbered years. To cast a ballot, a citizen must be a registered voter in the state in which they reside. To register, an individual must be a U.S. citizen at least eighteen years old and must register in advance of election day according to individual state rules. Maine, Minnesota, and Wisconsin permit citizens to register up to and on election day. Most states prohibit voting by convicted felons and people legally determined to be mentally incompetent. Registered voters are issued a voter registration card and informed of the designated voting location in their district or jurisdiction of residence. Voters can submit absentee ballots by mail if they will be away from their voting area on election day. Each state establishes a deadline for obtaining and submitting absentee ballots.

The voting ballot contains the names of the leading candidate for each political party, as selected by their national party conventions. All states allow Independent candidates to be listed on ballots. These candidates must obtain a minimum number of signatures on a petition to be placed on the ballot. Some states allow for write-in votes, which permits a voter to simply write the name of a candidate they wish to vote for on the ballot when that candidate is not listed on the ballot.

Voters actually choose electors according to which candidate they vote for and the electors in the Electoral College elect the president. If the majority of voters in a state vote for the Republican presidential candidate, that state's Republican electors are actually chosen. (The only exceptions to this process are in Maine and Nebraska, where two electors in each state are chosen based on the statewide vote and the other electors based on votes in congressional districts.) The number of electors equals each state's number of Representatives and Senators. There are 538 members of the Electoral

College: one for each of the 100 Senators, one for each of the 435 members of the House of Representatives, and 3 representing the District of Columbia. (The votes in the District of Columbia must equal those of the state with the fewest electoral votes.) Table 4.6 shows the number of electoral votes in each state as of 2007. The numbers range from three electoral votes in states with smaller populations and thus fewer Congressmen and Congresswomen such as Alaska, Montana, and North Dakota, to fifty-five electoral votes in California (the state with the largest population in the United States). The winning candidate needs a majority of electoral votes to win the general election, that is, 270. U.S. territories (such as American Samoa, Puerto Rico, Guam, and the Virgin Islands) do not have electoral members.

Members of the Electoral College are chosen by their political parties. For example, the Republican Party chooses its electors in each state. Being chosen as an elector is considered an honor and is often done to reward an individual's support, dedication, and service to the party. Article II, Section 1, of the U.S. Constitution states that

Table 4.6.   Total Number of Electoral Votes in Each State

State	Electoral votes	State	Electoral votes
Alabama	9	Montana	3
Alaska	3	Nebraska	5
Arizona	10	Nevada	5
Arkansas	6	New Hampshire	4
California	55	New Jersey	15
Colorado	9	New Mexico	5
Connecticut	7	New York	31
Delaware	3	North Carolina	15
District of Columbia	3	North Dakota	3
Florida	27	Ohio	20
Georgia	15	Oklahoma	7
Hawaii	4	Oregon	7
Idaho	4	Pennsylvania	21
Illinois	21	Rhode Island	4
Indiana	11	South Carolina	8
Iowa	7	South Dakota	3
Kansas	6	Tennessee	11
Kentucky	8	Texas	34
Louisiana	9	Utah	5
Maine	4	Vermont	3
Maryland	10	Virginia	13
Massachusetts	12	Washington	11
Michigan	17	West Virginia	5
Minnesota	10	Wisconsin	10
Mississippi	6	Wyoming	3
Missouri	11		

Total electors in the electoral college: 538

"no Senator or Representative, or Person holding an Office of Trust or Profit under the United States, shall be appointed an Elector." Parties normally choose elected officials at the state level or other leaders in their political party to serve as electors.

Electors meet on the first Monday after the second Wednesday in December and normally vote according to the votes of the largest number of people in their state. However, electors are free to vote as they choose. Because parties choose their electors, it is rare that an elector does not vote for his or her party's candidates. In the majority of the states, whoever receives the most electoral votes in the state is awarded the total number of electoral votes for that state. For example, California has fifty-five electoral votes. If the Democratic candidate receives twenty-eight or more electoral votes, they are automatically given all fifty-five votes for the state. The exceptions are in Maine and Nebraska, where the votes of citizens determine the number of electors from each political party. Therefore, the electoral votes in these two states can be split between the Democratic and Republican candidates for president.

Once electors complete their votes, the totals are collected by each state's governor and forwarded to the president of the Senate (the vice president). The results are announced before a joint session of Congress on the sixth day of January. There have been four elections where the president elected by the Electoral College did not receive the most votes from the actual voters: the presidential elections of John Adams in 1824, Rutherford B. Hayes in 1876, Benjamin Harrison in 1888, and George W. Bush in 2000. If no one candidate has more than half of all the states' electoral votes, the members of the House of Representatives choose the president. This has only occurred once. In 1801, the House of Representatives elected Thomas Jefferson as president after he and Aaron Burr tied in electoral votes in the 1800 presidential election. The Senate would elect the vice president in case of an electoral vote tie.

The entire Electoral College process is contained in Title 3 of the *United States Code*, Chapter 1, Sections 1–21.

HOW CONGRESSMEN AND CONGRESSWOMEN ARE ELECTED

Congressional Districts.   There are two senators allocated to each state, and they are elected by popular vote of the entire state. Representatives in the House of Representatives are elected from state congressional districts. In 1967, Congress passed legislation (found at Title 2 of the *United States Code*, Chapter 1, Sections 2a and 2c) that prohibited the continued use of "at-large" elections by states with more than one representative. In other words, representatives are elected in each state by the voters in the district the representative represents rather than by all voters in that state. Each state's population determines how many representatives they elect, so states with larger populations have more representative districts.

Apportionment is the process of dividing the seats in the U.S. House of Representatives (currently 435) among the fifty states. This process has been used since 1790 (except in 1920 because Congress could not agree on the apportionment process). Congress assigns each state one seat and then uses a formula to assign the remaining seats based on the decennial (i.e., ten-year) census. The states may gain or lose seats through reapportionment as their population changes every ten years.

The second column in Table 4.7 shows the population in each state that was used to determine the number of House seats each state was assigned after the 2000 census.

Table 4.7.   Apportionment Population According to the 2000 Census, Number of Representatives in 2000 Compared to 1990, and Total Number of Electoral Votes, by Each State

State	Apportionment population	Number of apportioned representatives	Change from 1990 census apportionment	Electoral votes (includes 2 for each state's senators)
Alabama	4,461,130	7	0	9
Alaska	628,933	1	0	3
Arizona	5,140,683	8	+2	10
Arkansas	2,679,733	4	0	6
California	33,930,798	53	+1	55
Colorado	4,311,882	7	+1	9
Connecticut	3,409,535	5	−1	7
Delaware	785,068	1	0	3
District of Columbia				3
Florida	16,028,890	25	+2	27
Georgia	8,206,975	13	+2	15
Hawaii	1,216,642	2	0	4
Idaho	1,297,274	2	0	4
Illinois	12,439,042	19	−1	21
Indiana	6,090,782	9	−1	11
Iowa	2,931,923	5	0	7
Kansas	2,693,824	4	0	6
Kentucky	4,049,431	6	0	8
Louisiana	4,480,271	7	0	9
Maine	1,277,731	2	0	4
Maryland	5,307,886	8	0	10
Massachusetts	6,355,568	10	0	12
Michigan	9,955,829	15	−1	17
Minnesota	4,925,670	8	0	10
Mississippi	2,852,927	4	−1	6
Missouri	5,606,260	9	0	11
Montana	905,316	1	0	3
Nebraska	1,715,369	3	0	5
Nevada	2,002,032	3	+1	5
New Hampshire	1,238,415	2	0	4
New Jersey	8,424,354	13	0	15
New Mexico	1,823,821	3	0	5
New York	19,004,973	29	−2	31
North Carolina	8,067,673	13	+1	15
North Dakota	643,756	1	0	3

(Continued)

Table 4.7.   (Continued)

State	Apportionment population	Number of apportioned representatives	Change from 1990 census apportionment	Electoral votes (includes 2 for each state's senators)
Ohio	11,374,540	18	−1	20
Oklahoma	3,458,819	5	−1	7
Oregon	3,428,543	5	0	7
Pennsylvania	12,300,670	19	−2	21
Rhode Island	1,049,662	2	0	4
South Carolina	4,025,061	6	0	8
South Dakota	756,874	1	0	3
Tennessee	5,700,037	9	0	11
Texas	20,903,994	32	+2	34
Utah	2,236,714	3	0	5
Vermont	609,890	1	0	3
Virginia	7,100,702	11	0	13
Washington	5,908,684	9	0	11
West Virginia	1,813,077	3	0	5
Wisconsin	5,371,210	8	−1	10
Wyoming	495,304	1	0	3
Total	281,424,177	435	0	538

The apportionment calculation is based on the total resident population (citizens and noncitizens) of each state, plus U.S. armed forces personnel and federal civilian employees stationed outside the United States (and their dependents living with them) that can be allocated back to a home state. The next column shows how many seats each state was given, followed by any changes in each state's seats as a result of population increases or decreases from 1990. Notice that a few states lost seats due to population decreases, while a few others gained an equal share of seats because of population gains. Ohio, Michigan, and New York lost seats because people had moved south and west to Florida and California. The last column shows the number of Electoral College votes each state has based on their number of House seats plus two votes for each state's two Senators.

State leaders can contest the apportionment process if they feel their state was not treated equitably. After the 2000 Census's apportionment, Utah disputed the extra seat given to North Carolina. Utah leaders believed Utah should have been given the extra seat because out-of-state Mormon missionaries should have been counted as residents. After pleading their case, the Supreme Court ruled in favor of then-Secretary of Commerce Donald Evans and North Carolina (*Utah et al. v. Evans, Secretary of Commerce*, 536 U.S. 452, 2002).

After Congress apportions seats, data from the decennial census is also used by each state legislature to create or realign existing districts. Redistricting involves revising the geographic areas of each district where citizens elect members of the U.S. House of Representatives, state congressional members, local councils, and school board members. Representatives may represent different parts of the state, and more or fewer people when districts are realigned. State and local governments ensure that districts are developed and aligned so that citizens are given fair and equal representation. In essence, no one representative is supposed to represent a population sizably larger than another. Most state commissions in charge of redistricting have open sessions where citizens can voice their concerns before final decisions are made. The average size of a congressional district based on the 2000 census apportionment population was 646,952 people, which was more than triple the average district size of 193,167 people based on the 1900 census apportionment.

Redistricting can have serious effects on the electoral prospects of candidates, particularly if the proportion of political party membership changes. For example, a Republican representative may have won a seat because most of the people in his or her district were Republican. If redistricting results in capturing areas composed of a large number of Democrats, he or she may not be reelected during the next election.

Gerrymandering is the attempt by one political party to influence the redistricting process to create districts that will include mostly its party members. If successful, that party would gain the majority vote in a particular district. Another gerrymandering tactic is to create districts that spread the members of the opposing party over disparate areas so that their collective voting power is dissipated. Parties that are negatively affected by gerrymandering normally take legal action to correct unfair redistricting.

Congressional Elections.   Each party has a national committee that oversees the campaigns of congressmen and congresswomen running for seats in the House of Representatives: the National Republican Congressional Committee (NRCC) and the Democratic Congressional Campaign Committee (DCCC). Each party also has a national committee that oversees candidates running for Senate seats: the National Republican Senatorial Committee (NRSC) and the Democratic Senatorial Campaign Committee (DSCC). These committees are composed of current members of the Senate and House of Representatives, political party members, and party supporters. They search for, endorse, and support candidates for open congressional seats. Each is led by a chairperson who oversees the operation of the committee, leads in the development of its policies, and oversees fund-raising.

State primaries are held to select party candidates for congressional elections. Just as in presidential elections, Independent or unaffiliated candidates must petition to have their names added to ballots. Often, local interest groups or large businesses play major roles in selecting congressional candidates because of their immense influence in congressional districts and on state economies. The president's personal endorsement of a candidate can also play a major role in congressional elections.

Elections take place on the second Tuesday in November of even-numbered years. All House seats are up for reelection during each congressional election, but only one-third of Senate seats. Members of the House of Representatives are elected by a majority of the voters in their respective districts. Members of the Senate are elected by a majority of votes in their states. Prior to the Seventeenth Amendment, senators were elected by their state legislatures.

If a senator cannot complete his or her term of office, the governor of that state chooses a temporary replacement until a special election can be held on the first November of the next even-numbered year. Vacated House seats are filled by a special election called by the governor of that state within six months of the date the seat is vacated. The governor does not temporarily fill the seat.

5

The Legislative Process

The responsibility for passing new laws is vested in the legislative branch per the United States Constitution. Congress is thus charged with all federal legislative powers. The process of passing a new law begins with the introduction of a bill in one chamber of Congress. After committee reviews and legislative debate in the Senate and House of Representatives, the final approval of a bill is sent to the president who may approve or reject (veto) the bill. However, Congress still has final approval of new laws and has the power to override the president's veto. The passage of new laws is impacted by input from outside the government through interest groups and lobbyists that attempt to sway the decisions of lawmakers through various means.

PURPOSE AND POWERS OF CONGRESS

The primary purpose and duty of Congress is to develop, evaluate, and pass laws. According to Article I, Section 1, of the United States Constitution, "All legislative Powers herein granted shall be vested in a Congress of the United States, which shall consist of a Senate and House of Representatives." The first Congress met on March 4, 1789, in New York City. It consisted of twenty Senators and fifty-nine Representatives. Today, Congress consists of 100 senators and 435 members of the House of Representatives. Each senator and representative has the power to recommend new laws or changes to existing laws, and each has one vote toward the passage of new laws.

Congress reviews and passes laws during each congressional session. A congressional session lasts for two years, beginning on January 3 of each odd-numbered (or biennial) year following a general election of its members. Each chamber of Congress abides by rules that govern its proceedings. These rules include the processes by which laws will be introduced, debated, and passed. The House adopts new rules on the opening day of each new session. The Senate maintains standing rules that are amended as needed.

Article I, Section 8, of the Constitution outlines the powers of Congress. The following is a summary of these powers:

- To access and collect taxes
- To borrow money for the United States

- To regulate commerce with foreign nations, among the states, and with Indian tribes
- To establish uniform rules for naturalization and bankruptcies
- To coin money and punish counterfeiters
- To establish post offices
- To approve patents and copyrights to inventors and authors
- To establish courts inferior to the Supreme Court
- To punish those convicted of treason
- To declare war
- To raise and maintain an army and navy
- To suppress rebellions, insurrections, and invasions
- To make laws that are necessary and proper for carrying out the powers of Congress

Each chamber of Congress has specific powers not granted to the other. Only the House of Representatives can originate a bill to raise revenues. Impeachment actions (against the president, vice president, Supreme Court justices, and all civil officers of the United States) must be taken by the House but impeachment trials must be held in the Senate. The Senate has final approval of all presidential appointments, such as for members of the president's cabinet, heads of executive branch departments, Supreme Court justices, and ambassadors. The Senate must also approve all U.S. treaties with foreign powers by at least a two-thirds vote.

Article I, Section 6, outlines the rights of members of Congress. These include protection from being arrested while attending sessions of Congress except in the cases of treason against the United States, in connection with committing a felony, or taking actions that breach the peace. This protection includes times when members are going to or returning from congressional sessions. Members cannot be questioned about remarks they make during speeches or congressional debates. Lastly, any member of Congress can be expelled by a of two-thirds vote of its members.

Section 9 of Article I outlines restrictions on Congress. The following is a summary:

- Congress cannot suspend a person's right to habeas corpus, that is, the right to seek relief for unlawful detention, except in connection with a rebellion or invasion.
- Congress cannot pass bills of attainder, declaring a person guilty without a trial, or ex post facto laws, declaring an act illegal when it was legal at the time the act was committed, or increasing the punishment for a crime beyond what is already in the law.
- Congress can only levy taxes based on the census or other means of counting the population.
- Congress cannot tax items exported from a state.
- Congress cannot give commercial regulation preference to one state's ports over another's or levy duties on international commerce.
- Congress can only use funds from the federal treasury for appropriations established by law, and must provide regular statements of treasury receipts and expenditures.
- Congress cannot grant a title of nobility to any person, and no public official can accept gifts, offices, or titles from royalty or a foreign state without congressional approval.

The last section of Article I, Section 10, outlines the powers of Congress over the states. States are not allowed to perform those duties that are the responsibilities of Congress or engage in certain actions that are also specifically prohibited by Congress. These include entering into treaties, coining money, borrowing money for the United States, passing any bills of attainder or ex post facto laws, invalidating contracts, or granting titles of nobility. The states must gain congressional approval to levy duties on imports and exports unless in connection with the costs of conducting inspections. The states must also obtain congressional approval to impose duties on shipments beyond those charged by Congress, maintain troops, enter into an agreement with another state, establish agreements with foreign powers, or engage in war unless invaded.

IMPETUS AND SOURCES OF NEW LAWS

The idea or impetus for new laws may originate from many sources. Often, they result from campaign promises made by representatives when they ran for election. Some originate from candidates who ran for office but did not win. Their ideas are then championed by members who did win the election. Some are the result of representatives recognizing the need to change existing laws due to changes in the economy, political environment, the general population, or the needs of a segment of the population. Major national or international events may result in new laws being introduced. These include international conflicts, changes in the global economy, or changes in the global environment. Congress must introduce a bill each year to develop the annual budget of the federal government. The budget affects the implementation of and changes to existing laws. Bills involving taxes (i.e., government revenues) must originate in the House (per Article I, Section 7). All other types of bills may originate in the House or Senate.

Legislators may also react in response to their constituents, including lobbyists, interest groups, and businesses. Ordinary citizens continually contact their representatives with recommended changes to legislation. Legislation often results from studies conducted by public, private, or nonprofit organizations. Specific studies that get legislative attention are those on such topics as environmental pollution, immigration, and the alleged misuse of federal funds.

Laws may originate from the states. The states may request Congress to consider laws required for them to govern. Congress may react in response to state actions that have an impact at the federal level, or Congress may determine the need for a federal law on an issue that affects two or more states. Congress may also pass a law to exercise legislative oversight of the executive branch, particularly when it feels the executive branch is exerting unconstitutional influence and a law is required to maintain the government's system of checks and balances. Congress may take similar actions when it feels the judicial branch is being too lenient or too harsh on a particular issue.

The president and members of his or her cabinet are sources of proposed legislation and legislative changes. They recommend new legislation for the same reasons as members of Congress. They forward drafts of new legislation to either the House or Senate for consideration. Ideas for new laws also come from heads of independent agencies. These agencies often have lawyers who develop drafts of legislation.

CONGRESSIONAL LAW MAKING

Introduction of New Legislation in Congress.   The introduction of a new law begins with the introduction of a formal document called a *bill* in either the Senate or the House of Representatives, although the majority of laws originate in the House of Representatives. A bill outlines the purpose and scope of a proposed law. This proposed law might be for the purpose of addressing a new issue or amending or repealing an existing law. A bill that affects the general public is called a *public bill*. A bill that addresses an individual, small group, or specific segment of the population is called a *private bill*. A *companion bill* is a similar or identical bill introduced concurrently in the House and Senate. A *temporary bill* is introduced for the passage of new legislation that will only be in effect for a specific period of time. All other bills are considered proposals for permanent legislation. Several bills may be packaged into one legislative package called an *omnibus bill*.

There are other types of legislative proposals that are similar to bills. These include joint, concurrent, and simple resolutions. Resolutions, just like bills, lead to the passage of new laws. However, resolutions may only affect Congress (i.e., not the general public).

Joint resolutions address similar or identical issues of concern in both chambers of Congress. They may be introduced in the Senate or the House, and may be proposed to solve specific or limited issues or to propose amendments to the Constitution. A joint resolution to amend the Constitution that is approved by a two-thirds vote in both chambers does not go to the president for approval. After being approved in Congress, it must be ratified (i.e., approved) by three-fourths of all the state legislatures within a specified time frame. Joint resolutions dealing with other topics are submitted to the president.

Concurrent resolutions address matters affecting operations in both chambers of Congress or are issued to express official positions of members in both chambers. Presidential review or approval is not required because concurrent resolutions express facts, principles, or purposes of the two chambers, and do not address matters affecting the general public. Concurrent resolutions do not become public law. The clerk of the House and the secretary of the Senate sign concurrent resolutions before sending them to the archivist of the United States for publication.

Simple resolutions address matters affecting operations in either the House of Representatives or the Senate or are issued to express official positions of either chamber. Presidential review or approval is not required because simple resolutions express facts, principles, or purposes of one chamber of Congress and do not address matters affecting the general public. Simple resolutions cannot become public law. Each is signed by the clerk of the House or secretary of the Senate and published in the *Congressional Record*, the official record of the proceedings and debates of Congress.

A bill may be introduced by a single senator, a group of senators, a single member of the House of Representatives, or a group of representatives. In the House, delegates or the resident commissioner from Puerto Rico may also introduce a bill. Only the primary sponsor of a bill is required to be identified on the bill itself with a signature. Sponsors rarely, if ever, write new legislation themselves. That task is completed by congressional staff members, or they may employ the services of the Office of Legislative Counsel in their respective chambers.

In the House, a new bill is given to the clerk of the House directly or placed in a box called a hopper and retrieved by the clerk. The clerk assigns the bill a number for tracking. In the Senate, a senator must be recognized by the presiding officer to introduce a new bill. A bill is passed to the clerk at the presiding officer's desk or verbally introduced on the floor of the Senate. This introduction of the bill in the House or Senate is the official "first reading" of the bill.

Bills are identified by a title designating their chamber of origin followed by an assigned number. Bills introduced in the House are assigned a tracking number beginning with "H.R." The H.R. stands for House of Representative, and not "House Resolution," which is often incorrectly assumed. The prefix "S." identifies bills introduced in the Senate. Joint resolutions are identified as "H.J. Res." or "S.J. Res." Concurrent resolutions are identified as "H. Con. Res." or "S. Con. Res." Simple resolutions are identified as "H. Res." or "S. Res."

The majority of bills introduced never become laws. Bill sponsors attempt to garner support from their colleagues by seeking cosponsors and rallying congressional voting support as early as possible. Support is sought from members of a congressman's or congresswoman's own political party as well as from members of other parties. Sponsors may also attempt to gain support from lobbyists, interest groups, and citizens to help them influence other members.

If there are no objections from other chamber members after the first reading, the bill is assigned to a committee for extensive review. In very rare cases, bills are not sent to a committee but rather directly to the chamber floor for review. In either case, the bill is forwarded to and printed by the U.S. Government Printing Office, and a copy is provided to all chamber members. It is also made available for viewing by the general public. If there are objections from chamber members after the first reading, the bill is placed on the calendar for further discussions.

Committee Review of Bills.   The Speaker of the House or the Senate Rules Committee (depending upon whether the bill is in the House of Representatives or the Senate) assigns the bill to a committee for review based on its subject matter. For example, the Senate Committee on Energy and Natural Resources has oversight over issues dealing with energy resources and development, including regulation, conservation, strategic petroleum reserves, and appliance standards; nuclear energy; Indian affairs; public lands and their renewable resources; surface mining; federal coal, oil, gas, and other mineral leasing; territories and insular possessions; and water resources. The various committees in each chamber of Congress include standing committees, special (or select) committees, and joint committees. Therefore, bills may be sent to more than one committee for review, or specific parts of a bill may be sent to various committees. The assigned committee may then send the bill to a subcommittee for extensive review and to develop recommendations to be reported back to the full committee for consideration.

The assigned committee or subcommittee closely reviews and debates the issues surrounding the bill. Input is received from executive and legislative branch agencies, and regulatory agencies that have information on the subject matter of the bill. Sometimes government agencies are asked to submit reports to Congress on issues pertinent to the bill's consideration. Public hearings are held for bills that have high public interest or those that will result in a substantive change to laws. Recommendations and testimonies are taken from subject matter experts, lobbyists, celebrities, ordinary citizens, and others with interests in or connection to the bill's topic. These witnesses may be in favor of or opposed to the passage of the bill under consideration. Some parts of hearings are closed if information pertinent to national security will be disclosed, personal rights will be violated, or if public disclosure of certain types of information is in violation of other laws or rules.

A markup session is held after hearings are completed to further deliberate and document the pros and cons of passing the bill. Revisions or amendments are made to the bill's wording as necessary. If substantial amendments are made, the committee may introduce a clean bill which contains all the changes but is assigned a new number.

After the markup session is completed, the committee submits a committee report that includes an explanation of the bill's purpose (i.e., goals and objectives), findings, and recommendations, a statement if new budget authority or change in revenues or expenditures will result, any proposed changes to existing laws, and votes of committee members. The committee can take several possible actions on the bill. It can release it (called *reporting*) back to the entire chamber with a recommendation to pass the bill without any changes, amend it and report back with a recommendation for passage, rewrite the bill and release it, report back with no recommendation, or table or ignore it (which kills the bill).

If the committee does report the bill back favorably, it is placed on the House or Senate calendar along with other bills awaiting action during upcoming sessions. Different types of bills are placed on different types of calendars. For example, in the House of Representatives most public bills are placed on the Union Calendar since they deal with appropriations or revenue. Public bills not dealing with money are placed on the House Calendar. In the Senate, bills are scheduled on the Calendar of Business also called the Legislative Calendar. Procedures allow high-priority bills to be heard quickly. Otherwise, bills would just be discussed according to when they were placed on congressional calendars. For example, the House will occasionally allow a bill to be heard based on the unanimous consent of all House members.

The House of Representatives has five calendars of business: the Union Calendar, the House Calendar, the Private Calendar, the Corrections Calendar, and the Calendar of Motions to Discharge Committees. Each calendar and their respective issues to be discussed, including the consideration of bills, are provided each day that the House is in session. The following is a summary of the types of issues placed on each calendar:

- Union Calendar: Schedule for consideration of bills impacting the entire nation, such as raising revenue, appropriations, and other bills directly or indirectly impacting the appropriation of money or property.
- House Calendar: Schedule for consideration of public bills and public resolutions that do impact raising revenue or have a direct or indirect impact on the appropriation of money or property.
- Private Calendar: Schedule for private bills to be considered in the House.
- Corrections Calendar: Schedule for consideration of bills to resolve specific problems with existing federal laws, rules, or regulations.
- Calendar of Motions to Discharge Committees: Used when a majority of House members sign a motion to discharge a committee from consideration of a public bill or resolution.

Within the Senate, there are the legislative and executive calendars. The consideration of legislation (bills and resolutions) is placed on the Legislative Calendar (also called the Calendar of Business). The consideration of executive resolutions, treaties, and nominations is scheduled on the Executive Calendar.

Once the calendar date is reached for a bill to be discussed, the committee makes a report to the full House or Senate session. The entire bill is read publicly to all members. According to the Ramseyer Rule in the House and the Cordon Rule in the Senate, any changes to existing laws, including the text of the law being repealed, must be outlined in the committee's official report. The bill is debated according to chamber rules. For example, the House Rules Committee establishes rules dictating how each bill will be addressed in debate and the process for amending it in the House of Representatives. The bill may be passed as recommended by the committee, amended and then passed, or defeated. A motion to recommit may also be passed to send the bill back to the committee with instructions. The committee must then hold further deliberations and report back to the chamber once complete.

Tactics to Expand or Block a Bill.   In the Senate, senators may try to take advantage of the popularity of a bill to attempt to pass additional legislation by attaching an amendment to the bill, called a *rider*, that may even be unrelated to the topic of the bill. The purpose is to secure the passage of the amendment along with the bill. Senators are routinely allowed to attach riders. The House of Representatives has rules forbidding riders, with exceptions.

When a bill is being debated on the House or Senate floor, a tactic that was once used to delay or prevent a bill's passage was *filibustering*. A member of Congress filibustered by engaging in extensive debate and using all available time. In the House, the five-minute rule is used in an attempt to prevent filibustering. A House member is only allowed five minutes to explain a proposed amendment to a bill. The member originally reading the bill or speaking before the member with the proposed amendment is allowed five minutes to rebut the proposal. Members can, however, still delay a bill by proposing an amendment to the amendment and speak for another five minutes. The House germaneness rule prevents members from making amendments on a subject or issue that is different from the bill being considered. In the Senate, a motion agreed upon by at least sixteen senators and then carried by three-fifths of the Senate ends debate. This process is called invoking cloture.

The following are additional tactics congressional representatives may take in attempts to slow or block the passage of new legislation:

- Persuade the Speaker of the House or president of the Senate to delay the consideration of a bill (i.e., delay its assignment to a committee).
- Convince fellow members in party conferences, caucuses, or other meetings to not support a particular bill.
- Convince congressional committee and/or subcommittee members to oppose a bill in committee hearings, debates, markup sessions, and voting.
- Persuade the Rules Committee to oppose applying a rule to a bill, which dictates the timing and terms of a bill's debate.
- Convince other congressmen and congresswomen not to support a bill once it reaches the floor for full debate.
- Build coalitions with lobbyists, interest groups, the media, and citizens to not support a bill.
- Propose amendments that will weaken a bill by making the entire package of legislation less popular.

Once a bill becomes a law, actions can still be taken to defeat or weaken it. A member of Congress can attempt to block or reduce funding to execute the law, thereby making it ineffective. A member of Congress can also propose new legislation that reverses the law. Lastly, the constitutionality of the law can be challenged in federal court.

Congressional Approval of Bills.   A *quorum call* is used to ensure there are enough members (i.e., a majority) present to vote on a bill's passage. Absent members may be requested to report. The House may hear a bill in the Committee of the

Whole, which means the House members consider a bill as one large committee. In the Senate, a quorum is not required unless a member insists that one is taken.

The bill is given a second reading in which the clerk reads the entire bill on the chamber floor. During debate, members may offer further amendments. After amendments are debated, the bill is read a third time (third reading).

Votes for bills are made by members responding "aye" or "no" and the majority wins. Members may be asked to stand to obtain an accurate vote count. Electronic votes are also taken. The House also uses yea-and-nay voting. A three-fifths majority vote of House members is needed to pass a bill, resolution, or amendment. A majority vote is required in the Senate. A bill dies if either chamber of Congress does not approve it. The same applies to amendments to the Constitution.

After a bill is passed in the chamber where it is introduced, it is passed to the other chamber for debate. An *engrossed bill* is the official copy of a bill or joint resolution that has passed in one chamber. When passed to the other chamber, the process of reviewing the bill begins again with the bill being assigned to the appropriate committee for review, and then a debated on the floor. If the second chamber amends the bill, it must be sent back the chamber where it originated for concurrence. In this case, a conference committee composed of members from both chambers of Congress will review the changes. Both the House and the Senate must approve their final Conference Report.

Once both chambers have finally approved the bill, the U.S. Government Printing Office prints a final copy of the bill (called *enrolling*) and sends it back to the originating chamber to verify it has been printed correctly. The Speaker of the House and the vice president sign the final, or enrolled bill. It then goes to the president for review and approval.

If both chambers do not approve a bill by the end of the congressional session, it is not carried over to the next session. A new bill must be introduced during the next session of Congress and the review process begins again.

PRESIDENTIAL APPROVAL OF BILLS

The president has ten days to take action on a bill approved by Congress and forwarded for presidential review and approval. If the president approves the bill by signing it and there are no changes to its language, it becomes a law. If the president takes no action at all, the bill becomes a law after ten days (excluding Sundays) if Congress is still in session. If Congress adjourns before the ten-day period is reached, the bill does not become a law (called a *pocket veto* if the president purposely holds the bill knowing Congress will end its session within the ten days) and it must be reintroduced as a new bill when Congress reconvenes. The president may veto the bill if he or she disagrees with it. If it is vetoed, the bill may be reviewed by Congress and amended according to the president's direction. Congress can, however, override the president's veto by a two-thirds vote in both chambers. The bill then becomes a law. For example, in 2007 Congress overrode President George W. Bush's veto of a $23 billion water resources bill (called the Water Resources Development Act). The president had vetoed the bill because he believed it included unnecessary projects.

Bills approved by the president or by congressional override of a presidential veto are sent to the archivist of the United States for publication. Each is initially published as a *slip law,* the unofficial form of the new law, until the end of the congressional session.

Once the congressional session ends and the new legislation is published, it officially becomes a new law. The National Archives and Records Administration (part of the Office of the Federal Register) maintains all laws in the *United States Statutes at Large* (also called the Statutes at Large), which has been printed since 1845. It is an annual publication listing all laws in the order in which they were passed. Congress moved the publication authority of laws from a private company (Little, Brown and Company) to the U.S. Government Printing Office in 1874. The *United States Statutes at Large* also includes the text of the Declaration of Independence, Articles of Confederation, the Constitution, treaties with Indians and foreign nations, and presidential proclamations.

All laws are also printed in the *United States Code*, published by the Office of the Law Revision Counsel of the U.S. House of Representatives. Since 1926, The *United States Code* has been published every six years, although annual supplements are published to provide the most current information on laws passed between these six-year cycles. Laws are arranged by subject; a law can also be found by searching on its name. The *Code* includes fifty subjects, called titles. Each law is assigned an identifying reference according to its title and section within that title. For example, "5 U.S.C. 2301" stands for Title 5, Section 2301 of the *United States Code*. The name of this code is "Merit System Principles." The *United States Code* is electronically maintained by the U.S. Government Printing Office and can be accessed on the Internet ("United States Code: Main Page, 2008).

The judicial branch does not routinely review new laws. However, the Supreme Court can rule a new law unconstitutional if it is reviewed in a court case. The Court will also analyze the law in light of past rulings the Court has issued during hearings on similar subject matters, using a process called the use of *precedent*. In reviewing laws, the Court will interpret the reason the law was passed and determine if it is written to meet the intent of its passage. For this reason, the Court may determine that while a law is not unconstitutional, it was not issued or is not being executed as per its intended purpose.

INTEREST GROUPS AND LOBBYISTS

Interest Groups.   Interest groups form to influence the government to support a particular issue. They represent the collective concerns of their members, and they ensure that elected officials are aware of issues affecting their members. Interest groups serve several purposes in American politics:

- Interest groups help close the divide between citizens and government and enable citizens to explain their views on policies.
- Interest groups help raise public awareness and push for actions on certain issues.
- Interest groups often provide public officials with specialized information that might be difficult to obtain to help make policy.
- Interest groups serve as a check on public officials to make sure that they are responsibly representing the needs of constituents.

There were concerns about the influence of interest groups even before the Constitution was ratified. Many of those who opposed the original Constitution believed that the new republic would not work because of factions or interest groups who would be fighting for power and control. In a 1787 edition of *The Federalist*, James Madison argued that the "mischief of factions" could be controlled and these groups are an inevitable part of a democratic government (Madison, 1787). He believed that small factions would simply be outvoted and the majority would rule. What Madison could not foresee was that intensely focused interest groups with enormous resources and influence representing large businesses, trade industries, and professional groups could indeed exert enormous influence on the legislative process and have a great impact on policy making.

Interest groups may be composed of individuals, groups, or organizations. Institutional interest groups represent businesses, foundations, or universities. Membership interest groups represent individuals. These individuals are called *patrons* and they provide financial backing to interest groups. Patrons finance interest groups through fees, donations, gifts, and grants. Interest groups can become very powerful if they have wealthy patrons or represent a large number of people. For instance, the AARP's annual budget surpasses $770 million (based on its 2003 budget reports).

Trade organizations are associations formed by members of a particular industry to develop standard goals for that industry. Trade organizations act as interest groups to gain government support for legislation or regulations that apply to their particular group. The National Association of Manufacturers and the National Education Association (NEA) are examples of trade organizations. Interest groups can be further segmented into other more specific categories. Other types of interest groups include agricultural interests, labor, the environment, consumers, and professionals.

Interest groups are further defined as private or public. Private interest groups (also called *special-interest groups*) form only to advance the concerns of their members or others with similar interests. For example, the American Medical Association (AMA) is composed of physicians and seeks to advance the interests of those in the medical profession. The outcome of actions by private interest groups may have consequences for other groups or the public at large. For example, lawsuits by the insurance industry against tobacco companies were aimed at recouping claims paid to injured claim holders. However, they also increased the general public's awareness of the possible harms of smoking.

Public interest groups form to advance concerns affecting the general public. They may focus on such issues as the environment, consumer product protection, and transportation. For example, Greenpeace is a public interest group. Some public interest groups claim to be representing the needs of the general public but are in fact only representing the personal views of its members. These include, for example, anti-abortion groups and those opposed to homosexuality.

The fund-raising arm of an interest group is called a Political Action Committee (PAC). These entities raise funds and make contributions to politicians on the interest group's behalf. Since the 1970s, there have been federal laws concerning how much money PACs can donate to campaigns. Although candidates do not vote on issues because of political donations from interest groups, the donations are given in an attempt to gain political favor with the candidate. (*See* Political Action Committees, below).

Lobbyists.   Interest groups work at all levels of government: local, state, and national. They use a variety of techniques, both direct and indirect, to influence policy and policy making. Most interest groups use direct techniques, making contacts with government officials to accomplish their goals. Some interest groups today use the indirect approach of hiring lobbyists, who make direct contact with elected officials in attempts to influence (or lobby support for) the passage of legislation that will benefit interest group members or the general public. Lobbyists then attempt to persuade legislative and executive branch leaders to propose, amend, approve, or disapprove of legislation, policies, and other decisions. The clients of lobbyists may be an individual, an organization, a group, or an industry. The term *lobbying* originated when groups and individuals who were interested in influencing policy would gather in the foyer or lobby of legislators to discuss their concerns and attempt to influence policy.

Due to their influence on elected officials, lobbyists are given substantial attention when new legislation is being considered. Lobbyists have influence for several reasons. Some lobbyist groups have a great deal of political influence. They represent very large groups of voters and have very influential members. Often their members include business leaders, actors, and community leaders. Lobbyists also have tremendous financial influence, spending billions of dollars each year. Some of the greatest spending for lobbying is in the pharmaceutical, insurance, electric utilities, computers, business, and education industries. Lobbyists exert their financial influence by providing or withholding financial contributions in election campaigns at national, state, and local levels. Lobbyists can also garner media attention. In addition to buying airtime and other forms of advertising, they can schedule press conferences, have demonstrations, and stage other events that attract the media. Finally, lobbyists are often experts in their field. Their members possess considerable knowledge and experience in their fields and can effectively gauge the short and long-term impact of federal, state, and local actions. They develop solutions and strategies to improve support to their areas, anticipate contingencies, develop cost estimates, and effectively articulate all of this information to legislatures. The results of their research are often useful in drafting legislation. Due to their expertise, lobbyists are often quite effective in providing sound and very persuasive justification for the passage of laws.

Direct lobbying techniques to persuade legislators include making direct contact, providing expert testimony and legal advice, and following up on laws passed by Congress. A lobbyist may meet with a legislator in the halls of the Congress, or during social occasions such as dinners, boating and fishing trips, and during golf outings. Legislators may not be familiar with a particular issue and may even seek expert information from an interest group on the issue. Lobbyists provide expert testimony before congressional committees in an effort to fight for or against proposed legislation. For example, the AARP would oppose any legislation proposed to cut benefits for the elderly, and would take advantage of any opportunity to testify before Congress on related issues. The group would then present as much evidence as possible to support their cause. Lobbyists may also provide legal advice to legislators. They may assist in drafting legislation or regulations. Finally, lobbyists follow up on passed legislation to ensure it is being implemented in support of their members. They establish contacts with agencies responsible for executing new laws and track how they implement resulting policies.

Lobbyists also influence legislation by influencing public opinion and using other legal means. They issue advertisements, gain celebrity endorsements, hold demonstrations, mobilize constituents, and utilize the courts. Lobbyists place ads supporting or opposing new legislation or candidates on television, radio, the Internet, and in print media such as newspapers and magazines. They also contact citizens through mass mailings. These methods are used to shape public opinion and garner grassroots (i.e., local or community) support for the organization. Lobbyists also use the influence of celebrity endorsements to sway public opinion. The National Rifle Association (NRA) has used actor Charlton Heston and rock star Ted Nugent as spokesmen. Lobbyists sometimes organize demonstrations, protest marches, and rallies to express concern for or against a particular issue or legislation. This method is most often used for more controversial issues in which there is heated debate, an example of which would be efforts to influence new immigration laws. The legal system has also proven to be an effective technique used by lobbyists. The Sierra Club has been successful in legally challenging industry and government actions that harm the environment.

There have been several legislative efforts to prevent lobbyists from exerting excessive and sometimes unlawful influence on the legislative process. The first legislation to control lobbying was the Federal Regulation of Lobbying Act of 1946. The purpose of the act was to curb senators and representatives from being influenced by lobbyists in the performance of their legislative duties. It was specifically intended to end corruption due to legislators taking bribes from lobbyists. Interest and lobbying groups were required to register with the clerk of the House of Representatives and the secretary of the Senate, and disclosure their financial reports. However the legislation contained loopholes that allowed lobbyists to still give excessive gifts to legislators. Many incidents occurred before and after this act was passed in which legislators were publicly criticized or punished for accepting extravagant gifts (including free trips and cash) from lobbyists in exchange for favorable votes. The act was repealed by the Lobbying Disclosure Act of 1995. The 1995 act defines contact by a lobbyist as any oral or written communication (including electronic communication) to a *covered* executive or legislative branch official that is made on behalf of a client regarding the formulation, modification, or adoption of federal legislation (including legislative proposals); formulation, modification, or adoption of a federal rule, regulation, executive order, or any other program, policy, or position of the United States Government; administration or execution of a federal program or policy (including the negotiation, award, or administration of a federal contract, grant, loan, permit, or license); or the nomination or confirmation of a person for a position subject to confirmation by the Senate. Covered officials include the president, vice president, members of the Executive Office of the President, members of Congress, other senior civilian and military officers, and any officer or employee in a confidential, policy-determining, policy-making, or policy-advocating position. Lobbyists are required to register with the secretary of the Senate and the clerk of the House of Representatives. The exception is if the total income from lobbying on behalf of a particular client does not exceed $5,000 or total expenses do not exceed $20,000.

6

THE EXECUTIVE PROCESS

The U.S. Constitution charged the executive branch with the responsibility of executing laws passed by the legislative branch. Executive orders and agency rules provide specific guidance on how executive officers and agencies will carry out their duties in order to effectively carry out laws. The Administrative Procedure Act provides specific guidance on agency rulemaking. To ensure citizens are afforded information about agency operations and rulemaking, the Freedom of Information Act requires agencies to publish information on their rulemaking procedures and grant public access to certain internal information. Other laws and regulations ensure agencies take steps to make sure rules are clearly understood by the general public and that citizens are afforded opportunities to provide input.

PURPOSE OF THE EXECUTIVE BRANCH

The primary purpose of the executive branch is to execute the laws passed by the legislative branch. One of the primary ways it does this is by establishing federal rules and regulations to oversee and direct the actions of agencies and other entities regulated by the executive branch. The act of establishing, revising, or eliminating rules and regulations is called *rule making*. Rules (which include regulations) are passed for several reasons. First and foremost, new rules are issued to provide guidance for laws passed by the legislative branch. Often laws passed by Congress are purposely stated in broad terms due to their general application to many or all government agencies. Therefore, more detailed interpretations of those laws and specific guidance on how they should be executed are issued. Because most rules are passed as a result of laws, they have the force of law. If not issued pursuant to a specific law, rules are subject to review by the legislative and judicial branches. Even when laws are not broad or do not require any further interpretation, some agencies have internal policies of issuing formal rules on any new laws that affect their operations. This is usually done as a standard process to officially recognize and execute a law.

Rules are also issued in response to internal and external events. Internally, changes in leaders or management, revised organizational structures, or internal policy reviews may prompt the need for rule making. Externally, changes in technology, scientific facts, or public needs may require the revision or issuance of new rules. The government establishes laws and rules when private sector organizations or companies cannot meet a public need or are harming citizens and government intervention is required. For example, a rule may be passed to protect the environment from pollution by businesses. Finally, rules are passed in response to citizens' actions or requests, activities in other agencies or branches of the government, or activities in state or local governments.

EXECUTIVE ORDERS

The president issues executive orders to provide direction to executive branch agencies and officers on specific matters. These orders establish policy and provide specific guidance based on laws passed by Congress. Each order is numbered consecutively for identification, a process begun in 1907 by the Department of State. Before then presidents issued executive orders but they were not published. All orders beginning with Executive Order 7316 (signed in 1937 by President Franklin D. Roosevelt) are posted sequentially in Title 3 of the *Code of Federal Regulations*, and arranged by subject.

Each signed executive order is received by the Office of the Federal Register and printed in the *Federal Register*. The *Federal Register*, known as the "daily newspaper" of the federal government, is a legal newspaper that is published each day by the National Archives and Records Administration. It contains federal agency regulations, proposed rules, public notices, executive orders, and other presidential documents. It can be obtained in paper form, on microfiche, and on the Internet.

The Office of the Federal Register maintains a record called *disposition tables* of all executive orders beginning with those issued by President Franklin D. Roosevelt, which can be accessed on the Internet ("Executive Orders Disposition Tables Index," 2008). The orders are arranged by presidential administration and year of signature, and include the following information:

- executive order number
- date signed by the president
- *Federal Register* volume, page number, and issue date
- title
- amendments (if any)
- current status

The president issues various types of executive orders. National Security directives deal with issues of national security or national defense. Homeland security matters are addressed in Homeland Security Presidential Directives. Proclamations are types of executive orders generally issued by the president as ceremonial announcements. For example, the president may formally recognize certain holidays or events such as Independence Day, Mother's Day, or National Physical Fitness and Sports Month. State governors also issue executive orders.

There have been long-standing concerns that executive orders issued by some presidents set rules that are beyond the powers granted to the executive branch.

For example, Attorney William J. Olson (1999) raised the following concerns in testimony to Congress in 1999:

> Congress and the courts have taken action from time to time to examine and, at times, challenge Presidential exercises of authority perceived to be unconstitutional: from President Washington's declaration of neutrality to the Louisiana Purchase, Jefferson's embargo, Jackson's removal of federal funds from the Second Bank of the United States, Polk's sending of Gen. Zachary Taylor's troops into contested territory before the declaration of war with Mexico, Lincoln's conduct of the Civil War without calling Congress into session, Lincoln's amnesty and reconstruction plans, the Tenure of Office Act and Andrew Johnson's impeachment . . . and the list goes on and on.

The checks and balances among the three branches of government control the passing of executive orders that truly are outside of the powers granted the president in the Constitution. If Congress feels the executive branch has overstepped its powers, it can revise existing laws or issue new laws. The Supreme Court can declare that an order is unconstitutional or that it deviates from the congressional intent of a law.

Presidents have made decisions based on the concept of *executive privilege*, the assertion that the president has inherent constitutional powers derived from his or her position as head of the executive branch to make decisions necessary to accomplish the duties of that office. Additionally, the assertion is that the president must be able to make decisions and take actions necessary to maintain checks and balances over the legislative and judicial branches.

The most notable and controversial use of executive privilege has been by presidents refusing to provide requested information. President Dwight D. Eisenhower invoked his right to this privilege perhaps more than any president due to the continual demands from Senator Joseph McCarthy to obtain testimonies from high ranking members of the executive branch. During the 1950s, the senator spent years asserting that communists and communist sympathizers were working within and subverting the U.S. government.

President Richard M. Nixon refused to provide tapes of conversations held in the Oval Office that were requested as part of the Watergate investigations. The Supreme Court upheld his refusal under the right of executive privilege in *United States v. Nixon*, 418 U.S. 683 (1974). President Bill Clinton attempted to use executive privilege in refusing to allow prosecutors to question his senior staff members during an investigation of the president's affair with a White House intern. A federal judge ruled against President Clinton. President George W. Bush invoked executive privilege several times, including his refusal to provide details of actions taken by former presidents.

AGENCY RULES AND RULEMAKING

Agencies develop rules and regulations based upon laws passed by Congress. Developing rules and regulations falls under *administrative law,* the body of bureaucratic law that results from the process of agencies making rules and regulations, enforcing these rules and regulations, and holding hearings (adjudication) when regulated parties violate rules or when parties believe they have been harmed by agency rules.

Administrative law is a combination of substantive law and procedural law. *Substantive law* is the part of administrative law resulting from the congressional statute creating an agency that outlines its duties and specifically outlines what the agency was developed to enforce. For example, the Federal Communications Commission (FCC) was established by the Communications Act of 1934, and given the responsibility and authority to regulate interstate and international communications by radio, and later television, wire, satellite, and cable. The FCC's jurisdiction covers the fifty states, the District of Columbia, and U.S. possessions. *Procedural law* outlines how an agency will enforce the provisions of statutory law. In other words, it is the specific method the agency will use to enforce the provisions of the statute or other laws it has been given the authority and responsibility to enforce. The FCC is comprised of bureaus that process applications for licenses and other filings, analyze complaints, conduct investigations, develop and implement regulatory programs, and take part in hearings. The rules and regulations passed by the FCC are codified in Title 47 of the *Code of Federal Regulations*.

Agencies issue rules in various forms, including guidance, regulations, and policy memorandums. There is a general process for the passage of rules. Proposed rules are first published in the *Federal Register*, as are subsequent interim and final rules. Comments from the public and the outcomes of formal agency hearings are then considered. Final rules are published in the *Code of Federal Regulations*, as required by the Federal Register Act of 1935. Once rules are passed, parties or individuals who believe they are or will be negatively affected can submit a formal dispute. Administrative law judges preside over disputes between agencies and individuals during administrative hearings.

The Administrative Procedure Act of 1946, Executive Order 12866, and the Congressional Review Act of 1996 govern agency rule making. Certain types of rule making are exempt from these regulations. For example, general policy statements that simply state general agency procedures or restate existing laws are exempt from the Administrative Procedure Act as these statements do not establish new rules.

Administrative Procedure Act of 1946.   The Administrative Procedure Act (APA) of 1946 (amended by the Electronic Freedom of Information Act of 1996) was passed as a result of the growth in number of agencies under President Franklin D. Roosevelt's New Deal legislation and the wide latitude they exercised in passing new regulations and hearing cases. Some agencies were exercising legislative, judicial, and executive powers by passing rules, hearing cases, and practicing administrative powers all at once. President Franklin D. Roosevelt established the Attorney General's Committee on Administrative Procedure to examine existing procedures and provide recommendations on how to provide improved oversight over agencies' activities. These recommendations and the outcomes of Senate hearings on the matter led to the passing of the APA. The *Attorney General's Manual on the Administrative Procedure Act* was issued in 1947 as a guide to the APA. It succinctly outlines the purpose of the APA as follows:

1. To require agencies to keep the public currently informed of their organization, procedures and rules. . . .
2. To provide for public participation in the rule making process. . . .
3. To prescribe uniform standards for the conduct of formal rule making . . . and adjudicatory proceedings . . . , i.e., proceedings which are required by statute to be made on the record after opportunity for an agency hearing. . . .
4. To restate the law of judicial review.

The *Attorney General's Manual on the Administrative Procedure Act* defines a rule and rule making as follows:

> *Rule and rule making.* "Rule" means the whole or any part of any agency statement of general or particular applicability and future effect designed to implement, interpret, or prescribe law or policy or to describe the organization, procedure, or practice requirements of any agency and includes the approval or prescription for the future of rates, wages, corporate or financial structures or reorganizations thereof, prices, facilities, appliances, services or allowances therefore or of valuations, cost, or accounting, or practices bearing upon any of the foregoing. "Rule making" means agency process for the formulation, amendment, or repeal of a rule.

Agencies adhere to the following "notice-and-comment" steps in making rules:

- An agency must publish a Notice of Proposed Rulemaking in the *Federal Register*.
- Other agencies and the general public may submit written comments on the proposed rule to the issuing agency for consideration (under Executive Order 12866, sixty days are allowed for comments to a proposed agency rule).
- The issuing agency reviews comments and makes adjustments to the proposed rule as necessary.
- The new rule is generally published thirty days before it takes effect.

Under revisions to the APA and the Freedom of Information Act of 1966 by the Electronic Freedom of Information Act of 1996, each agency is required to publish the following information in the *Federal Register*:

(A) Descriptions of its central and field organization and the established places at which, the employees (and in the case of a uniformed service, the members) from whom, and the methods whereby, the public may obtain information, make submittals or requests, or obtain decisions;

(B) Statements of the general course and method by which its functions are channeled and determined, including the nature and requirements of all formal and informal procedures available;

(C) Rules of procedure, descriptions of forms available or the places at which forms may be obtained, and instructions as to the scope and contents of all papers, reports, or examinations;

(D) Substantive rules of general applicability adopted as authorized by law, and statements of general policy or interpretations of general applicability formulated and adopted by the agency; and

(E) Each amendment, revision, or repeal of the foregoing.

The APA distinguishes between the rule making and adjudication processes within agencies. Rule making is similar to passing new legislation and is the process of developing new rules. Adjudication ends in the issuance of an order after reviewing actions (such as infractions) related to established agency rules and regulations. The *Attorney General's Manual on the Administrative Procedure Act* defines an order as a result of adjudication as follows:

> *Order and adjudication.* "Order" means the whole or any part of the final disposition (whether affirmative, negative, injunctive, or declaratory in form) of any agency in

any matter other than rule making but including licensing. "Adjudication" means agency process for the formulation of an order.

Agencies adjudicate through formal and informal procedures. Formal procedures involve documented hearings, the taking of witness testimonies, and other trial-like proceedings. Decisions made through the formal process are subject to judicial review by the courts. Informal procedures include holding negotiations or conferences.

Executive Order 12866, Regulatory Planning and Review.   Executive Order 12866 was signed by President Bill Clinton and went into effect on September 30, 1993, to make the regulatory process more efficient. Titled "Regulatory Planning and Review," the order's first paragraph outlines the problem it was passed to address:

> The American people deserve a regulatory system that works for them, not against them: a regulatory system that protects and improves their health, safety, environment, and well-being and improves the performance of the economy without imposing unacceptable or unreasonable costs on society; regulatory policies that recognize that the private sector and private markets are the best engine for economic growth; regulatory approaches that respect the role of state, local, and tribal governments; and regulations that are effective, consistent, sensible, and understandable. We do not have such a regulatory system today.

The order sets general standards that agencies should use when establishing regulations, and stipulates that all rules established by agencies are subject to presidential and congressional review. It specifies, "Federal agencies should promulgate only such regulations as are required by law, are necessary to interpret the law, or are made necessary by compelling public need, such as material failures of private markets to protect or improve the health and safety of the public, the environment, or the well-being of the American people."

It requires agencies to use scientific, technical, economic or other information to base their decisions. This not only ensures agencies are thoroughly evaluating new rules, but also adds specificity to broad laws passed by Congress. All costs and benefits should be analyzed in evaluating alternatives, including the alternative of not passing a regulation. Weighing these costs includes considering both quantitative and qualitative measures.

Under the order, the Office of Information and Regulatory Affairs (OIRA) carries out a regulatory review process on behalf of the president. The Office of Management and Budget (OMB) was given the responsibility of providing guidance to executive branch agencies and policy advisors, assisting the president and vice president, and reviewing individual regulations. OMB has issued additional guidance on rule making to agencies. The following are excerpts from that guidance (Graham, 2001):

> Agencies must prepare a Regulatory Impact Analysis (RIA) for each regulation that OIRA (Office of Information and Regulatory Affairs) or the agency designates as "economically significant." Section 3(f)(1) of the order defines an "economically significant" rule as one likely to "have an annual effect on the economy of $100 million or more or adversely affect in a material way the economy, a sector of the economy, productivity, competition, jobs, the environment, public health or safety, or state, local, or tribal governments or communities." This definition is functionally

equivalent to the definition of a "major" rule as that term is used in the Congressional Review Act.

The RIA must provide an assessment of benefits, costs, and potentially effective and reasonably feasible alternatives to the planned regulatory action (see section 6(a)(3)(C)). This is submitted to OIRA along with the applicable draft regulatory action. Preparing RIAs helps agencies evaluate the need for and consequences of possible Federal action. By analyzing alternate ways to structure a rule, agencies can select the best option while providing OIRA and the public a broader understanding of the ranges of issues that may be involved. Accordingly, it is important that a draft RIA be reviewed by agency economists, engineers, and scientists, as well as by agency attorneys, prior to submission to OIRA.

An important aspect of OIRA's review of a draft rule is an evaluation of its possible impact on the programs of other Federal agencies. This evaluation often involves an interagency review by specialists from affected agencies and the coordination of agency positions, as necessary.

The agencies prepare semi-annual regulatory agendas under E.O. 12866, section 4(b), outlining the agencies foreseeable regulatory priorities. OIRA plans to send, as occasion arises, what will be referred to as 'prompt' letters. The purpose of a prompt letter is to suggest an issue that OMB believes is worthy of agency priority. Rather than being sent in response to the agency's submission of a draft rule for OIRA review, a 'prompt' letter will be sent on OMB's initiative and will contain a suggestion for how the agency could improve its regulations. For example, the suggestion might be that an agency explore a promising regulatory issue for agency action, accelerate its efforts on an ongoing regulatory matter, or consider rescinding or modifying an existing rule. We will request prompt agency response to "prompt" letters, normally within 30 days.

Congressional Review Act of 1996.   The Congressional Review Act of 1996 is part of the Small Business Regulatory Enforcement Fairness Act of 1996, also called the Contract with America Advancement Act of 1996. It stipulates that Congress can review every new federal regulation and overrule regulations if necessary.

Before new rules can take effect, federal agencies are required to submit a report to the House of Representatives, the Senate, and the Comptroller General (head of the Government Accountability Office) that includes a description of the proposed rule and proposed effective date, and a cost benefit analysis of passing the rule. Just as each chamber of Congress does with congressional bills, each chamber passes proposed rules to standing committees with expertise and jurisdiction over the subject matter of the rule. The Comptroller General's report on the rule includes an assessment of the agency's compliance with procedural steps, and must be filed by the end of fifteen calendar days after receipt of the proposed rule.

Not all agency rules are subject to congressional approval. Rules can be put into effect by the president if necessary to counter an imminent threat to health or safety or other emergency, for the enforcement of criminal laws, for national security, or issued pursuant to any statute implementing an international trade agreement.

Other Applicable Rules and Regulations.   Executive Order 12988, entitled Civil Justice Reform, was signed February 5, 1996, under President Bill Clinton. The order established guidelines to promote fair and prompt hearings when disputes against agencies are filed. To expedite the hearing process, the order endorsed the use of settlement conferences and informal resolution techniques. It revoked Executive Order 12778 signed by President George H.W. Bush on October 23, 1991.

President Clinton's memorandum on *Plain Language in Government Writing* was issued June 1, 1998. It requires rule making documents to be written in plain language. It specifically states the following:

> The Federal Government's writing must be in plain language. By using plain language, we send a clear message about what the Government is doing, what it requires, and what services it offers. Plain language saves the Government and the private sector time, effort, and money.

The memorandum defines the use of plain language as the development of documents that use logical organization, easy-to-read design features, and "common, everyday words, except for necessary technical terms, 'you' and other pronouns, the active voice, and short sentences."

7

THE JUDICIAL PROCESS

The judicial branch, headed by the Supreme Court, has the responsibility of ensuring laws passed by the legislative branch and actions taken by the executive branch do not violate the U.S. Constitution. The branch operates under a three-tier system with district and circuit courts located throughout the United States that exist under the Supreme Court. The Supreme Court also has jurisdiction over all federal agencies and state courts. The U.S. federal court system is based on English common law, where two parties argue their positions in an adversarial system before a neutral party. When a party in the case is unsatisfied with a lower court's finding, he or she can appeal the case through the federal court system up to the Supreme Court.

APPOINTMENT OF FEDERAL JUDGES

The Supreme Court is the highest court in the United States. It is composed of the chief justice, who oversees the business of the Court and associate justices. Currently there are nine justices, but Congress can change that number if needed. Table 7.1 lists the Supreme Court justices as of 2007. Appendix K provides a list of the Supreme Court Chief Justices and Associate Justices since 1900 and brief information about each.

Justices are nominated by the president for life appointments and are confirmed (or approved) by the Senate. *For life* means until they die, voluntarily retire, or resign. An appointment to the Supreme Court is the ultimate form of presidential patronage for a federal judge. The president considers a potential justice's professional qualifications, personal background, ideologies in comparison to those of his or her political party, past decisions in cases on issues important to the president, the political climate of the Senate, and the concerns of constituents. Other factors affecting the president's nomination are a potential judge's race, sex, and age, taking into account the racial and gender composition of the Court. Senators consider these same factors during public confirmation hearings. Once a judge is chosen, neither the Senate nor the president can reduce his or her salary or remove the justice without due cause (i.e., legal justification). This ensures judges are able to make decisions impartially and without fear of political reprisal.

Table 7.1.   United States Supreme Court Justices, as of 2007

Judge	Position	Nominating president	Date seated
John G. Roberts, Jr.	Chief Justice	George W. Bush	September 29, 2005
John Paul Stevens	Associate Justice	Gerald R. Ford	December 19, 1975
Antonin Scalia	Associate Justice	Ronald W. Reagan	September 26, 1986
Anthony M. Kennedy	Associate Justice	Ronald W. Reagan	February 18, 1988
David Hackett Souter	Associate Justice	George H. W. Bush	October 9, 1990
Clarence Thomas	Associate Justice	George H. W. Bush	October 23, 1991
Ruth Bader Ginsburg	Associate Justice	William Clinton	August 10, 1993
Stephen G. Breyer	Associate Justice	William Clinton	August 3, 1994
Samuel Anthony Alito, Jr.	Associate Justice	George W. Bush	January 31, 2006

The appointment process begins with the collection of the names of qualified judges from which the president and presidential advisors derive a short list of top candidates for a vacant Supreme Court seat. This collection of names is provided to the president from congressional representatives, governors, other politicians, members of the federal court system, members of the legal profession, legal experts, and people professionally associated with possible nominees. The list may include both retired and active judges. If the vacant seat is for that of the chief justice, the Supreme Court associate justices are also on the list. A great deal of information is collected about each person on the list of candidates. This information includes a thorough background check of their personal and professional lives, including a check of their personal background by the Federal Bureau of Investigation. The president and a selection committee carefully consider the qualifications of each candidate.

Once a Supreme Court nominee is announced by the president, the Senate Judiciary Committee holds hearings to consider the candidate. The nominee may be called before the Senate committee to answer questions on his or her past court decisions and ideologies on specific issues. These issues may include capital punishment, abortion, and the torture of war criminals. The purpose of questions on these issues is to gauge how liberal or conservative a potential justice will be once appointed to the bench. Because of their political ideologies, members of the Senate Judiciary Committee may not approve of a nominee whose political or social ideologies are not compatible. For example, Harriet Miers was nominated by President George W. Bush in 2005 to replace retiring Associate Justice Sandra Day O'Conner. Many, particularly conservatives, objected to Miers's appointment because of questions about her qualifications and record. Her nomination was withdrawn less than six weeks into the confirmation hearing process. Other controversial Supreme Court nominations and confirmations have included those of Robert Bork (nominated by President Ronald W. Reagan but not confirmed by the Senate) and Clarence Thomas (nominated by President George H. W. Bush and confirmed by the Senate).

Judges are held to very high standards of behavior, and are expected to behave in an ethical manner when engaged in Court business and when off duty. They are expected to exhibit integrity, show no appearance of impropriety or partiality, exercise due diligence, and not engage in extra-judicial activities that conflict with their official duties. Congress can impeach a federal judge for treason, bribery, or other high crimes and misdemeanors.

Photograph of the Supreme Court justices (2007). *Courtesy of the U.S. Supreme Court.*

POWERS OF THE JUDICAL BRANCH

The powers of the U.S. judicial branch, specifically the Supreme Court, are granted in Article III of the Constitution, Sections 1 and 2. The Article also outlines the checks and balances exercised by other branches over the judicial branch. Section 1 establishes the Supreme Court as the highest court in the nation. It mandates that only Congress can establish lower courts, but Congress cannot terminate the appointment of a judge without due cause. Section 2 outlines the jurisdiction of federal courts, which includes all cases involving violations of the Constitution, all federal laws, and several categories of dispute under the jurisdiction of the federal courts. Section 1 states,

> The judicial Power of the United States, shall be vested in one supreme Court, and in such inferior Courts as the Congress may from time to time ordain and establish. The Judges, both of the supreme and inferior Courts, shall hold their Offices during good Behavior, and shall, at stated Times, receive for their Services a Compensation which shall not be diminished during their Continuance in Office.

Section 2 (modified by the Eleventh Amendment) states,

> The judicial Power shall extend to all Cases, in Law and Equity, arising under this Constitution, the Laws of the United States, and Treaties made, or which shall be made, under their Authority; to all Cases affecting Ambassadors, other public Ministers and Consuls; to all Cases of admiralty and maritime Jurisdiction; to Controversies to which the United States shall be a Party; to Controversies between two or more States; between a State and Citizens of another State; between Citizens of different States; between Citizens of the same State claiming Lands under Grants of different States, and between a State, or the Citizens thereof, and foreign States, Citizens or Subjects.

The federal courts are the guardians of the Constitution. Court decisions ensure that the liberties guaranteed citizens in the Constitution are protected. In accomplishing this, the courts often have to provide specific interpretations of the intent of Constitutional language. For example, the First Amendment of the Constitution includes a clause that prohibits Congress from establishing laws that infringe upon an individual's right to free speech. The Supreme Court has ruled the clause does not apply to offensive or obscene language, and the government can thus regulate how, where, and when it is used. In *Miller v. California*, 413 U.S. 15 (1973), the court ruled that material is considered obscene if it meets the following criteria:

(a) Whether "the average person, applying contemporary community standards" would find that the work, taken as a whole, appeals to the prurient interest, *Roth, supra*, at 489 (*Roth v. United States*, 354 U.S. 476 (1957))

(b) Whether the work depicts or describes, in a patently offensive way, sexual conduct specifically defined by the applicable state law, and

(c) Whether the work, taken as a whole, lacks serious literary, artistic, political, or scientific value.

The Supreme Court also ensures that members of the executive and legislative branches do not make decisions or take actions that are outside of their Constitutional powers. The federal courts are able to effectively protect citizens and provide judicial oversight of the other branches because of their independence. Judges are not subject to political compromises or punishment. In the Supreme Court, this independence is protected by justices being appointed for life, and by the president and Congress being prohibited from reducing the salaries of judges. Thus, federal judges decide cases based upon the law as neutral parties who are free from political influence and political retribution.

A practice that also gives the Supreme Court power is the authority to conduct judicial reviews as part of maintaining checks and balances. Judicial review is the Supreme Court's power to review all acts and decisions of the executive and legislative branches, and invalidate any that the Court rules are in conflict with the Constitution. The power of judicial review was officially established by the Court itself in the case of *Marbury v. Madison*, 5 U.S. 137 (1803). President John Adams appointed William Marbury as justice of the peace in the District of Columbia. His appointment was to be executed by Secretary of State John Marshall. President Thomas Jefferson refused to acknowledge several appointments made by Adams, including that of Marbury, because the appointments were made by Adams days before Jefferson was to take office. President Jefferson was a member of the Democratic-Republic party and President Adams was a Federalist. The judges appointed by President Adams were Federalists and were last-minute appointments made to create political havoc during Jefferson's term in office.

Marbury sued the government in an attempt to force the new Secretary of State, James Madison, to delivery his commission. The Supreme Court knew President Jefferson would ignore their decision if they ruled in favor on Marbury. This would make the Court appear weak. On the other hand, it would look as if the Court feared the president if it ruled against Marbury. The Court ruled that Madison should have appointed Marbury, but most importantly that the statute Marbury based his claim on (the Judiciary Act of 1789) was unconstitutional. The Act stated the Supreme Court could issue a "writ of mandamus," which meant it could force Madison to delivery

Marbury's commission. The Court ruled the statute violated the Constitution, rather than the actions of Presidents Adams or Jefferson. This ruling established the Supreme Court as the decision-making body on Constitutional law. Judicial review also applies to the state courts over state executive and legislative actions. Each state's supreme court can review all acts and decisions of its governors and state legislatures.

FOUNDATION OF THE U.S. JUDICIAL PROCESS

The U.S. judicial process is based upon English common law. Under this principle, laws evolve over time to meet the changing needs of society. Cases are decided based on the specific circumstances and facts of a trial. Rulings and decisions reached in previous cases are used to decide new cases. This use of precedent is an attempt by the courts to avoiding issuing contradictory decisions by reaching the same ruling in cases of similar facts unless there is a viable need to do otherwise.

The U.S. federal court system is based upon the simple concept of two parties arguing their positions in an adversarial system that allows them to present their disputes before a neutral party. This neutral party may be a judge or a jury, and the case is decided based on several sources of laws. First and foremost, the U.S. Constitution, as the primary legal document of the United States, is considered the supreme law of the land. New laws passed by Congress must either be in compliance with the Constitution, or Congress must amend the Constitution. The federal courts interpret the application of the Constitution to individual cases. Their interpretations of specific parts of the Constitution have changed over time.

Another source of federal law is rules passed by executive branch agencies and independent agencies. These rules collectively form the body of U.S. administrative law. They provide specific guidance on laws passed by Congress and are used to decide judicial cases. State constitutions provide more specific statutory guidance based on state rights granted by the U.S. Constitution, and are used by the courts in deciding cases involving issues within a single state. Finally, new laws are continually passed by state, city, county, and local governments. The federal courts will consider state and local laws in their decisions, specifically when considering cases involving a lawsuit brought against a state.

Except for specific exceptions, the majority of all U.S. court cases are heard in state and local courts. These include traffic violations, misdemeanor criminal cases, divorce proceedings, probate cases, and custody battles. These hearings take place in *limited-jurisdiction trial courts* (also called *inferior trial courts*), which hear specific types of cases. Within the states, cases from the lowest courts are appealed to the *state appellate courts*, also called the *intermediate appellate courts*. They can then be appealed to state supreme courts. The final level of appeal is to the U.S. Supreme Court.

FEDERAL COURT CASES

A case (civil or criminal) can only be heard in a federal court if it meets one of two criteria. The first is that it involves a federal law. Under this requirement of federal jurisdiction, federal courts can only hear cases involving a violation of the Constitution, a suit arising from an act of Congress or executive branch decision, a dispute under a treaty, controversies between states, or a dispute between the United States and a foreign government. The second criterion for a case being heard in federal court is cases that fall under the federal courts' "diversity of citizenship" jurisdiction. Here, a case must arise from a dispute between citizens of two different states where the amount in dispute is over $75,000, or a dispute between a U.S. citizen and a foreign government or foreign citizen. If these two conditions are not met, the case belongs in a state court. Cases brought to a federal court (or state courts) must not have exceeded their statute of limitations, the maximum amount of time allowed for a case to be brought to court depending upon the type of case. Some limitations are set by law. For example, in *Ledbetter v. Goodyear Tire & Rubber Co*, 550 U.S. ___ (2007) the Supreme Court ruled against a plaintiff because "an individual wishing to bring a Title VII lawsuit must first file an EEOC charge within, as relevant here, 180 days 'after the alleged unlawful employment practice occurred.'" (Note: the ___ in the title of the case is listed because this case had not been assigned to a page by the Court at the time this book was written.)

A party bringing a case to federal court must have *legal standing*, which is met if the following four conditions are met:

1. There must be an actual conflict between two or more parties. The Court cannot render decisions based on hypothetical scenarios.
2. The party bringing the case, the plaintiff, must have been harmed.
3. The issue surrounding the case cannot be "moot," that is, have been resolved before being heard by the court.
4. There must be a violation of Constitutional, statutory, or common law.

All bankruptcy cases are heard in federal courts. Congress has ruled that they cannot be addressed in state courts. These cases involve individuals or businesses seeking a legal relief from their debts (i.e., discharge of debt). A case is initiated by the filing of a bankruptcy petition. While many benefits exist for filing bankruptcy (as outlined below), there are also negative consequences. The main drawback is a negative impact on a filer's credit report. Bankruptcy filings remain on a filer's credit report for ten years. There are five types of bankruptcy cases allowed by Title 11 of the *United States Code*, also called the U.S. Bankruptcy Code:

> Chapter 7 (Liquidation): Individuals, companies, or corporations may file Chapter 7. Their assets (i.e., property) are taken over by a trustee and liquidated or sold, and the proceeds are distributed to their creditors. The filer is then relieved by the court from paying any further payments. The filer is allowed to keep some assets, as determined by the type of asset and bankruptcy law.
>
> Chapter 9 (Adjustment of Debts of a Municipality): Relief under Chapter 9 is only granted to a municipality such as a village, town, city, school district, county, or municipal utility. The municipality must reorganize and develop a plan to repay its debts.
>
> Chapter 11 (Reorganization): Chapter 11 allows businesses to continue their operations while paying off creditors under a court-approved plan. The business reorganizes its operations; it may repay a portion of its debts and have others discharged by the court, and also have the court terminate contracts and leases. The goal of a Chapter 11 filing is for the business to emerge from bankruptcy better organized and more profitable.

Chapter 12 (Adjustment of Debts of a Family Farmer or Fisherman with Regular Annual Income): Chapter 12 relates to relief available for farmers or fisherman that allows the filer to develop a repayment plan over a period of three to five years. *Regular annual income* means income that is sufficiently stable to allow the filer to make payments under the bankruptcy plan. A trustee is assigned to oversee the payments to the filer's creditors. The filer is allowed to continue operation of its business.

Chapter 13 (Adjustment of Debts of an Individual with Regular Income): Relief under Chapter 13 is available to individuals earning regular incomes from their jobs. The filer is allowed to keep some assets, such as their home, while paying off their creditors in installments over three to five years according to a court-approved plan. Creditors are not allowed to take any legal actions against the filer. All debts are relieved after the payment period ends. A trustee is assigned to oversee the payments to the filer's creditors.

The Bankruptcy Abuse Prevention and Consumer Protection Act of 2005 was passed by Congress and signed into law by President George W. Bush on April 20, 2005. It reformed the nation's bankruptcy system by making laws more stringent for filers. For example, the act increased the fees for filing bankruptcy, required filers to obtain credit counseling, increased compliance requirements for some businesses, and increased the length of time before a discharged filer can file for bankruptcy again.

The United States Trustee Program, the component of the Department of Justice that protects the integrity of the nation's bankruptcy system by overseeing case administration and litigating to enforce the bankruptcy laws, was given new responsibilities including:

- Implementing the new means test to determine whether a debtor is eligible for Chapter 7 (liquidation) or must file under Chapter 13 (wage-earner repayment plan)
- Supervising random audits and targeted audits to determine whether a Chapter 7 debtor's bankruptcy documents are accurate
- Certifying entities to provide the credit counseling that an individual must receive before filing bankruptcy
- Certifying entities to provide the financial education that an individual must receive before discharging debts
- Conducting enhanced oversight in small business Chapter 11 reorganization cases

Federal Civil Cases.   Federal civil cases involve a party who believes he or she has suffered some injury due to someone else's action. This action must have been in a violation of a federal law. An example would be an individual suing a company from another state for not delivering products according to a contract and the result created over $75,000 in damages to the individual. The injured party, the plaintiff, files a complaint in district court and pays the appropriate filing fee. The fee can be waived (called *forma pauperis*) if the plaintiff cannot afford the fee. The court is asked to force the party causing injury, the defendant, to provide compensation to the plaintiff, or to cease the actions that are causing the plaintiff harm. The judge tries to encourage the parties in civil cases to reach a settlement without a trial through such avenues as mediation or arbitration. *Mediation* involves a neutral third party meeting with and relaying information from one party to the other in an attempt to reach mutual agreement on a settlement. With *arbitration*, a neutral third party (an arbitrator) listens to the positions of each party and then renders a decision on the case. The parties in the case agree to abide by the arbitrator's decision in advance of any proceedings. The arbitrator listens to testimonies and is presented evidence during a trial-like proceeding. The Department of Justice represents the government if the government is the defendant in a civil case.

Each party in a civil case must provide the other party information on the case, such as a list of witnesses to be called and any case-related documents. This is part of the *discovery* process. Another part of discovery is the taking of depositions, or testimonies under oath, by witnesses while being questioned by attorneys.

Either party may request a jury trial, but if neither requests a jury, the judge decides the case alone. The plaintiff's job is to convince the judge and jury that a preponderance of the evidence supports being awarded the compensation or other judgment requested. Witnesses are brought into the courtroom as they testify. The opposing attorney may cross-examine any witness. An attorney may object if a witness is believed to be testifying based on nonpersonal knowledge, is prejudicial, is being coaxed to answer questions in a particular way by the questioning attorney, or is providing irrelevant information. The judge determines if the attorney's objection is valid (i.e., upheld) or has no basis (i.e., is overruled). Each side gives closing arguments once all evidence has been presented. The judge will explain to the jury laws that are relevant to the case and what decisions they need to reach, which generally include whether the defendant is responsible for damages, and, if so, what compensation should be given to the plaintiff.

Federal Criminal Cases.   Only the government can initiate a criminal case in federal court. An individual harmed by or a witness to criminal behavior must seek the assistance of the U.S. attorney's office, the Federal Bureau of Investigation, or some other legal enforcement office to have the case heard. Federal criminal cases involve individuals or organizations being tried on violations of federal law. For example, the federal government can prosecute a kidnapper who crosses state lines. After being arrested, the defendant is brought before a federal judge and advised of the charges filed by the government. The defendant is offered a court-appointed lawyer if they cannot afford an attorney on their own. The U.S. attorney represents the United States as the prosecutor. A grand jury decides whether there is enough evidence for the defendant to stand trial based upon the evidence presented by the U.S. attorney. The grand jury is composed of sixteen to twenty-three citizens who issue an indictment if they determine there is enough evidence to have a trial. A trial jury later hears the case when brought to trial.

During the next hearing (called the *arraignment*), the defendant enters a plea to the charges. The defendant can plead not guilty or guilty, and, in the latter case, seek a plea bargain, or compromise, with the U.S. attorney. This often to leads to some charges being dropped or a more lenient sentence. A trial is scheduled if the defendant pleads not guilty. It is up to the government to prove the defendant has committed a crime. The U.S. attorney must prove guilt beyond a reasonable doubt.

Unlike civil cases, restrictions may be put in place in criminal cases. The identity of some witnesses may be kept secret to protect them from harm for testifying. Certain evidence may not be allowed if the defendant's attorney can prove the government obtained it illegally. Additionally, the jury decides if the defendant is guilty but the judge decides the sentence.

If the defendant is found not guilty, the government cannot appeal the case. If the defendant is found guilty, the judge determines the appropriate sentence based upon guidelines issued by the United States Sentencing Commission. Either the defendant or the government may appeal the type of sentence levied if the defendant is found guilty. The U.S. attorney may feel the sentence is too lenient, or the defendant may feel it is too harsh.

The United States Sentencing Commission is an independent agency in the judicial branch created by the Sentencing Reform Act provisions of the Comprehensive Crime Control Act of 1984. Its principal purposes are to:

- Establish sentencing policies and practices for the federal courts, including guidelines to be consulted regarding the appropriate form and severity of punishment for offenders convicted of federal crimes
- Advise and assist Congress and the executive branch in the development of effective and efficient crime policy
- Collect, analyze, research, and distribute a broad array of information on federal crime and sentencing issues, serving as an information resource for Congress, the executive branch, the courts, criminal justice practitioners, the academic community, and the public.

Public Access to Federal Cases.   Most federal court cases are open to the public. While some lower court hearings are televised, Supreme Court hearings are not. However, they are recorded and these audio recordings are available to the public. Written transcripts of cases are also available from the Court clerk's office. Federal courthouses provide court calendars to citizens upon request. There are exceptions to making Court proceedings public. For example, cases involving juveniles are closed to the public.

The Supreme Court is open to the public when oral arguments are presented but seating is limited and granted on a first-come, first-seated basis. Lines to be seated are formed in the plaza in front of the Court building and are established separately for morning and afternoon sessions.

The details and opinions in Supreme Court cases can be found on their official Web site (http://www.supremecourtus.gov/opinions/06slipopinion.html). Cases are listed according to the year the case was heard by the Court. These are called "slip" opinions because they are the initial versions of rulings published within hours of the Court's rendering of decisions. The final version of the Court's opinions is printed in the bound volumes of the *United States Reports*. These include the full text of hearings, orders, opinions, and other materials issued since the 1991 Supreme Court term.

U.S. COURT OF APPEALS

An appeal from a district court or administrative agency is brought by the appellant to a U.S. Court of Appeals. The *appellant* is the party who disagrees with the decision of the lower court and believes a legal error was made. No additional evidence can be presented that was not part of the lower court hearing. The appeals court reviews the record of the case but does not hear witnesses. The appellant is allowed to present legal arguments in writing in a document called a *brief* to a panel of three appeal judges. The other party, the *appellee*, may submit a brief outlining why the decision of the lower court or administrative agency should be upheld. The judges may request oral arguments be presented before the court. Some cases are decided *en banc*, which means all of the appeal judges in a particular circuit hear a case while acting as a tribunal. This is done in highly publicized cases, cases with high legal importance, or when a decision by the panel of three appeal judges conflicted with a prior court decision.

During the hearing, each side is usually given fifteen minutes to present its arguments. The court of appeals will uphold or overturn the previous decision, or send it back to the lower court for additional consideration.

SUPREME COURT CASES

Once a case is determined to meet the criteria to be heard by a federal court, cases can reach the Supreme Court in one of two situations. The first is cases of original jurisdiction, in which the Supreme Court acts as the original trial court. These cases are very rare. Fewer than two hundred cases of original jurisdiction have been heard in the history of the Supreme Court. In these cases, the Supreme Court's decision cannot be appealed. The following are the types of cases that fall under this jurisdiction:

- Cases against the United States government
- All controversies between two or more states
- All actions or proceedings in which ambassadors, other public ministers, or consuls are parties
- All controversies between the United States and a state
- All actions or proceedings by a state against the citizens of another state or against aliens
- Cases between citizens of different states
- Cases between a state and a foreign country or foreign citizen
- Cases of maritime jurisdiction

The second type, and the majority of Supreme Court cases, are appeals of lower court decisions. These fall under the appellate jurisdiction of the Supreme Court and are appealed from lower federal or from state supreme courts when involving issues of federal laws or the Constitution. Cases from U.S. district courts are first appealed to one of the U.S. courts of appeals, based on jurisdiction. Cases from the states originate in a state trial court. State trial courts include state district courts, circuit courts, or courts of common appeal. The losing party can appeal to a state appeals court, then to the state supreme court, and finally to the U.S. Supreme Court.

Once appealed, cases are formally brought before the Supreme Court in one of four ways. Most are submitted by a Petition for a Writ of Certiorari in which the Supreme Court is asked to review the decision of a lower court. Most petitions are denied but those that are accepted make up the majority of cases that are heard by the Court. Under specific conditions, a petition can be resubmitted. Those that are accepted for review require affirmative votes from at least four justices, called the Rule of Four (or whatever number constitutes a majority if the number of justices is changed by Congress). The parties involved then present oral arguments before the Court. The Court issues a single majority opinion based on a majority vote that outlines the justification for its decision. Those justices in the minority who disagree with the decision usually issue a single document outlining the reasons for their dissenting opinions.

In the second way cases are brought before the Supreme Court, oral arguments are not heard. Instead, the appealing party files a legal brief to the Court citing the legal reasons the Court should overturn the decision of the lower court. The Justices review the brief in a private conference and issue a single decision called *per curiam*, which means *by the court*. The judges do not issue affirming and dissenting opinions.

The Supreme Court also provides assistance and insight on specific issues surrounding a lower court case. This process is called a *request for certification*. The lower court must follow any instructions handed down by the Supreme Court, including instructions to bring the entire case before the Court.

Finally, a case comes before the Supreme Court is at the Court's demand. The Court can issue a *petition for an extraordinary writ*, which shows that exceptional circumstances exist whereby only the Supreme Court can adequately review a particular case.

Supreme Court Process.   The Supreme Court's year begins the first Monday in October and it normally adjourns for the year in late June or early July. The year can run as late as the Sunday before the first Monday in October if the Court's caseload is large (i.e., the docket is not cleared). Cases are heard during two-week sessions each month. During these sessions, cases are heard Monday, Tuesday, and Wednesday mornings. The justices use the remainder of the week to deliberate, conduct research, and write opinions. The next two weeks of the month are recess periods the justices use to review new cases and prepare for the next two-week session.

The process of hearing cases in the Supreme Court predominantly applies to those brought under a Petition for a Writ of Certiorari, because that is the catalyst for the majority of cases heard. The following are the sequential steps:

1. The Petition for a Writ of Certiorari is sent to the clerk of the Court. The petitioner (or appellant) is the one who lost the case in a lower court and is asking the Supreme Court to review the case to reverse, it is hoped, the decision of the lower court. The other party is the respondent (or appellee), who argues for the Supreme Court to uphold the decision of the lower court. The clerk receives case documents and reviews them for accuracy. Each is returned if not correct. The clerk maintains all documents for the Court. The appealing party pays a fee to the Court for accepting the case unless the Court determines the party does not possess the financial means and it is thus waived. The petition is then assigned a number and placed on the Court docket.

2. The Justices must review all cases placed on the Court docket to determine which they will actually hear. They may have their clerks review the cases and provide case summaries for review.

3. The chief justice develops a "discussion list" of the cases he believes should be heard by the Court. After the list is reviewed by the associate justices, a private conference is held to agree upon the final list. An affirmative vote by at least four of the justices is required to grant a case a hearing (the Rule of Four.) The justices may actually reach a final decision on a case while reviewing it in conference. The Court provides notification of which cases will or will not be heard through certified orders. Those that do not make the discussion list are never heard. The Court very rarely provides justification for why a case is accepted or declined. When the Court refuses to hear a case, the decision of the lower court is upheld.

4. The clerk schedules oral arguments for the cases accepted by the Court. Cases are normally heard based on the sequence they were accepted for review. The petitioner and respondent must each file briefs with the Court outlining their legal arguments. The appellant must file a brief within forty-five days of the Court approving the Writ of Certiorari. The appellee has thirty days after the appellant's filing to file a brief.

5. The justices review the briefs and any other records received. Often with the assistance of their law clerks, they also review legal precedents and develop questions to be asked during oral arguments. Law clerks review documents, summarize cases, and may even write the first drafts of a justice's opinion.

6. During oral arguments, only one attorney may argue for each side. Often a party will hire a team of lawyers but the Court does not allow them all to speak. Cases are argued by lawyers who must have been licensed by the highest court in their state or U.S. territory for the last three years, have not been engaged in any type of disciplinary action, and then become a member of the bar of the Supreme Court. American and foreign attorneys may be granted temporary admission (called *pro hac vice*) to the bar of the Supreme Court for a specific case. The solicitor general of the Department of Justice argues cases on behalf of the United States if the government is a party in the case.

7. Attorneys are not allowed to read from a document, but rather argue extemporaneously. They must also clarify or further elaborate on the arguments cited in their briefs, rather than simply restate them. The appellant first presents arguments, and both sides have thirty minutes to be heard. The justices may interrupt for questions or remarks, which is then deducted from that side's thirty minutes. Parties with a stake in the case but who are neither the appellant nor appellee may also present arguments in the form of an *amicus curiae brief. Amicus curiae* means "a friend of the court." Their argument time is deducted from the time allotted to the side being supported by their testimony. Lights are used to advise each lawyer of how much time they have left.

8. The Court and a private company it contracts with tape and transcribe all oral arguments, and submit the tapes to the National Archives and Records Administration after the Court reaches a final decision.

9. The justices meet in private to discuss the case and oral arguments presented. During this conference, the chief justice leads the discussion and each associate justice speaks in the order of their seniority in the Court. At least six justices must be present to constitute a quorum and allow voting on the case. A simple majority vote decides the case. If a tie results, the decision of the lower court stands. The justices take as long as they need to decide a case. A decision may be rendered in one day or may take several months. However, the Court must render all decisions before its summer recess. The chief justice announces the decision from the bench.

10. The Court issues the majority opinion in writing as well as the dissenting opinions. The Court may render one of several decisions. The decision of the lower court may be approved, or affirmed. The Court may reverse the decision of the lower court. The case may be remanded (i.e., returned) to the lower court for further deliberation. Finally, the Court may vacate or dismiss the case completely.

11. The outcome of each case is published in the *United States Reports*, which is the official record of the Supreme Court (U.S. Supreme Court, 2008). Each report begins with a headnote, or syllabus, which summarizes the majority opinion of the Court. The report also shows how each justice voted.

12. The losing party may file for a rehearing of the case within twenty-five days of the announcement of the Court's decision if the case was brought before the Court on a Petition of Writ of Certiorari. Oral arguments are not heard if the Court agrees to review the case again.

Each time the Supreme Court decides a court case, its decision sets a precedent for future cases related to the same or a similar issue. The Court attempts to maintain the same decisions on specific issues over time to remain legally consistent. The Court decides against precedents as the needs of society change, new justices with different ideologies are appointed, or policies of the federal government change. For example, *Brown v. Board of Education of Topeka*, 347 U.S. 483 (1954) overturned *Plessy v. Ferguson*, 163 U.S. 537 (1896). While the Court ruled in *Plessy* that it was legal for states to provide separate but equal educational systems, in *Brown* the Court ruled against segregated schools.

The Court's decisions can lead to actions by or assistance from the legislative or executive branch. The Court's decision may result in new executive branch agency policies or new laws passed by Congress. The president may issue an executive order instructing agencies on new procedures to carry out the ruling of the Court. Congress can also pass or amend laws if it disagrees with Court decisions. Additionally, the Supreme Court does have not the power to enforce its decisions, but relies on Congress and the president to enforce them. However, not obeying a Supreme Court decision can have serious political implications, harming the legitimacy and respect of an office.

ADMINISTRATIVE HEARINGS

Article I, Section 8, of the Constitution grants Congress the authority and responsibility "To make all Laws which shall be necessary and proper for carrying into Execution the foregoing Powers, and all other Powers vested by this Constitution in the Government of the United States, or in any Department or Officer thereof." This clause, known as the Necessary and Proper Clause, has been interpreted to allow Congress to grant rule-making authority to agencies. Agencies receive their authorization through statutes, and the rules they pass often have the force of law. Executive branch agencies also receive their authority to make rules from those granted to the president. Along with rule-making authority, agencies have the authority to enforce rules they put into place. The body of administrative law, or regulatory law, includes making rules, executing rules, and holding hearings (or adjudication) when regulated parties violate rules or when parties believe they have been harmed by agency actions.

The powers given to an agency are conferred by the *delegation doctrine*. In other words, agencies are only permitted to exercise the specific powers granted by the legislative, executive, or judicial instrument granting its powers. This instrument may be a congressional law, presidential executive order, or the result of a judicial decision. The *nondelegation doctrine* specifies that Congress cannot delegate its law-making duties outlined in Article I, Section 8, to any other person or body, nor can it delegate authority it does not have (such as the authority to hold court hearings). However, it can authorize a person, body, or organization to carry out the laws it passes. The nondelegation doctrine has been the subject of controversy and the basis of many judicial proceedings. For example, in *A.L.A. Schecter Poultry Corp. v. United States*, 295 U.S. 495 (1935), the Supreme Court ruled that Congress could not authorize the president to establish codes of fair competition involving trade. The Court ruled that Congress must set some standards to guide the decisions of the executive branch. In a more recent case, the Court ruled in favor of Congress's delegation of powers on the following grounds (*Mistretta v. United States*, 488 U.S. 361 (1989)):

> The nondelegation doctrine is rooted in the principle of separation of powers that underlies our tripartite system of Government. The Constitution provides that "[a]ll

legislative Powers herein granted shall be vested in a Congress of the United States," U.S. Const., Art. I, 1, and we long have insisted that "the integrity and maintenance of the system of government ordained by the Constitution" mandate that Congress generally cannot delegate its legislative power to another Branch. We also have recognized, however, that the separation-of-powers principle, and the nondelegation doctrine in particular, do not prevent Congress from obtaining the assistance of its coordinate Branches. In a passage now enshrined in our jurisprudence, Chief Justice Taft, writing for the Court, explained our approach to such cooperative ventures: "In determining what [Congress] may do in seeking assistance from another branch, the extent and character of that assistance must be fixed according to common sense and the inherent necessities of the government co-ordination." So long as Congress "shall lay down by legislative act an intelligible principle to which the person or body authorized to [exercise the delegated authority] is directed to conform, such legislative action is not a forbidden delegation of legislative power." Applying this "intelligible principle" test to congressional delegations, our jurisprudence has been driven by a practical understanding that in our increasingly complex society, replete with ever changing and more technical problems, Congress simply cannot do its job absent an ability to delegate power under broad general directives. Accordingly, this Court has deemed it "constitutionally sufficient if Congress clearly delineates the general policy, the public agency which is to apply it, and the boundaries of this delegated authority."

The Internal Revenue Service (IRS) and Environmental Protection Agency (EPA) are examples of agencies that hear specific types of cases based on the subject matter and laws each is responsible for. For example, the Internal Revenue Service "is organized to carry out the responsibilities of the secretary of the Treasury under section 7801 of the Internal Revenue Code. The secretary has full authority to administer and enforce the internal revenue laws and has the power to create an agency to enforce these laws. The IRS was created based on this legislative grant. Section 7803 of the Internal Revenue Code provides for the appointment of a commissioner of Internal Revenue to administer and supervise the execution and application of the internal revenue laws" (Internal Revenue Service, 2007a, 2007b). The EPA "works to develop and enforce regulations that implement environmental laws enacted by Congress. The EPA is responsible for researching and setting national standards for a variety of environmental programs, and delegates to states and tribes the responsibility for issuing permits and for monitoring and enforcing compliance. Where national standards are not met, the EPA can issue sanctions and take other steps to assist the states and tribes in reaching the desired levels of environmental quality" (Environmental Protection Agency, 2007).

Administrative law judges preside over administrative hearings. These positions were established under the Administrative Procedure Act of 1946. These hearings are in essence trials but there are no juries. The judge hears facts presented from all parties involved. A judge may not hear a case until after it has been reviewed or heard by an agency's administrative board. During proceedings, the judge can issue subpoenas and administer oaths, regulate the hearing, listen to testimonies, and make a final decision based on the facts in the case. The decision reached by the judge is called an *order*, and outlines the ruling and reason(s) for the judge's decision. The decision reached is free of any pressures from individuals internal to the agency. Additionally, administrative law judges are immune from liability for their decisions in cases. The decision reached, which can include sanctions, must be in accordance with the enabling statute of the agency. Most agencies have an internal appeal process if a party does not agree with the decision of the judge. After all relief through agency procedures has been exhausted, a party can appeal to a federal court. The court can uphold the agency's decision, return the case to the agency for further review, or overturn the decision of the agency. Cases can be appealed up to the Supreme Court.

Under the Equal Access to Justice Act of 1980, an individual or small entity that feels it has been unjustifiably harmed by an agency action can sue in federal court to recover attorney's fees and other fees and expenses. Costs are not reimbursed if the court rules the actions of the agency were justified or circumstances surrounding the original decision on behalf of the plaintiff were unjust. Fees and other expenses include the reasonable expenses of expert witnesses; the reasonable cost of any study, analysis, engineering report, test, or project, which is found by the agency to be necessary for the preparation of the party's case; and reasonable attorney or agent fees. The following are the only parties covered by this act (with limited exceptions outlined in the act):

1. An individual whose net worth did not exceed $2 million at the time the adversary adjudication was initiated, or
2. Any owner of an unincorporated business, or any partnership, corporation, association, unit of local government, or organization, the net worth of which did not exceed $7 million at the time the adversary adjudication was initiated, and which had not more than 500 employees at the time the adversary adjudication was initiated.

8

United States Foreign Policy

Foreign policy is the official relationship a country's government establishes with other nations, both allies and enemies, and the stance it takes on issues. It includes the stance a government takes on issues involving foreign nations, groups, and individuals. Nations develop foreign policy based on outcomes that will benefit their own interests in both the short term and the long term. As nations have become more dependent on one another as a result of globalization, the development of broad and effective foreign policies has become a priority of most developed (i.e., industrialized) nations. Less-developed nations are growing more dependent on the foreign policies of developed nations to assist them in meeting the technological, economical, environmental, biological, and social challenges of the modern world.

Technological challenges include the necessity to use computers for basic communication, the technological complexities in manufacturing and using products, and the need for nations to become more engaged in space exploration to demonstrate future competitiveness. A negative side of technological advancement has been the vulnerability of electronic information, and the growing complexity and proliferation of weapons such as nuclear arms, missiles, and other weapons of mass destruction. Economic challenges include the growing costs of competing in a global environment, costs of obtaining needed resources (such as fuel), necessity to form alliances with groups of nations rather than individual countries (such as the European Union), and the evolution of the global economy from one based on products produced to one based on services provided. Environmental challenges include the growing harm to the global environment caused by global warming, the staggering increase in the extinction of different species of animal and plant life, and an increase in severe weather of all kinds. The resulting rise of the Earth's temperature over the coming centuries (and even decades) is expected to cause more recurring and severe droughts, fires, and diseases from biting insects. Biological challenges include providing health care for more complex diseases (such as AIDS, bird flu, and mad cow disease), and dealing with the growing use of biological weapons.

The social challenges are perhaps the most complex. Extremist groups and networks (such as al-Qaeda) that do not operate as part of an identifiable country or government are posing threats around the world. In addition, immigration and mass migration have become major issues for nations around the world, particularly for those gaining immigrants and for refugees seeking new nations in which to settle. Along with immigration is the concern over the inequitable treatment of diverse groups (such as people who are ethnically and racially different from the majority). Human trafficking has also become a growing international crime. Other social issues include organized crime, gang warfare, guns being used by children, political violence, poverty, and the need to improve education.

All of these challenges are causing strains on developed nations. The challenges to less-developed nations have been extremely difficult. International organizations and allied governments have agreed that these problems can only be tackled through international cooperation with the more developed nations taking the lead in developing and executing solutions. This underscores the importance of developing a sound strategic foreign policy, particularly for the United States as one of the wealthiest and the leading democratic country in the world.

Globalization has contributed to the difficulty of setting foreign policy. Private U.S. citizens and businesses have established relationships with foreign nations, individuals, and companies. However, the federal government must provide laws and policies to regulate these relationships. The Commerce Clause of the U.S. Constitution (Article I) authorizes the federal government to have exclusive power to regulate U.S. commerce with foreign countries. These exclusive powers mean the federal government's authority overrides the authority of the states, local governments, and private enterprises. For example, Congress passed the Foreign Corrupt Practices Act of 1977 that makes it illegal for U.S. companies, their employees, or their agents to bribe a foreign official, political party member, or person in office in an attempt to influence their decisions on business ventures.

THE PRESIDENT'S FOREIGN POLICY AGENDA

The president establishes U.S. foreign policy. The president's choice of the foreign policy issues to focus attention on and the administration's stance on those issues is called the *president's foreign policy agenda*. The agenda depends on world events and how the needs of the United States are affected by other nations and other external groups. Current needs include foreign supplies of food, oil, and other natural resources that are sold to the United States, and the demand for American-made products by other nations. The protection of future U.S. needs involves developing strategies today to ensure perceived threats to the United States do not materialize, such as hostile nations and forces developing nuclear weapons programs or deploying hostile forces within U.S. borders. It also involves executing strategies to protect the future health and welfare of U.S. citizens. For example, U.S. officials (both government and private individuals) are taking a leading role in developing global strategies to protect the environment to benefit future generations. As the needs of the United States and international conditions change, so does the president's foreign policy agenda.

While each president sets the foreign policy agenda for his or her term(s) of office, some agenda items do not change when a new president assumes office. For example, the Cold War was the major U.S. foreign policy issue from the late 1940s through the early 1990s. Each new president during those decades developed different strategies to address the cold war. For example, President Richard M. Nixon sought to develop a close working relationship with the Soviet Union and was successful in negotiating treaties whereby the United States and the Soviet Union would reduce their numbers of nuclear weapons. President Nixon was also able to develop a good relationship with China as part of his foreign policy agenda. President Jimmy Carter did not have the same level of success as President Nixon. President Carter focused on using diplomacy to promote human rights, especially with the governments of South Korea, Iran, Argentina, South Africa, and Zimbabwe. He was unable to maintain the diplomatic ties with the Soviet Union established by President Nixon because of a shift in foreign policy by the Soviet government. The Soviet Union supported revolutions in Africa, deployed medium-range nuclear weapons in Europe, and established a hostile occupation of Afghanistan. These actions were contrary to the foreign policy stance of President Carter. While U.S. diplomatic relations with the Soviets were dissolving, relations with China continued to improve. By 1979, the United States had granted full diplomatic recognition of China's government. The unrest in the Middle East has also been a major issue for years because of continuous conflicts in that area and its importance to the world in providing oil. The priority of these issues may change due to how much importance the president places on them.

The following are the predominant foreign policy categories that have been addressed in recent presidential agendas:

- The global economy, U.S. relationships with the nations that have the greatest impact on the global economy, and the impact and contribution of the United States to the global economy
- Trade with nations that supply and buy major U.S. goods and services
- The value of the U.S. dollar as measured against the currency of other nations
- Eliminating terrorism, tyranny, and threats to global peace, to include controlling the production and distribution of weapons (including nuclear and biological weapons)
- Coordinating with other nations to reduce or eliminate harm to the environment
- Ensuring the safe, ethical, and fair treatment of humans
- Combating dangers to global health, including fighting tuberculosis, AIDS, malaria, and pandemic flu
- Space exploration
- The sharing of advancements in information technology

The president attempts to gain support for his or her foreign policy agenda from Congress and the American public. Congress must provide approval for such things as funding, the passage of laws, the deployment of troops, and the appointment of ambassadors. Support is desired, but not always required, from the American people. For this reason, there have been instances when foreign policy agenda decisions and actions by the executive branch have been very controversial. For example, President Ronald W. Reagan undertook aggressive actions to carry out his foreign policies. He took a very firm stance toward the Soviet Union and called the communist nation an "evil empire." He spent billions (if not trillions) of dollars building up the U.S. military, including initiating the Strategic Defense Initiative (called Star Wars) that would build a shield around the United States to counter ballistic missile strikes. In 1983, President Reagan dispatched Marines to Lebanon to intervene in that nation's civil war in support of Lebanon's president. On April 28th of that year a suicide bomber drove a vehicle loaded with explosives into the Marine barracks. Almost twenty Americans were killed. A few months later in October another suicide bomber drove another vehicle full of explosives into a Marine building. Over two hundred Marines were killed in that attack. In 1997, members of President Reagan's administration were convicted of using funds from the sale of weapons to Iran in exchange for the release of American hostages in Lebanon to support the contras (i.e., rebels) attempting to overthrow the government of Nicaragua. In late 1996 and 1997, President Reagan denied that the events had taken place. In March 1996, he admitted that "what began as a strategic opening to Iran deteriorated, in its implementation, into trading arms for hostages." The Iran–Contra investigation did not officially end until President George H. W. Bush pardoned former members of the administration involved in the incident in 1992.

President George H. W. Bush attempted to be just as aggressive as President Reagan. Since he served as President Reagan's vice president for two terms, President Bush continued maintaining close diplomatic relations with then Soviet President Mikhail Gorbachev. President Bush ordered U.S. military forces to seize control of Panama and arrest its ruler, General Manuel Noriega, on charges of drug trafficking, money laundering, and racketeering charges against the United States. In 1990, Iraqi forces invaded Kuwait. The invasion threatened the sovereignty of Kuwait and the supply of oil to the United States from the Persian Gulf. Fearing that Iraq's aggression would expand to Saudi Arabia, President Bush organized a multinational coalition composed of forces from North Atlantic Treaty Organization (NATO) member nations and Arab countries. Under the auspices of the United Nations (UN), approximately five hundred thousand U.S. troops joined coalition forces in Saudi Arabia. This was the largest mobilization of United States military personnel since the Vietnam War. The event was named the Persian Gulf War and lasted less than a month. Coalition forces overthrew the Iraqi forces. Although the war was a success, it was not enough to bolster overall approval of President Bush's performance due to his inability to establish a successful domestic policy agenda. The suffering U.S. economy was a particularly troubling issue for his administration. President Bush lost his reelection bid to Democratic presidential candidate Bill Clinton.

Many of President Bill Clinton's foreign policy initiatives focused on restoring peace to embattled regions around the world. President Clinton was the first president to visit Vietnam since the Vietnam War. His visit was part of efforts to improve diplomatic relations with that nation. His administration succeeded in restoring Haitian President Jean-Bertrand Aristide to office in 1994 after he was ousted by a hostile military coup. President Clinton also committed U.S. troops to peacekeeping initiatives in Bosnia-Herzegovina, a country on the Balkan peninsula of Southern Europe facing internal genocide in the mid 1990s. The Clinton administration took a leading international role in initiatives to bring a permanent resolution to the dispute between Palestinians and Israelis. In 1993, Clinton invited Israeli Prime Minister Yitzhak Rabin and Palestine Liberation Organization Chairman Yasir Arafat to Washington to enter into an agreement that granted limited Palestinian self-rule in the Gaza Strip and Jericho. Rabin was later assassinated by religious fundamentalists who opposed any concession of land to create a Palestinian state. President Clinton's administration also faced criticism for not taking similar stances in other parts of the word, for example, for not getting involved to end the genocide and ethnic cleansing that took place in the African country of Rwanda in 1994.

During the Clinton administration, the United States was a target for international terrorists at home and abroad. This created a serious challenge for the president's foreign and domestic policies. President Clinton had to contend with protecting U.S. property and citizens around the world and the growing active aggression against the nation's basic philosophies of democracy and capitalism. In 1993, the World Trade Center in New York City was bombed by foreign terrorists acting as suicide bombers. On foreign soil, United States interests were also attacked. The United States' embassies in the African countries of Kenya and Tanzania were attacked in 1998. In 2000, the U.S. Navy ship *USS Cole* was attacked in Yemen by suicide bombers, killing seventeen soldiers. These attacks culminated with the events of September 11, 2001, when terrorists seized American airlines and used them to destroy the World Trade Center and fly into the Pentagon. A third plane was unsuccessful in hitting its target after passengers on board forced the terrorists to crash the plane into an uninhabited field in Pennsylvania.

Under President George W. Bush's administration some questioned the United States' involvement in the war in Iraq, and the government's idle stance on the genocides in some nations (e.g., Indonesia, Dufar, and Sudan) but active engagement in others (e.g., Kosovo). While many members of Congress and citizens called for the withdrawal of American troops from the Middle East, the president and his administration stood steadfast on keeping troops deployed until they were satisfied there was political stability in the area.

The Department of State assists the president in developing foreign policy, handles U.S. diplomatic ties and coalitions with other countries, mediates foreign conflicts, and oversees U.S. embassies and consulates. The mission statement of the Department of State under the administration of President George W. Bush was to "create a more secure, democratic, and prosperous world for the benefit of the American people and the international community." It attempted to meet this mission through the following three main strategies (U.S. Department of State, 2007a):

1. Build and maintain strong bilateral and multilateral relationships.
2. Protect the United States, its allies, and friends against the transnational dangers and enduring threats arising from tyranny, poverty, and disease.
3. Confront the intersection of traditional and transnational challenges by combining diplomatic skills and development assistance to act boldly to foster a more democratic and prosperous world integrated into the global economy.

While the secretary of state, ambassadors, and other members of the Department of State travel the world executing the president's foreign policy agenda, the president also spends a significant amount of time visiting other nations and receiving foreign dignitaries in the United States.

EVOLUTION OF FOREIGN POLICY DURING THE TWENTIETH CENTURY

U.S. foreign policy, in terms of the United States establishing relations with foreign nations, greatly evolved over the twentieth century. At the start of the century, the U.S. government maintained a relatively neutral or noninterventionist stance. The League of Nations was established in 1919 after World War I as a result of the Treaty of Versailles to "promote international cooperation and to achieve peace and security" throughout the world. Even though President Woodrow Wilson was the leading figure in establishing the League of Nations, the United States did not join because Congress and most citizens did not favor U.S. membership. There was general agreement that the United States did not want to be dragged into another international war. Congress passed the Neutrality Act of 1935 in an attempt to keep the United States out of the growing hostilities in Europe. One of its opening clauses forbade the export of U.S. goods to any nation involved in the hostilities:

> Resolved by the Senate and House of Representatives of the United States of America in Congress assembled, That upon the outbreak or during the progress of war between, or among, two or more foreign states, the President shall proclaim such fact, and it shall thereafter be unlawful to export arms, ammunition, or implements of war from any place in the United States, or possessions of the United States, to any port of such belligerent states, or to any neutral port for transshipment to, or for the use of, a belligerent country. (U.S. Department of State, 1943)

President Franklin D. Roosevelt realized future situations might require the United States to change its stance. Although he signed the Neutrality Act, he made the following statement:

> It is the policy of this government to avoid being drawn into wars between other nations, but it is a fact that no Congress and no executive can foresee all possible future situations. History is filled with unforeseeable situations that call for some flexibility of action. It is conceivable that situations may arise in which the wholly inflexible provisions of Section I of this Act might have exactly the opposite effect from that which was intended. In other words, the inflexible provisions might drag us into war instead of keeping us out. The policy of the government is definitely committed to the maintenance of peace and the avoidance of any entanglements which would lead us into conflict. At the same time it is the policy of the government by every peaceful means and without entanglement to cooperate with other similarly minded governments to promote peace. (Woolley and Peters, online)

Still, the United States only got involved in a foreign conflict if it was directly impacted. Many describe the United States as being "dragged" into world affairs in 1941. The United States watched the tyranny of Germany expand in Europe. On March 11, 1941, Congress passed the Lend-Lease Act. It was written as "An Act to Promote the Defense of the United States." It allowed President Roosevelt to provide military equipment and financial assistance to any country to help it defend against the Germans. An estimated $30 to $50 billion went to Great Britain by the end of World War II. The Soviet Union and China received lesser amounts, still estimated to be over $1 billion each. Many other nations received lesser support. Nonfinancial support to all of these nations included ammunition, tanks, trucks, airplanes, and food. The attack on Pearl Harbor on December 7, 1941, by Japan completely drew the United States into the war and permanently drew the United States into foreign affairs.

After World War II, the United States remained the world's leading economic power and primary defender of global democracy against communism. This was the basis of the cold war with the Soviet Union, the leading communist power in the world for most of the latter half of the twentieth century. During the early part of the twentieth century, the Soviet Union and the United States engaged in a politically ideological struggle. The United States' social philosophy was based the philosophies of capitalism and democracy, while the Soviet Union's was based on communism. Each nation sought

British Prime Minister Winston Churchill, U.S. President Franklin Roosevelt, and Soviet premier Joseph Stalin at Yalta, February 1945. *Courtesy of Franklin D. Roosevelt Library.*

to gain allies supporting their philosophies. The cold war escalated in 1949, when the Soviet Union exploded its first atomic bomb. While the NATO (see the section "U.S. Membership in NATO and the United Nations" below), SEATO (South-East Asia Treaty Organization), and other organizations, perceived it as passive containment, the United States viewed this action as hostile. War between the two nations seemed imminent on several occasions. For example, during the Cuban missile crisis of 1962, the United States staged a blockade and threatened retaliation before the Soviet Union moved its intermediate-range ballistic weapons out of Cuba.

The arms race between the Soviet Union and the United States continued through the 1970s. President Ronald W. Reagan's policies in the early 1980s moved the United States ahead of the Soviets because his foreign policy centered on investing in the military and military equipment. This aided in leading to the collapse of the Soviet Union as it went bankrupt in its attempts to also heavily invest in its military.

The purpose of U.S. involvement in the Korean and Vietnam Wars was to help stop the spread of communism into the democratic southern regions of Korea and Vietnam. The policies of President Richard M. Nixon exemplified the policies of U.S. presidents in dealing with communist nations during the twentieth century. President Nixon sought to fortify the United States' status as a "super power." The president's national security adviser, Henry Kissinger, became the principal advocate for the Nixon Doctrine, which called for allied nations (especially in Asia) to take more responsibility for their own defense. One example of this was a desire for South Korea to assume more control and responsibility for fighting the Vietnam War so American troops could be withdrawn. The doctrine also called for improved relations with the Soviet Union to reduce each nation's military strength.

"I Want YOU for U.S. Army Nearest Recruiting Station" (1917), World War I recruiting poster by James Montgomery Flagg. *Courtesy of Library of Congress Prints and Photographs Division/Gift of the Talbot County Public Library.*

President Nixon's policy led to the Strategic Arms Limitation Talks, which resulted in a treaty with the Soviet Union to significantly reduce the number of antiballistic missile systems held by each nation. The president and Kissinger later negotiated an interim agreement that limited the number of strategic offensive missiles each country could deploy in the future. Kissinger made a secret trip to Peking, China, in 1971 that led to a presidential visit the following year. This created strong ties between the United States and China. President Nixon then visited Moscow to show he sought to establish relations with both communist nations. However, the relationship with the Soviet Union was tested during the Arab-Israeli War in 1973 in which the United States supported Israel and the Soviet Union supported the Arabs. President Nixon was able to negotiate a cease-fire that improved Israeli–Egyptian relations.

The United States' involvement in the Vietnam War expanded, causing strong opposition in the United States. Student protests were held at colleges around the country. Demonstrations at Kent State University in Ohio and Jackson State University in Mississippi both led to confrontations with National Guard troops. This increased opposition to the administration's policies on the war. Further antiwar demonstrations followed the 1971 U.S. invasion of Laos and President Nixon's decision to resume bombing of North Vietnam in 1972. By the end of 1972, negotiations to end the Vietnam War slowly progressed. A cease-fire agreement was finally brokered and signed with North Vietnam on January 27, 1973. Other conflicts occurred after the Vietnam War. The United States invaded Panama in December 1989 to end the dictatorial rule of Manuel Noriega.

By the end of the twentieth century, the government's view was that the United States must maintain a strong global influence in any issue involving democracy. For that reason, foreign policy became a major part of the agendas of the executive and legislative branches. This is evidenced in the mission of the U.S. Department of State (2007):

American diplomacy in the 21st century is based on fundamental beliefs: our freedom is best protected by ensuring that others are free; our prosperity depends on the prosperity of others; and our security relies on a global effort to secure the rights of all.

The history of the American people is the chronicle of our efforts to live up to our ideals. In this moment in history, we recognize that the United States has an immense responsibility to use its power constructively to advance security, democracy, and prosperity around the globe.

The events of September 11, 2001, changed the global focus of the U.S. government from communism to terrorism and created one of the greatest historical foreign policy challenges for the U.S. government for two reasons. First, the attackers were not part of a unified force or identifiable country. Members of al-Qaeda were located throughout the world, even within the United States. Second, the attackers obtained support from numerous nations but there was no definitive proof of the level of support or exactly how the governments of suspected nations were providing support. For these reasons the U.S. war on terrorism was established as a war based on a concept of fighting terrorism rather than a declared war against a specific foe. This challenge is expected to continue to affect U.S. foreign policy for years to come.

FOREIGN ASSISTANCE

Providing financial assistance to foreign nations is a major part of U.S. foreign policy. As the wealthiest nation in the world, the United States provides assistance to nations in need of financial and humanitarian support. For example, the Millennium Challenge Corporation is a U.S. government corporation established in 2004 to provide sustainable economic support to poor nations in support of transportation, water, and industrial infrastructure; agriculture; education; private-sector development; and capacity building. The United States also supports efforts to battle diseases and support political and social reforms through many other programs. As a champion of global democracy and leading combater of global terrorism (since September 11, 2001), the United States provides military assistance as a major portion of its foreign aid. The United States leads the world in economic aid. In 2003, the United States provided $16.25 billion in aid. The next three leading providers were Japan ($8.68 billion), France ($7.25 billion), and Germany ($6.78 billion). The United States' closest ally, the United Kingdom, provided $6.28 billion. In 2005, the United States provided some form of foreign assistance to approximately 150 countries. This assistance amounted to $21.197 billion or 1.2 percent of U.S. spending. This is compared to $16.66 billion in 2000, $14.71 billion in 1995, and $14.82 billion in 1990.

Table 8.1 shows the countries that received the largest amounts of U.S. foreign aid in 2005. Israel, Egypt, Afghanistan, and Pakistan received the largest amounts for a combined total exceeding $6 billion. Each of these countries received funds as part of U.S. support of the Middle East. Other programs that received the highest amount of U.S. support in 2005 were U.S. efforts to battle narcotics, HIV/AIDS, and terrorism (Tarnoff and Nowels, 2005).There are five categories of foreign aid (Tarnoff and Nowels, 2005):

• Bilateral development aid:

> Direct support to developing countries for sustainable economic and social stability, mostly through the U.S. Agency for International Development
> Includes debt relief, funding to fight diseases, and economic reform

Table 8.1.   Countries Receiving The Largest Amounts Of U.S. Foreign Aid In 2005

Country	Amount of aid	Primary reason for aid
Israel	$2.58 Billion	Middle East Support
Egypt	$1.84 Billion	Middle East Support
Afghanistan	$980 Million	Middle East Support
Pakistan	$700 Million	Middle East Support
Colombia	$570 Million	Counter-Narcotics
Sudan	$500 Million	Emerging From Internal Crisis
Jordan	$480 Million	Combat Terrorism
Uganda	$250 Million	HIV/AIDS
Kenya	$240 Million	HIV/AIDS
Ethiopia	$190 Million	HIV/AIDS
South Africa	$190 Million	HIV/AIDS
Peru	$190 Million	Counter-Narcotics
Indonesia	$180 Million	Combat Terrorism
Bolivia	$180 Million	Counter-Narcotics
Nigeria	$180 Million	HIV/AIDS
Zambia	$180 Million	HIV/AIDS

Source: Curt Tarnoff And Larry Nowels (2005). *Foreign Aid: An Introductory Overview Of U.S. Programs And Policy.*
The Library Of Congress Congressional Research Service, Washington, Dc. Retrieved November 1, 2007, From
http://shelby.senate.gov/legislation/foreignAid.pdf

Aid Sectors include economic growth, agriculture and trade; global health; and democracy, conflict, and humanitarian
34.7% (or $7.35 billion) of U.S. aid in fiscal year (FY) 2005

• Military aid:

Funds provided to U.S. allies and friendly nations to assist them in acquiring U.S. military
equipment and training
Three main programs are foreign military financing, the international military education
and training program, and peacekeeping funds
23.6% (or $4.75 billion) of U.S. aid in FY 2005

• Economic political and security aid:

Assistance to support U.S. interests in international economic, political, or security programs, mostly through the economic support fund ($3.9 billion in FY 2005)
Most of these funds from 1995 through 2005 were to support the Middle East Peace
Process
Other programs support former Soviet Union states and Central European countries to
develop democratic systems and free market economies, antiterrorism efforts, and to
combat illegal drugs, crime, and weapons proliferation
21.8% (or $4.62 billion) of U.S. aid in FY 2005

- Humanitarian aid:

  Majority of funds from 1995 through 2005 were to support refugee programs under the Department of State

  Supports relief from manmade and natural disasters, provides agricultural goods to developing countries, funds U.S. farmers to provide training to foreign groups, and finances school feeding and nutrition programs

  12.5% (or $2.68 billion) of U.S. aid in FY 2005

- Multilateral aid:

  Funds from partnering nations are given to an international agency such as the World Bank and the United Nations Children's Fund (UNICEF) to support needy countries

  7% (or $1.54 billion) of U.S. aid in FY 2005

The United States provides assistance mostly in the form of grants rather than loans. The grants include cash transfers; commodity import programs where foreign private businesses gain U.S. dollars to import goods; and supplied equipment and commodities, training, and expertise. The United States does provide some loans, and loaned approximately $108 billion to foreign countries from 1946 through 2002, of which $25 billion was still outstanding in 2002. Some debt is forgiven. The United States forgave or reduced approximately $18.66 billion in debt owed by forty-six countries from 1990 through 2003.

Laws covering foreign aid include the Agricultural Trade Development and Assistance Act of 1954, the Foreign Assistance Act of 1961, and the Arms Export Control Act of 1976. The Agricultural Trade Development and Assistance Act of 1954 (also known as Public Law 480, Food for Peace) was passed under President Dwight D. Eisenhower. The act established the U.S. policy of providing agricultural food, resources, and training to developing countries. President George H. W. Bush signed the latest pertinent amendment to the act, Executive Order 12752, in 1991. It provided the following (House Committee on International Relations, 2003):

- A program under Title I of the Agricultural Trade Development Act to provide for the sale of agricultural commodities to developing countries and private entities to be implemented by the secretary of agriculture
- A program under Title II of the Agricultural Trade Development Act to provide for the donation of agricultural commodities to foreign countries and least developed countries to be implemented by the administrator of the Agency for International Development
- The establishment of a Food Assistance Policy Council to ensure policy coordination of assistance provided under the Agricultural Trade Development Act and the Food for Progress Act (1985), to include senior representatives from the Department of Agriculture, the Agency for International Development, the Department of State, and the Office of Management and Budget

The United States was facing criticism for its dwindling foreign assistance program and it became a major issue during the 1960 presidential campaign. As a result, the Foreign Assistance Act of 1961 was passed by Congress on September 4, 1961, and reorganized assistance programs into military and nonmilitary aid. The act was created to promote U.S. foreign policy, security, and welfare by assisting other nations in their economic development, and internal and external security. It also recognized the interdependence of nations around the world, the need to support civil and economic rights, and the need to work with other nations to use resources more wisely. It reaffirmed the humanitarian ideals of the United States and its people in eliminating hunger, poverty, illness, and ignorance in developing countries.

According the act's mandate for the creation of an agency to administer economic assistance programs, President John F. Kennedy established the U.S. Agency for International Development (USAID) on November 3, 1961. He stated the following in justifying the need to strengthen the government's foreign assistance program:

> The answer is that there is no escaping our obligations: our moral obligations as a wise leader and good neighbor in the interdependent community of free nations—our economic obligations as the wealthiest people in a world of largely poor people, as a nation no longer dependent upon the loans from abroad that once helped us develop our own economy—and our political obligations as the single largest counter to the adversaries of freedom. To fail to meet those obligations now would be disastrous; and, in the long run, more expensive. For widespread poverty and chaos lead to a collapse of existing political and social structures which would inevitably invite the advance of totalitarianism into every weak and unstable area. Thus our own security would be endangered and our prosperity imperiled. A program of assistance to the underdeveloped nations must continue because the Nation's interest and the cause of political freedom require it. (Woolley and Peters, [online])

The USAID was able to provide direct support to nations as a separate agency. It combined the multiple functions previously and separately provided by the International Cooperation Agency, Department of Loan Fund, the Export-Import Bank, and the Department of Agriculture. The following excerpt from the act lists its five principal goals:

(1) the alleviation of the worst physical manifestations of poverty among the world's poor majority;
(2) the promotion of conditions enabling developing countries to achieve self-sustaining economic growth with equitable distribution of benefits;
(3) the encouragement of development processes in which individual civil and economic rights are respected and enhanced;
(4) the integration of the developing countries into an open and equitable international economic system; and
(5) the promotion of good governance through combating corruption and improving transparency and accountability.

The Arms Export Control Act of 1976 was passed to further world peace and security. It provides and outlines the authority of the president to control the export and import of defense articles and services to and from foreign parties by any government or private entity. Nongovernment entities must obtain an export license from the government to export articles and services, and continually keep the government informed of all current and future negotiations. The act forbids the export of weapons contributing to the (nuclear) arms race, development of weapons of mass destruction, international terrorism, outbreak or escalation of conflict, or prejudice in the development of bilateral or multilateral arms control or nonproliferation agreements or other arrangements. The act also provides a detailed list of approved weapons (included on the U.S. Munitions List) and outlines specific punishment for violators. Various parts of the president's authority have been delegated to the Departments of State, Defense, Treasury and Homeland Security, and the attorney general under President Gerald R. Ford's Executive Order 11958 in 1977 and President George W. Bush's Executive Order 13284 in 2003.

U.S. HUMANITARIAN ASSISTANCE

A major part of the U.S. government's foreign policy is providing humanitarian assistance to other nations, particularly those with high levels of poverty. Congress appropriates funding to several sources that the executive branch can then use to provide humanitarian assistance. These sources include the Office of Foreign Disaster Administration within the Agency for International Development, which provides nonfood humanitarian assistance such as cash and material. The U.S. Department of Agriculture has food aid programs. The State Department provides refugee support through its Emergency Refugee and Migration Account. The Department of Defense's Overseas Humanitarian and Disaster and Civic Aid (OHDACA) program includes three segments: the Humanitarian Mine Action Program, the Humanitarian Assistance Program, and Foreign Disaster Relief Assistance. OHDACA programs fund assistance programs by military forces. Through these and other sources, the United States contributed almost $3 billion in global disaster relief from October 1, 2005, through September 30, 2006.

Figure 8.1 displays major global incidents in which the United States provided relief from 1978 through 2006. As shown, the United States provides humanitarian assistance in many forms. It first provides medical, food, shelter, personnel, and financial assistance to nations that have been damaged by such natural disasters as tsunamis, earthquakes, droughts, floods, and volcanoes. The United States also provides assistance to nations affected by man-made disasters such as fires, wars, and mass murders. The United States provides funds to private volunteer organizations that support humanitarian relief efforts such as the American National Red Cross and Feed the Children, Inc. Through the Denton Program, nongovernmental organizations or private citizens can use space available on U.S. military cargo planes to send goods and equipment to countries in need.

The United States also provides assistance to foreign nationals fleeing persecution in their home nations. For example, the government provided almost $1 billion in humanitarian assistance for displaced Iraqi citizens in 2007. The United States also assists nations in strengthening or rebuilding their infrastructures. The government pledged $230 million in humanitarian, reconstruction, and security assistance to Lebanon in 2006. This assistance included assisting in the rebuilding of bridges and roads, homes and other private infrastructures, schools, and the environment.

ALLIES, ENEMIES, AND TREATIES

The United States does not officially declare a country an enemy unless there is an active conflict or war. In this case, the president declares war against a specific country or group. Declarations of war require congressional approval. In times of peace, the United States does not maintain formal diplomatic relations with countries it does not

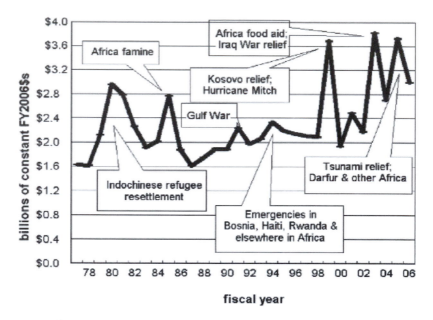

Figure 8.1. U.S. humanitarian assistance spending (in billions of dollars). Expressed in constant FY2006 dollars. *Source:* Margesson (2006). *International Crisis and Disasters: U.S. Humanitarian Assistance, Budget Trends, and Issues for Congress.* Library of Congress Congressional Research Service, Washington, DC. Retrieved July 4, 2007, from http://italy.usembassy.gov/pdf/other/RL33769.pdf.

consider allies because of such issues as support to terrorism or communism, or the abuse of human rights. As of 2007, the United States did not maintain direct diplomatic relations with Bhutan, Cuba, Iran, North Korea, Somalia, the Republic of China (Taiwan), and the Sahrawi Arab Democratic Republic. Dictators and/or communist governments ran most of these nations. The nations the United States considers allies and enemies changes over time. During World War I, the primary allies to the United States were France, the Soviet Union, Great Britain, and Italy. The United States, the Soviet Union, and Great Britain were the main allied forces in World War II. However, the United States and the Soviet Union remained locked in the cold war for decades to follow.

The United States establishes formal alliances with friendly or allied nations in the forms of treaties or executive agreements. Both types have the force of law and are established by the president, the authority for which is granted under Article II, Section 2, of the Constitution ("He shall have Power, by and with the Advice and Consent of the Senate, to make Treaties, provided two thirds of the Senators present concur"). Levels of partnering are outlined in treaties and executive agreements. The United States may declare a nation a full partner on almost every aspect of global relations from trade, to maintaining world peace, to fighting for democracy around the world. In other cases, there may only be an alliance on one issue such as controlling the production of nuclear weapons. An alliance may be a completely new agreement with a nation or it may result from an existing agreement. For example, an agreement may emanate from the existing North Atlantic Treaty. The North Atlantic Treaty was originally signed in 1949 by the founding members of NATO. These nations included Belgium, Canada, Denmark, France, Iceland, Italy, Luxembourg, the Netherlands, Norway, Portugal, the United Kingdom, and the United States. It established these nations as allies and stipulated an attack against one member nation would be considered an attack against all of them. Its aim was also to foster economic, political, and social cooperation among member nations. Later other nations joined the treaty. Two or more of these member nations can establish an agreement emanating from the North Atlantic Treaty but the agreement is only pertinent to specific concerns they share.

There are two types of executive agreements. Congressional-executive agreements (also called statutory agreements) result from legislation previously passed by Congress. Based on existing law, the executive branch then forms an agreement with a foreign nation(s). The executive branch must still submit the final agreement to the Senate for final approval. Presidential or sole-executive agreements are made by the president and not submitted to Congress for approval. The president makes these agreements based upon the argument that this sole authority is granted in the following sections of the Constitution (Congressional Research Service, 2001, p. 5):

- Executive power in Article II, Section 1
- Power as Commander-in-Chief of the armed forces in Article II, Section 2
- Power to negotiate treaties in Article II, Section 2
- Authority to receive Ambassadors and other public Ministers in Article II, Section 3
- Duty to "take care that the laws be faithfully executed" in Article II, Section 3

A treaty or executive agreement originates with a desired need being identified. This need addresses a gap or deficiency in current laws covering a specific issue where two or more nations have a stake or interest in the issue. The originating party or parties conduct a cost-benefit analysis of establishing and executing the agreement, consider the likelihood an alliance will actually be established, the time it will take to form the alliance in relation to the problem at hand, and any laws or agreements already in place. The following steps outline how U.S. treaties and executive agreements are put into place after the need for an alliance has been determined and there is some level of agreement in principle between the United States and another nation(s). Notice that the steps in the process of establishing a treaty or an executive agreement are the same until step 5.

1. The executive branch formally initiates negotiations with another nation or nations that will be partners in the treaty or executive agreement. The secretary of state authorizes a U.S. representative to negotiate on behalf of the United States. The U.S. representative is often a U.S. ambassador or other member of the U.S. Foreign Service. They obtain negotiating authority and instructions from the president on the executive branch's position on issues and the expected objectives to be reached by developing the alliance.
2. The negotiation process is the most difficult part of establishing an alliance. The parties negotiate based on the instructions they have been given by their governments (and gain additional guidance as needed throughout the negotiation process), and consider the likelihood that the terms and conditions of the alliance will be accepted by their respective legislative bodies.
3. The United States and foreign representatives agree on the terms, wording, and form of the agreement.
4. Once negotiations are concluded, each party signs the formal document. The U.S. representative signs per authorization granted by the secretary of state.

5. The secretary of state passes the document to the president for submission to the Senate for review and approval. For sole-executive agreements, the president is the final approving authority. However, even these agreements must be transmitted to Congress within sixty days of the agreement entering into force according to the Case-Zablocki Act of 1972. *Entering into force* means the agreement goes into effect and becomes binding international law between the signing parties.

6. The Senate Foreign Relations Committee reviews the treaty. It passes it to the full Senate body with a resolution of ratification (i.e., recommendation for approval) as written or with amendments, or it does not pass it to the Senate at all (i.e., disapproves).

7. A treaty requires a two-thirds majority vote in the Senate to be approved. If the treaty is not approved or not considered by the end of the Senate session, it is either returned to the Senate Foreign Relations Committee or the president for reconsideration and re-submittal.

8. Once approved by the Senate, the signature of the president ratifies the treaty. If the Senate recommended amendments, further negotiations with the foreign partner(s) may be required to agree on the amendments. The president may choose not to ratify the treaty at this stage due to disagreement with the Senate's amendments, changes in international conditions, or other issues.

9. Once all parties to the treaty agree, it enters into force. The treaty may require Congress to pass new legislation to execute its terms. For example, Congress may need to appropriate new funds or establish a new agency to execute the treaty. If new legislation is required, it goes through the full congressional legislative approval process.

10. The executive branch monitors the execution of the treaty and negotiates any disputes that arise. Congress provides oversight.

11. Any modification or extension of the original treaty is considered a new agreement and requires the treaty to go through the entire approval process again.

12. The treaty is terminated according to the duration and method outlined in the language of the treaty, or by mutual consent of all parties who signed the document.

The relationship of the United States with specific nations has dominated the foreign policy agendas of presidents. Some of these nations are considered allies and others have been considered long-standing enemies. The close relationship between the United States and Israel has been a constant of American foreign policy since Israel was founded. U.S. support for Israel is primarily based upon the latter's support for the United States and security interests in that region. The United States sends approximately $3 billion in military and economic aid to Israel annually. These appropriations are rarely challenged by the U.S. Congress. There continues to be general political agreement within the U.S. government that Israel has advanced U.S. interests in the Middle East. In return for this support, the U.S. government has provided aid, weapons, and political support to the Israeli state, which has been critical to that nation's survival.

Domestic relations with some South American countries have been hampered by those countries supporting or taking an idle stance on drug trade. For example, the U.S. government has severed its ties with Venezuela because it believes that nation has aided the shipments of cocaine manufactured in neighboring Colombia. While Venezuelan officials argue their nation is unable to stop drug traffickers, some U.S. officials have countered that the Venezuelan government has taken a purposefully complacent stance toward drug trade. U.S. diplomatic ties with Venezuela worsened under the administration of Venezuelan President Hugo Chavez. In 1998, following

Chavez's decision to run for the president of Venezuela, the State Department turned down his request for a visa that to allow him to present his political platform to multi-national representatives in New York and Washington, DC. Then-Secretary of State Madeleine Albright defended the refusal because Chavez had participated in a failed coup against Venezuelan President Carlos Andres Perez in 1992. However, this explanation was criticized because the U.S. government granted a visa to Francisco Arias Cardenas, a known participant in the same coup attempt. Cardenas later became a rival of Chavez during the presidential campaign and criticized Chavez's anti-American rhetoric and pro-Cuban comments.

Chavez's negative comments about the United States and the denial of a U.S. visa increased his popularity within Venezuela during the campaign and helped him win the election. Since his time in office, members of President George W. Bush's administration have criticized Chavez for damaging U.S. foreign policy by providing oil to Cuba (another so-called enemy of the United States), opposing a plan that includes $1.3 billion in United States counternarcotics aid for South America, and by giving political support to guerrillas and antigovernment forces in neighboring Andean nations. Chavez used his nation's oil export power as leverage against the United States. In 2000–2007, Venezuela was the fourth largest supplier of oil to the United States, accounting for 13 percent of American oil imports. Rising oil prices during the period gave the nation additional economic and political clout. Chavez further challenged the policies of the United States and other democratic nations by being the only Latin American head of state to visit Iraq since the end of the Persian Gulf War. He ignored the U.S. international economic blockade of Cuba and invited Cuban dictator Fidel Castro to visit the Venezuelan capital of Caracas. Diplomatic relations were officially severed when Chavez called President Bush "the devil" during a speech before the UN in 2006 and criticized the foreign policies of the United States. He also characterized the UN as an ineffective body. Chavez has continually accused the Bush administration of taking subversive action to remove him from office, yet made continuous promises to the American people that he would increase the supply of oil to the United States to assist poor Americans in being able to afford gas in the wake of rising gas prices.

Diplomatic ties with Iran reached a crisis situation when American diplomats in the U.S. embassy in Tehran were taken hostage in 1979. The hostages were taken to protest U.S. involvement in that nation's affairs and in support of the recently ousted Shah of Iran, Mohammad Reza Pahlavi, who was placed in power in 1953 as the result of a coup funded by the U.S. Central Intelligence Agency. The hostages were released within minutes of President Ronald W. Reagan taking office in 1981. In retaliation, the United States enforced economic sanctions against Iran. Iranian anger at the United States increased due to U.S. support of Iraq during the Iran-Iraq War from 1980 to 1988. During the administration of President George W. Bush, the U.S. government claimed Iran had been developing a nuclear weapons program. Seeking international support to counter any Iranian efforts, U.S. Secretary of State Condoleezza Rice called for the International Atomic Energy Agency to take aggressive actions against any Iranian nuclear program in 2005. The agency responded by sending inspectors to Iran, but no evidence of nuclear weapon technology was found. The U.S. government also believed Iran was supporting international terrorist groups, and imposed sanctions on the Iranian Bank in 2006 that barred it from dealing with U.S. financial institutions directly or indirectly. In 2007 and 2008, there were a series of naval stand-offs between Iranian speedboats and U.S. warships in the Strait of

Hormuz. U.S. officials accused Iran of harassing and provoking its naval vessels. Iran denied these allegations.

TRADE AGREEMENTS

Established in 1963, the Office of the United States Trade Representative (USTR), which is part of the executive office of the president, negotiates trade agreements between the United States and foreign governments. The USTR participates in global trade policy organizations, coordinates with public and private individuals and groups on trade issues, resolves trade disputes, and is the principal coordinator on the president's trade policy positions. The following are the trade sectors in which the United States establishes treaties: agriculture, the environment, government procurement, intellectual property and innovation, investment, labor, manufacturing, services, small business, telecommunications and e-commerce, and textiles and apparel.

The United States has established several free-trade agreements. These allow open trade with a partnering nation, eliminate or reduce tariffs, and remove regulations that favor national businesses over foreign businesses. The following are examples, taken from the official Web site of the USTR (http://www.ustr.gov/Trade_Agreements/Section_Index.html):

- The United States-Israel Free Trade Area (FTA) Agreement took effect September 1, 1985, and is designed to stimulate trade between the United States and Israel. The agreement, which has no expiration date, provides for the elimination of duties for merchandise from Israel entering the United States. As of January 1, 1995, all eligible reduced rate imports from Israel were accorded duty-free treatment. The FTA does allow the two countries to protect sensitive agricultural subsectors with nontariff barriers including import bans, quotas, and fees.
- By strengthening the rules and procedures governing trade and investment on this continent, the NAFTA (North American Free Trade Agreement) has allowed trade and investment flows in North America to skyrocket. According to figures of the International Monetary Fund, total trade among the three NAFTA countries (the United States, Canada, and Mexico) has more than doubled, passing from US$306 billion in 1993 to almost US$621 billion in 2002. That's US$1.2 million every minute. NAFTA is an outstanding demonstration of the rewards to outward-looking countries that implement policies of trade liberalization as a way to increase wealth and improve competitiveness. NAFTA is an example of the benefits that all countries could derive from moving forward with multilateral trade liberalization. Farmers, workers, and manufacturers benefit from the reduction of arbitrary and discriminatory trade rules, while consumers enjoy lower prices and more choices.
- The United States-Jordan Free Trade Agreement (FTA) was signed on October 24, 2000. It was America's third free-trade agreement, and the first ever with an Arab state. The Jordan FTA achieves significant and extensive liberalization across a wide spectrum of trade issues. It will eliminate all tariff and nontariff barriers to bilateral trade in virtually all industrial goods and agricultural products within ten years.
- (The) United States-Bahrain Free Trade Agreement [which was passed in 2004 and went into effect in 2006] is an important step in implementing the president's economic reforms in the Middle East and pursuing the goal of a Middle East Free Trade Area. U.S. goods exports to Bahrain in 2003 totaled $509 million, including aircraft, machinery, vehicles, pharmaceutical

products, and toys, games, and sports equipment. The United States is seeking to eliminate tariffs and other duties on trade between Bahrain and the United States on the broadest possible basis, improve intellectual property rights protection, and eliminate barriers in Bahrain's services markets.

- The Central America-Dominican Republic-United States Free Trade Agreement, which was signed on August 5, 2004, is designed to eliminate tariffs and trade barriers and expand regional opportunities for the workers, manufacturers, consumers, farmers, ranchers, and service providers of all the countries. CAFTA-DR will immediately eliminate tariffs on more than 80 percent of U.S. exports of consumer and industrial products, phasing out the rest over ten years. In all, 80 percent of CAFTA-DR imports already enter the United States duty free under the Caribbean Basin Initiative, Generalized System of Preferences, and Most Favored Nation programs; the CAFTA-DR will provide reciprocal access for U.S. products and services.

The United States also has free-trade agreements in place with Chile, Singapore, Australia, and Morocco. According to the USTR, in 2007, free-trade agreements with Peru, Colombia, Panama, and the South Korea (the Republic of Korea) were pending congressional approval.

Countries the United States does free trade with may be designated with a Permanent Normal Trade Relations (PNTR) status. This title replaced the formal designation of Most Favored Nation in 1998. The United States does not grant PNTR status to most communist nations, or those that support terrorism. One concern raised by some government officials is that the PNTR status is permanent. For example, human rights advocates were opposed to the United States granting China PNTR status in 2001 because of that country's history of imposing restrictions on its citizens' labor, human, religious, and free speech rights. Granting that nation PNTR removed the annual review Congress conducted on China's policies and actions. China then was granted membership into the World Trade Organization (WTO). Non-PNTR status nations may be granted trading rights with the United States but the relationship is reviewed annually by Congress, specifically to examine the practices of that nation.

The WTO is located in Geneva, Switzerland. It was established on January 1, 1995, and provides trade agreements for the world's leading nations. Its 151 members (as of July 2007) represent over 95 percent of global trade and abide by the General Agreement on Tariffs and Trade (GATT) originally signed in 1947, as amended by the Uruguay Round negotiations of 1986–1994. The GATT was an agreement establishing a forum for international discussion and agreement on issues of the free trade of products between member nations. These negotiations led to the creation of the WTO and expanded GATT coverage from just goods to include trade for services, inventions, and intellectual property such as creations and designs. WTO members "operate a non-discriminatory trading system that spells out their rights and their obligations. Each country receives guarantees that its exports will be treated fairly and consistently in other countries' markets. Each promises to do the same for imports into its own market. The system also gives developing countries some flexibility in implementing their commitments" (WTO Information and Media Relations Division, 2007). Members guarantee each other most-favored-nation status, and imported goods are treated as equally as locally produced goods. The United States has permanent free trade with all other members of the WTO. (See Appendix M for a list of all WTO members as of July 27, 2007.)

U.S. AMBASSADORS

According to Article II, Section 1, of the Constitution, the president has the authority to appoint ambassadors and other public ministers and consuls to represent the United States throughout the world. The Senate must approve these appointments. Ambassadors, ministers, and consuls are all now members of the U.S. Foreign Service. The Foreign Service was created by the Foreign Service Act of 1946 (also called the Rogers Act) and is part of the Department of State. Its members are the primary diplomats for the United States. The following statement from the Department of State describes the roles of ambassadors, ministers, and consuls who are collectively referred to as foreign service officers (U.S. Department of State, 2007b):

> Foreign Service Officers (FSOs) advocate American foreign policy, protect American citizens, and promote American business interests throughout the world. FSOs staff our Embassies, consulates and other diplomatic missions devoted to strengthening peace, stability, and prosperity. Their perceptiveness, dedication, and creativity drive the formulation and achievement of American foreign policy objectives. Increasingly, transnational issues such as the environment, science and technology; the global struggle against diseases such as AIDS; international law enforcement cooperation and counter narcotics trafficking; counter proliferation and international action against trafficking in persons have gained stature among American foreign policy objectives.

FSOs are hired into general positions along five career tracks: consular officer, economic officer, management officer, political officer, and public diplomacy officer. The United States is also represented by foreign service specialists (FSSs) who are hired into specific types of positions such as health practitioners. While potential FSOs take complex oral and written exams, an FSS candidate is recommended for a position after an oral assessment by experts in a particular field.

The following are the qualifications to become an FSO or FSS:

- Must be a U.S. citizen
- Must be at least twenty years of age but no older than fifty-nine at time of application
- Must be at least twenty-one years of age but no older than sixty on date of appointment
- Must be able to accept assignments worldwide

(See Appendix N for a complete list of United States Embassies.)

U.S. MEMBERSHIP IN NATO AND THE UNITED NATIONS

The United States attempts to become involved in foreign matters together with other countries rather than alone. The two primary means of doing this are through its membership in the NATO and the UN. Each organization was established to create an alliance of nations that work together to peacefully develop solutions to issues of international importance. They each rely on their members to execute its policies and programs, including providing military support when that is a decision of last resort.

Table 8.2.   Member Countries of the North Atlantic Treaty Organization (NATO) in 2007

Belgium	Hungary	Portugal
Bulgaria	Iceland	Romania
Canada	Italy	Slovakia
Czech Republic	Latvia	Slovenia
Denmark	Lithuania	Spain
Estonia	Luxembourg	Turkey
France	Netherlands	United Kingdom
Germany	Norway	United States
Greece	Poland	

Source: "NATO Member Countries." Available at http://www.nato.int/structur/countries.htm

NATO is an alliance of twenty-six countries formed to fulfill the goals of the North Atlantic Treaty (see Table 8.2 for a list of the member countries of NATO as of 2007). The North Atlantic Treaty was signed April 4, 1949, to reaffirm the principles of the charter of the United Nations in uniting the efforts of its members in providing for collective defense through the preservation of global peace and security. NATO addresses issues of common concern to its members and develops consensual strategies to resolve them. This consensual decision making requires each member country to concur with a decision before it can take effect. Members do not cast votes. Instead, each member has a chance to state its position, the NATO Secretary General provides consultation, and negotiations continue until an acceptable resolution is reached. NATO's headquarters are located in Brussels, Belgium.

The U.S. government provides a special designation to nations it establishes major alliances with that are not members of NATO. Each of these nonmember nations is designated as a *major non-NATO ally* (MNNA). This term originated in 1989 with the addition of Section 2350a to Title 10 of the *United States Code*. It defines MNNA as "a country (other than a member nation of the North Atlantic Treaty Organization) that is designated as a major non-NATO ally for purposes of this section by the Secretary of Defense with the concurrence of the Secretary of State." In July 1996, Public Law 104-164 amended the Foreign Assistance Act of 1961 to allow the president to designate MNNAs. The president must notify Congress thirty days before designating a country as a MNNA or terminating a MNNA designation.

While MNNA nations do not receive the same level of military and financial aid as NATO nations, they do receive some level of support. For example, the following are provisions of the alliance with Thailand:

- Permits firms of the country to bid on certain U.S. government contracts for maintenance, repair, or overhaul of Department of Defense equipment outside of the Continental United States
- Makes the country eligible for certain joint counterterrorism research and development projects
- Allows the Department of Defense to enter into cooperative research and development projects with the country to improve conventional defense capabilities on an equitable cost-sharing basis

Other MNAA nations include Argentina (the first Latin American MNNA), Australia, Bahrain, Egypt, Israel, Japan, Jordon, Kuwait, Morocco, New Zealand, Pakistan, Philippines, South Korea, and Taiwan.

The United Nations, a name coined by President Franklin D. Roosevelt, was officially established on October 24, 1945, by a conference of over fifty countries. Its headquarters are located in New York, New York. The following are the established purposes of the UN (United Nations, 1945):

1. To maintain international peace and security, and to that end: to take effective collective measures for the prevention and removal of threats to the peace, and for the suppression of acts of aggression or other breaches of the peace, and to bring about by peaceful means, and in conformity with the principles of justice and international law, adjustment or settlement of international disputes or situations which might lead to a breach of the peace
2. To develop friendly relations among nations based on respect for the principle of equal rights and self-determination of peoples, and to take other appropriate measures to strengthen universal peace
3. To achieve international co-operation in solving international problems of an economic, social, cultural, or humanitarian character, and in promoting and encouraging respect for human rights and for fundamental freedoms for all without distinction as to race, sex, language, or religion
4. To be a center for harmonizing the actions of nations in the attainment of these common ends.

The United Nations Security Council (UNSC) has the primary responsibility for developing strategies for maintaining international peace and security. The UNSC is comprised of five permanent seats: the United States, Great Britain, China, Russia, and France. Permanent seat members have veto power over proposed resolutions. The UNSC is also comprised of ten additional seats that are temporary and held for two-year terms. The presidency of the Council rotates each month according to the alphabetical listing of the Council's member states. The following lists the official roles of the UNSC (United Nations Security Council, 2007):

- Maintain international peace and security in accordance with the principles and purposes of the United Nations
- Investigate any dispute or situation which might lead to international friction
- Recommend methods of adjusting such disputes or the terms of settlement
- Formulate plans for the establishment of a system to regulate armaments
- Determine the existence of a threat to the peace or act of aggression and to recommend what action should be taken
- Call on Members to apply economic sanctions and other measures not involving the use of force to prevent or stop aggression
- Take military action against an aggressor
- Recommend the admission of new Members
- Exercise the trusteeship functions of the United Nations in strategic areas
- Recommend to the General Assembly the appointment of the Secretary-General and, together with the Assembly, elect the Judges of the International Court of Justice

The UNSC carries out its mission in several ways. If a conflict arises, the Council attempts to have the parties reach agreement through peaceful means and sometimes acts as a mediator. It may levy economic sanctions, such as trade embargos, against nations

United Nations Security Council meeting on the deployment of the African Union–United Nations Hybrid Operation in Darfur, November 27, 2007. *Evan Schneider/UN Photo*.

in violation of UN policies or it may decide military intervention is required. The council can send UN peacekeeping forces to an area to keep opposing sides apart while peace can be restored. It may also recommend a nation be expelled from the United Nations for serious or consistent violation of the terms of the UN Charter. According to the UN Charter, the decisions, called *resolutions,* of the UNSC must be carried out by member nations. (See Appendix L for a complete list of UN member nations.)

THE GROUP OF EIGHT (G8)

The Group of Eight (better known as the G8) is composed of the heads of state and governments of the leading industrialized nations in the world. It is an international forum for these leading nations to deal with global issues. Its membership currently consists of representatives from Canada, France, Germany, Italy, Japan, Russia, the United Kingdom, and the United States. The European Commission, the executive branch of the European Union, is also represented in all meetings of the group. The presidency of the G8 is rotated among its members. In 2007, the member from Germany served as president. The collective member nations of the G8 produce approximately two-thirds of the world's products, account for nearly half of world trade, provide three-quarters of the global development aid, and are the major contributors to international organizations.

In 1975, the G8 (then the G6; in 1976, the addition of Canada formed the G7, and Russia's participation in summit conferences from 1998 created the G8) first met in Rambouillet, France, to discuss the global economy. It was established as a result of the oil crisis of the mid-1970s and the resulting global recession. Some of the issues its members discussed were monetary cooperation, macroeconomic control, trade, and energy. It has since developed policies to address crises in the Middle East, education as a prerequisite for economic prosperity in industrialized and developing countries, overcoming the digital gap, climate protection, debt relief in the world's poorest countries, and fighting AIDS around the world. The G8 meetings, called *summits*, have grown from private meetings among its members to a developed system of year-round meetings at different levels.

The members continually develop joint positions on key issues of foreign policy. These initiatives are crafted into G8 joint initiatives executed by member nations and other countries affected. The G8 often hires experts to conduct studies on issues of importance. G8 members also hold meetings among themselves. For example, during a summit meeting two heads of state may take the opportunity to reach agreement on an issue that only affects their nations. There are also submeetings of member nations on specific areas. For example, foreign ministers meet to discuss foreign policy, those responsible for environmental issues hold separate meetings, and finance ministers from each nation coordinate on financial policies and issues impacting affecting the global economy. Sherpas and Sous-sherpas meet several times during the year to plans the agendas for summit meetings.

The following is a list of some of the issues and policies on which the G8 is focusing its efforts, as well as some of its achievements (Press and Information Office of the Federal Government, 2008):

- The G8's New Partnership for Africa's Development (NEPAD) supports reforming African nations.
- Through its Global Health Fund, the G8 has made over $1.4 billion available for combating disease since 2000.
- The Global G8 Partnership aims at preventing the spread of weapons and material of mass destruction. Its priorities include the destruction of chemical weapons, and the disposal of decommissioned nuclear submarines and fissile material.
- A G8 experts group has been dealing with combating organized crime since 1995. The G8-Senior Experts Group on Transnational Organized Crime implements proposed recommendations.
- At the 2005 G8 Summit in Gleneagles an action plan was signed to increase energy efficiency.
- The G8 is developing policies to deal with the problem of climate change, challenges of energy security, economic growth, and environmental protection.

THE UNITED STATES AS THE WORLD POLICE

The United States has taken a leading role in so many international conflicts and the internal affairs of so many other nations that it has gained the title the "world police." Starting with the Korean and Vietnam Wars, the United States has gotten involved in numerous conflicts where America was not directly attacked but the government determined a threat to democracy existed, human rights were being violated, or a present or future threat to the United States existed. In some cases, the United States simply provided assistance, such as serving as a mediator. In 1978, for example, President Jimmy Carter mediated twelve days of peace talks between Egyptian President Anwar al-Sadat and Israeli Prime Minister Menachem Begin. The negotiations at Camp David led to the Israel-Egypt Peace Treaty in 1979, the first peace treaty between Israel and an Arab state. In other cases, the United States established a military presence.

From December 1979 through February 1989, the United States deployed troops to support Islamic Afghan guerilla fighters when the Soviet Union invaded Afghanistan. A prime minister, whom the Soviet Union helped install after the assassination of the former leader, led the pro-Soviet Afghan communist leadership. The Soviet Union withdrew in 1989.

An excerpt from the Department of State's mission statement exemplifies the role the United States has assumed in providing global support and protection:

> We must protect our nation, our allies, and our friends against the transnational dangers and enduring threats arising from tyranny, poverty, and disease. Global terrorism, international crime, and the spread of weapons of mass destruction are new challenges born of traditional ambitions.

There is disagreement on whether the United States should maintain the role of a world police. Events during the administration of President George W. Bush intensified the debate. In his State of the Union address on January 29, 2002, President Bush announced a dramatic shift in American foreign policy. In addition to the war on terrorism, he stated that the United States was committed to very ambitious foreign policy goals. Specifically. the president stated, "Our . . . goal is to prevent regimes that sponsor terror from threatening America or our friends and allies with weapons of mass destruction." During the address, he named countries from the so-called "axis of evil," which included Iraq, Iran, and North Korea, deemed as significant threats to the security of the United States because of their supposed connections to terrorists and the development of weapons of mass destruction. North Korea was considered a threat to the United States and international peace because of its development of nuclear weapons during the 1990s. North Korea defended its actions as in defense of South Korea's development of new weapons with the support of the United States. The North Korean government admitted to successfully conducting a nuclear test in 1996. President Bush's administration did not take action to conduct diplomatic talks with North Korea.

After the State of the Union address, President Bush laid out his strategy in a report entitled *The National Security Strategy of the United States of America* (The White House, 2002). The key new strategy in this report centered on preemptive actions, which meant that the United States would reserve the right to strike first against terrorist groups and tyrants that may harbor weapons of mass destruction and that had the potential to pass these weapons to terrorists. The report specifically states, "While the United States will constantly strive to enlist the support of the international community, we will not hesitate to act alone, if necessary, to exercise our right of self defense by acting preemptively against such terrorists, to prevent them from doing harm against our people and our country." Although the idea of preemptive intervention was not generally opposed in the United States, some countries who were American allies, such as Germany and France, were not pleased with this announcement because they believed the United States should have consulted with their governments before making a statement that could have consequences for the international community. A year later the new strategy was put into action when United States armed forces were used to initiate a war with Iraq and remove Saddam Hussein from power. The war with Iraq stimulated debate over whether the United States should utilize a unilateralist foreign policy or the traditional foreign policy method of multilateralism. With multilateralism, foreign and military policy is based on consultation and cooperation with a broad range of allies, whereas a unilateralist stance supports the view that the United States is acting as the world police.

Those in favor of the United States' policing role point out that the United States is the world's largest democratic power and should therefore take whatever actions are needed to ensure those nations embracing democratic principles are provided assistance in fighting enemies of democracy. They believe protecting democracy globally is vital to the future safety and security of the United States. Others argue that because the United States is the strongest economic power in the world and possesses the strongest military, it has a duty to provide some level of protection to the rest of the world, particularly poor nations. Another argument is that there are no other nations or groups able to provide the level and speed of protection the United States can provide. These advocates criticize the United Nations as acting too slowly in crisis situations, not possessing a military force, and being unable to act without agreement from all its members.

One argument against the United States being the world police is that the United States does not have the responsibility or authority to police other nations. This action impedes on and interferes with the sovereignty of other nations. Another argument is that the U.S. government practices "cowboy diplomacy" in this role. In other words, it ignores true diplomatic relations and the collaborative missions of the United Nations and NATO. Instead, the United States acts in whatever manner it wants to forcefully reach the ends it wants to see globally. A third argument is that the United States is maintaining a "holier than thou" attitude in policing other nations. The government is imposing its view of ethics and morality on other nations, and ignoring their cultural norms. For example, a U.S. promise of medicines to battle AIDS in Africa carried the stipulation that any program utilizing U.S. support must promote abstinence versus safe sex. A fourth argument is that the United States has enough of its own internal problems to contend with, such as poverty and racism. The financial and personnel strains of providing worldwide support are stretching this nation too thin. This is intensified when short-term support turns into long-term commitments. The United States continues to provide support to both South Korea and South Vietnam against threats from their northern counterparts decades after wars in both regions have ended. An additional argument is that the United States makes enemies when it attempts to police other nations. History has shown this sometimes includes the enemies of those we were protecting, and in other cases those we were protecting become our enemies. For example, many experts have pointed out that al-Qaeda became an enemy of the United States after the continued presence of U.S. troops in Afghanistan after the Soviet-Afghan war ended in 1989. The United States entered the war to assist the Afghan rebels in driving Soviet troops from the region. The rebels later complained they traded one occupation for another when U.S. troops remained stationed in their nation. Enemies are also made when the United States does not provide comparable support to different nations in similar situations.

MILITARY TRIBUNALS

After the terrorist attacks on the United States on September 11, 2001, military tribunals were used to try those held for terrorist crimes or who are suspected of having ties with terrorist groups. A military tribunal is a type of military court used during times of war to try members of the enemy force. Tribunals operate outside the scope of the normal court system. The judges and jurors are military officers, and all charges and sentencing are based on military rules. Additionally, they fall under the executive branch because of the president's authority as commander-in-chief of the armed forces. On November 13, 2001, President George W. Bush issued an military order authorizing the use of military tribunals based on his authority as "President and as Commander in Chief of the Armed Forces of the United States by the Constitution and the laws of the United States of America, including the Authorization for Use of Military Force Joint Resolution (Public Law 107-40, 115 Stat. 224) and sections 821 and 836 of title 10, United States Code." In the order entitled "Detention, Treatment, and Trial of Certain Non-Citizens in the War Against Terrorism," the president ordered the use of military tribunals to try those accused of terrorist activities and provided types of legal remedies for those being tried (U.S. Department of State, 2001).

The order specifically mandated, "military tribunals shall have exclusive jurisdiction with respect to offenses by the individual; and the individual shall not be privileged to seek any remedy or maintain any proceeding, directly or indirectly, or to have any such remedy or proceeding sought on the individual's behalf, in any court of the United States, or any State thereof, any court of any foreign nation, or any international tribunal." The order applied to any individual not a U.S. citizen who was a current or former member of al-Qaeda; who engaged, aided, abetted, or conspired to commit terrorist acts against the United States; or who harbored terrorists.

Al-Qaeda (also spelled Al-Qaida or Al-Qadr) is an extremist Islamic group founded during the 1980s by Usama bin Laden. The group's goal at that time was to push Soviet troops out of Afghanistan during the Soviet-Afghan war. When the war ended, al-Qaeda became even more vigilant about pushing non-Muslims (especially those from Western nations) out of Muslim countries. The United States was a major target of this group, which recruits, trains, and transports thousands of members around the world. Al-Qaeda is considered extremist because it justifies such tactics as assassination, kidnapping, suicide attacks, and hijacking, as warranted in its view of *jihād*, the Muslim religious principle of struggle or striving against evil (sometimes broadly translated as Holy War) against those who do not live according to Islamic teachings. Al-Qaeda often chooses prominent targets for destruction, such as embassies, office complexes, and shopping centers, in order to kill as many people as possible with each strike. In 2008, bin Laden remains the "Most Wanted Terrorist" in the world on the FBI's list of most sought-after criminals. He also remains one of the FBI's ten most wanted fugitives, and is sought after by law enforcement agencies around the world.

The actions of President Bush were similar to those employed by President Franklin D. Roosevelt during World War II. Eight German saboteurs reached the United States by submarine with the intent of blowing up U.S. railroads, bridges, factories, and other targets. They were tried and found guilty by a military tribunal. The Germans attempted to seek a writ of habeas corpus, or release for being imprisoned unlawfully, in the civil courts. The Supreme Court upheld President Roosevelt's use of the military tribunal in *Ex Parte Quirin,* 317 U.S. 1 (1942).

There are several arguments against the use of military tribunals. These arguments focus mostly on how prisoners are treated before, during, and after being brought before tribunals. Some contest alleged human rights abuses against those held. Beyond not being told of their crimes, provided a timely trial, or provided legal representation, those detained are sometimes held in deplorable conditions or subjected to humiliating interrogations. Another argument tied to the first is that the United States should treat foreign criminals being held in U.S. custody the same as the United States would expect foreign nations to treat U.S. citizens being held in a foreign detention center or prison. An issue that arose in 2007 connected to both of these issues was the use of an interrogation technique, called "water boarding," by U.S. interrogators to interrogate terrorist suspects. The technique involves laying a suspect on his back and forcing water into his mouth, causing a gag reflex. The suspect feels the sensation of drowning. Some members of the executive branch and others in the federal government argued water boarding was an effective practice to force suspects to confess to crimes and give other important information about possible terrorist activities. Many others criticized the use of the technique as a blatant form of inhumane torture.

The federal courts have also expressed concern that military tribunals may allow the executive branch to overstep its Constitutional authority by exercising the powers of all three branches of the government. Beyond executing laws, it enacts legislation to create military tribunals, and exercises judicial powers in holding trials and prosecuting criminals. This concentration of power in one branch of government threatens the rights and liberties of individuals who have no recourse for appeal and overrides the Constitutional safeguard of checks and balances.

A major argument against the use of military tribunals in connection with the war on terrorism is that some actions may be in violation of the Geneva Conventions. The Geneva Conventions are four conventions that outline how nations are to engage during times of war, specifically with respect to the humanitarian treatment of prisoners of war and civilians not actively engaged in a battle. The first Geneva Convention was held in 1864 in Geneva, Switzerland, by a convention of world leaders, statesmen, and diplomats with the goal of reducing the suffering and deaths that result during times of war. The most recent modification to the treaty was made in 1949 due to the extreme amount of destruction caused during World War II and the use of nuclear weapons during the war. The following are just a few provisions of the treaty:

> Persons taking no active part in the hostilities, including members of armed forces who have laid down their arms and those placed hors de combat by sickness, wounds, detention, or any other cause, shall in all circumstances be treated humanely, without any adverse distinction founded on race, colour, religion or faith, sex, birth or wealth, or any other similar criteria.
>
> To this end the following acts are and shall remain prohibited at any time and in any place whatsoever with respect to the above-mentioned persons: (a) Violence to life and person, in particular murder of all kinds, mutilation, cruel treatment and torture; (b) Taking of hostages; (c) Outrages upon personal dignity, in particular, humiliating and degrading treatment; (d) The passing of sentences and the carrying out of executions without previous judgment pronounced by a regularly constituted court affording all the judicial guarantees which are recognized as indispensable by civilized peoples. . . .
>
> Prisoners of war must at all times be humanely treated. Any unlawful act or omission by the Detaining Power causing death or seriously endangering the health of a prisoner of war in its custody is prohibited, and will be regarded as a serious breach of the present Convention. In particular, no prisoner of war may be subjected to physical mutilation or to medical or scientific experiments of any kind which are not justified by the medical, dental or hospital treatment of the prisoner concerned and carried out in his interest. Likewise, prisoners of war must at all times be protected, particularly against acts of violence or intimidation and against insults and public curiosity. Measures of reprisal against prisoners of war are prohibited.

Detainees in the exercise yard in Camp 4, the medium-security facility within Camp Delta at Naval Station Guantanamo Bay, Cuba. *U.S. Army Sgt. Sara Wood/U.S. Department of Defense.*

No prisoner of war may be convicted without having had an opportunity to present his defence and the assistance of a qualified advocate or counsel.

IMMIGRATION

Immigration involves the long-term or permanent relocation of a person from one nation to another. This geographical move may be illegal or legal. Legal immigrants follow the prescribed rules of the country they relocate to. Illegal immigrants establish residence without following the immigration laws of a country. Some illegally enter a country by crossing its border on foot or by vehicle, others by air, and others do so by boat. Some obtain work or student visas, which are temporary permits allowing them into the country, but then stay in the country after their visas expire. *Naturalization* is the process by which an immigrant, or alien, becomes a U.S. citizen. The Immigration and Nationality Act (INA) of 1952 governs this process. The INA, also known as the McCarran-Walter Act, also outlines the rules for the employment of aliens. It codified the various statutes that existed prior to its passing. It has been amended several times since its original passing.

Immigration was moved under the U.S. Immigration and Customs Enforcement (ICE) branch of the Department of Homeland Security after the events of September 11, 2001. It combined the law enforcement responsibilities of the former Immigration and Naturalization Service (INS) and the former U.S. Customs Services. The purpose of ICE is to protect the United States against terrorist attacks by targeting illegal immigrants, and the people, money, and materials that support terrorism and other criminal activities.

Immigration is one of the most controversial U.S. foreign policy issues. It has been at the forefront of domestic and foreign policy debates since the early twentieth century. Because of a continued influx of foreign citizens, the Immigration Act of 1924 was passed. It included the National Origins Act and Asian Exclusion Act. It set an immigration limit per country of no more than 2 percent of the number of its immigrants already living in the United States. It excluded any further immigration of Asians. The quotas remained in effect until the passing of the Immigration and Nationality Act of 1965, which was one of the amendments to the Immigration and Nationality Act of 1952. Also known as the Hart-Cellar Act, it allowed more immigrants from third world countries, set a separate quota for refugees, and allowed one hundred seventy thousand immigrants from the eastern hemisphere with no more than twenty thousand per country.

There continues to be a debate over whether legal immigration laws should be more restrictive, whether existing laws should be strengthened to fight illegal immigration, how those laws should be executed, and what additional laws are needed. The controversy in the United States has reached a peak due to the number of illegal immigrants in this nation and the expected growth of the Hispanic population over the coming century.

The immigration debate can be separated along the lines of the arguments for relaxing immigration laws and in favor of strengthening laws:

Arguments for more lenient immigration laws:

- Immigrants increase the diversity of a nation's citizenship.
- Immigrants provide needed lower-cost labor.
- Allowing free labor markets (i.e., allowing workers from other nations to compete for jobs around the world) boosts the global economy.
- Immigration provides opportunities to those from poorer nations.
- Stricter immigration laws lead to *xenophobia* or fear and hatred of foreigners.

Arguments for stricter immigration laws:

- Immigrants disrupt the established culture of the nation.
- Illegal immigrants strain the systems supported by taxpaying citizens such as medical assistance, police protection, public transportation, and public education.
- Immigrants provide unfair competition to citizens because they offer cheaper labor.
- Illegal immigrants are exploited because they have no citizen rights.
- Illegal immigrants lead to overpopulation and drain the nation's resources (e.g., oil, gas, food, etc.).
- Illegal immigrants cannot be held accountable for abiding by laws.
- Illegal immigration is a threat to national security and increases the risk of terrorism.

The number of illegal immigrants in the United States has grown substantially over the past few decades. The estimated number of illegal immigrants in the United States in 2007 ranges from seven million to twenty million. It is nearly impossible to know exactly how many are actually in the United States. However, it is also estimated that approximately five hundred thousand new illegal immigrants enter the United States annually and most illegal immigrants come from Mexico. In recent years, the government has attempted to adopt much stricter immigration laws that would increase border patrols, utilize National Guard troops to help protect the border, and even build a fence to separate the United States from Mexico. The Immigration Reform and Control Act of 1986 (IRCA) provides a legal means for illegal immigrants who have been continuously in the country since 1982 to become residents; it prohibits employment discrimination based on a potential employee's national origin or citizenship; it establishes penalties for employers who knowingly hire illegal workers; and increases enforcement of U.S. borders. The act also provides protections for immigrants. For example, an employer must obtain employment verification from all employees and not just individuals of a particular national origin or those who appear to be or sound foreign.

The Illegal Immigration Reform and Immigrant Responsibility Act of 1996 was signed by President Bill Clinton. The act is over 200 pages long and addresses a host of issues associated with immigration. The act is divided into the following sections, which provide specific laws in these areas:

- Title I—Improvements to Border Control, Facilitation of Legal Entry, and Interior Enforcement
- Title II—Enhanced Enforcement and Penalties Against Alien Smuggling; Document Fraud
- Title III—Inspection, Apprehension, Detention, Adjudication, and Removal of Inadmissible and Deportable Aliens
- Title IV—Enforcement of Restrictions Against Employment
- Title V—Restrictions on Benefits for Aliens
- Title VI—Miscellaneous Provisions

The Border Protection, Anti-terrorism, and Illegal Immigration Control Act of 2005 (also called the Sensenbrenner Bill after Wisconsin Republican Jim Sensenbrenner) was passed in the House but failed in the Senate. Several similar bills were later introduced. These attempts to strengthen legislation have met with protests across the country. Some proposed laws would require employer fines and sanctions for hiring an employee whose social security numbers did not match government records. Passports would be required to exit and enter the United States, even for U.S. citizens. This new law would have a serious impact on the agricultural, hotel, cleaning, and restaurant industries, and have the greatest impact on California.

Another law passed in 2005 as a result of the events of September 11, 2001, which also affects immigration, is the REAL ID Act of 2005. The act was passed as part of the government's attempt to improve its system of issuing secure identification documents. It requires that a REAL ID license (i.e., new identification requirements on state issued driver's licenses and identification cards) be used for official purposes, as defined by the Department of Homeland Security. These official purposes include accessing a federal facility, boarding a federally-regulated commercial aircraft, and entering nuclear power plants. The Department is expanding the categories under the title "official purposes." The states have been granted an extension until December 31, 2009, to begin issuing new licenses. All licenses and identification cards held by individuals from a state must be compliant by May 10, 2013. The face of the new REAL ID must contain space available for thirty-nine characters for full legal name, address of principal residence, digital photograph, gender, date of birth, signature, document number, and machine-readable technology.

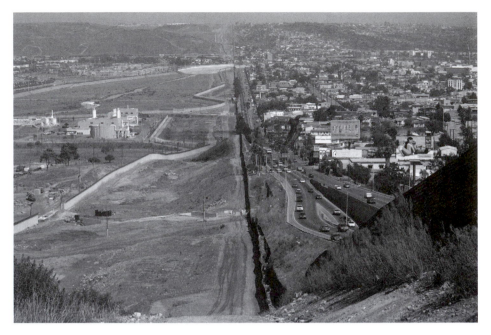

The U.S.-Mexican border (the U.S. is on the left side of the photo). *Gerald L. Nino/U.S. Customs and Border Protection, Department of Homeland Security.*

While the federal government is still debating which laws to pass, state and local governments are passing stricter immigration laws, including those that suspend business licenses of companies hiring illegal immigrants and stricter laws to keep illegal immigrants out of state colleges and universities.

U.S. Citizenship: Becoming a Legal Immigrant and Permanent U.S. Resident. The following is a summary of the basic steps required to become a legal immigrant in the United States and then to obtain permanent residence:

1. Petition is filed with the U.S. Citizenship and Immigration Services (USCIS) by a relative or employer on behalf of the immigrant.
2. Petition is approved by the USCIS.
3. Immigrant visa number is assigned.
4. Immigrants already inside the United States may apply for permanent residence status. Immigrants outside the United States must go to their local U.S. consulate to complete the processing for the immigrant visa.
5. Applicants for permanent residence status may apply for a work permit while their case is pending.
6. While the permanent residence status is pending, permission, called *advance parole*, must be granted before an applicant can leave the United States; if not obtained, the applicant's application for permanent residence will be abandoned and they may not be able to reenter the country.
7. A permanent residence card is given; if not granted, the only applications that can be appealed are those based on a marriage that occurred while the application was under review

or those under the Foreign Operations Appropriations Act of 2001 for certain Vietnam, Cambodian, or Laotian nationals.
8. Permanent residence status is conditional if based on a marriage less than two years old on the day permanent residence is granted.

If sponsored by a relative, the relative must meet the following criteria:

• Be a U.S. citizen or lawful permanent U.S. resident
• Provide proof they can support the applicant at one hundred and twenty-five percent above the poverty line

If the sponsor is a U.S. citizen, he or she can sponsor an alien who is a

• husband or wife
• unmarried child under twenty-one years of age
• unmarried son or daughter over twenty-one years old
• married son or daughter of any age
• brother or sister, if the sponsor is at least twenty-one years old
• parent, if the sponsor is at least twenty-one years old

If the sponsor is a lawful permanent resident, they may sponsor an alien who is a(n)

• husband or wife
• unmarried son or daughter of any age

The following preferences are given to aliens seeking U.S. residence:

• First preference: Unmarried adult sons and daughters of U.S. citizens (twenty-one years of age or older)
• Second Preference: Spouses of lawful permanent residents, their unmarried children (under twenty-one), and the unmarried sons and daughters of lawful permanent residents
• Third Preference: Married sons and daughters of U.S. citizens
• Fourth Preference: Brothers and sisters of adult U.S. citizens

The following are four categories for granting permanent residence status based on employment.
Priority workers:

• Foreign nationals of extraordinary ability in the sciences, arts, education, business, or athletics
• Foreign nationals that are outstanding professors or researchers
• Foreign nationals that are managers and executives subject to international transfer to the United States

Professionals with advanced degrees or persons with exceptional ability:

• Foreign nationals of exceptional ability in the sciences, arts, or business
• Foreign nationals that are advanced degree professionals
• Qualified alien physicians who will practice medicine in an area of the United States that is underserved

Skilled or professional workers:

- Foreign national professionals with bachelor degrees (not qualifying for a higher preference category)
- Foreign national skilled workers (minimum two years training and experience)
- Foreign national unskilled workers

Special immigrants:

- Foreign national religious workers
- Employees and former employees of the U.S. government abroad

The State Department has an annual Diversity Lottery Program in which fifty-five thousand immigrant visas are granted to people from countries with low immigrant rates. The department selects one hundred ten thousand applicants to the program because most will not complete the visa process. The program is closed once fifty-five thousand visas are issued or the fiscal year ends. Those chosen are authorized permanent U.S. residency, and may bring their spouse and unmarried children under twenty-one years of age.

Aliens may also apply for permanent residence based on Title 8 of the *Code of Federal Regulations* if they meet the following criteria:

- Entered the United States prior to January 1, 1972
- Have continuously resided in the United States since entry
- Are of good moral character
- Are neither ineligible for citizenship, except for the requirement of five years of lawful permanent residence, nor inadmissible for participation in terrorist activities, certain criminal or security grounds, or for alien smuggling
- Never participated in Nazi persecutions or genocide

The Immigration and Nationality Act also allows for ten thousand immigrant visas to be made annually available to qualified individuals seeking permanent resident status on the basis of their engagement in a new commercial enterprise. The criteria for a new commercial enterprise include the following.

Aliens who establish a new commercial enterprise by

- creating an original business;
- purchasing an existing business and restructuring or reorganizing the business so that a new commercial enterprise results; or
- expanding an existing business by 140 percent of the pre-investment number of jobs or net worth, or retaining all existing jobs in a troubled business that has lost 20 percent of its net worth over the past twelve to twenty-four months; and

Who have invested or are in the process of investing in a new commercial enterprise:

- at least $1,000,000, or
- at least $500,000 where the investment is being made in a "targeted employment area," which is an area that has experienced unemployment of at least 150 percent of

the national average rate or a rural area as designated by the Office of Management and Budget; and

Who are engaged in a new commercial enterprise that will benefit the U.S. economy and

- create full-time employment for at least ten qualified individuals; or maintain the number of existing employees at no less than the pre-investment level for a period of at least two years, where the capital investment is being made in a "troubled business," which is a business that has been in existence for at least two years and that has lost 20 percent of its net worth over the past twelve to twenty-four months.

9

United States Domestic Policy

Domestic policy focuses on developing programs to sustain and improve a country's citizens, businesses, environment, and infrastructure. These programs are established under laws supporting and regulating government agencies, individuals, businesses, and organizations. Laws and regulations provide support to every aspect of citizens' lives including health, social security, social welfare, transportation, environmental protection, equal rights, and emergency assistance. Unlike foreign policy, which is developed by the president and executed by the Department of State, both the executive and legislative branches develop domestic policy. Each of the cabinet-level departments and major independent agencies serves some key role in domestic policy.

The development of domestic policy laws and regulations has become a very complex task for the U.S. government, mainly because of the continual increase in the country's population, its diverse composition, and its evolving economy. In 2007, the U.S. population exceeded three hundred million as compared to seventy-six million in 1900. That is almost a 400 percent increase in a little over a century. The population is composed of groups distinguishable by different races, ethnic groups, age groups, income groups, sexual orientations, and religions. Along with general support from the government, they each seek specific laws and regulations to meet their respective needs. Some of the most controversial issues resulting from such diverse needs include the legalization of gay marriage, abortion rights, the separation of church and state, and the uneven treatment of minorities in the legal system. As the population has grown in size and become more diverse, the United States has evolved from an agricultural economy to an industrial economy to a technological and service-oriented economy. This has required a continuous change in laws to meet the needs of businesses, workers, citizens, and the environment. For example, technological improvements have given way to the need for laws governing the use of e-mail, protecting Internet users from identity theft, regulating electronic business transactions, and prosecuting cyber stalkers.

The political diversity in this nation has also complicated the creation of domestic policies. The passage of laws on such issues as social security, gun control, stem cell research, and the war on drugs has been divided along political lines. Even though the need for strategies to reduce inflation and protect the environment are agreed upon, there is political disagreement on what laws should be developed and then how they should be executed. Even with these and other challenges, each president focuses on key domestic issues and works diligently to obtain congressional support for the passage of associated laws. Agencies interpret laws passed, institute programs, and execute strategies to meet the goals of domestic policies established.

THE EXECUTIVE BRANCH AND U.S. DOMESTIC POLICY

Presidential Domestic Policies.   Each president establishes domestic policy based on pertinent issues during their time in office. Some have only focused on a few issues due to the circumstances of their term in office. For example, President Abraham Lincoln's domestic policies were chiefly focused on the issues surrounding the Civil War and the war itself. President George W. Bush's primary focus was on combating foreign terrorist threats to the United States after the events of September 11, 2001. Other presidents have focused on a variety of issues under the umbrella of a large plan to improve the nation. For example, President Franklin D. Roosevelt's New Deal included a sequence of programs and policies to reform the economy due to the Great Depression of 1929. It included laws to improve social welfare, reform the banking system, provide reforms for businesses and workers, and led to the creation of numerous federal agencies to execute programs developed. He approved many legislative acts, including the Agricultural Adjustment At of 1933 (which paid farmers not to produce goods that were already in over-supply), the National Housing Act of 1934 (which increased bank loans to businesses building homes and business establishments), and the Federal Securities Act of 1934 (which required stocks to be sold with full and true information). Some of the agencies established were the Tennessee Valley Authority, Federal Housing Administration, and the Securities and Exchange Commission.

Domestic policy is more difficult for the president to develop than foreign policy because the issues directly affect citizens and are generally more controversial because citizens generally have a much better understanding of and increased attention toward the issues and impact of domestic policies. For example, the average citizen may not understand the repercussions of imposing sanctions on a foreign country but will be very interested in a proposed tax increase on wages. The president carefully chooses which events outside of the United States to respond to, but must provide more urgent attention to major events inside the country. For example, the United States tries to avoid getting involved in civil wars within the boundaries of a foreign country but cannot ignore conflicts between two U.S. states. The following are examples of domestic policies under various presidents (during their term in office).

President John Adams's presidency (1797–1801) was engrossed in trying to continue the nation's democratic growth after the Revolutionary War, while dealing with bipartisan disputes between the Federalists (Adams's Party) and Democratic-Republicans (founded by Thomas Jefferson and James Monroe). He issued four laws that were collectively called the Alien and Sedition Acts. These acts set stringent laws for aliens, including deportation during peacetime, longer years in the United States before being eligible to apply for citizenship, and strong legal actions (including imprisonment and deportation) for aliens of nations with which the United States was at war. It also made it illegal to speak or publish "false, scandalous, and malicious" statements against the government or federal officials. Although the laws were partly passed due to the U.S. conflict with France, it was also intended to end political opposition from the Democratic-Republicans. The grandson of Benjamin Franklin, a Democratic-Republican, was even arrested for printing negative comments about President Adams. The laws were extremely unpopular and President Thomas Jefferson pardoned those convicted under the Sedition Act when he won the next election, and Congress restored the fines they were forced to pay as part of their punishment.

President Theodore Roosevelt (1901–1909) focused on protecting citizens by fighting business corruption and trusts. Trusts were large companies that created monopolies by implementing strategies to curb or prevent competition. President Roosevelt's policies were called the Square Deal because he sought to force large companies to develop honest relationships with their workers and customers. For example, the Hepburn Act of 1906 expanded the powers of the nation's first regulatory agency, the Interstate Commerce Commission, to regulate railroad rates so customers would be charged fairly. In 1902, he used the Sherman Antitrust Act of 1890 to successfully break up the Northern Securities Company, a large railroad conglomerate. He filed suits against almost fifty other major corporations over the next seven years. He pushed Congress to pass laws to improve the safety of food and drugs. The Pure Food and Drug Act of 1906 required products to be labeled properly, and established laws for the safe production and distribution of food, drugs, medicines, and liquors. The Meat Inspection Act of 1906 allowed the government to inspect meat production facilities. All animals had to be inspected by the U.S. Drug Administration before being slaughtered, and standards of cleanliness were established for slaughterhouses and processing plants. President Roosevelt also focused on environmental conservation. He created wildlife preserves, urged Congress to create the National Forest Service in 1905, and established National Parks throughout the United States. He appointed a professional conservationist, Gifford Pinchot, to oversee the national forests as head of the National Forest Service. Pinchot is known today as the Father of American conservation.

President Harry S. Truman's (1945–1953) Fair Deal policies were an extension of President Roosevelt's New Deal. He attempted to implement housing for low-income families, conservation initiatives, stronger social security, and civil rights for African Americans. Among the legislation passed under his administration was the Social Security Act of 1935 (which increased benefits to the elderly), the Fair Labor Standards Act of 1938 (which increased the minimum wage), the GI Bill of Rights of 1944 (which provided tuition assistance to veterans), the Employment Act of 1946 (which helped stabilize the economy after World War II), the Agriculture Act of 1949 (which provided support to farmers), and the Housing Act of 1954 (which provided affordable housing). President Truman created the first President's Committee on Civil Rights in 1946 under Executive Order 9808. The passage of the National Security Act of 1947 created the Central Intelligence Agency. President Truman's Executive Order 9981, signed in 1948, barred discrimination in the federal government and the armed forces.

President Lyndon B. Johnson (1963–1969) focused on the passage of legislation that was part of President John F. Kennedy's New Frontier program after President Kennedy was assassinated. President Johnson was his vice president and assumed the Presidency in 1963. He succeeded in getting President Kennedy's Civil Rights bill passed in 1964 (Civil Rights Act of 1964). He reduced the U.S. budget from $101.5 billion to $97.9 billion due to the passage of an $11.5 billion tax cut. He also began the War on Poverty in 1964 and later pushed through other legislation that was part of his Great Society program. This program focused on improving the social and personal welfare of the American people. Some of the programs established and legislation passed included Medicare (medical insurance for senior citizens), Medicaid (hospital care for poor senior citizens), the Economic Opportunity Act of 1964 (which provided training for disadvantaged youths and volunteers to work in low-income areas), the Higher Education Act of 1965 (which gave funds to colleges and universities), the Voting Rights Act of 1965 (which ended literacy tests as a qualification to vote), the Omnibus Housing Act of 1965 (which provided funds for low-income housing and assistance to small businesses), and the Air Quality Act of 1967 (which created automobile emission standards). The financial obligations and national opposition to the Vietnam War later affected the ability of the executive branch to execute President Johnson's policies. President Johnson faced growing antiwar sentiment by individuals and groups in the United States and was unsuccessful in negotiating a peace settlement to end the war.

President Richard M. Nixon (1969–1974) focused on welfare policy, civil rights, law enforcement, and the environment. In 1969, he passed the Philadelphia Plan, the first affirmative action legislation, which required a percentage of jobs on federally funded construction projects to be set aside for minorities. He increased funding to the Equal Employment Opportunity Commission, and proposed legislation that created the Occupational Safety and Health Administration (1970) and the Environmental Protection Agency (1970). Under his administration, Supplemental Security Income was established in 1972 to provide guaranteed income for the elderly, blind, and disabled. Cost-of-living adjustments for Social Security recipients were established, and programs such as food stamps and low-income family health insurance were expanded. Under his New Federalism program, President Nixon attempted to restore more power to the states and municipalities because he disliked large government programs, and believed the federal bureaucracy hindered entrepreneurship and created social dependency on government services. For example, he successfully established biracial state committees to resolve the desegregation of public schools in the south rather than attempt to force desegregation using federal force.

After the Watergate scandal and the resignation of President Nixon, President Gerald R. Ford's (1974–1977) was a "caretaker administration" in regard to domestic policy. In other words, the executive branch was viewed so negatively because of Watergate that it found it difficult to gain the confidence of the American people. President Ford further angered many in the American public when he granted Nixon a full pardon for his role in the scandal in 1974. However, President Ford believed a pardon was the only way the country could move away from the scandal. While Henry Kissinger (appointed by President Nixon as secretary of state) remained in office and continued to focus on foreign policy directives established under President Nixon, President Ford turned his attention to the U.S. economy. The Arab oil embargo by the Organization of the Petroleum Exporting Countries (OPEC) led to a quadrupling of oil prices. This caused *stagflation* in the U.S. economy, a combination of rising inflation and a national recession. In 1974, prices on goods rose more than 10 percent and unemployment exceeded 9 percent. President Ford and the majority-led Democratic Congress were at odds on economic strategies. He vetoed at least fifty new bills that he believed unnecessarily increased federal spending but did little to help the economy recover. He appealed to citizens to help fight inflation as part of his Whip Inflation Now initiative. In a televised speech on October 8, 1974, he stated, "Here is what we must do, what each and every one of you can do: To help increase food and lower prices, grow more and waste less; to help save scarce fuel in the energy crisis, drive less, heat less. Every housewife knows almost exactly how much she spent for food last week. If you cannot spare a penny from your food budget, and I know there are many, surely you can cut the food that you waste by five percent." The initiative was a public relations and policy failure. The economy did eventually begin to show signs of improvement by mid-1976. However, President Ford lost his incumbent campaign for reelection.

President Jimmy Carter's (1977–1981) domestic policy strategies were mostly ineffective at improving rising inflation and the energy crisis of the time. He was viewed as indecisive because of his frequent changes in policies. President Carter's appointment of Paul Volcker as chairman of the Federal Reserve Board in 1979 further harmed the U.S. economy. In an effort to control inflation, Volcker raised interest rates to unprecedented levels, which caused a severe recession. President Carter was easily defeated during his bid for reelection. Republican candidate Ronald W. Reagan received 91 percent of the electoral college votes. The Republicans also gained control of the Senate for the first time since 1954.

When President Ronald W. Reagan (1981–1989) took office, he pledged to reduce the size of government. He also pledged to rejuvenate the economy by cutting taxes, which would lead to increased consumer spending. In 1981, Congress approved his program to reduce income taxes by 25 percent over a three-year period, cut federal spending on social programs, and greatly increase military spending. The economy experienced a recovery from the high inflation and the recession of the 1970s and President Reagan's popularity soared. The only major political harm to his popularity resulted in 1987 as an outcome of the Iran-Contra Scandal, when it was revealed that the Reagan administration had secretly sold arms to Iran in exchange for American hostages and illegally used the profits to fund the contras (rebels fighting the government in Nicaragua). The revenue projections made by President Reagan's administration did not materialize and the United States' debt reached record levels. By the end of his administration, the United States had the world's largest national debt.

Many of the domestic initiatives launched by President George H. W. Bush's (1989–1993) administration were in an adversarial role against a majority-led Democratic Congress. As the economy suffered and the federal deficit increased, President Bush was forced to retract his "no new taxes" campaign pledge of 1988. This caused him to lose political support, particularly from previously loyal conservatives, and led to reelection challenges from within his Republican party during the 1992 election. However, President Bush did achieve some domestic policy successes. One of his greatest domestic accomplishments was the passage of the Americans with Disabilities Act of 1990, which eased legal and physical obstacles to citizens with disabilities and was one of the most sweeping pieces of civil rights legislation in a decade. He worked to increase federal spending for education, child care, and advanced technology research and development. He signed legislation improving the nation's interstate highway system. In 1989, Bush released a comprehensive plan to bail out the suffering savings and loan industry. Congress reacted by rewriting regulations and creating the Resolution Trust Corporation to take over bankrupt savings and loan associations and sell off their assets. The Clean Air Act of 1990 established higher standards for air quality and required cleaner burning fuels.

In 1991, Bush proposed the North American Free Trade Agreement (NAFTA) among the United States, Mexico, and Canada, which would lower or eliminate tariffs on trade among the three nations. The proposal was designed to help North America compete against the growing free-trade zones of Europe and Asia. The agreement was not reached under President Bush but was later championed by President Bill Clinton and enacted in 1993. President Bush's administration also faced the challenge of dealing with the greatest business failures in history. In 2001, Enron declared bankruptcy because of accounting fraud. At that time it was the biggest business failure in history. Its failure was surpassed by WorldCom in 2002, which also failed because of accounting fraud. WorldCom had improperly recorded over $3 billion in expenses. At the time it filed for bankruptcy, it reported assets of $107 billion and had accumulated $41 billion in debt. Enron had reported approximately $63 billion in assets when it filed for bankruptcy. The government responded to these and other major business failures by passing the Sarbanes-Oxley Act of 2002. Also known as the Public Company Accounting Reform and Investor Protection Act of 2002, the act established the Public Company Accounting Oversight Board to regulate accounting and auditing firms to ensure the proper disclosure of accounting and financial records.

President Bill Clinton (1993–2001) focused on a diverse array of domestic policy issues during his two terms in office. The nation was facing a slow economy, violent drug-related crime, poverty, a need for welfare reform, issues with race relations, and high health care costs. The president tackled the issue of gays being open in the military but faced strong opposition from conservatives and military leaders. The end result was a compromise described by the phrase "don't ask, don't tell."

The president attempted to tackle the sluggish economy and campaign reforms with an economic stimulus package and a campaign finance reform bill. Both pieces of proposed legislation were blocked by a Republican filibuster in the Senate. He also faced challenges in reducing health care costs. While campaigning for the presidency, President Clinton promised to institute a system of universal health insurance. He appointed his wife, Hillary R. Clinton, to chair a task force on health care reform. This appointment was criticized as a conflict of interest. None of the task force's recommendations were ever formally submitted to Congress. President Clinton was, however, able to achieve numerous domestic policy successes. He achieved the most diverse federal government in history. He appointed women and minorities to significant posts throughout his administration, including Janet Reno as the first female Attorney General, Donna Shalala as secretary of health and human services, Joycelyn Elders as surgeon general, Madeleine Albright as the first female secretary of state, and Ruth Bader Ginsburg as a Supreme Court justice. The president signed over thirty bills related to women and family issues, including the Family and Medical Leave Act of 1993 and the Brady Handgun Violence Prevention Act of 1993. The Family and Medical Leave Act required covered employers to grant an eligible employee up to a total of twelve work weeks of unpaid leave during any twelve-month period for the birth and care of a newborn child; placement with the employee of a son or daughter for adoption or foster care; to care for an immediate family member (spouse, child, or parent) with a serious health condition; or to take medical leave when the employee was unable to work because of a serious health condition. The Brady Handgun and Violence Prevention Act strengthened laws to acquire a hand gun. President Clinton's policies also resulted in the nation achieving the longest period of economic expansion in decades, and the first balanced budget in thirty years.

President George W. Bush (2001–2009) also focused on an array of domestic policy issues, including immigration and border control, the reforming of the nation's tax code, legal liability procedures covering medical malpractice, and class-action lawsuits. He attempted to reform the Social Security retirement system by proposing workers be given their Social Security withholdings to fund their own private retirement accounts. This plan was never instituted. President Bush's national approval rating suffered as a result of deployed U.S. troops to the war in Iraq, but decreased even more because of the slow response of the government to the devastation caused by Hurricane Katrina in Louisiana, Alabama, Mississippi, and Florida. The president responded by promising government reforms, particularly in the Department of Homeland Security, and federal assistance to those harmed. President Bush attempted to tackle illegal immigration by proposing a "guest worker" program that would grant immigrants legal status and the opportunity for eventual citizenship. His proposal was criticized by many conservatives as an ineffective means to solve the problem. One significant piece of legislation passed by Congress under the Bush administration included a bankruptcy-reform law (the Bankruptcy Abuse Prevention and Consumer Protection Act of 2005). The president's overall focus on domestic policy was overshadowed by the war in the Middle East and War on Terrorism after the events of September 11, 2001.

Members of the president's cabinet may also develop policies or take actions as part of the executive branch's domestic policy agenda. Each head of the executive branch departments formulates policies to support the areas their departments are in charge of. These actions may have positive or negative consequences. For example, President Woodrow Wilson appointed Alexander Mitchell Palmer as the U.S. attorney general from 1919 to 1921. In 1920, Palmer ordered the arrest of persons within the United States suspected of being involved in communist activities. He based his authority on the Espionage Act of 1917 and the Sedition Act of 1918. During this "Red Scare," federal agents and local law enforcement officials arrested up to six thousand people. Agents searched homes without search warrants, held suspects for long periods of time without formally charging them, and denied them legal representation. Aliens were deported to Finland and Russia.

The Espionage Act of 1917 had been passed after World War I and made it illegal to spread any information that interfered with the operation and success of the military to promote enemies. Persons in violation of the act faced a $10,000 fine and twenty years in prison. Additional penalties were levied on anyone refusing to perform their military duties. After its enactment almost one thousand people were charged with violating the act and sentenced to prison. The Sedition Act of 1918 was passed as an amendment to the Espionage Act, making it illegal when the United States is at war to interfere with the military, promote the success of enemies, obstruct the government's raising of war funds, or attempt to cause "insubordination, disloyalty, mutiny, or refusal of duty" of military forces, or make negative statements about the government, Constitution, military, or the U.S. flag. Members of the U.S. government committing any disloyal act or uttering any unpatriotic language would be immediately fired. The postmaster general was given the authority to suspend mail delivery to anyone suspected of sending or receiving mail in violation of the act.

Presidential Executive Orders.   The president issues executive orders to execute domestic policies. Presidents issue these orders under statutory authority granted by congressional legislation and their explicit executive power granted in Article II, Section 1, of the Constitution. Executive orders give specific guidance to executive branch departments, federal officers, and agencies. Agencies issue rules and regulations to further outline how executive orders will be implemented. The president cannot issue an executive order that contradicts an existing law. Orders specifically cannot make new laws.

There have only been two executive orders overturned by the courts. Using Executive Order 10340 President Harry S. Truman sought to place all U.S. steel mills under the possession and operation of the Department of Commerce to avert a national catastrophe from the possible stoppage of steel production due to labor disputes. In *Youngstown Sheet and Tube Co. v. Sawyer*, 343 U.S. 579 (1952), the Supreme Court ruled the order was invalid because its mandate created a new law that had not been authorized by congressional enactment. On March 8, 1995, President Bill Clinton issued Executive Order 12954 that banned the federal government from contracting with companies that permanently replaced lawfully striking employees. The stated purpose of the order was "to ensure the economical and efficient administration and completion of Federal Government contracts" because the costs of produced goods would increase when skilled striking workers were replaced by less skillful workers. The order explained, "By permanently replacing its workers, an employer loses the accumulated knowledge, experience, skill, and expertise of its incumbent employees. These circumstances then adversely affect the businesses and entities, such as the Federal Government, which rely on that employer to provide high quality and reliable goods or services." The order was struck down by the Court of Appeals for the District of Columbia Circuit on February 2, 1996, in the case *Chamber of Commerce of the United States, et al. v. Reich*, 74 F.3d 1322 (D.C. Cir 1996). The Court ruled the order violated laws passed by Congress, specifically the National Labor Relations Act of 1935, and overstepped the authority granted to the president in the Procurement Act of 1949 (also called the Federal Property and Administrative Services Act of 1949), and was therefore unconstitutional. The 1935 act guaranteed the right of employees to organize and collectively bargain with employers, and to engage in such protected activities as peaceful strikes. The 1949 act gave the president authority to prescribe policies and directives to ensure an economical and efficient system for the procurement of federal goods and supplies, but not to pass laws.

The following are examples of executive orders related to domestic policy issued by other presidents. President Franklin D. Roosevelt established the Rio Grande Wild Life Refuge in New Mexico under Executive Order 6086 in 1933. This refuge area covering approximately seventy-three thousand acres was established for the protection of native birds and wild animals. It made the following acts unlawful:

> (a) to hunt, trap, capture, willfully disturb, or kill any wild animal or bird of any kind whatever, to take or destroy the nests or eggs of any wild bird, to occupy or use any part of the reservation or to enter thereon for any purpose, except under such rules and regulations as may be prescribed by the Secretary of Agriculture; (b) to cut, burn, or destroy any timber, underbrush, grass, or other natural growth; (c) willfully to leave fire or to suffer it to burn unattended near any forest, timber, or other inflammable material; (d) after building a fire in or near any forest, timber, or other inflammable material, to leave it without extinguishing it; and (e) willfully to injure, molest, or destroy any property of the United States.

Executive Order 10925, signed by President John F. Kennedy in 1961, used the term "affirmative action" for the first time. It required federal contractors to take "affirmative action to ensure that applicants are employed, and that employees are treated during employment, without regard to their race, creed, color, or national origin," and established the Committee on Equal Employment Opportunity. The committee was tasked to "recommend additional affirmative steps which should be taken by executive departments and agencies to realize more fully the national policy of nondiscrimination within the Executive Branch of the Government," enforce all provisions of the order, and recommend sanctions and penalties to the Department of Justice for action.

Executive Order 11246, originally signed by President Lyndon B. Johnson in 1965 and amended in 1967, prohibited employment discrimination by federal contractors and subcontractors who do over $10,000 in annual business with the federal government. The U.S. Department of Labor's Office of Federal Contract Compliance Programs was assigned the responsibility of administering and enforcing the order. The order mandated that contractors;

> will not discriminate against any employee or applicant for employment because of race, color, religion, sex, or national origin. The contractor will take affirmative action to ensure that applicants are employed, and that employees are treated during employment, without regard to their race, color, religion, sex or national origin. Such action shall include, but not be limited to the following: employment, upgrading, demotion, or transfer; recruitment or recruitment advertising; layoff or termination; rates of pay or other forms of compensation; and selection for training, including apprenticeship. The contractor agrees to post in conspicuous places, available to employees and applicants for employment, notices to be provided by the contracting officer setting forth the provisions of this nondiscrimination clause.

President Jimmy Carter issued Executive Order 12138 in 1979. It mandated that executive branch departments and agencies take actions to "facilitate, preserve and strengthen women's business enterprise and to ensure full participation by women in the free enterprise system." It created the Interagency Committee on Women's Business Enterprise. The order stated the following:

> For purposes of this Order, affirmative action may include, but is not limited to, creating or supporting new programs responsive to the special needs of women's business enterprise, establishing incentives to promote business or business-related opportunities for women's business enterprise, collecting and disseminating information in support of women's business enterprise, and insuring to women's business enterprise knowledge of and ready access to business-related services and resources. If, in implementing this Order, an agency undertakes to use or to require compliance with numerical set-asides, or similar measures, it shall state the purpose of such measure, and the measure shall be designed on the basis of pertinent factual findings of discrimination against women's business enterprise and the need for such measure.

President Ronald W. Reagan's Executive Order 12358, issued in 1982, established the Presidential Commission on Drunk Driving to aid the states in combating drunk driving. The order established the commission to heighten public awareness of the seriousness of drunk driving; persuade the states and local communities to develop more organized and systematic strategies to arrest and sentence drunk drivers; ensure that states and localities use the latest techniques and methods to solve the problem; and generate public support for the increased enforcement of state and local drunk driving laws.

Executive Order 13160, signed by President Bill Clinton on June 23, 2000, mandated nondiscrimination in federally conducted education and training programs on the basis of race, sex, color, national origin, disability, religion, age, sexual orientation, and status as a parent. Examples of areas covered under the order include, but are not limited to, access to formal schools, extracurricular activities, academic programs, occupational training, scholarships and fellowships, student internships, training for industry members, summer enrichment camps, and teacher training programs.

President George W. Bush issued Executive Order 13410 in 2006 to improve the quality and efficiency of health care services provided by the federal government. The order mandated agencies to:

> Ensure that health care programs administered or sponsored by the Federal Government promote quality and efficient delivery of health care through the use of health information technology, transparency regarding health care quality and price, and better incentives for program beneficiaries, enrollees, and providers. It is the further purpose of this order to make relevant information available to these beneficiaries, enrollees, and providers in a readily useable manner and in collaboration with similar initiatives in the private sector and non-Federal public sector. Consistent with the purpose of improving the quality and efficiency of health care, the actions and steps taken by Federal Government agencies should not incur additional costs for the Federal Government.

Domestic Policy Council.   The president develops domestic policy with the assistance of the Domestic Policy Council (DPC). The DPC is part of the White House office and advises the president on domestic policy issues, coordinates policy making across the executive branch, ensures domestic policy is implemented, and represents the president to the other branches. The foundation of the DPC was created under President Lyndon B. Johnson by a senior-level aide who developed domestic policy. However, there was not a formal staff of personnel dedicated to domestic issues. President Richard M. Nixon created the Domestic Council under Executive Order 11541 in 1970. It merged various functions by replacing the Council for Urban Affairs, the Cabinet Committee on the Environment, and the Council for Rural Affairs. As part of the executive office of the president, the Domestic Council was charged with the following responsibilities:

1. Receive and develop information necessary for assessing national domestic needs and defining national domestic goals, and develop for the president alternative proposals for reaching those goals
2. Collaborate with the Office of Management and Budget and others in the determination of national domestic priorities for the allocation of available resources
3. Collaborate with the Office of Management and Budget and others to assure a continuing review of ongoing programs from the standpoint of their relative contributions to national goals as compared with their use of available resources
4. Provide policy advice to the president on domestic issues

President Bill Clinton issued Executive Order 12859 on August 16, 1993, which created the current DPC. Under the order, the following are the principal functions of the DPC:

> (1) coordinate the domestic policy-making process; (2) coordinate domestic policy advice to the president; (3) ensure that domestic policy decisions and programs are consistent with the president's stated goals, and to ensure that those goals are being

effectively pursued; and (4) monitor implementation of the president's domestic policy agenda.

The DPC has a large membership. It consists of the president (who serves as the chairman), the vice president, secretary of health and human services, attorney general, secretary of labor, secretary of veterans affairs, secretary of the interior, secretary of education, secretary of housing and urban development, secretary of agriculture, secretary of transportation, secretary of commerce, secretary of energy, secretary of the treasury, administrator of the environmental protection agency, chair of the council of economic advisers, director of the office of management and budget, assistant to the president for economic policy, assistant to the president for domestic policy, assistant to the president and director of the office of national service, senior advisor to the president for policy development, director of office of national drug control policy, aids policy coordinator, and other officials within the executive branch as designated by the president. The DPC's staff is headed by the assistant to the president for domestic policy.

Some of the major issues the council addressed under President Bill Clinton included health care, education, crime, consumer protection, children and families, tobacco, and welfare reform. Under President George W. Bush, the council oversaw such domestic policy areas as education, health, housing, welfare, justice, federalism, transportation, environment, labor and veteran's affairs.

THE LEGISLATIVE BRANCH AND U.S. DOMESTIC POLICY

Legislatures have a major stake in the outcomes of domestic policy programs and are actively involved in domestic politics. They have the potential of losing elections due to the passing of unpopular policies (including laws and regulations), or because policies have a negative impact on their constituents. Congressmen are elected based on the beliefs of their constituents that their interests will be represented in Congress. Lobbyists get directly involved in domestic issues on behalf of their clients and interest groups expend considerable resources attempting to protect their needs. They exert energy in attempting to influence domestic policy laws passed by Congress (see section, "Interest Groups and Lobbyists" in Chapter 5).

The legislative branch has influence in affecting domestic policy because Congress must approve any proposals by the president through the passage of laws. The political party makeup of Congress has a significant impact on whether policies issued by the president will be accepted or rejected by Congress. The president must gain support both from members of their own party as well as from members of the opposing party to gain passage of proposed legislation. This is sometimes a difficult task and requires skillful negotiation on the part of the president and the president's staff to reach compromise. Table 9.1 shows the political parties of the majority of members (i.e., political party control) of each chamber of Congress since 1901 versus that of the president in office during each session of Congress. As shown, there have been many sessions of Congress where the party control of the House of Representatives, the Senate, or both chambers differed from that of the president. For example, Republican President Gerald R. Ford and the majority-led Democratic Congress were at odds on economic strategies. He vetoed at least fifty new bills that he believed unnecessarily increased federal spending but did little to help the economy recover.

Table 9.1. Political Party Control in Each Session of Congress, 1900–2008

Session of Congress	Session years	President in office	President's political party	Majority party in the House	Majority party in the Senate
57	1901–1903	Theodore Roosevelt	Republican	Republican	Republican
58	1903–1905	Theodore Roosevelt	Republican	Republican	Republican
59	1905–1907	Theodore Roosevelt	Republican	Republican	Republican
60	1907–1909	Theodore Roosevelt	Republican	Republican	Republican
61	1909–1911	William H. Taft	Republican	Republican	Republican
62	1911–1913	William H. Taft	Republican	Democrat	Republican
63	1913–1915	Woodrow Wilson	Democrat	Democrat	Democrat
64	1915–1917	Woodrow Wilson	Democrat	Democrat	Democrat
65	1917–1919	Woodrow Wilson	Democrat	Democrat	Democrat
66	1919–1921	Woodrow Wilson	Democrat	Republican	Republican
67	1921–1923	Warren G. Harding	Republican	Republican	Republican
68	1923–1925	Calvin Coolidge	Republican	Republican	Republican
69	1925–1927	Calvin Coolidge	Republican	Republican	Republican
70	1927–1929	Calvin Coolidge	Republican	Republican	Republican
71	1929–1931	Herbert C. Hoover	Republican	Republican	Republican
72	1931–1933	Herbert C. Hoover	Republican	Democrat	Republican
73	1933–1935	Franklin D. Roosevelt	Democrat	Democrat	Democrat
74	1935–1937	Franklin D. Roosevelt	Democrat	Democrat	Democrat
75	1937–1939	Franklin D. Roosevelt	Democrat	Democrat	Democrat
76	1939–1941	Franklin D. Roosevelt	Democrat	Democrat	Democrat
77	1941–1943	Franklin D. Roosevelt	Democrat	Democrat	Democrat
78	1943–1945	Franklin D. Roosevelt	Democrat	Democrat	Democrat
79	1945–1947	Harry S. Truman	Democrat	Democrat	Democrat
80	1947–1949	Harry S. Truman	Democrat	Republican	Democrat
81	1949–1951	Harry S. Truman	Democrat	Democrat	Democrat
82	1951–1953	Harry S. Truman	Democrat	Democrat	Democrat
83	1953–1955	Dwight D. Eisenhower	Republican	Republican	Republican
84	1955–1957	Dwight D. Eisenhower	Republican	Democrat	Democrat
85	1957–1959	Dwight D. Eisenhower	Republican	Democrat	Democrat
86	1959–1961	Dwight D. Eisenhower	Republican	Democrat	Democrat
87	1961–1963	John F. Kennedy	Democrat	Democrat	Democrat
88	1963–1965	John F. Kennedy / Lyndon B. Johnson	Democrat	Democrat	Democrat
89	1965–1967	Lyndon B. Johnson	Democrat	Democrat	Democrat
90	1967–1969	Lyndon B. Johnson	Democrat	Democrat	Democrat
91	1969–1971	Richard M. Nixon	Republican	Democrat	Democrat
92	1971–1973	Richard M. Nixon	Republican	Democrat	Democrat

(*Continued*)

Table 9.1.   (Continued)

Session of Congress	Session years	President in office	President's political party	Majority party in the House	Majority party in the Senate
93	1973–1975	Richard M. Nixon / Gerald R. Ford	Republican	Democrat	Democrat
94	1975–1977	Gerald R. Ford	Republican	Democrat	Democrat
95	1977–1979	Jimmy Carter	Democrat	Democrat	Democrat
96	1979–1981	Jimmy Carter	Democrat	Democrat	Democrat
97	1981–1983	Ronald W. Reagan	Republican	Democrat	Republican
98	1983–1985	Ronald W. Reagan	Republican	Democrat	Republican
99	1985–1987	Ronald W. Reagan	Republican	Democrat	Republican
100	1987–1989	Ronald W. Reagan	Republican	Democrat	Democrat
101	1989–1991	George H. W. Bush	Republican	Democrat	Democrat
102	1991–1993	George H. W. Bush	Republican	Democrat	Democrat
103	1993–1995	Bill Clinton	Democrat	Democrat	Democrat
104	1995–1997	Bill Clinton	Democrat	Republican	Republican
105	1997–1999	Bill Clinton	Democrat	Republican	Republican
106	1999–2001	Bill Clinton	Democrat	Republican	Republican
107	2001–2003	George W. Bush	Republican	Republican	Democrat
108	2003–2005	George W. Bush	Republican	Republican	Republican
109	2005–2007	George W. Bush	Republican	Republican	Republican
110	2007–2008	George W. Bush	Republican	Democrat	Democrat

Democratic President Bill Clinton faced a majority Republican Congress for most of his two terms in office. His health care reform proposals were a major part of his domestic policy agenda, but he was unable to gain support from the Republican controlled Congress. President George W. Bush faced the first congressional override of one of his vetoes after seven years in office after the Democrats gained control of Congress. This process of opposing issues based on political parties is called *partisanship*. Legislatures can also propose laws affecting domestic policy, but must gain support from the president to prevent a presidential veto (which Congress can override with a two-thirds vote in each chamber).

The Committee on Oversight and Government is located within the House of Representatives. It has jurisdiction over the investigation of any federal program or policy. One of its subcommittees is the Domestic Policy Subcommittee, which conducts investigations, holds hearings, and provides reports that identify waste, fraud, and abuse, and the need for new legislation on domestic policy issues. The subcommittee attempts to "act as the eyes and ears of consumers, workers and businesses." Some examples of issues the committee has focused attention include law enforcement in New Orleans after Hurricane Katrina, deficiencies in state and federal gun purchase laws, predatory lending, and Medicaid programs providing dental care access to children.

Interstate 10 in New Orleans, looking toward Lake Pontchartrain, after Hurricane Katrina in late August 2005. *Petty Officer 2nd Class Kyle Niemi/U.S. Coast Guard.*

Specific issues are addressed by the applicable committees and subcommittees within the House and Senate. For example, the Senate Committee on Commerce, Science, and Transportation oversees issues including communications, highways, aviation, rail, shipping, transportation security, merchant marine, the Coast Guard, oceans, fisheries, climate change, disasters, science, space, interstate commerce, tourism, consumer issues, economic development, technology, competitiveness, product safety, and insurance. Its subcommittees include Aviation Operations, Safety, and Security; Consumer Affairs, Insurance, and Automotive Safety; Interstate Commerce, Trade, and Tourism; Oceans, Atmosphere, Fisheries, and Coast Guard; Science, Technology, and Innovation; Space, Aeronautics, and Related Sciences; and Surface Transportation and Merchant Marine Infrastructure, Safety, and Security.

THE INFLUENCE OF CITIZENS ON DOMESTIC POLICY: EXAMPLES

Citizens have considerable impact on domestic policy decisions made by the executive and legislative branches. The foundation of citizens' power lies in the ability to vote for those they believe will best represent their interests. Beyond this, citizens can organize to influence political decisions. The collective power of citizens acting in informal and formal groups and organizations to influence government action is perhaps the most profound aspect of the democracy. The United States was founded by the colonists acting as a unified body to end British control. Many instances of groups influencing change by the U.S. government have occurred since. Two examples of have been the civil rights movement and the women's suffrage movement.

The Civil Rights Movement's Influence on Domestic Policy.   In 1892, a group of Louisiana citizens challenged segregated laws that required African Americans to ride in separate rail cars. Homer Plessy, an African American who sat in the "Whites Only" rail car, was arrested for violating segregation laws that were common across much of the South. The case was taken to court and reached the Supreme Court four years later. In *Plessy v. Ferguson*, 163 U.S. 537 (1896), the Court's decision provided legal support for segregation by ruling "separate but equal" accommodations supported the Equal Protection Clause of the Fourteenth Amendment. In other words, it supported segregation as long as the separate accommodations provided blacks were equal to those provided to whites. The lone dissenter on the Court was Justice John Marshall Harlan. In his dissent he wrote, "Our constitution is colorblind, and neither knows nor tolerates classes among citizens." The separate but equal doctrine was used across America to justify segregation. During the 1930s and 1940s, the Court began to change its position and finally ended segregation in *Brown v. Board of Education of Topeka*, 347 U.S. 483 (1954). The case arose from a suit by Mr. and Mrs. Oliver Brown who wanted their daughter, Linda Carol Brown, to attend the school that was the nearest to their home. This school was designed for whites only, so the couple was forced to send their daughter to a school approximately twenty-one blocks from their home. The National Association for the Advancement of Colored People (NAACP) assisted the family in filing suit against the local board of education. The Supreme Court ruled segregation by race in public education was unconstitutional, even if separate but equal accommodations were provided. The Supreme Court's ruling was challenged, and, due to legal loopholes, desegregation did not take affect across the country for years.

A year after the *Brown* decision, Rosa Parks, a forty-two-year-old seamstress, challenged segregation laws in Montgomery, Alabama. She boarded a public bus and refused to be reseated in the "colored section" after the bus became crowded. After her arrest, the African American citizens of Montgomery organized and began a boycott of city buses that lasted 381 days. This became the beginning of the civil rights movement to end racial segregation. The bus boycott was led by a twenty-six-year-old Baptist minister who was a new resident to Montgomery, the Reverend Dr. Martin Luther King, Jr. The bus boycott was successful in ending segregation of public transportation in the city and grew into a national movement. It unified the actions of several groups, including the Southern Christian Leadership Conference, Congress of Racial Equality, Student Nonviolent Coordinating Committee, and the NAACP.

Dr. King adopted two strategies to challenge segregation. The first was the use of nonviolent civil disobedience. Civil disobedience is the deliberate and public act of refusing to obey laws that are believed to be unjust. An example of this tactic used during the 1960s were "sit ins," in which demonstrators entered a business, school, or other public place and remained seated until they were forcibly removed or their demands were met. In February 1960, a group of African American students from North Carolina A&T University sat at the "whites only" lunch counters at Woolworth's. Rather than serve the students, the establishment closed the store. More students returned the next day to picket and were verbally and psychically assaulted. Within months, however, the establishment changed its policy and ended segregation practices.

The second, and perhaps most effective, tactic used by Dr. King was to gain media attention to rally national support for the movement. This would focus attention at the federal government level and lead to changes in federal laws. These federal laws would then invalidate local and state segregation laws. This tactic proved to be a success. The civil rights movement gained national and international media attention. In August 1963, Dr. King led the March on Washington for Jobs and Freedom. A. Phillip Randolph developed the idea for the march and it was organized by Bayard Rustin. The purpose of the march was to demonstrate and gain widespread support for legislation that would ban discrimination in every sector of American life. It culminated symbolically on the steps of the Lincoln Memorial and a number of speakers addressed the crowd of two hundred fifty thousand assembled. The highlight of the event was Dr. King's "I Have A Dream" speech, in which he challenged the federal government to end discrimination for all people regardless of color.

The efforts of Dr. King and the millions of others involved in the civil rights movement led to the passage of the Civil Rights Act of 1964. The act banned discrimination on the basis of race, color, religion, gender, and national origin. It outlawed discrimination in public places, mandated federal funds could be withheld from any federal and state project if discrimination was practiced, banned discrimination in employment, outlawed discrimination in voting, and authorized the federal government to sue to desegregate public schools. A year later, Dr. King and other civil rights leaders organized a march from Selma to Montgomery, Alabama, to protest voting rights restrictions still in existence in Alabama. One day of the march became known as "Bloody Sunday" when marchers were attacked with clubs and tear gas by police. The violence was televised around the country and horrified many viewers who were unaware of the treatment of African Americans in some parts of the South. President Lyndon B. Johnson reacted by submitting proposed legislation to Congress that led to the passage of the Voting Rights Act of 1965, which made it illegal to interfere with any citizen's right to vote.

The Influence of the Women's Suffrage Movement on Domestic Policy.   Women have fought for the same rights granted men since the founding of the United States. In 1776, Abigail Adams wrote to her husband, John Adams, one of the nation's founders, and asked that the framers of the Declaration of Independence "remember the ladies" when drafting the document. Women were discriminated against in almost every aspect of public and private American life. They were not allowed equal access to education, paid lower wages for equal work, not allowed to hold public office, and denied the right to vote. Lucretia Mott and Elizabeth Cady Stanton, two American activists in the movement to end slavery, organized the first convention to address

Suffrage parade on Pennsylvania Avenue, Washington, D.C., on March 3, 1913. *George Grantham Bain Collection/Library of Congress Prints and Photographs Division.*

women's right to vote in Seneca Falls, New York, in 1848. Approximately three hundred women attended the Women's Rights Convention and approved a Declaration of Sentiments and Resolutions, based on the Declaration of Independence, which declared that men and women should be treated as equals. The declaration declared, among other things, the following (Stanton, 1889, pp 70–71):

> The history of mankind is a history of repeated injuries and usurpations on the part of man toward woman, having in direct object the establishment of an absolute tyranny over her. To prove this, let facts be submitted to a candid world.
>
> He has never permitted her to exercise her inalienable right to the elective franchise
>
> He has compelled her to submit to laws, in the formation of which she had no voice.
>
> He has withheld from her rights which are given to the most ignorant and degraded men—both natives and foreigners.
>
> Having deprived her of this first right of a citizen, the elective franchise, thereby leaving her without representation in the halls of legislation, he has oppressed her on all sides.

In the years to follow, Mott and Stanton held conventions in various East and Midwest cities to raise awareness of women's suffrage. However, the Civil War slowed the movement. In 1869, the movement regained momentum when Susan B. Anthony and Elizabeth Cady Stanton formed the National Women Suffrage Association (NWSA) in New York. The organization was considered radical in its open criticism of the Fourteenth and Fifteenth Amendment as being discriminatory toward women. The former declared citizens and voters as male, and the latter gave voting rights to black men but not women. The NWSA called for easier means to obtain a divorce, and support for an end to employment and pay discrimination. Its members were also radical in their approach to gain attention to their cause. For example, Susan B. Anthony was arrested and brought to trial in Rochester, New York, for attempting to vote for Ulysses S. Grant in the presidential election. Fifteen other women were arrested for illegally voting.

Believing a more conservation approach was needed to gain voting rights for women, Lucy Stone, Henry B. Blackwell, and Julia Ward Howe formed the American Women Suffrage Association (AWSA) in Boston, Massachusetts, in 1890, focusing solely on suffrage. Also in 1890, Wyoming became the forty-fourth state and was admitted to the United States of America with its suffrage law in place. The NWSA and AWSA merged in 1890 in order to combine their efforts. They formed the National American Woman Suffrage Association (NAWSA), led by Elizabeth Candy Stanton, Susan B. Anthony, Carrie Chapman Catt, Frances Willard, Mary Church Terrell, Matilda Joslyn Gage, and Anna Howard Shaw. The NAWSA represented millions of women and was the national head of hundreds of local and state groups. Gains were made in individual states, but not at the national level. Suffrage was temporarily gained in Utah, but later invalidated by the U.S. Congress. Women first gained the right to vote in the state of Colorado in 1893, and then later in Utah in 1896, Idaho (1896), Washington (1910), and California (1911). The first vote on woman suffrage was introduced in the U.S. Congress in 1878 but was defeated in the Senate.

Many demonstrations occurred in the early twentieth century and other suffrage organizations were formed. In 1903, Mary Dreier, Rheta Childe Dorr, and Leonora O'Reilly formed the Women's Trade Union League of New York, comprised of middle- and working-class women dedicated to unionizing working women and gaining the right to vote. In 1915, forty thousand women marched in a suffrage parade in New York City. Many of the women were dressed in white and carried signs identifying the states they represented. Alice Paul and Lucy Burns organized the Congressional Union in 1913, which later became known as the National Women's Party in 1916. The group borrowed aggressive tactics from the militant Women's Social and Political Union in England and held hunger strikes, picketed the White House, and engaged in other forms of civil disobedience to publicize the suffrage cause. Members were arrested for picketing in front of the White House in 1917, but unconditionally released due to public disapproval of their arrest.

Organizations also formed to oppose voting rights for women. The National Association Opposed to Woman Suffrage was organized in 1911. Its members included wealthy, influential women and Catholic clergymen. They joined with brewers and distillers in contributing to Congressmen and businesses to gain support against women being given voting rights.

In 1916, Jeanette Rankin of Montana became the first woman elected to Congress, in the House of Representatives. She opened debate on a suffrage amendment in the House in 1918, but it failed to gain passage in the Senate. President Woodrow Wilson publicly supported the amendment and personally addressed the Senate at the end of World War I. During the war as men went to war, women served as volunteers and held jobs traditionally held by men. The president believed women should be rewarded for their support of the nation. The Senate passed the Nineteenth Amendment in 1919, granting women the right to vote, and the state legislatures ratified it in 1920. The wording of the amendment was unchanged from the original legislation introduced in 1878. The NAWSA was dissolved in 1920 but became the foundation of the League of Women Voters.

The struggle for women gaining the right to vote was not just a national challenge. American suffragists worked with organizations struggling for the same rights in other countries. New Zealand was the first nation to give women the right the vote in 1893. New Zealand was followed by Australia (1902), Norway (1913), Great Britain (1918), Canada (1918), Germany (1919), the United States (1920), South Africa (1930), Brazil (1932), France (1944), Italy (1945), Japan (1945), Argentina (1947), India (1950), Greece (1952), Mexico (1953), Egypt (1956), Kenya (1963), Switzerland (1963), and Yemen (1984). In some countries, particularly in Middle Eastern countries such as Saudi Arabia, women are still not allowed to vote.

PROTECTING U.S. CITIZENS

The primary goals of each president's domestic policy agenda have been to protect U.S. citizens from harm, and sustain and improve their social welfare. Once these goals are formalized into laws and executive orders, they are executed by executive branch departments and agencies. The following are examples of departments and agencies that execute domestic policy orders, rules, and laws.

Department of Homeland Security. The Department of Homeland Security was established by the National Strategy for Homeland Security and the Homeland Security Act of 2002. This cabinet level department is responsible for preventing terrorist threats and attacks against the United States, and minimizing the damage from attacks and natural disasters. Many executive branch independent agencies and offices have been brought under the Department of Homeland Security into one of its four major directorates. The following outlines the reassignment of operations to the department and indicates (in parenthesis) which Department or agency the operation was moved from:

- The Border and Transportation Security directorate combined major border security and transportation operations:
  - The U.S. Customs Service (Treasury)
  - The Immigration and Naturalization Service (part from Justice)
  - The Federal Protective Service (General Services Administration)
  - The Transportation Security Administration (Transportation)
  - Federal Law Enforcement Training Center (Treasury)
  - Animal and Plant Health Inspection Service (part from Agriculture) and
  - Office of Domestic Preparedness (Justice)

- The Emergency Preparedness and Response directorate oversees domestic disaster preparedness training and coordinates federal disaster response:
  - The Federal Emergency Management Agency
  - Strategic National Stockpile and the National Disaster Medical System (Health and Human Services)
  - Nuclear Incident Response Team (Energy)
  - Domestic Emergency Support Teams (Justice)
  - National Domestic Preparedness Office (FBI)

- The Science and Technology directorate utilizes science and technology in protecting the United States:
  - Chemical, Biological, Radiological, and Nuclear (CBRN) Countermeasures Programs (Energy)
  - Environmental Measurements Laboratory (Energy)

A U.S. Department of Homeland Security Hermes 450 Unmanned Aerial Vehicle (UAV). The UAVs were launched under the Arizona Border Control Initiative of June 25, 2004. *Gerald L. Nino, U.S. Customs and Border Protection, Department of Homeland Security.*

- National BW Defense Analysis Center (Defense)
- Plum Island Animal Disease Center (Agriculture)

- The Information Analysis and Infrastructure Protection directorate analyzes intelligence and information from other agencies (including the CIA, FBI, Defense Intelligence Agency, and National Security Agency) involving threats to homeland security and evaluates infrastructure vulnerabilities:
  - Federal Computer Incident Response Center (GSA)
  - National Communications System (Defense)
  - National Infrastructure Protection Center (FBI)
  - Energy Security and Assurance Program (Energy)

The Secret Service and the Coast Guard were also placed under Homeland Security, but remain separate operations outside the four directorates.

The Homeland Security Council. The Homeland Security Council (HSC) is part of the White House office. It was created in October 2001 by President George W. Bush's Executive Order 13228 after the events of September 11, 2001, to advise and assist the president in all aspects of homeland security. For example, President Bush met with the HSC on June 1, 2007, to discuss the preparedness of the federal government for the upcoming hurricane season. The responsibilities of the HSC were further outlined in the President's Homeland Security Presidential Directive-1 and in Title IX of the Homeland Security Act of 2002. Under the act, the responsibilities of the HSC are defined as follows:

(1) assess the objectives, commitments, and risks of the United States in the interest of homeland security and to make resulting recommendations to the President;
(2) oversee and review homeland security policies of the Federal Government and to make resulting recommendations to the President; and
(3) perform such other functions as the President may direct.

The HSC also coordinates all homeland security–related activities among executive branch departments and agencies, and promotes the effective development and implementation of all homeland security policies. The membership of the Council includes the president, vice president, secretary of homeland security, attorney general, secretary of defense, and other executive branch officers the president chooses to designate.

National Security Council. The National Security Council (NSC) was created under President Harry S. Truman by the National Security Act of 1947 (which also created the secretary of defense, National Military Establishment, Central Intelligence Agency, and National Security Resources Board). The act was amended by the National Security Act Amendments of 1949 and the Council was moved under the executive office of the president. The NSC advises the president on issues of national security and foreign policy. According to the act, "The function of the Council shall be to advise the President with respect to the integration of domestic, foreign, and military policies relating to the national security so as to enable the military services and the other departments and agencies of the Government to cooperate more effectively

Secretary of Defense Robert M. Gates (left) and Vice Chairman of the Joint Chiefs of Staff Gen. James Cartwright, U.S. Marine Corps, conduct a media roundtable in the Pentagon, January 17, 2008. *Petty Officer 2nd Class Molly A. Burgess, U.S. Navy/U.S. Department of Defense.*

in matters involving the national security." The president chairs the Council. Its meetings are regularly attended by the vice president, the secretary of state, the secretary of the treasury, the secretary of defense, chairman of the joint chiefs of staff, director of national intelligence, and the assistant to the president for national security affairs. Other executive department officials also attend as invited or required by the president.

Federal Bureau of Investigation.   The Federal Bureau of Investigation (FBI) was established in 1908 by the U.S. attorney general as part of the Department of Justice. The FBI enforces U.S. criminal laws, and defends the United States against terrorist and foreign intelligence threats. Its National Security Priorities include counterterrorism (international and domestic), counterintelligence (including espionage), and fighting such cyber crimes as computer intrusion, online predators, and Internet fraud. The following are the categories of the agency's criminal priorities and examples of crimes investigated by the FBI under each the agency (Federal Bureau of Investigation, 2003):

- Public Corruption

    Government fraud
    Election fraud

- Civil Rights

    Hate crime
    Human trafficking
    Freedom of access to clinics

- White-Collar Crime

    Antitrust
    Bankruptcy fraud
    Identity theft

- Organized Crime

    Italian mafia
    Middle Eastern
    Sports bribery

- Major Thefts/Violent Crime

    Art theft
    Bank robberies
    Crimes against children
    Vehicle theft
    Violent gangs

Central Intelligence Agency.　The Central Intelligence Agency (CIA) was created by the National Security Act of 1947 under President Harry S. Truman. The Intelligence Reform and Terrorism Act of 2004 amended the original act to provide for a Director of National Intelligence. The director also serves over the director of the CIA. The duties of the director of the CIA include the following (Central Intelligence Agency, 2007):

- Collecting intelligence through human sources and by other appropriate means, except that he shall have no police, subpoena, or law enforcement powers or internal security functions;
- Correlating and evaluating intelligence related to national security and providing appropriate dissemination of such intelligence;
- Providing overall direction for and coordination of the collection of national intelligence outside the United States through human sources by elements of the Intelligence Community authorized to undertake such collection and, in coordination with other departments, agencies, or elements of the United States Government which are authorized to undertake such collection, ensuring that the most effective use is made of resources and that appropriate account is taken of the risks to the United States and those involved in such collection; and
- Performing such other functions and duties related to intelligence affecting the national security as the President or the Director of National Intelligence may direct.

Bureau of Alcohol, Tobacco and Firearms.　The Bureau of Alcohol, Tobacco and Firearms (ATF) is located in the Department of Justice. The law enforcement functions were transferred from the Department of the Treasury in 2003 under the Homeland Security Act of 2002. The taxation and trade functions remained in the Department of the Treasury in the newly established Alcohol Tobacco Tax and Trade Bureau. The agency was initially created in 1972 when the original functions performed by the ATF were transferred to the Department of the Treasury from the Internal Revenue Service.

As a law enforcement agency, the ATF enforces federal laws and regulates the firearms and explosive industries. It also investigates acts of arson, and the illegal trafficking of alcohol and tobacco products. The following are the ATF's major programs (Bureau of Alcohol, Tobacco and Firearms, 2007):

- Firearms—Investigates armed violent offenders and career criminals, narcotics traffickers, narcoterrorists, violent gangs, and domestic and international arms traffickers; issues firearms licenses and conducts firearms licensee qualification and compliance inspections.
- Arson and Explosives—Provides resources to local communities to investigate explosives incidents and arson-for-profit schemes, and uses National Response Teams, International Response Teams, and Arson Task Forces; prevents both the criminal use and accidental detonations of explosives materials; conducts inspections to ensure that explosives are safely and securely stored and by issuing permits and licenses; plays a lead role in the investigations of arson and bombing incidents directed at abortion clinics; provides expertise internationally in the areas of post-blast examination, and cause and origin determination; maintains the Explosives Incident System which is a computerized repository for historical and technical data on national explosives.
- Alcohol/Tobacco Programs—Regulates the qualification and operations of distilleries, wineries, and breweries, as well as importers and wholesalers in the industry; protects consumers through such programs as the ATF National Laboratory Center to test new products and the health risk of existing products; ensures the collection of alcohol beverage excise taxes, provides for accurate deposit and accounting for these taxes, prevents entry into the industry by criminals or persons whose business experience or associations pose a risk of tax fraud, and suppresses label fraud, commercial bribery, diversion and smuggling, and other unlawful practices in the alcohol beverage marketplace; ensures the collection of tobacco excise taxes and to qualify applicants for permits to manufacture tobacco products or operate tobacco export warehouses; conducts tobacco inspections; investigates the trafficking of contraband tobacco products in violation of federal law and sections of the Internal Revenue Code.

Food Safety and Inspection Service.   The Food Safety and Inspection Service (FSIS) is an agency located in the U.S. Department of Agriculture. It oversees the safety, proper packaging, and correct labeling of commercial meat, poultry, and egg products. The FSIS implements programs to educate consumers on the importance of handling food safely to reduce the risks of illnesses. It also helps other agencies and industry respond to natural disasters and intentional food contamination. The agency was established as the Food Safety and Quality Service in 1977 to replace the Animal and Plant Health Service. The name was changed to the Food Safety and Inspection Service in 1981.

One of the most significant achievements of the FSIS has been the issuance of the Pathogen Reduction/Hazard Analysis and Critical Control Point (HAACP) Systems rule. It holds industries accountable for food safety, while the government is responsible for setting food safety standards, conducting inspections of adherence to standards, and maintaining enforcement plans for plants that do not meet regulatory standards. The implementation of the rule was completed in 2000. According to the FSIS, "the Pathogen Reduction/HACCP rule applied to approximately 6,500 federally-inspected and 2,550 State-inspected meat and poultry (slaughter and processing) plants in the United States. The CDC has attributed HACCP implementation as an important factor in the overall decline in bacterial food-borne illnesses from 1996 through 2001" (Food Safety and Inspection Service, 2007).

U.S. Food and Drug Administration.   The U.S. Food and Drug Administration (FDA) is an agency within the Department of Health and Human Services.

It began under the Department of Agriculture as the Division of Chemistry. The modern FDA originated with the passage of the Federal Food and Drugs Act in 1906, also called the Wiley Act. Harvey Wiley was a chief chemist and conducted experiments to expose the dangers of chemical preservatives. He unified a variety of groups to spearhead the passing of a federal law to end the misbranding of food and drugs.

The FDA protects the public health by assuring the safety and security of human and animal drugs, biological products, medical devices, food, cosmetics, and products that emit radiation. It advances innovations in these areas, and ensures public access to health information. This includes ensuring products are accurately labeled to provide information on their contents, and food and drug manufacturers meet government safety standards.

The FDA consists of eight centers or offices:

- Center for Biologics Evaluation and Research (CBER)
- Center for Devices and Radiological Health (CDRH)
- Center for Drug Evaluation and Research (CDER)
- Center for Food Safety and Applied Nutrition (CFSAN)
- Center for Veterinary Medicine (CVM)
- National Center for Toxicological Research (NCTR)
- Office of the Commissioner (OC)
- Office of Regulatory Affairs (ORA)

According to the FDA's official history (U.S. Food and Drug Administration, 2007), "the agency grew from a single chemist in the U.S. Department of Agriculture in 1862 to a staff of approximately 9,100 employees and a budget of $1.294 billion in 2001, comprising chemists, pharmacologists, physicians, microbiologists, veterinarians, pharmacists, lawyers, and many others. . . . Agency scientists evaluate applications for new human drugs and biologics, complex medical devices, food and color additives, infant formulas, and animal drugs. Also, the FDA monitors the manufacture, import, transport, storage, and sale of about $1 trillion worth of products annually at a cost to taxpayers of about $3 per person. Investigators and inspectors visit more than 16,000 facilities a year, and arrange with State governments to help increase the number of facilities checked."

Federal Communications Commission. The Federal Communications Commission (FCC) is an independent agency that reports directly to Congress. It was established under the Communications Act of 1934 to perform the following functions:

For the purpose of regulating interstate and foreign commerce in communication by wire and radio so as to make available, so far as possible, to all the people of the United States, without discrimination on the basis of race, color, religion, national origin, or sex, a rapid, efficient, Nationwide, and world-wide wire and radio communication service with adequate facilities at reasonable charges, for the purpose of the national defense, for the purpose of promoting safety of life and property through the use of wire and radio communication, and for the purpose of securing a more effective execution of this policy by centralizing authority heretofore granted by law to several agencies and by granting additional authority with respect to interstate and foreign commerce in wire and radio communication.

The act was amended by the Telecommunications Act of 1996 under President Bill Clinton to promote competition by reducing regulation. This act was passed to allow more businesses and individuals to enter into the communication market. The new act was the first major communications legislation passed since 1934. It provides guidance and regulation for radio, television (including cable and satellite television), telephone services, and online computer services. While the act reduced barriers for entry into the communications market, it also instituted stricter regulations and penalties for transmitting obscene or indecent material.

The following are some of the functions performed by the FCC's various bureaus and offices:

- Enforce the Communications Act of 1934
- Process applications for communication licenses
- Investigate complaints
- Conduct investigations
- Regulate radio and television broadcast stations
- Oversee the use of cellular and Personal Communications Services (PCS) phones
- Regulate telephone companies
- Hold administrative hearings for violations

Other Agencies Supporting Domestic Policy. The following are other agencies (and the year they were created) that play roles in enforcing laws and regulations important to domestic policy:

- Federal Trade Commission (1914)—Ensures advertising is truthful, requires products to be properly labeled, prohibits price fixing, prevents unfair competition, and prohibits unfair and deceptive business acts or practices.
- Centers for Disease Control and Prevention (1946)—Part of the Department of Health and Human Services, the CDC was initially established to battle the spread of malaria by killing mosquitoes. It has grown into the nation's leading promoter of health, including fighting infections, diseases, injuries, disabilities, workplace hazards, and environmental health issues. The agency conducts research and investigations, and partners with the States and other nations to implement prevention strategies. It also maintains and reports national health statistics.
- Environmental Protection Agency (1970)—Protects human health and the environment by developing and enforcing regulations that implement environmental laws enacted by Congress, and issuing sanctions and taking other steps against those not in compliance. Also researches and sets national standards for a variety of environmental programs, and delegates to States and tribes the responsibility for issuing permits and for monitoring and enforcing compliance.
- Consumer Product Safety Commission (1972)—Protects the public from unreasonable risks of serious injury or death from products that pose a fire, electrical, chemical, or mechanical hazard or can injure children.
- Drug Enforcement Administration (1973)—Enforces controlled substances laws and regulations, and apprehends groups and individuals involved in the growing, manufacture, or distribution of controlled substances. Also recommends and supports programs aimed at reducing the availability of illicit controlled substances on the domestic and international markets.

Domestic Policy Legislation.   Congress passes laws to protect the needs of U.S. citizens, business, animals, and the environment. These laws regulate, protect, and provide oversight of people, businesses, and other organizations. They also protect and sustain the country's infrastructure, such as its highways and waterways. For examples, laws set standards for businesses selling potentially dangerous products (such as dangerous drugs), prohibit organizations from infringing on the civil liberties of citizens, and provide citizen protection through such laws as speed limits. These laws often stipulate which federal agency will provide oversight and enforcement. Statutes, for example, establish agencies and provide them chartered missions to guide the accomplishments of their missions. Agencies use these statutes to develop detailed functions they will accomplish and regulations for the entities they are established to regulate. Laws are then amended or rescinded as required. For example, the minimum wage has been adjusted to keep pace with inflation. This entire process is the foundation of the legislative process of that supports domestic policy. This includes passing laws to support the domestic policies established by the executive branch. The following are examples of laws supporting domestic policy.

The Federal Trade Commission Act of 1914 created the Federal Trade Commission and empowered it to (a) prevent unfair methods of competition, and unfair or deceptive acts or practices in or affecting commerce; (b) seek monetary redress and other relief for conduct injurious to consumers; (c) prescribe trade regulation rules defining with specificity acts or practices that are unfair or deceptive, and establishing requirements designed to prevent such acts or practices; (d) conduct investigations relating to the organization, business, practices, and management of entities engaged in commerce; and (e) make reports and legislative recommendations to Congress.

The Truth in Lending Act of 1968 was passed by Congress as part of the Consumer Protection Act. It requires creditors to provide consumers clear disclosures of credit terms and all costs associated with a lending arrangement. This information will allow consumers to compare the terms and costs of different loans. Creditors are required to use the same credit terminology and method of computing interest rates. Consumers are protected against inaccurate credit billing practices, given the right to cancel certain credit arrangements against their principal residence, and provided a means for the fair and timely resolution of billing disputes. The act is executed by the Federal Reserve Board.

The Consumer Product Safety Act of 1972 was passed to protect the public against unreasonable risks of injury associated with consumer products, to assist consumers in evaluating the comparative safety of consumer products, to develop uniform safety standards for consumer products and to minimize conflicting state and local regulations, and to promote research and investigation into the causes and prevention of product-related deaths, illnesses, and injuries. The U.S. Consumer Product Safety Commission (CPSC) was established to enforce the act through such actions as setting standards to reduce or eliminate risks associated with dangerous consumer products, and pursuing recalls for products that present a substantial product hazard. The CPSC is charged with protecting the public from unreasonable risks of serious injury or death from more than fifteen thousand types of consumer products under the agency's jurisdiction.

The Endangered Species Act of 1973 was passed to protect endangered and threatened species of fish, wildlife, and plants. It repealed the Endangered Species Conservation Act of 1969. The 1973 Act provides a means whereby the ecosystems upon which

Endangered Species: Adult male black-footed ferret (*Mustela nigripes*) in an outdoor pen at the National Black-Footed Ferret Conservation Center. *Paul Marinari/U.S. Fish and Wildlife Service.*

endangered species and threatened species depend may be conserved, to provide a program for the conservation of endangered and threatened species, and to take appropriate steps to achieve the purposes of the treaties and conventions set forth in the Act. The Department of Commerce determines species that fall under the act by analyzing the present or threatened destruction, modification, or curtailment of their habitat or range; overutilization of their habitats for commercial, recreational, scientific, or educational purposes; disease or predation; the inadequacy of existing regulatory mechanisms; or other natural or manmade factors affecting their continued existence.

The Nutrition Labeling and Education Act of 1990 (NLEA) gives the FDA authority to require producers to place nutrition labels on most foods regulated by the agency. All nutrient content claims (such as "low fat" or "high in fiber") and health claims by these producers must be consistent with agency regulations. Specific labeling requirements include (1) the serving size or other common household unit of measure customarily used; (2) the number of servings or other units per container; (3) the number of total calories derived from any source and derived from total fat; (4) the amount of total fat, saturated fat, cholesterol, sodium, total carbohydrates, complex carbohydrates, sugars, dietary fiber, and total protein contained in each serving or other unit of measure; and (5) any vitamin, mineral, or other nutrient required by the FDA to assist consumers in maintaining healthy dietary practices.

RELIGION AND GOVERNMENT

One of the most controversial domestic policy issues since the founding of the United States has been the relationship of religion and government. The founders of the nation wanted to ensure the two remained separate because European rulers attempted to exert control over religious practices through government actions, including persecuting those whose beliefs were not in agreement with government leaders. Therefore, religious freedom was one of the main reasons many immigrants came to this country. The founding fathers established the First Amendment to ensure Congress did not pass laws establishing or supporting any official religion, and that citizens were free to practice their religious beliefs. The Supreme Court has interpreted the Amendment to apply to the entire federal government.

The debate over the separation religion and government, or church and state, has not been resolved. The phrase "separation of church and state" originated from a letter from President Thomas Jefferson to the Danbury Baptist Association in 1802. The association complained that their religious freedom in Connecticut were seen as "favors granted" by the State rather than guaranteed rights. President Jefferson replied that at the federal level there was a "wall of separation between church and state."

The debate over the relationship of religion and the government stems from how the First Amendment has been interpreted by different readers. It reads as follows:

> Congress shall make no law respecting an establishment of religion, or prohibiting the free exercise thereof; or abridging the freedom of speech, or of the press; or the right of the people peaceably to assemble, and to petition the government for a redress of grievances.

The first part of the Amendment forbidding the government from establishing a religion is known as the Establishment Clause, and the second part is known as the Free Exercise Clause. Based upon its reading, many argue that questions such as the following are not answered:

- Should the government support prayer in public schools?
- Should government funds be used to aid religious schools?
- Should religious displays or symbols be on government property or products (buildings, currency, etc.)?
- Should public officials be allowed to accept political contributions from religious groups?
- Should politicians be allowed to campaign in churches or at religious events?
- Should politicians accept the political endorsement of religious groups or leaders?
- Should the government be allowed to pass laws on issues that are religious in nature (such as abortion and gay marriage)?

As a result of these and other questions, two opposing viewpoints have developed in the debate over the proper interaction of church and state. The following are arguments supporting the separation of religion and government:

- The First Amendment bars the government from establishing or regulating religion.
- If the two are not separated, the government may favor religious over nonreligious people and organizations.
- The government should not be allowed to criticize religious beliefs or practices.
- The government should not fund religions or religious activities, particularly since taxpayers are from various religious groups and some are atheist or agnostics. There is consequently no equitable way of ensuring all of these groups obtain equal funding.
- The government would require exposure to religious practices during its normal operation of government business if it had to address religious issues.
- Religious beliefs will affect or control the passage and execution of laws.
- Churches are built upon personal beliefs and thus must maintain their independence from government control or influence.
- Religious beliefs lead to varying moral and ethical beliefs, rather than neutrality strictly based upon the law.

The following are arguments against the separation of religion and government:

- The First Amendment bars the government from establishing a church but allows the government to regulate some aspects of religion.
- The government can support religion as long as it is accomplished equitably.
- The U.S. government should not be a secular establishment, especially since this nation was established based on religious principles. This is evidenced by such phrases as "In God We Trust" being printed on national currency and "One Nation Under God" being included in the Pledge of Allegiance.
- The U.S. people are religious, and the government must represent the needs and beliefs of its people.
- The government should encourage ethical and moral beliefs found in religious teachings.

The Supreme Court has consistently ruled against the sponsoring of religious activities by the government or public officials:

- In *Torcaso v. Watkins*, 367 U.S. 488 (1961), the Court ruled it was unconstitutional for the state of Maryland to require a state official to declare his belief in God. This invaded an individual's freedom of belief and religion guaranteed by the First Amendment and protected by the Fourteenth Amendment.
- In *Engel v. Vitale*, 370 U.S. 421 (1962), the Court ruled against state-sponsored school prayer. The Court wrote in its decision, "Because of the prohibition of the First Amendment against the enactment of any law 'respecting an establishment of religion,' which is made applicable to the States by the Fourteenth Amendment, State officials may not compose an official State prayer and require that it be recited in the public schools of the State at the beginning of each school day—even if the prayer is denominationally neutral and pupils who wish to do so may remain silent or be excused from the room while the prayer is being recited."
- In *Stone v. Graham*, 449 U.S. 39 (1980), the Court ruled that a Kentucky statute requiring the posting of the Ten Commandments was unconstitutional and in violation of the Establishment Clause of the First Amendment. The Court also ruled that it did not matter that the Ten Commandments were posted rather than read aloud.
- The Court ruled against religious teachings in schools in *Edwards v. Aquillard*, 482 U.S. 578 (1987). The state of Louisiana's Creationism Act forbade the teaching of the theory of

evolution in public elementary and secondary schools unless it was accompanied by a teaching of the theory of creation science. The Court ruled the Act violated the Establishment Clause of the First Amendment.

• In *Allegheny County v. Greater Pittsburgh ACLU*, 492 U.S. 573 (1989), the Court ruled that the display of the Christian Nativity scene on public property in downtown Pittsburgh as unconstitutional because it was a government endorsement and promotion of religious beliefs.

The executive branch has taken a stance that religious activities providing social service programs should be allowed to obtain federal support as long as that support is provided indiscriminately. In 1996, President Bill Clinton passed several laws that allowed and outlined the procedures for the receipt of federal funds by faith-based organizations. These laws were collectively named "charitable choice" and include the Personal Responsibility and Work Opportunity Reconciliation Act established in 1996, the Welfare-to-Work Program in 1997, the Community Services Block Grant in 1998, and legislation that created the Substance Abuse and Mental Health Services Administration in 2000. The oversight of funds provided for specific types of services was placed under specific agencies. Temporary Assistance to Needy Families (TANF) and the Community Services Block Grant (CSBG) programs are overseen by the Administration for Children and Families in the U.S. Department of Health and Human Services. Programs for substance abuse and mental health are overseen by the Substance Abuse and Mental Health Services Administration. The Welfare-to-Work program is overseen by the Department of Labor. The following statement from the White House under President George W. Bush further outlines the purposes and goals of these laws (White House Office of Faith-Based and Community Initiatives, 2003):

> These laws clarify both the rights and the responsibilities of faith-based organizations that receive Federal funds. They specify that faith-based organizations cannot be excluded from the competition for Federal funds simply because they are religious. These laws also provide that faith-based organizations that receive Federal funds may continue to carry out their missions consistent with their beliefs. For example, they may maintain a religious environment in their facilities, and they may consider their religious beliefs in hiring and firing employees. The Charitable Choice laws also impose certain restrictions on faith-based organizations. They spell out specific "do's" and "don'ts" for faith-based groups receiving Federal money. The laws specify that religious organizations that receive Federal funds must serve all eligible participants, regardless of those persons' religious beliefs. They also prohibit religious organizations from using Federal funds to support any inherently religious activities (such as worship, religious instruction, or proselytizing). In addition, recipients of services provided under Charitable Choice laws have a right to be provided with services from a non-religious provider. President Bush believes that recipients of Federal services should be offered a choice of providers. That is why it is preferable to have a range of providers, both secular and faith-based.

President Bush expanded on the laws issued by President Clinton through two executive orders issued in December 2002. Executive Order 13279 provides "Equal Protection of the Laws for Faith-based and Community Organizations." It was established "to guide Federal agencies in formulating and developing policies with implications for faith-based organizations and other community organizations, to ensure equal protection of the laws for faith-based and community organizations, to further the national effort to expand opportunities for, and strengthen the capacity of, faith-based and other community organizations so that they may better meet social needs in America's communities, and to ensure the economical and efficient administration and completion of Government contracts." Executive Order 13280 outlines the "Responsibilities of the Department of Agriculture and the Agency for the International Development with Respect to Faith-based and Community Initiatives." It established the Centers for Faith-Based and Community Initiatives at the Department of Agriculture and the Agency for International Development to coordinate agency efforts to eliminate regulatory, contracting, and other programmatic obstacles to the participation of faith-based and other community organizations in the provision of social services.

Under laws and executive orders, funds are not set aside for faith-based organizations. Rather, they must apply for funds just as all other types of organizations. These organizations cannot refuse to provide federally funded services to anyone needing help. Federal funds cannot be used to pay for any activity connected with the practice or advertisement of their religions (i.e., inherently religious activities). Faith-based organizations can continue to perform their religious activities separate from any activities conducted using federal funds. They may display their religious symbols and can briefly describe their religious practices only if specifically asked by a service recipient. They can also hire employees providing services based upon religious criteria. They must file financial reports according to federal standards.

Under President Bush, the White House Office of Faith-Based and Community Initiatives coordinated government-wide efforts to expand partnerships with nonprofit organizations. Programs were implemented by eleven Agency Centers for Faith-Based and Community Initiatives located within major agencies across the federal government. These agencies were part of the Agency for International Development, Department of Agriculture, Department of Commerce, Department of Education, Department of Health and Human Services, Department of Homeland Security, Department of Housing and Urban Development, Department of Justice, Department of Labor, Small Business Administration, and Department of Veterans Affairs.

EQUAL RIGHTS

The first ten Amendments to the Constitution are called the Bill of Rights. These Amendments were specifically established to protect citizens from infringements against their basic rights and liberties by the government and other citizens. These basic rights and liberties are collectively called *civil liberties*. The founding fathers established the Bill of Rights to establish equal opportunity for all individuals based on equal treatment under the law. In summary, the Bill of Rights guarantees individuals freedom of speech, freedom of assembly, freedom of religion, the right to bear arms, protection from home seizure by the military, protection from unreasonable search and seizure, due process under the law, the right to a speedy and public trial, trial by a jury of one's peers, protection from cruel and unusual punishment for crimes committed, other rights implicitly retained by the people, and a delegation of powers to the states and the people those implicit rights not otherwise specifically stated in the Constitution or prohibited by the States.

In addition to the rights guaranteed in the Bill of Rights and other Amendments of the Constitution, Congress has passed other laws that provide additional rights to individuals. These laws provide clarifications of or elaborations on the basic rights guaranteed in the Constitution. The following paragraphs outline key laws addressing equal rights.

The Civil Rights Act of 1866 declared that all persons born in the United States were citizens, regardless of their race, color, or previous condition as a slave. As citizens, they could sue and be sued, enforce contracts, give evidence in court proceedings, and inherit, purchase, lease, sell, hold, and convey property. President Andrew Johnson vetoed the act, but his veto was overridden by Congress. The act provided penalties for violators of a fine not exceeding $1,000 or imprisonment not exceeding one year, or both.

The Civil Rights Act of 1870, also called the Enforcement Act, gave all citizens the right to vote without regard to their race, color, or previous condition of servitude (i.e., as a slave). The act covered the right of all citizens to register to vote. Any person or group that infringed on these rights would be charged with a misdemeanor carrying a fine of no less than $500, or imprisonment of no more than one year, or both. Felony charges could be levied against any group of two or more persons who banded together, conspired, or disguised themselves on a public highway or someone's premises with the intent to violate any part of the act, or to injure, oppress, threaten, or intimidate any citizen with the intent of preventing or hindering that citizen from freely exercising any right or privilege granted by the Constitution or U.S. law.

The Civil Rights Act of 1871 prohibits any group of two or more persons from conspiring to overthrow, declare war against, oppose the authority of, or seize the property of the U.S. government. It also prohibits any group from intimidating or threatening any person from accepting or holding a U.S. office, including threatening or inducing a U.S. officer from leaving a state, district, or any other location where that officer is required to perform the duties of that office. This includes injuring the officer or destroying their property, interfering with a person being a witness in a court proceeding, or interfering with the verdict in a court case. Those attempting to protect a citizen from threats or intimidation are also protected. Citizens are also protected from being coerced to vote a particular way in an election.

Under the Civil Rights Act of 1875, Congress recognized the equality of all people in the eyes of the law, and therefore all are guaranteed equal justice regardless of their nativity (i.e., nation of origin), race, color, religion, or political affiliation. All citizens are entitled to the full and equal enjoyment of public facilities (i.e., the accommodations, advantages, facilities, and privileges of inns, public conveyances on land or water, theaters, and other places of public amusement). Those found guilty of violating this act are subject to a fine of $500 to be paid to the person aggrieved, and deemed guilty of committing a misdemeanor carrying a fine of at least $500 or no less than thirty days imprisonment. The act also deems it a misdemeanor to deny a citizen the right to serve as a juror, or to interfere with the process of selecting or summoning jurors. This offense carries a fine of not more than $5,000.

The Civil Rights Act of 1964 prohibits segregation in schools and public places. Segregation is defined as the intentional denial and separation of equal access to facilities because of an individual's race, color, religion or national origin. The act mandates each U.S. citizen's constitutional right to vote, provides the district courts the ability to levy injunctive relief against public establishments convicted of discrimination, authorizes the attorney general to institute suits against violators of the act, and makes it illegal for programs receiving federal assistance to engage in discriminatory acts. Title VII of the act prohibits employment discrimination. Specifically it states:

> It shall be an unlawful employment practice for an employer (1) to fail or refuse to hire or to discharge any individual, or otherwise to discriminate against any individual with respect to his compensation, terms, conditions, or privileges of employment, because of such individual's race, color, religion, sex, or national origin; or (2) to limit, segregate, or classify his employees in any way which would deprive or tend to deprive any individual of employment opportunities or otherwise adversely affect his status as an employee, because of such individual's race, color, religion, sex, or national origin.

The act also extended the powers of the U.S. Commission on Civil Rights and established the Equal Employment Opportunity Commission (EEOC). The Commission on Civil Rights is an independent agency whose mission includes the following (U.S. Commission on Civil Rights, 2007):

- To investigate complaints alleging that citizens are being deprived of their right to vote by reason of their race, color, religion, sex, age, disability, or national origin, or by reason of fraudulent practices.
- To study and collect information relating to discrimination or a denial of equal protection of the laws under the Constitution because of race, color, religion, sex, age, disability, or national origin, or in the administration of justice.
- To appraise federal laws and policies with respect to discrimination or denial of equal protection of the laws because of race, color, religion, sex, age, disability, or national origin, or in the administration of justice.
- To serve as a national clearinghouse for information in respect to discrimination or denial of equal protection of the laws because of race, color, religion, sex, age, disability, or national origin.
- To submit reports, findings, and recommendations to the president and Congress.
- To issue public service announcements to discourage discrimination or denial of equal protection of the laws.

The EEOC cooperates with regional, state, local, and other agencies and individuals to investigate complaints of discrimination under the terms of the act. It can also conduct technical studies of discrimination and make these reports available to the public. The agency has the authority to enforce the act and hold hearings, without having to forward them to the Department of Justice for action as it did when first established. The EEOC also enforces the provisions of the following acts:

- Equal Pay Act of 1963: prohibits employers from engaging in wage discrimination based on sex for employees working in the same establishment performing equal work. Employers may not reduce the wages of male or female employees to make pay more equitable.
- Age Discrimination in Employment Act of 1967: prohibits employment discrimination based on age, specifically for those 40 years of age or older. Employees may not make statements or specifications of age preferences or limitations in job notices or advertisements. An age limit can only be specified in cases where there is a bona fide occupational qualification. Employer can also not discriminate on the basis of age in apprenticeship programs or deny benefits to older employees.

- Rehabilitation Act of 1973: prohibits discrimination against qualified individuals with disabilities who work in the federal government.
- Americans with Disabilities Act of 1990: Title I and Title V prohibit employment discrimination in the private sector, state, and local governments against individuals with mental or physical disabilities. This applies to accepting job applications, hiring, advancement, discharge, employee compensation, job training, and other terms, conditions, and privileges of employment.
- Civil Rights Act of 1991: amended the Civil Rights Act of 1964 to strengthen and improve federal civil rights laws, including providing for damages in cases of intentional employment discrimination.

Title VIII of the Civil Rights Act of 1964 barred housing discrimination on the basis of race, color, religion, sex, or national origin. The Fair Housing Amendments Act of 1988 amended Title VIII and bars discrimination in the selling or renting of a dwelling to any person based on race, color, religion, sex, familial status, disability, or national origin. Familial status covers families with children. Disability covers those with mental or physical challenges.

The Pregnancy Discrimination Act of 1975 amended Title VII of the Civil Rights Act of 1964 to also prohibit employment discrimination based on pregnancy, childbirth, or related medical conditions. The following are some specific guidelines contained in the Act, according to the EEOC:

- An employer cannot refuse to hire a woman because of her pregnancy related condition as long as she is able to perform the major functions of her job.
- If an employee is temporarily unable to perform her job due to pregnancy, the employer must treat her the same as any other temporarily disabled employee; for example, by providing modified tasks, alternative assignments, disability leave or leave without pay.
- Any health insurance provided by an employer must cover expenses for pregnancy related conditions on the same basis as costs for other medical conditions.
- Pregnancy related benefits cannot be limited to married employees.

The Civil Service Reform Act of 1978 prohibits federal employees in an authority position from taking personnel actions that discriminate against other employees on the basis of race, color, national origin, religion, sex, age, or disability. It also stipulates that certain personnel actions cannot be taken based on an employee's marital status, political affiliation, or other conditions, resulting in a negative impact on the employee's job performance. The Office of Personnel Management, which oversees the employment of federal employees, has interpreted the act to prohibit discrimination based on sexual orientation. The act is enforced by the Office of Special Counsel (OSC) and the Merit Systems Protection Board.

The Equal Rights Amendment is a proposed amendment to the Constitution to guarantee equal legal rights to all Americans regardless of sex. The original amendment was sent to the states in 1972 and did not pass. The latest proposed amendment in 1982 also did not pass.

FREEDOM OF INFORMATION ACT

Citizens are allowed to obtain information on agencies through the Freedom of Information Act of 1966 (FOIA). FOIA (5.U.S.C 552) was created to provide citizens access to information from and about the federal government. The law applies to agencies. Congress, the judicial branch, and the president and the president's immediate staff and advisors are excluded. The act was amended by the Government in the Sunshine Act of 1976 to provide exemptions for some information being provided. This includes information associated with national defense, a breach of privacy, and information related to an agency's involvement in legal proceedings. The act was amended again by the Electronic Freedom of Information Act of 1996, and today requires agencies to make the following information available to the public:

(A) descriptions of its central and field organization and the established places at which, the employees (and in the case of a uniformed service, the members) from whom, and the methods whereby, the public may obtain information, make submittals or requests, or obtain decisions;

(B) statements of the general course and method by which its functions are channeled and determined, including the nature and requirements of all formal and informal procedures available;

(C) rules of procedures, descriptions of forms available or the places at which forms may be obtained, and instructions as to the scope and contents of all papers, reports, or examinations;

(D) substantive rules of general applicability adopted as authorized by law, and statements of general policy or interpretations of general applicability formulated and adopted by the agency; and

(E) each amendment, revision, or repeal of the foregoing.

Each agency must also make the following information available for public inspection and copying:

(A) final opinions, including concurring and dissenting opinions, as well as orders, made in the adjudication of cases;

(B) those statements of policy and interpretations which have been adopted by the agency and are not published in the Federal Register;

(C) administrative staff manuals and instructions to staff that affect a member of the public;

(D) copies of all records, regardless of form or format, which have been released to any person and which, because of the nature of their subject matter, the agency determines have become or are likely to become the subject of subsequent requests for substantially the same records; and

(E) a general index of the records

Records created one year after November 1, 1996, must be made available through electronic means. In the statement issued by President Bill Clinton upon signing the 1996 amendment, he emphasized the need for the modernization of providing federal information (White House Office of the Press Secretary, 1996):

Since 1966, the world has changed a great deal. Records are no longer principally maintained in paper format. Now, they are maintained in a variety of technologies, including CD ROM and computer tapes and diskettes, making it easier to put more information on-line. . . . The legislation I sign today brings FOA into the information and electronic age by clarifying that it applies to records maintained in electronic format. This law also broadens public access to government information by placing more material on-line and expanding the role of the agency reading room. As the Government actively disseminates more information, I hope that there will be less need to use FOIA to obtain government information.

There are types of information this act does not apply to and that agencies do not release to the public. This includes information that must remain secret in the interest of national defense or foreign policy, related solely to internal agency rules, trade secrets or private financial information, personnel and medical files, records compiled for law enforcement purposes, and geological and geophysical information and data concerning wells.

The Government in the Sunshine Act of 1976 expanded public access to information originally provided under the Freedom of Information Act (FOIA) of 1966. It requires most federal agency meetings to be open to the public. Agencies must also make promptly available to the public, in a place easily accessible to the public, the transcript, electronic recording, or minutes of the discussion of any item on the agenda, or of any item of the testimony of any witness received at the meeting. The act provides lengthy exceptions to having public meetings. Agencies shall not make meetings public that:

(1) Disclose matters that are:
   (A) specifically authorized under criteria established by an Executive order to be kept secret in the interests of national defense or foreign policy and
   (B) in fact properly classified pursuant to such Executive order;
(2) Relate solely to the internal personnel rules and practices of an agency;
(3) Disclose matters specifically exempted from disclosure by statute . . . , provided that such statute
   (A) requires that the matters be withheld from the public in such a manner as to leave no discretion on the issue, or
   (B) establishes particular criteria for withholding or refers to particular types of matters to be withheld;
(4) Disclose trade secrets and commercial or financial information obtained from a person and privileged or confidential;
(5) Involve accusing any person of a crime, or formally censuring any person;
(6) Disclose information of a personal nature where disclosure would constitute a clearly unwarranted invasion of personal privacy;
(7) Disclose investigatory records compiled for law enforcement purposes, or information which if written would be contained in such records, but only to the extent that the production of such records or information would
   (A) interfere with enforcement proceedings,
   (B) deprive a person of a right to a fair trial or an impartial adjudication,
   (C) constitute an unwarranted invasion of personal privacy,
   (D) disclose the identity of a confidential source and, in the case of a record compiled by a criminal law enforcement authority in the course of a criminal investigation, or by an agency conducting a lawful national security intelligence investigation, confidential information furnished only by the confidential source,
   (E) disclose investigative techniques and procedures, or
   (F) endanger the life or physical safety of law enforcement personnel;

(8) Disclose information contained in or related to examination, operating or condition reports prepared by, on behalf of, or for the use of an agency responsible for the regulation or supervision of financial institutions;

(9) Disclose information the premature disclosure of which would—

    (A) in the case of an agency which regulates currencies, securities, commodities, or financial institutions, be likely to lead to significant financial speculation in currencies, securities, or commodities, or significantly endanger the stability of any financial institution; or

    (B) in the case of any agency, be likely to significantly frustrate implementation of a proposed agency action.

except that subparagraph (B) shall not apply in any instance where the agency has already disclosed to the public the content or nature of its proposed action, or where the agency is required by law to make such disclosure on its own initiative prior to taking final agency action on such proposal; or

(10) Specifically concern the agency's issuance of a subpoena, or the agency's participation in a civil action or proceeding, an action in a foreign court or international tribunal, or an arbitration, or the initiation, conduct, or disposition by the agency of a particular case of formal agency adjudication pursuant to the procedures in section 554 of this title or otherwise involving a determination on the record after opportunity for a hearing.

The Intelligence Authorization Act for Fiscal Year 2003 amended FOIA to prohibit information from agencies associated with gathering or maintaining intelligence from being disclosed to foreign governments or international governmental organizations. Intelligence agencies include the Central Intelligence Agency, the National Security Agency, agencies of the Department of Defense, and agencies of the Department of State.

10

THE UNITED STATES
FEDERAL BUDGET

The U.S. economy operates as a mixed system of free trade and government management. Private companies supply goods and services to meet consumer demand, while the government establishes policies to maintain economic growth. The government fosters economic growth by eliminating barriers to commercial competition, protecting consumer rights and welfare, and taking actions to maintain a stable U.S. economy. The federal budget of the United States is the largest in the world, and represents approximately 20 percent of the U.S. Gross Domestic Product. A complex process is used to develop the budget, beginning with input from the president and ending with the final passage of the budget by Congress.

THE U.S. ECONOMY

The U.S. economy is most often characterized as operating on the basis of *capitalism*, in which production and trade take place with little or no government intervention. However, it is more accurately described as a *mixed economy* of free enterprise and government management. Free enterprise allows for the ownership of private property, pursuit of self-interests, and operation of free markets. Private businesses use resources and labor to produce goods and services. They then sell these goods and services based on the demands from buyers in order to earn a profit. The prices charged by sellers are controlled by what buyers are willing to spend. This is the basic premise of supply and demand. Two-thirds of these buyers in the U.S. economy are private citizens. The rest are other businesses and the government. The government provides some products and services, particularly those that a private company is unwilling or unable to provide. These include disaster relief, national defense, space exploration, interstate transportation networks, and a system of justice. The government also provides social support through such programs as Social Security, welfare programs, Medicare, and unemployment support. Citizens vote for officials they feel will make policy decisions they favor thus controlling the products and services provided by the government.

The government manages the economy by providing oversight and regulations through policies that ensure equity in business transactions to sustain economic growth. Two major components of economic growth are high levels of employment and stable prices. A high rate of unemployment results in fewer buyers able to buy what businesses produce, fewer people able to make products, and an increase in the number of people relying on government social support programs such as unemployment insurance. The absence of stable prices can lead to businesses placing an economic burden on citizens. For example, the high price of gasoline in 2008 resulted in consumers cutting their spending on other goods such as food, clothing, and new homes. The government thus establishes policies to influence the economy when the economy is not operating normally, that is, when supply and demand are not at equilibrium.

Government policies fall into two categories: fiscal and monetary. *Fiscal policy* aims to influence the economy by adjusting government spending and the federal tax system. During times of high inflation, for example, reduced spending by businesses and citizens is required to drive prices back down. If their spending continues to rise, the government will decrease its spending or raise tax rates. *Monetary policy* aims to influence the economy by the Federal Reserve (see the section, "The Federal Reserve System," below) adjusting the government's buying and selling of U.S. government securities, the money supply, or credit and interest rates. For example, the lowering of interest rates is often used to increase borrowing when the government determines the housing market is suffering from low sales of new homes.

Gross national product (GNP) is the dollar value of all goods and services produced in any given year. It includes all output by any citizen regardless of where he or she resides. The output of an American company located overseas is thus included. It is used to measure the economic welfare of a country. Measuring GNP according to aggregate (or total) spending includes the sum of spending by households, investments by businesses, government spending, and the net value of export spending (value of exports minus imports). GNP is raised by households buying more appliances, businesses building new office complexes, the government increasing road construction, and an increase in goods being exported. Since two-thirds of all spending in the U.S. is done by individuals, household spending determines GNP. Therefore government policies to influence spending take primary aim at household spending.

The size of a country's economy is measured by its *gross domestic product* (GDP). GDP is the market value of all goods and services produced within a nation each year. GDP is used to measure the economy in the U.S. rather than GNP. The United States has the largest economy in the world. The GDP of the U.S. is computed and reported by the Bureau of Economic Analysis (BEA) within the U.S. Department of Commerce. According to the BEA, in 2006 the GDP of the U.S. was approximately $13 trillion. This is compared to a GDP of $91.2 billion in 1930, $526.4 billion in 1960, $2.8 trillion in 1980, and $5.8 trillion in 1990. According to the World Bank, the nations with the next highest GDPs in 2006 were Japan ($4.3 billion), Germany ($2.9 billion), China ($2.7 billion), the United Kingdom ($2.3 billion), and France $2.2 billion (World Bank, 2007).

The U.S. economy continues to grow more complex due to the interdependence of nations around the world. The global economy has resulted from nations and private business forming partnerships. As a result, U.S. companies have moved jobs overseas, foreign producers have taken over some U.S. markets (such as automobile sales and electronics), U.S. dependence on some foreign made products has increased, and the value of the U.S. dollar is more dependent on the economies of other countries.

As more nations are becoming economically developed, the U.S. share of the global market is shrinking, which has a negative impact on the global strength of the U.S. economy. All of these factors have significantly contributed to the complexity that the federal government is faced with when attempting to successfully manage the U.S. economy.

The top U.S. industries in terms of annual sales are wholesale trade, retail trade, finance and insurance, health care and social assistance, information, and professional, scientific, and technical services. Some of the top U.S. exports are wheat, corn, other grains, fruits, vegetables, and cotton. Some of the primary imports are crude oil and petroleum products, machinery, and automobiles. Table 10.1 shows the top countries the U.S. exported goods to and received imports from in 2006, excluding services. Fifteen nations comprised approximately 73 percent of all U.S. trade. In total, the U.S. exported $1.037 trillion in goods (excludes services) and imported $1.855 trillion in goods. The top five trading partners (export and import partners) were Canada, China, Mexico, Japan, and Germany.

Government Influence on the Economy.   The federal government manages and influences the economy through economic and social regulation. Economic regulation

Table 10.1.   Top U.S. Trading Partners in 2006 (total trade, exports, and imports for goods only, excludes services), in Billions of Dollars

Country	Exports	Imports	Total, all trade	Rank	Percent of total trade
Total, all countries	$1,037.3	$1,855.4	$2,892.7		
Total, top fifteen countries	755.2	1,369.1	2,124.3		73.4
Canada	230.6	303.4	534.0	1	18.5
China	55.2	287.8	343.0	2	11.9
Mexico	134.2	198.3	332.4	3	11.5
Japan	59.6	148.1	207.7	4	7.2
Germany	41.3	89.1	130.4	5	4.5
United Kingdom	45.4	53.4	98.8	6	3.4
South Korea	32.5	45.8	78.3	7	2.7
France	24.2	37.1	61.4	8	2.1
Taiwan	23.0	38.2	61.2	9	2.1
Malaysia	12.6	36.5	49.1	10	1.7
Netherlands	31.1	17.3	48.4	11	1.7
Venezuela	9.0	37.2	46.2	12	1.6
Brazil	19.2	26.4	45.6	13	1.6
Italy	12.6	32.7	45.2	14	1.6
Singapore	24.7	17.8	42.5	15	1.5

Source: U.S. Census Bureau (2007). *Foreign Trade Statistics.* U.S. Census Bureau, Washington, D.C. Retrieved September 27, 2007, from http://www.census.gov/foreign-trade/statistics/highlights/top/top0612.html

attempts to control prices to ensure they are fair and reasonable for consumers and do not allow companies to earn excessive profits. It includes strict regulation over some industries. For example, government regulation of utilities ensures these companies do not charge excessive prices and do provide continuous service to their customers. Companies are also monitored to prevent them from engaging in harmful collusive activities such as price fixing, in which companies work together to set prices higher than the market would normally demand. The government also deregulates some industries to stimulate the economy and foster competition. For example, the government lifted rules affecting the airline industry to allow new service providers to enter the market.

Antitrust laws are economic regulations that attempt to prevent companies from engaging in activities that purposely stifle competition. These include engaging in activities the government believes create a monopoly within an industry, collusive joint ventures, and the hostile acquisition of vulnerable companies. For example, *United States v. Microsoft*, 87 F. Supp 2d 30 (2000) was a consolidation of cases in which the U.S. Department of Justice and twenty states brought suit against Microsoft for allegedly acting as a monopoly in the computer industry. The argument in the case was that Microsoft's extremely large and stable share of the market was protected by a high barrier to competitors being able to enter the market, and Microsoft's customers were therefore unable to obtain a commercially viable alternative to Windows (Microsoft's computer operating system). The Court of Appeals ruled that Microsoft was a monopoly, but should not be split into two companies. The case was sent back to the District Court for the District of Columbia, because the court had altered the requirements of liability and the district court judge had acted with bias in interviews with reporters about the case. This last action violated the *Code of Conduct for United States Judges* so the original judge was not allowed to hear the case the second time. The Supreme Court refused to hear Microsoft's appeal from the circuit court. Microsoft eventually reached a settlement agreement with the Department of Justice to share its programming with other companies but maintain its marketing rights. In essence, it was not required to change the way it conducted business.

The Sherman Antitrust Act of 1890 was the first major government law that attempted to control monopolies. It stated,

> Every contract, combination in the form of trust or otherwise, or conspiracy, in restraint of trade or commerce among the several States, or with foreign nations, is declared to be illegal. Every person who shall monopolize, or attempt to monopolize, or combine or conspire with any other person or persons, to monopolize any part of the trade or commerce among the several States, or with foreign nations, shall be deemed guilty of a felony, and, on conviction thereof, shall be punished by fine not exceeding $10,000,000 if a corporation, or, if any other person, $350,000, or by imprisonment not exceeding three years, or by both said punishments, in the discretion of the court.

American Telephone and Telegraph (AT&T) was dissolved in 1982 for violating the act.

Many other laws have been passed in addition to the Sherman Antitrust Act. The Clayton Act of 1914 was passed to strengthen the Sherman Antitrust Act and forbade such practices as price cutting to keep competitors out of a local market, a company selling products to another with the stipulation the company does not do business with competitors, and offering different prices to affect competition. It legalized peaceful labor strikes, picketing, and boycotts.

The Federal Trade Commission Act of 1914 created the Federal Deposit Insurance Corporation (FDIC). The FDIC is an independent agency that was created in response to the thousands of bank failures during the Great Depression. It insures deposits in banks and thrift institutions for at least $100,000. During the 1980s, thousands of savings and loan banks became insolvent as a result of risky and bad investments. The government contributed to the problem because it deregulated the savings and loan industry. Investors lost billions of dollars. As a result, Congress passed the Financial Institutions Reform Recovery and Enforcement Act of 1989 that established the Resolution Trust Corporation to liquidate the assets of failed savings and loans and use the proceeds to repay investors. Regulation of the industry was moved under the Office of Thrift Supervision in the Department of the Treasury. New regulations were established to protect investors, including insuring investors through the FDIC.

The Hart-Scoss-Rodino Antitrust Improvement Act of 1976 made it easier for the FTC to investigate mergers in order to determine if they violated antitrust laws by requiring that all major mergers and acquisitions be reported to the FTC. Congress passed the Foreign Trade Antitrust Improvement Act of 1982 to apply U.S. antitrust laws to foreign commerce when actions have a "direct, substantial, and reasonably foreseeable effect" on U.S. export trade and commerce. The International Antitrust Enforcement Assistance Act of 1994 allows the U.S. attorney general and the Federal Trade Commission to establish agreements with foreign antitrust authorities, and provide information and support to assist the foreign antitrust authorities in determining whether a person has violated or is about to violate any of the foreign antitrust laws administered or enforced by the foreign antitrust authority, or in enforcing foreign antitrust laws.

The government's use of social regulation sets rules and standards for businesses to protect employees, citizens, and the environment. Companies must abide by emissions and pollution standards that protect the environment (water, air, and land), people, and animals from harmful goods and byproducts of production. These standards include regulations for the storage, transportation, and disposal of products. Laws ensure employees are provided safe working conditions. This includes ensuring employees do not work excessive hours that would put them and others in danger, and children are protected from being forced to work in adult conditions. Laws and regulations ensure employees are paid fair and equitable wages, and are not discriminated against based upon nonwork-related factors such as their age, sex, disability, or race. Finally, federal actions are taken to protect the finances of citizens.

The federal, state, and local governments use many other methods to maintain or stimulate the economy. Opposite actions are taken when the government desires to slow down the economy. The following are examples.

- Increase federal spending and government investments
- Increase the supply of money
- Lower tax rates so consumers will spend more
- Lower interest rates to increase borrowing
- Provide tax cuts and other incentives to businesses
- Increase government support for specific programs (such as farming, student loans, low interest business loans, and social programs for the poor)
- Increase the minimum wage to provide consumers more money

Since spending by households comprises almost two-thirds of all U.S. spending, the government attempts to influence household spending when the economy is not performing well (i.e., during recessions, when spending is lower than production, when businesses maintain excess inventory, etc.) One tactic used by the executive branch has been to reduce income taxes so that consumers will have more money to spend. This increases money in the economy to businesses, leading to a growth in jobs and an increase in the flow of revenues to the government from business taxes. Under President Ronald W. Reagan, the Economic Recovery Tax Act of 1981 reduced income taxes by 25 percent over a three-year period in order to stimulate the economy. Fearing an economic recession, President George W. Bush introduced an economic stimulus package in January 2008 that would provide up to $150 billion in tax relief for consumers and businesses. The plan included giving rebate checks to taxpayers in the amount of $600 for individuals, $1,200 for couples, and an additional $300 per child for families. The plan included restrictions as to how much income tax filers would receive. The full amounts of the rebates were capped for individuals with an annual income of $75,000 and joint tax filers with an income of at $150,000. Income tax filers who earned at least $3,000 in 2007 but paid less than $300 in income taxes would receive $300. The goal of the plan was for consumers to then spend the money and therefore provide a boost to the economy. The House approved the proposal in January 2008.

The Federal Reserve System.   The Federal Reserve System, an independent agency also called the Central Bank of the United States, is responsible for U.S. monetary policy. It was created in 1913 by the Federal Reserve Act. It has four major duties (Board of Governors of the Federal Reserve System, 2005):

- conducting the nation's monetary policy by influencing the monetary and credit conditions in the economy in pursuit of maximum employment, stable prices, and moderate long-term interest rates
- supervising and regulating banking institutions to ensure the safety and soundness of the nation's banking and financial system and to protect the credit rights of consumers
- maintaining the stability of the financial system and containing systemic risk that may arise in financial markets
- providing financial services to depository institutions, the U.S. government, and foreign official institutions, including playing a major role in operating the nation's payments system

The Federal Reserve takes actions to maintain the stability of the U.S. economy and foster its growth. For example, low consumer spending causes businesses to lose money and reduce their number of workers. The Federal Reserve lowers interest rates and/or increases the supply of money to increase spending. If spending is too high, business may also suffer by not being able to maintain production at the pace of consumer demand. The Federal Reserve then increases interest rates and/or reduces the money supply to slow down spending.

The Federal Reserve controls the U.S. supply of money. The Federal Reserve's monetary notes (or paper currency) are printed by the U.S. Bureau of Engraving and Printing in Washington, D.C., and Fort Worth, Texas. Coins are produced at the U.S. Mints in Philadelphia, Pennsylvania, and Denver, Colorado. The currency is shipped and stored in the Federal Reserve Banks and branches, and ordered as needed from banking institutions. The Federal Reserve is also the bank for the federal government. It issues the government's checks, such as Social Security and federal employee paychecks. U.S. securities (such as savings bonds and treasury bills) are issued and redeemed by the Federal Reserve. It also redeems food stamps for banking institutions that receive them as deposits from grocery stores.

The Federal Reserve is financially independent of the government in that it uses funds it earns as interest from bank loans, interest from investments in government securities, and payments received from services provided to financial institutions to fund its operations. Any excess money remaining is turned over to the U.S. Treasury.

The Federal Reserve System is comprised of a central governing body called the Board of Governors and twelve regional Federal Reserve Banks. The Board of Governors is headquartered in Washington, D.C., and is composed of seven members appointed by the president for fourteen years and confirmed by the Senate. The president selects the Chairman and Vice Chairman of the Board for four-year terms, subject to approval by the Senate. The Board oversees all federal banks, and those state banks that elect to join the Federal Reserve System and meet the requirements of membership, that is, a bank must maintain at least 6 percent of its capital or surplus in its regional Federal Reserve Bank. In 2005, the Board of Governors supervised the twelve reserve banks, nine hundred state member banks, and five thousand bank holding companies (i.e., companies that control banks). The Board establishes the minimum amounts of reserve (i.e., capital on hand) all member banks must maintain on hand, and sets the discount rate for the Reserve Banks.

The twelve Federal Reserve Banks and their respective branches are strategically located in major cities around the country. They distribute currency, regulate member banks and holding companies in their regions, and serve other functions on behalf of the system for the region assigned to them. Table 10.2 shows the Federal Reserve Banks and their branches as of 2007. Each has its own board of nine directors chosen from outside the Bank as provided by law.

Table 10.2. The Federal Reserve Banks and Their Respective Branches, as of 2007

Federal Reserve Bank	Branches
Boston	
New York	Buffalo, New York
Philadelphia	
Cleveland	Cincinnati, Ohio; Pittsburgh, Pennsylvania
Richmond	Baltimore, Maryland; Charlotte, North Carolina
Atlanta	Birmingham, Alabama; Jacksonville, Florida; Miami, Florida; Nashville, Tennessee; New Orleans, Louisiana
Chicago	Detroit, Michigan
St. Louis	Little Rock, Arkansas; Louisville, Kentucky; Memphis, Tennessee
Minneapolis	Helena, Montana
Kansas City	Denver, Colorado; Oklahoma City, Oklahoma; Omaha, Nebraska
Dallas	El Paso, Texas; Houston, Texas; San Antonio, Texas
San Francisco	Los Angeles, California; Phoenix, Arizona; Portland, Oregon; Salt Lake City, Utah; Seattle, Washington

(a)   (b)

American eagle gold bullion coins, in circulation since 1986. (a) Obverse, modified design of Augustus Saint Gaudens's high-relief U.S. $20 gold coin design of 1907, "Standing Liberty." (b) Reverse, "Family of Eagles" motif, symbolizing family tradition and unity. Designed by Ms. Miley Frances Busiek. *U.S. Mint.*

The Federal Reserve System is also composed of a Federal Open Market Committee (FOMC) that oversees the operations of the open market, and advisory committees that provide advice and consultation to the Board of Governors. The open market is where the Federal Reserve issues or buys securities. The FOMC is composed of seven members of the Board of Governors and five members selected from the Federal Reserve Banks.

U.S. Money Supply.   The U.S. money supply consists of currency (i.e., bills and coins) and various types of public deposits in financial institutions. The United States once used gold as a measure of its money supply. In simple terms, the amount of money in the country was a measure of how much could be exchanged for gold. Under President Richard M. Nixon, the value was converted into *fiat money*, which is the amount of money the government has the legal authority to issue.

The supply of money has a direct effect on the economy. An increase in the supply of money allows more to be available for consumers to spend. Increased consumer spending causes businesses to increase their use of resources and labor to produce more goods, stimulating the economy. If too much money is supplied, prices rise because production cannot increase at the same pace, which eventually leads to inflation (i.e., a period of rising prices). Inflation causes lenders to charge higher interest rates for loans because of an expected decrease in the purchasing power of money due to increased prices. If there is not enough money available and production is not able to decrease at an equal pace, prices fall and disinflation or deflation (falling prices) results.

The Federal Reserve attempts to use monetary policy to achieve the economic goals of stable prices, sustainable economic growth, and high employment. It does this through controlling the supply of money, that is, how much money is allowed to be in circulation in the United States at any given time. The Full Employment and Balanced Growth Act of 1978 (also known as the Humphrey-Hawkins Act) requires the Federal Reserve to establish annual target ranges for money supply growth and to report these targets to Congress. The Federal Reserve uses two measures to determine the size of the money supply. Each is based on the how liquid various forms of money are, that is, how easy it is to spend. The first measure, M1, measures the most liquid of assets and includes the value of currency in circulation (i.e., bills and coins in the hands of the public), traveler's checks, and demand deposits and other deposits against which checks can be written. The second measure, M2, includes liquid assets and those that are less liquid. It therefore includes all of M1, plus the value of savings accounts, and money in retail money market mutual fund accounts (i.e., investments that are relatively available, therefore excluding money in retirement accounts). In 2006, M1 was approximately $1.4 trillion, which mostly consisted of currency. M2 was approximately $6.8 trillion and consisted mostly of savings deposits.

The Federal Reserve uses three methods to control the money supply: open market operations, changes to reserve requirements, and changes in the discount rate. With the first method, the Federal Reserve can increase reserves by buying government securities. This occurs because the seller of the securities then deposits the funds from the sale to the Federal Reserve into his or her bank account. The bank's amount of money increases and it must therefore maintain more reserves as a percent of their increased deposits. The Federal Reserve sells securities to reduce reserve levels. The buyer uses money to buy the securities, which reduces their deposits. Banks therefore have less money and are required to maintain smaller reserve amounts. With the second method, changing the reserve requirements, the Federal Reserve alters the requirements of bank deposits. The Federal Reserve requires its member banks to maintain a specific percent of their deposits in reserve accounts. For example, it may stipulate that 6 percent of all bank deposits are held and not used for investments or loans. Banks place these reserves in their vaults or deposit them in their local Federal Reserve branch. The Federal Reserve can increase the required reserve percent to decrease money supply, or decrease the rate to increase money supply. Finally, the Federal Reserve also increases the money supply by changing the discount rate. This is the rate the Federal Reserve charges banks. If it increases the discount rate, banks will decrease their interest rates on savings. People will be less interested in placing money in savings accounts and will spend more, driving up prices.

There are instances when the Federal Reserve issues new currency not in direct connection with influencing the economy. In these cases, the actual amount of money in supply does not increase. When a bank requires additional currency (additional cash), the Federal Reserve issues them money and deducts the amount of currency from the bank's reserve. This may happen, for instance, when a bank does not have enough currency on hand to meet demands from customers for loans or withdrawals. The Federal Reserve also takes old money out of circulation and replaces it with new bills. The old money is destroyed. New currency is also issued when counterfeiting of older bills increases. The Federal Reserve adds extra safeguards to new currency, such as special variants in colors, to make counterfeiting more difficult. Finally, the government issues commemorative coins of special events in American history or to celebrate the life of a well-know U.S. figure (such as a former president).

THE U.S. FEDERAL BUDGET

Size of the U.S. Budget.   The U.S. federal budget is the largest in the world. The next largest are Japan, Germany, the United Kingdom, France, and Italy. As shown in Table 10.3, in 2005 the federal government spent $2.4 trillion on thousands of

Table 10.3. Summary of U.S. Government Receipts, Outlays, and Surpluses or Deficits, 1905–2010 (in millions of dollars)

Year	Total			On-budget			Off-budget		
	Receipts	Outlays	Surplus or deficit (–)	Receipts	Outlays	Surplus or deficit (–)	Receipts	Outlays	Surplus or deficit (–)
1905	544	567	–23	544	567	–2	—a	—a	—a
1910	676	694	–18	676	694	–18	—a	—a	—a
1915	683	746	–63	683	746	–63	—a	—a	—a
1920	6,649	6,358	291	6,649	6,358	291	—a	—a	—a
1925	3,641	2,924	717	3,641	2,924	717	—a	—a	—a
1930	4,058	3,320	738	4,058	3,320	738	—a	—a	—a
1935	3,609	6,412	–2,803	3,609	6,412	–2,803	—a	—a	—a
1940	6,548	9,468	–2,920	5,998	9,482	–3,484	550	–14	564
1945	45,159	92,712	–47,553	43,849	92,569	–48,720	1,310	143	1,167
1950	39,443	42,562	–3,119	37,336	42,038	–4,702	2,106	524	1,583
1955	65,451	68,444	–2,993	60,370	64,461	–4,091	5,081	3,983	1,098
1960	92,492	92,191	301	81,851	81,341	510	10,641	10,850	–209
1965	116,817	118,228	–1,411	100,094	101,699	–1,605	16,723	16,529	194
1970	192,807	195,649	–2,842	159,348	168,042	–8,694	33,459	27,607	5,852
1975	279,090	332,332	–53,242	216,633	270,780	–54,148	62,458	61,552	906
1980	517,112	590,941	–73,830	403,903	477,044	–73,141	113,209	113,898	–689

Year									
1985	734,088	946,396	−212,308	547,918	769,447	−221,529	186,171	176,949	9,222
1990	1,032,094	1,253,130	−221,036	750,439	1,028,065	−277,626	281,656	225,065	56,590
1995	1,351,932	1,515,884	−163,952	1,000,853	1,227,220	−226,367	351,079	288,664	62,415
2000	2,025,457	1,789,216	236,241	1,544,873	1,458,451	86,422	480,584	330,765	149,819
2005	2,153,859	2,472,205	−318,346	1,576,383	2,069,994	−493,611	577,476	402,211	175,265
2010 (est.)	2,954,724	3,049,085	−94,361	2,201,442	2,540,528	−338,086	753,282	508,557	244,725

a$500 thousand or less.

Note: Budget figures prior to 1933 are based on the "administrative budget" concepts rather than the "unified budget" concepts.

Source: Office of Management and Budget (2007b). *Historical Tables, Budget of the United States Government, Fiscal Year 2008*. Superintendent of Documents, U.S. Government Printing Office, Washington, DC. Retrieved December 30, 2007, from http://origin.www.gpoaccess.gov/usbudget/fy08/pdf/hist.pdf

programs. This is compared to $92 billion in 1960 and $567 million in 1905. U.S. receipts or revenue in 2005 were $2.1 trillion, compared to $92 billion in 1960 and $544 million in 1905. The federal budget represents a sizable portion of the U.S. economy. It is almost 20 percent of the U.S. GDP. By 2010, the spending and revenues are each expected to reach $3 trillion.

The U.S. budget is divided between off-budget and on-budget categories. Off-budget revenues and spending are for two Social Security trust funds (the Old-Age and Survivors Insurance Trust Fund and the Disability Insurance Trust Fund) and the transactions of the Postal Service. Trust funds are monies that are accounted for separately, set aside for specific purposes, and deposited in trust fund accounts. These include funds for civil service retirement, Social Security, Medicare, unemployment benefits, and infrastructure construction improvements (such as highways and airports). All budgetary accounts that are not off-budget are designated by law as on-budget.

The difference between what is raised by the government (i.e., revenues) and spent (i.e., outlays) results in either a surplus or a deficit. A budget surplus results if federal spending is less than what is raised. The only presidents to achieve and maintain a surplus since World War II have been President Harry S. Truman from 1947–1949, President Dwight D. Eisenhower in 1956 and 1957, and President Bill Clinton from 1998–2001. A budget deficit results if more is spent than raised. As shown in Table 10.3, government outlays have mostly outpaced receipts, resulting in the annual U.S. budget being at a deficit for most of the twentieth century. The U.S. deficit was $318 billion in 2005. The government uses debt to make up the deficit needed to fund spending (see section on *U.S. Debt*).

As shown in Table 10.4, the largest amount of federal receipts comes from individual income taxes, taxes paid by citizens from their wages and salaries. It has accounted for over 40 percent of the government's annual revenue since 1960 and is expected to reach $1.4 trillion in 2010 (compared to $892 million in 1940). The second highest source of revenues is from Social Security and retirement receipts. These revenues are expected to reach $1 trillion by 2010, compared to approximately $1.8 billion in 1940. Income taxes from corporations, excise taxes, and receipts from miscellaneous (or "other") sources make up the remainder of government receipts. Excise taxes are taxes on such products as alcohol, tobacco, crude oil windfall profits, telephones, ozone depleting chemicals/products, and transportation fuels. The "other" category includes estate and gift taxes, customs duties, and Federal Reserve deposit earnings. It also includes funds from borrowing.

Table 10.5 shows government spending by major categories called superfunctions, (shown in boldface type in the table) and subcategories called functions for select years from 1940 through 2010. For example, physical resources is a superfunction, or primary, category of spending. Its functions, or subcategories, include energy, natural resources and environment, commerce and housing credit, transportation, and community and regional development. Since 1980, the majority of spending has been on functions under human resources. Spending on this superfunction increased from $4.1 billion in 1940 to $1.1 trillion in 2000 and is expected to reach $2 trillion in 2010. This is due to Social Security, Income Security, and Medicare outlays. The second largest outlays have been for national defense. Spending here increased from $1.6 billion in 1940 to $294 billion in 2000. Spending is expected to reach $565 billion in 2010, predominantly due to increased spending as a result of the War on Terrorism. Of the remaining functions, the largest amounts have been on net

Table 10.4. United States Government Receipts by Source, Select Years 1940–2010 (in millions of dollars)

Fiscal year	Individual income taxes	Corporate income taxes	Social Security and retirement receipts			Excise taxes	Other	Total receipts		
			Total	On-budget	Off-budget			Total	On-budget	Off-budget
1940	892	1,197	1,785	1,235	550	1,977	698	6,548	5,998	550
1950	15,755	10,449	4,338	2,232	2,106	7,550	1,351	39,443	37,336	2,106
1960	40,715	21,494	14,683	4,042	10,641	11,678	3,923	92,492	81,851	10,641
1970	90,412	32,829	44,362	10,903	33,459	15,705	9,499	192,807	159,348	33,459
1980	224,069	64,600	157,803	44,594	113,209	24,329	26,311	517,112	403,903	113,209
1990	466,884	93,507	380,047	98,392	281,656	35,345	56,311	1,032,094	750,439	281,656
2000	1,004,462	207,289	652,852	172,268	480,584	68,865	91,989	2,025,457	1,544,873	480,584
2005	927,222	278,282	794,125	216,649	577,476	73,094	81,136	2,153,859	1,576,383	577,476
2010 (est.)	1,428,317	325,459	1,029,309	276,027	753,282	63,600	108,039	2,954,724	2,201,442	753,282

Note: Beginning in 1987, includes trust fund receipts for the hazardous substance superfund. The trust fund amounts are as follows (in millions of dollars): 1987: 196; 1988: 313; 1989: 292; 1990: 461; 1991: 591; 1992: 380; 1993: 886; 1994: 653; 1995: 612; 1996: 323; 1997: 4; 1998: 79; 1999: 10; 2000: 3.

Source: Office of Management and Budget (2007a). *Historical Tables, Budget of the United States Government, Fiscal Year 2008.* Superintendent of Documents, U.S. Government Printing Office, Washington, D.C. Retrieved December 30, 2007, from http://origin.www.gpoaccess.gov/usbudget/fy08/pdf/hist.pdf

Table 10.5. Outlays by Superfunction (in boldface type) and Function, Select Years 1940–2010 (in millions of dollars)

	1940	1950	1960	1970	1980	1990	2000	2010 (est.)
National Defense	**1,660**	**13,724**	**48,130**	**81,692**	**133,995**	**299,331**	**294,394**	**565,309**
Human Resources	**4,139**	**14,221**	**26,184**	**75,349**	**313,374**	**619,345**	**1,115,665**	**2,009,444**
Education, training, employment, and social services	1,972	241	968	8,634	31,843	37,179	53,789	87,175
Health	55	268	795	5,907	23,169	57,716	154,533	312,310
Medicare				6,213	32,090	98,102	197,113	439,334
Income security	1,514	4,097	7,378	15,655	86,557	148,668	253,724	399,313
Social Security	28	781	11,602	30,270	118,547	248,623	409,423	682,505
Veterans benefits and services	570	8,834	5,441	8,669	21,169	29,058	47,083	88,807
Physical resources	**2,312**	**3,667**	**7,991**	**15,574**	**65,985**	**126,037**	**84,954**	**124,685**
Energy	88	327	464	997	10,156	3,341	–761	2,169
Natural resources and environment	997	1,308	1,559	3,065	13,858	17,080	25,031	30,950
Commerce and housing credit	550	1,035	1618	2,112	9,390	67,600	3,208	2,291
Transportation	392	967	4,126	7,008	21,329	29,485	46,853	73,803
Community and regional development	285	30	224	2,392	11,252	8,531	10,623	15,472
Net interest	**899**	**4,812**	**6,947**	**14,380**	**52,533**	**184,347**	**222,949**	**280,847**
(On-budget)	–941	5069	7,511	15,948	54,872	200,338	282,745	417,339
(Off-budget)	–42	257	–563	–1,568	–2,339	–15,991	–59,796	–136,492

202

Other functions	775	7,955	7,760	17,286	44,996	60,686	113,835	151,631
International affairs	51	4,673	2,988	4,330	12,714	13,764	17,216	34,898
General science, space and technology		55	599	4,511	5,831	14,443	18,633	28,886
Agriculture	369	2,049	2,623	5,166	8,774	11,806	36,459	19,791
Administration of justice	81	193	366	959	4,702	10,185	28,499	46,518
General government	274	986	1,184	2,320	12,975	10,488	13,028	20,517
Allowances								1,021
Undistributed offsetting receipts	**−317**	**−1,817**	**−4,820**	**8,632**	**−19,942**	**−36,615**	**−42,581**	**−82,831**
Total, fderal outlays	**9,468**	**45,562**	**92,191**	**195,649**	**590,941**	**1,253,130**	**1,789,216**	**3,049,085**
(On-budget)	−9,482	42,038	81,341	168,042	477,044	1,028,065	1,458,451	2,540,528
(Off-budget)	−14	524	10,850	27,607	113,898	225,065	330,765	508,557

Source: Office of Management and Budget (2007a). *Historical Tables, Budget of the United States Government, Fiscal Year 2008.* Superintendent of Documents, U.S. Government Printing Office, Washington, DC. Retrieved December 30, 2007, from http://origin.www.gpoaccess.gov/usbudget/fy08/pdf/hist.pdf

interest on government debt, health programs, veterans benefits and services, and transportation.

U.S DEBT

The government uses debt to fund its operations when spending exceeds revenues. This debt is in the form of U.S. treasury securities, which include loans to the government through treasury bills, bonds, and notes the government sells. Treasury bills are short-term securities that mature (i.e., reach full value) one year after their date of issue. Bonds provide interest until reaching maturity in ten years or more. Treasury notes mature between one and ten years. The holders of these loans are paid interest by the government.

In 1940 the U.S. debt was $50 billion. In 2005 it had reached nearly $8 trillion, the highest of any nation in the world. This dollar amount was 63 percent of the U.S. GDP. The government attempts to control debt by setting statutory limits mandating a debt ceiling. This ceiling is the maximum amount the government is allowed to borrow without obtaining additional approval from Congress. If the debt ceiling is not raised, cuts in spending must be made. Over the years this limit has been changed to accommodate the size of the government's debt, inflation, and other related factors. In 1940 the debt limit was $49 billion (per 54 Stat. 526, dated June 25, 1940). Under 120 Stat. 289, dated March 20, 2006, the debt limit reached $8.965 trillion.

Of the $8.17 trillion in federal debt as of December 2005, approximately $4.2 trillion was held by the Federal Reserve and government accounts, and the remaining $3.9 trillion was owed to private investors. In the former case, the government borrowed money from government sources. Of the funds owned by private investors, the following outlines the owners of private U.S. treasury securities:

Foreign and international	**$2.041 billion**
Debt held by U.S. investors	**$1.930 billion**
State and local governments	$455 million
Mutual funds	$254 million
U.S. Savings Bonds	$205 million
Private pension funds	$162 million
Insurance companies	$161 million
State and local government pension funds	$120 million
Depository institutions	$117 million
Other investors	$456 million

As shown, debt is held by investors within and outside the United States. A concern is the growing amount of U.S. debt owed to foreign entities. In 2005, foreign ownership of U.S. debt was approximately 25 percent of all U.S. debt. This was up from approximately 17 percent in 1996. Foreign ownership was 52 percent of all privately held debt. The top foreign investors in U.S. securities were Japan, China, the United Kingdom, Luxembourg, Cayman Islands, and Canada (Board of Governors of the Federal Reserve System, 2007). There are two main concerns over foreign investment. The first concern is that the U.S. economy could be in crisis if foreign countries stopped investing. This removes a large amount of control of the U.S. economy away from its government, businesses, and citizens. A second concern is that there is uncertainty over exactly who is funding some of these investments. For example, some experts have questioned if investments being made by the Cayman Islands are really on behalf of Middle Eastern governments. It is not known if all investors are allies or enemies.

INDIVIDUAL INCOME TAXATION

Individual income taxes are the federal government's largest source of revenue. Individuals paid $927 billion in income taxes in 2005. This total amount includes taxes on the worldwide income of U.S. citizens and resident aliens, and on certain U.S. income of nonresidents. The first income tax law was put into effect under the Revenue Act of 1861 to finance the Civil War. It levied a tax of 3 percent on all incomes over $800 a year. In 1862, Congress established a two-tiered tax structure of 3 percent for incomes up to $10,000 and 5 percent for incomes over $10,000. The income tax was then repealed in 1872. Congress attempted to establish it again with the Income Tax Act of 1894 with a flat tax for all citizens but it was challenged and struck down by the Supreme Court in *Pollock v. Farmers' Lock & Trust Co.*, 157 U.S. 429 (1895). The Court ruled that the Constitution only allowed Congress to levy direct taxes if it was done according to each state's population.

Congress passed the Sixteenth Amendment, which was ratified in 1913. It removed the requirement that taxation must be based on state populations. It states, "The Congress shall have power to lay and collect taxes on incomes, from whatever source derived, without apportionment among the several states, and without regard to any census or enumeration." The government levied an excise tax on business income and an income tax on individuals' incomes. Congress established a tax rate of 1 percent to 7 percent for incomes over $500,000. Form 1040 was used as the standard tax reporting form. Less than 1 percent of the population paid taxes when the law was first introduced, mainly because the Congress stipulated only "lawful income" could be taxed. It was difficult to define "lawful" and some citizens were making illegal incomes from such activities as bootlegging. The word "lawful" was removed in 1916 and all income was subject to taxation.

The tax rates have changed many times over the years and have become very complex. The tax law is contained in Title 26 of the *United States Code* (26 U.S.C.) under the Internal Revenue Code. Chapter 1 of Subtitle A defines such elements as what is included and excluded in income, and what deductions are allowed for individuals and corporations. Table 10.6 shows the Internal Revenue Service tax rate schedules for individuals as of 2006.

THE U.S. FEDERAL BUDGET PROCESS

Overview of the U.S. Budget Process.   The federal government is not allowed to spend money without a budget. Article I, Section 9, of the U.S. Constitution states, "No money shall be drawn from the Treasury, but in Consequence of Appropriations made by law." Congress must therefore consider all budgetary requests and pass an annual budget into law for the federal government. The budget includes the sources and methods of raising money (i.e., taxation), approved appropriations (i.e., specific programs for which money is set aside), and actual expenditures (i.e., where money is

Table 10.6. 2006 Federal Tax Rate Schedules for Individuals, Based on Filing Status and Income

If taxable income is over	But not over	The tax is
Filing Status: Single		
$0	$7,550	10% of the amount over $0
$7,550	$30,650	$755 plus 15% of the amount over $7,550
$30,650	$74,200	$4,220 plus 25% of the amount over $30,650
$74,200	$154,800	$15,107.50 plus 28% of the amount over $74,200
$154,800	$336,550	$37,675.50 plus 33% of the amount over $154,800
$336,550	No limit	$97,653 plus 35% of the amount over $336,550
Filing Status: Married Filing Jointly or Qualifying Widow(er)		
$0	$15,100	10% of the amount over $0
$15,100	$61,300	$1,510.00 plus 15% of the amount over $15,100
$61,300	$123,700	$8,440.00 plus 25% of the amount over $61,300
$123,700	$188,450	$24,040.00 plus 28% of the amount over $123,700
$188,450	$336,550	$42,170.00 plus 33% of the amount over $188,450
$336,550	No limit	$91,043.00 plus 35% of the amount over $336,550
Filing Status: Married Filing Separately		
$0	$7,550	10% of the amount over $0
$7,550	$30,650	$755.00 plus 15% of the amount over $7,550
$30,650	$61,850	$4,220.00 plus 25% of the amount over $30,650
$61,850	$94,225	$12,020.00 plus 28% of the amount over $61,850
$94,225	$168,275	$21,085.00 plus 33% of the amount over $94,225
$168,275	No limit	$45,521.50 plus 35% of the amount over $168,275
Filing Status: Head of Household		
$0	$10,750	10% of the amount over $0
$10,750	$41,050	$1,075.00 plus 15% of the amount over $10,750
$41,050	$106,000	$5,620.00 plus 25% of the amount over $41,050
$106,000	$171,650	$21,857.50 plus 28% of the amount over $106,000
$171,650	$336,550	$40,239.50 plus 33% of the amount over $171,650
$336,550	No limit	$94,656.50 plus 35% of the amount over $336,550

Source: Internal Revenue Service (2007a). *2006 Federal Tax Rate Schedules.* U.S. Department of the Treasury, Washington, DC. Retrieved December 1, 2007, from http://www.irs.gov/formspubs/article/0,,id=150856,00.html

spent). The Constitution provides a very broad outline of the budget process in parts of Article I, Sections 7 and 8:

Section 7—Revenue Bills, Legislative Process, Presidential Veto
    All bills for raising Revenue shall originate in the House of Representatives; but the Senate may propose or concur with Amendments as on other Bills. . . .

Section 8—Powers of Congress

The Congress shall have Power To lay and collect Taxes, Duties, Imposts and Excises, to pay the Debts and provide for the common Defence and general Welfare of the United States; but all Duties, Imposts and Excises shall be uniform throughout the United States;

To borrow money on the credit of the United States; . . .

To coin Money, regulate the Value thereof, and of foreign Coin, and fix the Standard of Weights and Measures; . . .

To provide for the Punishment of counterfeiting the Securities and current Coin of the United States.

The basic budget process that exists today originated with the Budget and Accounting Act of 1921. Prior to the act, agencies went directly to Congress for funds. The act involved the president in the budget making process, and created the Bureau of Budget within the Department of the Treasury to assist the president. Under the act, the president submits a budget proposal to Congress for approval. Once the budget is approved, the president ensures that funds set aside for specific purposes, or appropriated, are spent. The Bureau of Budget was renamed the Office of Management and Budget (OMB) in 1970. OMB is part of the executive office of the president and the following is its published mission (Office of Management and Budget, 2007):

> OMB's predominant mission is to assist the President in overseeing the preparation of the federal budget and to supervise its administration in Executive Branch agencies. In helping to formulate the President's spending plans, OMB evaluates the effectiveness of agency programs, policies, and procedures, assesses competing funding demands among agencies, and sets funding priorities. OMB ensures that agency reports, rules, testimony, and proposed legislation are consistent with the President's Budget and with Administration policies. In addition, OMB oversees and coordinates the Administration's procurement, financial management, information, and regulatory policies. In each of these areas, OMB's role is to help improve administrative management, to develop better performance measures and coordinating mechanisms, and to reduce any unnecessary burdens on the public.

The act also created the General Accounting Office (GAO) to assist Congress as the primary auditing and investigative agency of the government. The name of the agency was changed to the U.S. Government Accountability Office in 2004.

The Congressional Budget and Impoundment Control Act of 1974 established dual roles for the president and Congress. Also known simply as the Budget Act, it requires Congress to develop an annual concurrent budget resolution, that is, a resolution developed jointly by the House of Representatives and the Senate. This is done independently of the president's proposal. The act provides specific guidance on the procedures Congress follows to develop annual legislation for raising revenue and spending. It established the House and Senate Budget Committees, and the Congressional Budget Office to provide information and estimates required for the congressional budget process. Table 10.7 outlines the timetable of the budget process as outlined in Title III of the act. Figure 10.1 provides the process flow of the entire budget process.

The Budget Act has been amended several times. For example, the Byrd Rule of 1990 allows Senators to protest amendments to the budget reconciliation bill that are "extraneous." This rule prevents Senators from trying to use a filibuster to delay the passing of an appropriation bill by raising issues or points that do not affect or deal

Table 10.7. The Congressional Budget Process Timetable

Date	Action to be completed
First Monday in February	President submits budget to Congress
February 15	Congressional Budget Office submits economic and budget outlook report to Budget committees
Six weeks after President submits budget	Committees submit views and estimates to budget committees
April 1	Senate budget committee reports budget resolution
April 15	Congress completes action on budget resolution
May 15	Annual appropriations bills may be considered in the House, even if action on budget resolution has not been completed
June 10	House Appropriations Committee reports last annual appropriations bill
June 15	House completes action on annual appropriations bills
June 30	House completes action on annual appropriations bills
July 15	President submits mid-session review of his budget to Congress
October 1	Fiscal year begins

Source: Heniff, Bill Jr. (2003). *The Congressional Budget Process Timetable.* The Library of Congress Congressional Research Service, Washington D.C.

with appropriations or reducing the deficit. This includes the following types of proposed amendments (Committee on Rules, 2008):

> Do not produce a change in outlays or revenues; do not produce changes in outlays or revenue which are merely incidental to the non-budgetary components of the provision; are outside the jurisdiction of the committee that submitted the title or provision for inclusion in the reconciliation measure; increase outlays or decrease revenue if the provision's title, as a whole, fails to achieve the Senate reporting committee's reconciliation instructions; increase net outlays or decrease revenue during a fiscal year after the years covered by the reconciliation bill unless the provision's title, as a whole, remains budget neutral; or contain recommendations regarding the OASDI (social security) trust funds.

There are exceptions to the Byrd Rule. These include the following (Committee on Rules, 2008):

> A provision that mitigates direct effects attributable to a second provision which changes outlays or revenue when the provisions together produce a net reduction in outlays; the provision will result in a substantial reduction in outlays or a substantial increase in revenues during fiscal years after the fiscal years covered by the reconciliation bill; the provision will likely reduce outlays or increase revenues based on actions that are not currently projected by CBO for scorekeeping purposes; or such provision will likely produce significant reduction in outlays or increase in revenues, but due to insufficient data such reduction or increase cannot be reliably estimated.

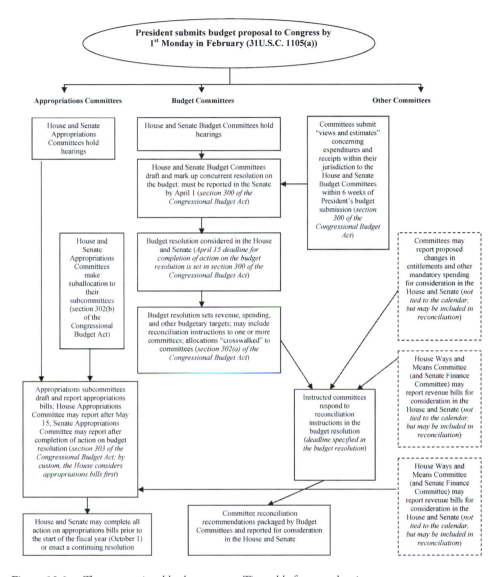

Figure 10.1.   The congressional budget process: Timetable for annual action.
(*Source:* Saturno (2004). *The Congressional Budget Process: A Brief Overview.* The Library of Congress Congressional Research Service, Washington D.C.)

The Byrd rule can be waived by a three-fifth majority of the Senate.

President's Budget Proposal.   The annual budget process begins with the development of the president's budget proposal. The proposal is developed by OMB based on input from each agency. Each agency issues internal instructions to each of its components (divisions, branches, etc.) on its budget process and begins working on its submission up to three years in advance of the president's deadline to Congress. The agencies work directly with OMB and submit their final inputs to their executive branch department. For example, the Army's, Navy's and Air Force's budgets are part of the total budget for the Department of Defense. By at least January, OMB submits the aggregated budget proposal to the president for review and approval.

The president's proposal outlines requests for spending on discretionary, or appropriated, programs. The president does not have to submit budget changes to permanent programs contained in the budget unless there are proposed changes. These programs are funded by mandatory spending and established under permanent laws. They include spending for such purposes and programs as interest on the national debt and entitlement programs such as Social Security, Medicaid, and Medicare.

The proposal also outlines how much the government should spend, estimates revenues from taxes, and outlines how much of a resulting surplus or deficit is acceptable. It includes specific information on historical spending, projected spending for the next five or more years, how spending should be prioritized, and supporting documentation that provides justification for funds requested. It outlines spending on such domestic policy programs as crime prevention, health care, and education. It also includes spending on programs supporting foreign policy such as economic growth in poor nations, health care, and funding to combat terrorism. The president must also outline proposed changes to the tax code.

The president submits the proposal to Congress by the deadline of the first Monday in February for the upcoming fiscal year, which runs from October 1 through September 30. The president can alter the budget proposal at any time but must submit one budget update by July 15.

Congressional Budget Process.   The Congressional Budget Office (CBO) reviews the president's budget proposal and submits a report to the House of Representatives and Senate budget committees. Congress may reject the president's budget proposal (via a majority vote in each chamber) for several reasons. Congress may feel the president's categories of spending are unacceptable or spending amounts are too high. Congress may not support the president's request to take funds from one agency to fund a new program. The proposal may not support programs favored by a majority of congresionnal representatives. For example, Congress may favor reduced government spending to provide tax cuts to citizens.

The House and Senate budget committees then meet to develop a concurrent resolution that sets limits on revenues and spending for the upcoming fiscal year, and outlines very broad categories of spending, rather than detailed information. This resolution can be made completely independently of the president's recommendations. Hearings are held to develop the resolution, and the committees can request testimonies from executive branch departments, agencies, and the OMB on funds requested. The CBO assists the budget committees in developing their budget estimates and in developing a budget baseline.

The House and Senate budget committees submit the concurrent resolution to the full House and Senate for review. Each chamber reviews the resolution and votes to pass or reject it. If rejected, a joint conference of members from each chamber is held to resolve issues of disagreement and a conference report is developed to reach agreement on any differences. The full House and Senate meet again to pass the conference report. The House and Senate budget committees then meet again to amend the concurrent resolution based upon agreements reached in the conference report. The full House and Senate meet once again to pass the final concurrent resolution.

As a concurrent resolution where money has yet to be appropriated, the president's approval and signature is not yet needed. The budget resolution must be completed by April 15 and is made up of budget functions outlined in Table 10.5. These include national defense, health, energy, transportation, agriculture, administration justice, and allowances. Each function is broken down into more defined categories of spending called line items.

While the budget resolution is pending or if it is not completed by May 15, the House and Senate appropriations committees must still formulate appropriations bills for discretionary spending required for part of the upcoming year's budget. This spending is outlined in thirteen appropriation bills developed by the House and Senate appropriations subcommittees to basically keep the government operating. Appropriation subcommittees hold hearings with agencies, analyze past years' spending, and work from the president's budget proposal to develop the following appropriation bills:

1. Defense
2. Veteran's Administration, Independent Agencies and Housing and Urban Development
3. Labor, Education, and Health and Human Services
4. Energy and Water
5. Commerce, Justice, State, and the Judiciary
6. Interior
7. Agriculture, Rural Development, and Food and Drug Administration
8. Transportation, Treasury, Postal Service, and General
9. Foreign Operations
10. Military Construction
11. Legislative Branch
12. District of Columbia
13. Homeland Security

Once the House and Senate appropriations subcommittees complete their budget formulations, their draft bills are sent to the House and Senate appropriations committees for review and finalization. These committees are chaired by the some of the most influential members in Congress. Each committee can hold hearings and mark-up sessions, and the House and Senate floors must again meet to concur on the appropriation bills. Under the Constitution, the House must approve appropriations bills before the Senate. A joint House and Senate conference committee is held to resolve any differences.

The final budget is sent to the president for approval. The president may sign each bill or veto any he or she chooses. The president will veto a bill if it is substantially different from the presidential budget proposal submitted by OMB. If a bill is vetoed, it is sent back to the chamber of origin for review. A veto can be overridden by a two-thirds vote in each chamber.

If the budget is not agreed to by October 1 (i.e., the president vetoes appropriation bills and Congress cannot obtain enough votes to override the vetoes), the U.S. government is not allowed to spend money. In essence, the government must shut down noncritical offices due to lack of funding. Congress can pass continuing appropriations acts to keep agencies temporarily running until the final budget is approved.

Once the budget is finally passed, Congress monitors how funds are spent. Congressional committees and subcommittees monitor agencies to ensure each is spending their allocated funds as required by law. If not, hearings are held and witnesses can be subpoenaed to testify before Congress on spending violations. Each agency is expected to spend all of its appropriated funds. Congress must pass a law if funds are required to be transferred from one appropriated account to another. If an agency runs out of funds before the year is over, Congress can pass a supplemental appropriations bill to provide additional funding through the remainder of the fiscal year.

Appendix A

TIMELINE OF U.S. FEDERAL GOVERNMENT HISTORY

The following timelines lists major events that have shaped the history of the federal government of the United States. This timeline lists people, organizations, events, and legislative actions that have affected the formation, operation, and policies of the United States government. Note that the events are not listed chronologically within each year, but rather by category of events (e.g., legislative acts are listed together).

1215   The Magna Carta is adopted in England

1513   Juan Ponce de Leon of Spain establishes the first colony in North America in what is now St. Augustine, Florida

1565   The first permanent European settlement in North America—St. Augustine, Florida—is founded by Spanish explorer Pedro Menendez de Aviles

1584   Sir Walter Raleigh founds the Roanoke Colony in Virginia, the first English settlement in the New World

1590   The Roanoke Colony is found deserted; becomes known as the Lost Colony

1607   The first permanent English colony is settled, in Jamestown, Virginia

1614   The Dutch claim and establish New Netherland, a series of towns, forts, and trading posts along the Hudson River, governed from New Amsterdam (now New York City)

1619   The first slaves are sold in Virginia

The first legislature of elected representatives, the House of Burgesses, meets in Jamestown

1620   The Pilgrims arrive on the *Mayflower*, establish the Mayflower Compact and found Plymouth Colony

1639   Three Connecticut towns adopt the first written constitution in America, the Fundamental Orders

1643   The Toleration Act is passed in Maryland, allowing freedom of worship

1676   Bacon's Rebellion, considered to the first colonial rebellion against Great Britain, takes place in Virginia

1682   The Pennsylvania Frame of Government is established; later it is used as a basis for the Bill of Rights

1701   The Pennsylvania Charter of Privileges, later used as a basis for the Bill of Rights, is established

1712   The Carolina colony is divided into North Carolina and South Carolina

1751   The British Parliament passes the Currency Act, banning the New England colonies from issuing paper currency [unless publicly funded]

1754   The Colonial Congress meets in Albany, New York, with seven colonies and Iroquois Indians and proposes a Union of Colonies

The French and Indian War begins between France and Great Britain in America over land disputes in the Ohio River Valley

1763   The French and Indian War formally ends with the signing of the Treaty of Paris

A British Royal Proclamation forbids the colonists from purchasing land west of the Appalachian Mountains so that Native Americans can keep their land unless the British Crown purchases land from the Indians in an open and "legal" manner

1764   The British Sugar Act places duties on imports of sugar, textiles, coffee, wines, and dye to the colonies

The British Currency Act places the currency system of the colonies under British control

The British Revenue Act enforces British taxation of goods and control of colonial exports

Boston merchants begin boycotting British imports

James Otis raises the issue of taxation without representation by Great Britain and calls for the colonies to take action against the British acts

1765   Patrick Henry presents seven Virginia Resolutions, stating only the Virginia Assembly (rather than Great Britain) can legally tax Virginia residents

The Sons of Liberty form and use violence to force British stamp agents to resign

The British Quartering Act requires British soldiers to be housed by the colonists and provided free supplies

The British Stamp Act places a direct tax on such paper products as legal documents, newspapers, bills, licenses, almanacs, playing cards, pamphlets, and permits

The Stamp Act Congress meets in New York City, with representatives from nine Colonies, and prepares a resolution requesting Great Britain repeal the taxation acts

1766   Great Britain repeals the Stamp Act but passes the Declaratory Act stating the British government has total power over the colonies

1767   The Townshend Acts tax colonial imports, establishes courts to try colonists in violation of the Act, and gives tax collectors power to search for smuggled goods

1770   The Boston Massacre occurs when British troops kill three colonists when firing on a disgruntled crowd of settlers upset over British military occupation in Boston

The Townsend Acts are repealed, and the Quartering Act is not renewed

1772   The British vessel *Gaspee* is seized, stripped, and burned by settlers in protest of British trade regulations; Britain demands the capture of the perpetrators and their shipment to England for trial, further upsetting the colonists

Samuel Adams calls Boston town meetings, which endorse three proclamations outlining the rights of the colonies to self-rule

1773   The Boston Tea Party occurs, in which settlers disguised as Indians dump tea in Boston Harbor in protest of British taxes on tea

1774   Great Britain declares martial law in Massachusetts

Great Britain passes the Intolerable Acts to punish those responsible for the Boston Tea Party and to gain control of the colonists

The Quartering Act is re-enacted

The colonists establish the Minute Men, members of the colonial militia who vow to be ready to fight within minutes of being called

The First Continental Congress meets in Philadelphia

1775   Patrick Henry gives his "Give me liberty or give me death" speech in the Virginia assembly

The Revolutionary War officially begins with the battles of Lexington and Concord in Massachusetts

The Second Continental Congress meets in Philadelphia

The Continental Congress establishes the Continental Army and appoints George Washington as its commander-in-chief

The Continental Congress establishes the Continental Navy and appoints Esek Hopkins as commodore of the Navy

King George III officially declares a state of open rebellion in the American colonies

1776   The colonies pass the Declaration of Independence, formally declaring independence from British rule

1777   The Second Continental Congress adopts the Articles of Confederation

Congress adopts the American flag of stars and stripes

1778   The colonies establish the Treaty of Alliance with France

1781   The Articles of Confederation are ratified, and John Hanson is elected the first president by the Continental Congress

The Revolutionary War ends with the surrender of British General Charles Cornwallis to George Washington at Yorktown, Virginia

1783   The Treaty of Paris is signed by Great Britain and the United States, officially ending the Revolutionary War and establishing the United States as a sovereign nation

As a result of the Treaty of Paris, the United States gains what today is Indiana, Illinois, Kentucky, Michigan, Ohio, Tennessee, Wisconsin, and parts of Alabama, Georgia, Minnesota, Mississippi, North Carolina, Pennsylvania, Virginia, and West Virginia

The Continental Army is disbanded

1784   The state of Frankland (or Franklin) secedes from North Carolina, but is denied statehood by Congress in 1785

Thomas Jefferson proposes a total ban on slavery; it is narrowly defeated in Congress

The United States and China begin trading goods

1785   Congress moves to New York City and it becomes the temporary U.S. capital

1786   The Continental Congress adopts the dollar and coinage system, replacing U.S. use of the British monetary system based on the pound

Shays's Rebellion takes place in Massachusetts in protest of state taxes and farm debt, eventually leading to a reevaluation of the Articles of Confederation

1787   The Constitutional Convention meets in Philadelphia to reevaluate the Articles of Confederation, which leads to the development of the United States Constitution

George Washington is elected president of the Constitutional Convention

The first of the *Federalist Papers*, arguing for ratification of the U.S. Contitution, is published in New York, calling for a Bill of Rights to be added to the Constitution

Congress bars slavery in the new western states

Delaware gains the title First State by being the first colony to ratify the Constitution

Pennsylvania ratifies the Constitution and becomes the second state

New Jersey ratifies the Constitution and becomes the third state

1788 Georgia ratifies the Constitution and becomes the fourth state

Connecticut ratifies the Constitution and becomes the fifth state

Massachusetts ratifies the Constitution and becomes the sixth state

Maryland ratifies the Constitution and becomes the seventh state

South Carolina ratifies the Constitution and becomes the eighth state

New Hampshire becomes the ninth state to ratify the Constitution, therefore securing its adoption

Virginia ratifies the Constitution and becomes the tenth state

New York ratifies the Constitution and becomes the eleventh state

1789 George Washington is inaugurated as the first president of the United States of America, in New York City

John Adams is sworn in as the first vice president of the United States of America

The United States Constitution goes into effect

The House of Representatives holds its first meeting, in New York City

The United States Congress adopts the Bill of Rights and sends it to the states for ratification

The United States Army is established

The Department of State is established

The Department of Treasury is established

Congress and President George Washington establish a Day of Thanksgiving, and it is celebrated as an official national holiday for the first time (but not made permanent)

The Judiciary Act is passed by Congress, creating federal district and circuit courts and other provisions of the federal judicial system

North Carolina ratifies the Constitution and becomes the twelfth state

1790 The seat of the United States government is moved from New York to Philadelphia

The United States Coast Guard is established

The first United States census is taken: the population is 3,929,214. Blacks make up nineteen percent of the total, and Indians are not counted. The average family consists of eight children

Rhode Island ratifies the Constitution and becomes the thirteenth state

1791 Vermont (formerly part of New York) becomes the fourteenth state, the first after the original thirteen colonies to become a state

The Bill of Rights is ratified by three-fourths of the states and officially becomes part of the United States Constitution

1792   Kentucky (formerly part of Virginia) becomes the fifteenth state, the first from the western wilderness

Thomas Jefferson founds the Democratic (Republican-Democratic) Party

United States Postal Service is established

The United States Mint is established

The military draft is established

The first Presidential Succession Act is passed, establishing a line of succession if the president or vice president cannot complete their terms in Office

1793   President George Washington is sworn in for a second term in Office, and John Adams is sworn in for a second term as vice president

Congress passes the Fugitive Act, making it illegal to harbor or assist escaped slaves

1794   The United States Navy is established

1796   Tennessee (formerly part of North Carolina) becomes the sixteenth state

1797   John Adams becomes the second president of the United States, and Thomas Jefferson becomes the second vice president

1798   The United States Marine Corps is established

The Alien and Sedition Acts are passed, establishing laws against aliens and criticism of the United States government

The Eleventh Amendment is added to the Constitution, limiting the ability of citizens to sue states

1799   The Logan Act is passed, forbidding unauthorized citizens to negotiate on behalf of the United States with foreign governments

1800   The Library of Congress is founded

The United States capital is moved from Philadelphia to Washington, DC

Thomas Jefferson and Aaron Burr tie in Electoral College votes

1801   The House of Representatives elects Thomas Jefferson as the third president of the United States of America, with Aaron Burr as vice president

1803   In *Marbury v. Madison*, 5 U.S. 137 (1803), the Supreme Court invalidates a law passed by Congress for the first time and establishes its power of judicial review

Ohio (formerly part of Connecticut) becomes the seventeenth state

The United States purchases the Louisiana territory from France for $15 million, which contained what is today Arkansas, part of Colorado, Iowa, Louisiana, part of Minnesota, Missouri, part of Montana, part of North Dakota, part of Oklahoma, South Dakota, and part of Wyoming

1804   Aaron Burr kills Alexander Hamilton in a duel

The Twelfth Amendment is added to the Constitution, allowing members of the Electoral College to cast separate ballots for the president and vice president

1805   President Thomas Jefferson is sworn in for a second term in Office

1808   The United States ends the importation of slaves

1809   James Madison becomes the fourth president of the United States

William Maclure, known as the Father of American geology, publishes the first geologic map of the United States

1810   The Supreme Court invalidates a state passed legislative act for the first time in *Fletcher v. Peck*, 10 U.S. 87 (1810)

1812   Louisiana becomes the eighteenth state

The United States declares war on Great Britain, starting The War of 1812, for Britain supporting the American Indians, blocking trade routes to Europe, and abducting Americans to serve in the British fleet

1813   President James Madison is sworn in for a second term in Office

1814   The British set fire to Washington, DC

The War of 1812 ends with the United States and Great Britain signing the Treaty of Ghent

1816   Indiana becomes the nineteenth state

1817   James Monroe becomes the fifth president of the United States

The New York Stock Exchange opens

Mississippi becomes the twentieth state

1818   Illinois becomes the twenty-first state

The rebuilt president's home in Washington, DC, which was burned by the British during the War of 1812, becomes known as the "White House" because it is painted a gleaming white

1819   Alabama becomes the twenty-second state

The United States acquires Florida from Spain through the Adams-Onis Treaty

1820   Maine becomes the twenty-third state

The Missouri Compromise forbids slavery north of Missouri's southern border

1821   President James Monroe is sworn in for a second term in Office

Missouri becomes the twenty-fourth state

1822   Joseph Marion Hernandez of Florida is the first Hispanic to serve in Congress

1823   The Monroe Doctrine forbids European nations from colonizing in or interfering with the new United States

1825   John Quincy Adams becomes the sixth president of the United States

1826   Thomas Jefferson and John Adams both die on Independence Day

1828   The Tariff of Abominations is passed by Congress, levying heavy duties on imports to protect United States manufacturers

1829   Andrew Jackson becomes the seventh president of the United States

1832   South Carolina unsuccessfully attempts to nullify a federal law instituting tariffs on the grounds that the federal law is unconstitutional

1833   President Andrew Jackson is sworn in for a second term in Office

1834   The Whig Party is formed

1835   Texas's war for independence from Mexico begins

1836   The Battle of the Alamo takes place in San Antonio, Texas between Texans fighting for independence from Mexico

Arkansas becomes the twenty-fifth state

1837   Martin Van Buren becomes the eighth president of the United States and the first president actually born in the United States

Michigan becomes the twenty-sixth state

In *Charles River Bridge v. Warren Bridge,* 36 U.S. 420 (1837), the Supreme Court rules the public good outweighs private property

1841   William Henry Harrison becomes the ninth president of the United States and dies in Office within a month from pneumonia

Vice President John Tyler becomes the tenth president of the United States

1844   The United States acquires property from Spain in what are now parts of Colorado, New Mexico, Kansas, Oklahoma, and Texas under the Adams-Onis Treaty

1845   James K. Polk becomes the eleventh president of the United States

Florida becomes the twenty-seventh state

Texas becomes the twenty-eighth state

1846   The Mexican-American War begins with the Battle of Palo Alto due to disputes over border lines between the United States and Mexico

Iowa becomes the twenty-ninth state

1848   The Democratic National Convention is established

The Mexican-American War ends with the signing of the Treaty of Guadalupe Hidalgo, and the United States gains what are now California, Nevada, Utah, and parts of Arizona, Colorado, New Mexico, and Wyoming

The first women's rights convention is held in Seneca Falls, New York

Wisconsin becomes the thirtieth state

1849   Zachary Taylor becomes the twelfth president of the United States

The Department of Interior is established

1850   President Zachary Taylor dies in office

Vice President Millard Fillmore becomes the thirteenth president of the United States

California becomes the thirty-first state

1853   Franklin Pierce becomes the fourteenth president of the United States

The United States purchases what is now part of Arizona and New Mexico from Mexico under the Gadsden Purchase for $10 million

1854   The Kanagawa Treaty establishes a trade relationship between the United States and Japan

1856   The Republican Party is established

1857   James Buchanan becomes the fifteenth president of the United States

1858   Minnesota becomes the thirty-second state

1859   Edwin L. Drake makes the first commercial oil strike in Titusville, Pennsylvania

Oregon becomes the thirty-third state

1860   South Carolina secedes from the United States (the Union) over slavery

1861   Abraham Lincoln is sworn in as the sixteenth president of the United States of America

Other states secede from the Union over slavery: Mississippi, Florida, Alabama, Georgia, Louisiana, Texas, Virginia, Arkansas, North Carolina, and Tennessee

Seceding states from the Union form the Confederate States of America

Richmond, Virginia becomes the capital of the Confederate States of America

Jefferson Davis becomes president of the Confederate States of America, with Alexander Stevens as vice president

The Confederate Congress adopts its own Constitution

The Civil War begins at Fort Sumter, South Carolina

Forty-eight counties in western Virginia rejoin the United States after seceding

Kansas becomes the thirty-fourth state

The United States government makes the first attempt to establish an income tax law with the Revenue Act (repealed in 1872)

1862   Slavery is abolished within the city of Washington, DC

The Department of Agriculture is established

1863   President Abraham Lincoln issues the Emancipation Proclamation

West Virginia becomes the thirty-fifth state

President Abraham Lincoln delivers the Gettysburg Address

1864   The Geneva Convention is established as a treaty to address the humanitarian treatment of the victims and prisoners of war

Nevada becomes the thirty-sixth state

1865   President Abraham Lincoln is sworn in for a second term in Office

The Civil War ends with Confederate General Robert E. Lee's surrender to Union General Ulysses S. Grant at Appomattox, Virginia

President Abraham Lincoln is assassinated

Vice President Andrew Johnson becomes the seventeenth president of the United States

The Thirteenth Amendment is added to the Constitution, abolishing slavery

1866   Tennessee is the first state readmitted to the Union from those that seceded

The Civil Rights Act of 1866 is passed, giving all persons the right to sue and be sued, enforce contracts, give evidence in court, and own property

1867   The United States purchases the Alaska Territory from the Russian Empire for $7.2 million

Nebraska becomes the thirty-seventh state

The United States annexes the Midway Islands, located in the northwestern part of the Hawaiian archipelago

1868   The United States House of Representatives impeaches President Andrew Johnson, but he is later acquitted of all Eleven Articles of Impeachment by the United States Senate

The Fourteenth Amendment is added to the Constitution, making all U.S. born persons citizens of the United States

President Andrew Johnson issues an unconditional pardon to those who participated in the Southern rebellion against the Union

Jon Willis Menard of Louisiana is the first African American elected to Congress

1869   Ulysses S. Grant becomes the eighteenth president of the United States

The number of Supreme Court Justices is increased from seven to nine

The Pacific Railroad is completed, forming the first transcontinental railroad

Wyoming is the first state to grant women suffrage

1870   The Department of Justice is established

The United States Weather Bureau is established

The Civil Rights Act of 1870 is passed, giving all citizens the right to vote and prohibiting the infringement of any citizen's rights guaranteed under the Constitution or United States law

The Fifteenth Amendment is added to the Constitution, prohibiting race, color or previous status as a slave from being used as a qualification to vote

1871   The Civil Rights Act of 1871 is passed, prohibiting any group from attacking the United States or interfering with the duties of any United States officer

1872   Victoria Clafin Woodhull is the first female presidential candidate

Susan B. Anthony is the first woman in the United States to register to vote, later becoming the first to cast a ballot (for which she was arrested)

1873   President Ulysses S. Grant is sworn in for a second term in Office

1875   Congress passes the Civil Rights Act of 1875, prohibiting discrimination in public places

1876   The Supreme Court rules in *Munn v. Illinois*, 94 U.S. 113 (1877), that the states can regulate utilities

Colorado becomes the thirty-eighth state

1877   Rutherford B. Hayes becomes the nineteenth president of the United States

1878   The Bland-Allison Act is passed, allowing the coinage of silver

1881   James A. Garfield becomes the twentieth president of the United States

President James A. Garfield is assassinated in July 1881

Vice President Chester A. Arthur becomes the twenty-first president of the United States

1883   United States railroads begin using four time zones across the United States

Segregation is legalized by the Supreme Court in the *Civil Rights Cases*, 109 U.S. 3 (1883), a group of five Supreme Court cases consolidated and ruled upon at one time by the Court

The Pendleton Civil Service Reform Act is passed, ending the "spoils system" in federal employment

1885   Grover Cleveland becomes the twenty-second president of the United States

1886   The second Presidential Succession Act is passed, reestablishing a line of succession in the event the president is unable to complete his term in Office

1887   The Interstate Commerce Act is passed, creating the Interstate Commerce Commission

1889   Benjamin Harrison becomes the twenty-third president of the United States

North Dakota becomes the thirty-ninth state

South Dakota becomes the fortieth state

Montana becomes the forty-first state

Washington becomes the forty-second state

1890   Idaho becomes the forty-third state

Wyoming becomes the forty-fourth state

The McKinley Tariff sets rates on foreign imports to protect goods provided by American businesses

The Sherman Antitrust Act is passed, the first major government law that attempted to control monopolies

1892   The first immigrants arrive in the United States through Ellis Island

1893   Grover Cleveland becomes the twenty-fourth president of the United States

1894   The Income Tax Act is passed as an attempt by Congress to levy a flat income tax rate (it was ruled illegal by the Supreme Court in 1895)

1896   Utah becomes the forty-fifth state

In *Plessy v. Ferguson*, 163 U.S. 537 (1896), the Supreme Court rules segregated public accommodations are lawful as long as they are "separate but equal"

1897   William McKinley becomes the twenty-fifth president of the United States

The Dingley Tariff raises the tariff on imports into the United States to extreme levels

1898   Congress declares war on Spain (the Spanish-American War)

The United States annexes Hawaii

The United States and Spain sign a peace treaty in Paris

1899   The United States annexes Guam, the Philippines, and Puerto Rico following the end of Spanish-American War

The United States, Great Britain and Germany sign the Treaty of Berlin, recognizing the independence of Samoa

1900   The Gold Standard Act is passed, establishing gold as the only standard for valuing money

1901   President William McKinley is sworn in for a second term in Office

President William McKinley is assassinated

Vice President Theodore Roosevelt becomes the twenty-sixth president of the United States

1903   President Theodore Roosevelt establishes the first national wildlife refuge in Pelican Island, Florida

The Department of Commerce is established

The Departments of Labor is established

The Panama Canal Treaty is established between the United States and Columbia

1904   The National Child Labor Committee is established to protect children in the workplace

1905   President Theodore Roosevelt is sworn in for a second term in office

1906   Theodore Roosevelt receives the Nobel Peace Prize for negotiating the Treaty of Portsmouth

The Pure Food and Drug Act (also called the Wiley Act) is passed, establishing laws for the safe production and distribution of food, drugs, medicines and liquors

The Meat Inspection Act is passed, allowing the government to inspect meat production

The Hepburn Act is passed, allowing the Interstate Commerce Commission to monitor and change railroad rates determined as unfair and unreasonable

1907   The Department of State begins officially numbering and publishing presidential executive oders

The Tillman Act is passed, prohibiting corporations and banks from making political contributions to federal campaigns

Oklahoma becomes the forty-sixth state

1908   The Federal Bureau of Investigation is established

1909   William H. Taft becomes the twenty-seventh president of the United States

W.E.B. Du Bois forms the National Association for the Advancement of Colored People

1910   The Federal Corrupt Practices Act is passed, establishing campaign spending limits and financial disclosure of campaign funds

1911   The Supreme Court rules that Standard Oil is a monopoly and therefore in violation of the Sherman Antitrust Act in *Standard Oil Co. of New Jersey v. United States*, 221 U.S. 1 (1911), and the company is dissolved

1912   The United States begins maintaining troops in Nicaragua to support the government, and protect American people and property

New Mexico becomes the forty-seventh state

Arizona becomes the forty-eighth state

1913   Woodrow Wilson becomes the twenty-eight president of the United States

The Department of Labor is established

The Federal Reserve Act is passed, creating the Federal Reserve System

The Sixteenth Amendment is added to the Constitution, establishing a federal income tax

The Seventeenth Amendment is added to the Constitution, establishing direct elections of senators by the people rather than state legislatures

1914   Archduke Ferdinand of the Ottoman Empire is assassinated in Europe, starting World War I with the Ottoman Empire declaring war on Bosnia

President Woodrow Wilson issues a proclamation of neutrality, attempting to keep the United States out of World War I

The United States Army Air Corps is established

The Federal Trade Commission Act is passed, establishing the Federal Trade Commission to regulate market competition

The Clayton Act is passed, prohibiting such monopolistic practices as price cutting

1916   Germany declares unrestricted submarine warfare against all ships

The United States purchases the West Indies, including the Virgin Islands, from Denmark for $25 million

The United States establishes a military government over the Dominican Republic

The United States signs the Bryan-Chamorro Treaty with Nicaragua to build a canal

Jeannette Rankin from Montana is the first female elected to the United States House of Representatives

The United States National Park Service is established

1917   President Woodrow Wilson is sworn in for a second term in office

Puerto Rico becomes a United States territory

The United States joins the Allies in World War I

The United States National Guard is established

The Espionage Act is passed, making it illegal to spread any information that interferes with the operation of the military or to promote enemies

1918   World War I ends with the Allied Forces and Central Powers signing an armistice

The Sedition Act is passed, making it illegal to interfere with the military, promote enemies, or cause disloyalty against the United States

1919   The Treaty of Versailles is signed, officially ending World War I

Congress does not allow the United States to enter the League of Nations

The Eighteenth Amendment is added to the Constitution, prohibiting the production, distribution and transportation of alcohol (the start of prohibition)

1920   Under the orders of United States Attorney Alexander General Mitchell Palmer during the Red Scare, six thousand people suspected of subversive communist activities are arrested

The Nineteenth Amendment is added to the Constitution, giving women the right to vote

1921   Warren G. Harding becomes the twenty-ninth president of the United States

The Budget and Accounting Act is passed, outlining the federal budget process with the president's proposal and congressional approval, and establishing the Bureau of Budget

1922   Rebecca Felton is the first female to serve in the United States Senate, due to a temporary vacancy

The Lincoln Memorial is completed and opens to the public

1923   President Warren G. Harding dies of a heart attack while in office

Vice President Calvin Coolidge becomes the thirtieth president of the United States

1924   The Indian Citizenship Act (also called the Snyder Act) gives citizenship to all United States indigenous people, i.e., Indians

The Immigration Act of 1924 limits the number of immigrants to the United States per country but prohibits the further immigration of Asians into the United States

1925   President Calvin Coolidge is sworn in for a second term in office

1927   United States citizenship is granted to residents of the Virgin Islands

1928   Octavian Larrazolo of New Mexico is the first Hispanic elected to the United States Senate

1929   Herbert C. Hoover becomes the thirty-first president of the United States

The Great Depression begins after the crash of the New York Stock Market

The American Samoa becomes a United States territory

1931   Congress adopts The Star Spangled Banner as the National Anthem

1932   Hattie Wyatt Caraway of Arkansas is the first female elected to the United States Senate

The Norris-LaGuardia Act is passed, making it legal for employees to form and join Unions without employer interference

1933   Franklin D. Roosevelt becomes the thirty-second president of the United States

President Franklin D. Roosevelt launches his "New Deal" programs

President Franklin D. Roosevelt appoints the first female to the President's Cabinet, Frances Perkins as Secretary of Labor

The Farm Credit Administration is established

The Home Owners Loan Corporation is established

The Tennessee Valley Authority is established

The Twentieth Amendment is added to the Constitution, establishing the end of the term of office for the President and congressmen and a presidential line of succession

The Twenty-first Amendment is added to the Constitution, ending prohibition

1934   The Securities and Exchange Commission is established

The Federal Housing Administration is established

The Indian Reorganization Act is passed, providing expanded rights to Indians

The Communications Act is passed, establishing the Federal Communications Commission

1935   The United States grants the Philippines its independence, and Manuel Quezon is elected as its first president during the nation's election

The first of a series of Neutrality Acts is passed in an attempt by the United States government to keep the United States out of growing turmoil in Europe

The Social Security Act is passed, providing benefits for retired and disabled workers

The Federal Register Act is passed, governing the passage and publication of agency rules and regulations

The National Labor Relations Act (also called the Wagner Act) is passed, creating the National Labor Relations board and establishing working relationships between Unions and employers in the private sector

The Revenue Act is passed, reforming federal income taxation

1937   President Franklin D. Roosevelt is sworn in for a second term in office

1938   The Fair Labor Standards Act is passed, establishing a national minimum wage

1939   President Theodore Roosevelt creates the Executive Office of the president to assist him in dealing with the increased government responsibilities of dealing with the Great Depression

France and Great Britain declare war on Germany, beginning World War II

The White House Office is established

The Hatch Act is passed, prohibiting federal workers from engaging in partisan political activities

1940   Benjamin Davis becomes the first Black General in the United States Army

The Selective Training and Service Act is passed, requiring men between twenty-one and thirty years old to register for the draft

The Alien Registration Act is passed, making it illegal to attempt to overthrow the government and requiring aliens to register

1941   President Franklin D. Roosevelt is sworn in for a third term in office

Atomic bomb research begins with the Manhattan project

The Atlantic Charter is signed between President Franklin D. Roosevelt and British Prime Minister Winston Churchill, setting goals for after the war

Japan attacks the United States at Pearl Harbor, Hawaii

The United States declares war on Japan and enters World War II

The United States places Japanese-Americans in internment camps

Germany and Italy declare war on the United States

The Lend-Lease Act is passed, permitting the president to provide financial and material support to nations combating Germany

1942   Women are allowed to serve in all branches of the armed services

The Revenue Act is passed, reforming income taxation

1943   Income tax withholdings is introduced

1944   United States diplomat and government advisor George F. Kennan argues for a "containment" policy to curb the inherently expansionist policies of the Soviet Union

The Bretton Woods Conference establishes the International Monetary Fund and the World Bank

D-Day: Allied forces invade Normandy

Allied forces defeat German troops

1945   President Franklin D. Roosevelt is sworn in for a fourth term in office

President Franklin D. Roosevelt dies in office

Vice President Harry S. Truman becomes the thirty-third president of the United States

American forces liberate the Philippines from Japan

The United Nations is established

The United States joins the United Nations

The United States drops the first atomic bomb on Hiroshima, Japan

The United States drops the second atomic bomb on Nagasaki, Japan

World War II ends with Japan surrendering to the United States

1946   President Harry S. Truman creates the first President's Committee on Civil Rights

The Philippines, protected by the United States, gains independence

The Center for Disease Control is established

The Council of Economic Advisers is established

The Cold War begins as Winston Churchill proclaims "an iron curtain has swept across the continent" in Europe

The Employment Act is passed in an attempt by the government to stimulate the economy

The Administrative Procedure Act is passed, governing the process federal agencies use to establish regulations

The Federal Regulation of Lobbying Act is passed as the first (but unsuccessful) attempt to control lobbying

The Foreign Service Act (also called the Rogers Act) is passed, establishing the United States Foreign Service

The Atomic Energy Act is passed to govern how the United States will manage its development and control of atomic energy

1947   The Department of Defense is established

The United States establishes the Truman Doctrine, a policy of providing assistance to any nation threatened by Communism

The third Presidential Succession Act is passed, revising the line of presidential and vice presidential succession established under the Presidential Succession Act of 1886

The Taft-Hartley Act (also called the Labor-Management Relations Act) is passed, limiting the power of Unions, particularly to have labor strikes that affect national security or safety

The National Security Act is passed, establishing the National Security Council and the Central Intelligence Agency

The General Agreement on Tariffs and Trade (GATT) is passed, establishing a forum for international discussion of free trade between member nations

1948   President Harry S. Truman's Executive Order 9981 desegregates the armed forces

The Economic Cooperation Act of 1948 (Marshall Plan) is passed to provide economic assistance to European nations devastated by World War II

1949   President Harry S. Truman is sworn in for a second term in office

The Soviet Union tests its first atomic bomb

Germany is divided into East Germany and West Germany

The North Atlantic Treaty is signed and the North Atlantic Treaty Organization (NATO) is established

The Agriculture Act is passed, providing for agricultural aid to foreign nations

1950 The Korean War begins with North Korea (backed by China) invading South Korea

The United Nations declares war on North Korea

Senator Joseph McCarthy begins accusing government officials and citizens of being communists

1951 The Mutual Security Act is passed, expanding United States foreign aid

The Twenty-second Amendment is added to the Constitution, limiting the presidents to two terms in office

1952 The United States detonates the first hydrogen bomb

Puerto Rico becomes a United States commonwealth

The Immigration and Nationality Act is passed, reforming and combining immigration and citizenship laws

1953 Dwight D. Eisenhower becomes the thirty-fourth president of the United States

The Korean War ends

The Department of Health and Human Services is established

1954 The *Nautilus*, the first atomic submarine, is launched by the United States Navy

In *Brown v. Board of Education*, 347 U.S. 483 (1954), the Supreme Court rules segregated schools violate the Fourteenth Amendment

The Wiley-Dondero Act (commonly called the Saint Lawrence Seaway Act) is passed, approving the U.S.-Canadian construction of a system of canals, damns and locks in the St. Lawrence River connected to the Great Lakes to provide a passage for ships

Ellis Island is closed as an immigration point of entry

The Agricultural Trade Development and Assistance Act is passed, expanding agricultural assistance by the United States to other nations

The Housing Act is passed, establishing laws for urban housing improvement

1955 Rosa Parks refuses to give up her seat on a bus and begins the Montgomery Bus Boycott

The AFL and CIO merge to form the largest union in the United States

1956 The President's Foreign Intelligence Advisory Board is established

The Interstate Highway Act is passed, providing billions of dollars to construct highways across the United States

1957   President Dwight D. Eisenhower is sworn in for a second term in office

President Dwight D. Eisenhower sends troops to enforce school desegregation in Little Rock, Arkansas

The space race begins with the Soviet Union's launch of Sputnik

The Civil Rights Act of 1957 is passed, establishing voting rights for all citizens

1958   The United States sends its first satellite, Explorer I, into orbit

The National Aeronautics and Science Administration (NASA) is established

The National Defense Education Act is passed, providing educational assistance for public and private education

1959   Fidel Castro takes control of Cuba

Alaska becomes the forty-ninth state

Hawaii becomes the fiftieth state

1960   The Organization of the Petroleum Exporting Countries (OPEC) is formed between Iran, Iraq, Kuwait, Saudi Arabia and Venezuela

The first televised presidential debates take place in Chicago, Illinois between Democratic candidate Senator John F. Kennedy and Republican candidate Vice President Richard M. Nixon

The Civil Rights Act of 1960 is passed, providing voting rights protection

1961   John F. Kennedy becomes the thirty-fifth president of the United States

The United States Agency for International Development is established

The Foreign Assistance Act is passed, expanding United States support to foreign nations

The Twenty-third Amendment is added to the Constitution, giving the District of Columbia presidential electors in the Electoral College

1962   The Supreme Court rules in *Baker v. Carr*, 369 U.S. 186 (1962), that the federal courts can intervene in state reapportionments of legislative districts

The Supreme Court forbids state sanctioned school prayer in *Engel v. Vitale*, 370 U.S. 421 (1962)

1963   President John F. Kennedy is assassinated

Vice President Lyndon B. Johnson becomes the thirty-sixth president of the United States

American and Vietnamese forces stage a coup in Vietnam

The March on Washington for Jobs and Freedom takes place, and Dr. Martin Luther King Jr. delivers his "I Have a Dream" speech

The Nuclear Test Ban Treaty is established between the United States and the Soviet Union, creating the "red phone" or "Hot Line" between the two nations' leaders

The Office of the United States Trade Representative is established

The Equal Pay Act is passed, prohibiting wage discrimination based on sex

1964   The Economic Opportunity Act is passed, providing health, education and welfare programs for the poor

The Civil Rights Act of 1964 legally ends segregation in the United States

The Twenty-fourth Amendment is added to the Constitution, prohibiting the use of a poll tax

1965   President Lyndon B. Johnson is sworn in for a second term in office

Patsy Takemoto Mink of Hawaii is the first Asian American elected to Congress

The United States officially enters the Vietnam War by sending troops to Vietnam

President Lyndon B. Johnson's Executive Order 11246 prohibits employment discrimination by federal contractors

The Department of Housing and Urban Development is established

Medicaid and Medicare are enacted

The Immigration Act of 1965 is passed, allowing more immigrants into the United States

The Higher Education Act is passed, providing financial aid to college students

The Voting Rights Act is passed, outlawing poll taxes and literacy tests as requirements for voting

The Omnibus Housing Act is passed, providing housing assistance to the poor

1966   Robert C. Weaver is the first African American in the President's Cabinet, appointed as Secretary of the Department of Housing and Urban Development

The Department of Housing and Urban Development is established

The Department of Transportation is established

The Supreme Court's decision in *Miranda v. Arizona*, 384 U.S. 436 (1966), establishes the Miranda Rights

The National Traffic and Motor Vehicle Safety Act is passed, allowing the government to set safety standards for motorists

The Freedom of Information Act is passed, allowing public access to government information

The Presidential Election Campaign Fund Act is passed, providing matching federal funds for presidential candidates during the general election campaign

1967   Thurgood Marshall is appointed as the first Black Supreme Court Justice

The Supreme Court ends all laws forbidding interracial marriage in *Loving v. Virginia*, 388 U.S. 1 (1967)

The Age Discrimination in Employment Act is passed, prohibiting employment discrimination of anyone forty years of age or older

The Air Quality Act is passed, establishing clean air standards

The Twenty-fifth Amendment is added to the Constitution, updating the presidential line of succession and establishing steps to remove the president and vice president from office

1968   Civil Rights leader Dr. Martin Luther King Jr. is assassinated

Robert F. Kennedy is assassinated during his run for president of the United States

The United States signs the Nuclear Non-Proliferation Treaty with other nations, agreeing to limit the spread of nuclear weapons

The Civil Rights Act of 1968 is passed, prohibiting housing discrimination

The Truth in Lending Act is passed, requiring creditors to provide consumers clear disclosures of credit terms and all costs associated with a lending arrangement

1969   Richard M. Nixon becomes the thirty-seventh president of the United States

Shirley Chisholm of New York is the first African American woman to serve in Congress, in the House of Representatives

President Richard M. Nixon passes the Philadelphia Plan, the first affirmative action legislation

The United States Department of Defense invents ARPANET, the predecessor of the INTERNET

The Council of Environmental Quality is established

1970   Anna Mae Hays becomes the first female General in the United States Army

The Occupational Safety and Health Administration is established

The Office of Management and Budget is established

The Clean Air Act is passed, establishing the Environmental Protection Agency to set and monitor standards to reduce air pollution

1971   The Federal Election Campaign Act is passed, establishing rules for campaign funding disclosure

The Twenty-sixth Amendment is added to the Constitution, granting the right to vote to any United States citizen at least eighteen years of age

1972   Shirley Chisholm is the first African American to campaign for president of the United States

The Department of Defense invents the Global Positioning System (GPS)

The United States establishes the Anti-Ballistic Missile Treaty with the Soviet Union

Supplemental Security Income is passed

The Bureau of Alcohol, Tobacco and Firearms is established

The Consumer Product Safety Act is passed, establishing the Consumer Product Safety Commission to regulate consumer product safety

1973   President Richard M. Nixon is sworn in for a second term in office

Vice President Spiro T. Agnew resigns due to tax evasion charges

Congressman Gerald R. Ford becomes the first vice president appointed under the Twenty-fifth Amendment

The Vietnam War ends with a peace treaty between the United States and Vietnam

The last American forces leave Vietnam

The Senate Watergate hearings begin

The Supreme Court makes abortion legal in *Roe v. Wade*, 410 U.S. 113 (1973)

The Drug Enforcement Administration is established

The Rehabilitation Act is passed, establishing protections for the disabled

The Endangered Species Act is passed to protect endangered and threatened species of fish, wildlife, and plants

1974   The House Judiciary Committee votes to impeach President Richard M. Nixon

President Richard M. Nixon resigns on August 9 as a result of the Watergate scandal

Vice President Gerald R. Ford becomes the thirty-eighth president of the United States

Nelson A. Rockefeller becomes the second vice president appointed under the Twenty-fifth Amendment

President Gerald R. Ford pardons Richard M. Nixon

The Congressional Budget and Impoundment Control Act is passed, setting rules for how Congress passes the annual federal budget

The Presidential Primary Matching Payment Account is passed, providing federal matching funds for presidential candidates during their primary race

1975   The first meeting of the Group of Eight (G8) takes place in Rambouillet, France

The Federal Election Commission is established

The Pregnancy Discrimination Act is passed, prohibiting employment discrimination against pregnant employees

1976   The Office of Science and Technology Policy is established

The Supreme Court rules in *Gregg v. Georgia*, 428 U.S. 153 (1976), that capital punishment is not cruel and unusual, and is constitutionally admissible

The Government in the Sunshine Act is passed, expanding public access to information originally provided under the Freedom of Information Act (FOIA) of 1966

The Arms Export Control Act is passed, expanding Congressional control of arms sales and exports

The Hart-Scoss-Rodino Antitrust Improvement Act is passed, requiring all mergers and acquisitions to be reported to the Federal Trade Commission

1977   Jimmy Carter becomes the thirty-ninth president of the United States

Patricia Roberts Harris is the first African American female in the President's Cabinet, appointed as Secretary of Housing and Urban Development

President Jimmy Carter pardons draft evaders of the Vietnam War

The Office of Administration is established

The Department of Energy is established

The Food Safety and Inspection Service is established

1978   The Supreme Court bars quotas but upholds affirmative action in higher education in *Regents of the University of California v. Bakke*, 438 U.S. 265 (1978)

The Civil Service Reform Act is passed, reforming the civil service employment system

The Ethics in Government Act is passed, requiring government officials to disclose their financial holdings by filing financial disclosure statements

1979   The Israel-Egypt Peace Treaty is signed as a result of the Camp David Accords

Iranian forces seize the American Embassy in Tehran, Iran and take fifty-two hostages

The Department of Education is established

1980   The Refugee Act is passed, establishing immigration reforms

The Equal Access to Justice Act is passed, allowing individuals or small entities that feel unjustifiably harmed by an agency action to sue to recover attorney's fees, and other fees and expenses

1981   The hostages being held in the American Embassy in Tehran, Iran are released minutes before President Ronald W. Reagan takes Office

Ronald W. Reagan becomes the fortieth president of the United States

Sandra Day O'Connor is sworn in as the first female Supreme Court Justice

President Ronald W. Reagan orders striking air traffic controllers back to work, and later fires some of those who do not

The Economic Recovery Tax Act is passed, reducing income taxes by twenty-five percent over a three-year period in an attempt to stimulate the economy

1982   President Ronald W. Reagan sends Marines to help stabilize Lebanon

AT&T is broken up after being declared a monopoly and in violation of the Sherman Antitrust Act of 1890

The Foreign Trade Antitrust Improvement Act is passed, making United States antitrust laws applicable to foreign commerce when actions have a direct effect on U.S. export trade and commerce

1983 Two hundred and forty-nine United States Marines are killed by a suicide bomber in Lebanon

The United States invades Grenada after its government is overthrown

Martin Luther King Day becomes an official national holiday, the first national holiday for an African American

1984 The Comprehensive Crime Control Act is passed, creating the United States Sentencing Commission

1985 President Ronald W. Reagan is sworn in for a second term in Office

President Ronald W. Reagan announces the Strategic Defense Initiative, nicknamed the Star Wars initiative

The United States-Israel Free Trade Area agreement takes effect

The Food for Progress Act is passed, providing United States agricultural commodities to developing nations

1986 The Tax Reform Act of 1986 is passed, modifying the United States tax system

The Immigration Reform and Control Act is passed, amending immigration laws

1987 Alan Greenspan is appointed chairman of the Board of Governors of the Federal Reserve

The Iran-Contra scandal is unveiled, revealing funds from secret United States arms sales to Iran were used to fund rebels in Nicaragua

The Commission on President Debates is established

The United States and Soviet Union sign an agreement to reduce nuclear weapons

1988 Lauro Fred Cavazos, Jr. is the first Hispanic member of the President's Cabinet, appointed as Secretary of Education

The Department of Veterans Affairs is established

The Fair Housing Amendments Act is passed, expanding laws to prohibit housing discrimination

The Worker Adjustment and Retraining Notification (WARN) Act (also called the Plant Closing Act) is passed, requiring employers with at least one hundred employees to notify their employees at least sixty days in advance of a plant closing or layoffs

1989 George H.W. Bush becomes the forty-first president of the United States

Ileana Ros-Lehtinen of Florida is the first Hispanic female elected to Congress, in the United States House of Representatives

The federal government is forced to bail out hundreds of failed savings and loans institutions

The United States invades Panama and arrests General Manuel Noriega

The Exxon Valdez spills eleven million gallons of oil off the coast of Alaska

The Supreme Court rules in *City of Richmond v. Croson*, 488 U.S. 469 (1989), that affirmative action programs must be subject to "strict scrutiny"

The Office of National Drug Control Policy is established

The Financial Institutions Reform Recovery and Enforcement Act is passed, establishing the Resolution Trust Corporation to liquidate the assets of failed savings and loans

1990   English developer Sir Timothy John Berners-Lee implements the World Wide Web

The American with Disabilities Act is passed, establishing civil rights for disabled employees

The Nutrition Labeling and Education Act is passed, giving the U.S. Food and Drug Administration (FDA) authority to require producers to place nutrition labels on most foods regulated by the Agency

The Clean Air Act establishes higher standards for air quality and requires cleaner burning fuels

1991   United Nations forces launch an air strike on Iraq in the Gulf War (also called the Persian Gulf War)

United Nations ground forces liberate Kuwait from Iraq

A cease-fire is signed between the United Nations and Iraq

The Soviet Union collapses

The Civil Rights Act of 1991 is passed, expanding prohibitions against employment discrimination

1992   Carol Moseley-Braun of Illinois is the first African American female elected to the United States Senate

California elects two women to the United States Senate, Dianne Feinstein and Barbara Boxer

The United States prison population reaches one million

The Cold War ends with a treaty between the United States and the Soviet Union

The Twenty-seventh Amendment is added to the Constitution, limiting Congressional pay raises

1993   William "Bill" Clinton becomes the forty-second president of the United States

Janet Reno is the first female United States Attorney General

Jocelyn Elders is the first African American United States Surgeon General

Sheila Widnall is the first female Secretary of a branch of the United States military, the Air Force

The Brady Handgun and Violence Prevention Act (Brady Bill) is passed, strengthening laws to acquire a hand gun

The Hatch Act Reform Amendments are passed, giving federal employees greater freedom to engage in the political process

The Family and Medical Leave Act is passed, requiring employers to grant eligible employees up to twelve workweeks of unpaid leave in a year for family related reasons such as childbirth, adoption, and health care of a family member

1994   The North American Free Trade Agreement (NAFTA) goes into effect

The International Antitrust Enforcement Assistance Act is passed, allowing the United States Attorney General and the Federal Trade Commission to establish agreements with foreign authorities in combating antitrust laws

1995   The World Trade Organization (WTO) is established

The Lobbying Disclosure Act is passed, establishing guidelines for lobbyist groups to disclose funding of federal campaigns

1996   The Electronic Freedom of Information Act Amendment is passed, amending the Freedom of Information Act to include public access to electronic information

The Telecommunications Act is passed, establishing rules for telecommunication providers

The Congressional Review Act is passed, requiring agencies to send rules and regulations to Congress for review

The Illegal Immigration Reform and Immigrant Responsibility Act is passed, amending immigration laws

The Personal Responsibility and Work Opportunity Reconciliation Act is passed, establishing stricter requirements for recipients of federal welfare assistance

1997   President Bill Clinton is sworn in for a second term in Office

Madeleine Albright is the first female secretary of state

President Bill Clinton bars the use of federal money to fund human cloning research

Nations around the world sign the Kyoto Protocol, agreeing to reduce greenhouse gases

California becomes the first state to ban all forms of affirmative action with Proposition 2009, leading other states to follow

The Welfare-to-Work Program legislation is passed, establishing guidelines to provide employment to welfare recipients

1998   The United States House of Representatives approve two of four Proposed Articles of Impeachment against President Bill Clinton for charges in connection with sexual misconduct with a White House intern

The Community Services Block Grant legislation is passed, providing federal funding to community programs assisting those in poverty

The Supreme Court rules in *Oncale v. Sundowner Offshore Services, Incorporated*, 523 U.S. 75 (1998), that Title VII of the Civil Rights Act covers sexual discrimination when both parties in a case are of the same sex

1999   President Bill Clinton announces a second year of budget surplus, the first two-year consecutive surplus since 1957

The Senate acquits President Bill Clinton of impeachment charges

Panama takes control of the Panama Canal from the United States

2000   The percent of United States population living in suburbs reaches fifty percent, up from thirty-eight percent in 1970

In the presidential election, George W. Bush wins more Electoral College votes although Albert A. Gore Jr. wins the most popular votes

The Supreme Court rules against a manual recount of presidential election votes in Florida

The Jordan Free Trade Agreement is signed

2001   George W. Bush becomes the forty-third president of the United States

Colin Powell is the first African American secretary of state

Al Qaeda terrorists use commercial planes to attach the United States, destroying the World Trade Center and damaging the Pentagon on September 11

The War in Afghanistan begins as the United States declares a War on Terrorism as a result of the events of September 11

President George W. Bush issues a military order authorizing the use of military tribunals to try suspected terrorists

The Homeland Security Council is created

The Patriot Act is passed, establishing stronger laws against terrorists

The Foreign Operations Appropriations Act of 2001 is passed, granting special immigration appeal rights for certain Vietnamese, Cambodian or Laos nationals

2002   The Unite States prison population reaches two million

The United States withdraws from the Anti-Ballistic Missile Treaty

WorldCom becomes the biggest business failure in United States history due to accounting fraud

The Bipartisan Campaign Reform Act is passed, amending laws governing the financing of election campaigns

The Homeland Security Act is passed, establishing the Department of Homeland Security and strengthening laws against terrorism

The Sarbanes-Oxley Act is passed, establishing the Public Company Accounting Oversight Board to regulate accounting and auditing firms to ensure the proper disclosure of accounting and financial records of companies

The No Child Left Behind Act becomes law, increasing the accountability of schools in educating children

2003   United States forces capture Iraqi President Saddam Hussein

The Supreme Court rules in *Grutter* v. *Bollinger*, 539 U.S. 306 (2003), that race can be used as one of many individual applicant selection factors used by colleges and universities

The Intelligence Authorization Act for Fiscal Year 2003 is passed, prohibiting information from intelligence agencies from being disclosed to foreign governments or international governmental organizations

2004   Massachusetts becomes the first state to legalize gay marriage

The Central America-Dominican Republic-United States Free Trade Agreement is signed

The United States-Bahrain Free Trade Agreement is signed

The Intelligence Reform and Terrorism Act is passed, expanding laws against terrorism

2005   President George W. Bush is sworn in for a second term in Office

Condoleezza Rice is the first African American female secretary of state

The United States trade deficit with China exceeds $200 billion

Hurricane Katrina devastates New Orleans, Louisiana

The Central America-Dominican Republic-United States Free Trade Agreement (CAFTA-DR) is established between the United States, Costa Rica, Dominican Republic, El Salvador, Guatemala, Honduras, and Nicaragua

The Border Protection, Anti-terrorism, and Illegal Immigration Control Act is passed, strengthening laws against illegal immigration

The Bankruptcy Abuse Prevention and Consumer Protection Act is passed, making the bankruptcy laws stricter for individuals and businesses

2006   Keith M. Ellison is the first Muslim elected to the United States Congress

Due to increased gas prices, Exxon Mobil posts the largest profit of any company in United States history

Protests against proposed illegal immigration reforms are staged across the United States

2007   Nancy Pelosi of California is the first female Speaker of the House of Representatives

The United States Climate Action Partnership USCAP) calls for the federal government to enact legislation to achieve significant reductions of greenhouse gas emissions

The United States trade deficit reaches a record $764 billion

New Jersey is the first state to legally end capital punishment

The Energy Independence and Security Act is passed, establishing stricter energy standards for automobile, appliance, and light bulb manufacturers

The Water Resources Development Act is passed, providing for $23 billion for the development of water and related resources, after Congress overrides President George W. Bush's veto

2008   The price of oil reaches an all-time record of $147 a barrel

Exxon announces another year of record profits, $46.6 billion in 2007, mainly due to profits earned as a result of high gas prices

The United States Supreme Court overrules case in which a Louisiana man was sentenced to death even though the victim was not killed (but was raped), testing the constitutionality of the death penalty for crimes other than murder

The two leading Democratic presidential candidates are an African American male and a woman

Appendix B

GLOSSARY

Act.   Legislation that has been approved by both chambers of Congress and signed by the president, or passed by at least two-thirds of the members of Congress if the president vetoed the proposed law (same as a **law**).

Adjudication.   The hearing and passage of an order after the review of actions (such as infractions) relating to established agency rules and regulations.

Administrative law.   Cumulative body of bureaucratic law that results from the process of agencies making rules and regulations, outcomes of the enforcement of these rules and regulations, and rulings made in administrative hearings (adjudication) when regulated parties violate rules, or when parties bring complaints that they have been harmed by agency rules.

Affirmative action.   A policy for the establishment of programs that involve giving preferences in employment, contracting, and education to members of groups that have historically been discriminated against.

Amendment.   The legislative process of changing the language of a proposed law (i.e., bill) or an existing law.

Amicus curiae brief.   Legal arguments before the Supreme Court by parties that are not direct participants in a case but have a stake in its outcome and are in support of either the defendant or plaintiff.

Appellant.   Party who disagrees with the decision of the lower court, believing a legal error was made, and appeals the case to the next highest court.

Appellate jurisdiction.   Authority of the Supreme Court to hear cases brought to the Court through appeals from lower federal courts or from state supreme courts when involving issues of federal law.

Apportionment.   The process of dividing the seats in the U.S. House of Representatives among the fifty states based on each state's population.

Appropriation.   Funds set aside by Congress from government revenues for specific uses.

Arbitration.   Informal legal proceeding in which a neutral third party listens to the positions of each party in a dispute and then renders a decision after a trial-like proceeding.

Arraignment. Hearing in a federal criminal case in which the defendant offers a plea of guilty or not guilty to the charges being brought by the government.

Attack ad. In political campaigns, an attack ad is a negative political advertisement whose message is intended as an attack against another candidate or political party.

Bilateral development aid. U.S. foreign assistance in the form of direct support to developing countries for sustainable economic and social stability, mostly through the U.S. Agency for International Development.

Bill. Congressional document outlining the purpose and scope of a proposed law.

Bill of Rights. The first ten Amendments of the U.S. Constitution that outline the civil rights and liberties of all U.S. citizens.

Bipartisanship. The tendency marked by or involving cooperation, agreement, and compromise between the two major political parties on legislation or a plan of action.

Bonds. Government securities that provide interest until reaching maturity (i.e., reach full value) in ten years or more after their date of issue.

Budget deficit. Government financial position when more funds are spent than raised.

Budget surplus. Government financial position when less funds are spent than raised.

Bureaucracy. A large, complex, hierarchically structured administrative organization that carries out a specific function.

Bureaucrat. An individual who works in a bureaucracy, usually referring to a government employee.

Capitalism. Economic and social system where production and trade take place with little or no government intervention.

Case of original jurisdiction. Cases that are brought directly to the Supreme Court where the Supreme Court acts as a trial court.

Caucus. A political party convention held in a state to choose a political party's candidate where voters select delegates to choose the candidate.

Chamber. One of the two sections or houses of Congress; the Senate or the House of Representatives.

Checks and balances. Constitutional power granted to each branch of the federal government to monitor and provide oversight to the other two branches to ensure they do not take actions beyond their constitutionally granted authority.

Civil liberties. Basic rights and liberties guaranteed to all citizens, specifically through the Bill of Rights of the U.S. Constitution.

Civil rights. The rights of all Americans to equal treatment under the law as stipulated in the First Amendment of the U.S. Constitution and further protected by the Fourteenth Amendment.

Civil rights movement. The social and political movement in the United States during the 1950s and 1960s led by minorities to end racial segregation.

Civil servants.   Members of the U.S. civil service who are the employees that carry out the daily work of the federal government.

Clean bill.   A bill after it has gone through so many amendments to its original language that it is assigned a new tracking number.

Cloture.   A method of ending debate in the Senate for a bill under consideration to place it to a vote by the entire chamber.

Cold war.   The verbal and military conflict of ideologies between the United States and the Soviet Union that lasted from the late 1940s through the early 1990s.

Commander in chief.   The role of the president of the United States as commander of the military forces.

Commerce clause.   Power of the federal government to collect taxes, coin money, and regulate commerce accordinig to Article I, Section 8, of the U.S. Constitution.

Committee of the whole.   The meeting of all members of the House of Representatives as one large committee, normally to consider a bill.

Common law.   Decisions reached by judges in court cases that become precedent for future cases of the same or similar subject matter.

Companion bill.   Similar or identical bill introduced concurrently in the House of Representatives and the Senate.

Concurrent powers.   Authority and duties shared by the federal government and the state governments, such as the power to levy taxes.

Concurrent resolution.   Legislative proposal not requiring the president's approval that addresses matters affecting operations in both chambers of Congress or are issued to express official positions of members in both chambers.

Conference committee.   Committee comprised of members of the Senate and House of Representatives formed to resolve legislative differences raised by each chamber.

Confirmation.   Process by which the Senate approves a nomination of the president for an ambassador, member of the judicial branch, member of the president's cabinet, or other senior level official, as required by the U.S. Constitution.

Congressional caucus.   Informal or unofficial congressional group formed because its members share common concerns, interests, or ideologies.

Congressional charter.   Law passed by Congress that states the mission and authority of a group or organization, such as a nonprofit organization; does not mean Congress provides the group any funding or federal powers.

Conservative.   Political ideology defined as being in favor of tradition and gradual change, where tradition refers to religious, cultural, or nationally defined beliefs and customs.

Constitutional law.   Rulings by the federal courts based upon the U.S. Constitution.

Debt ceiling.   The maximum amount the government is allowed to borrow without obtaining additional approval from Congress.

De facto segregation.   Racial segregation that occurs because of past inferior social and economic conditions and residential patterns, rather than deliberate actions by an opposing individual, group, or organization.

Delegation doctrine.   Principle that agencies are only permitted to exercise the specific powers granted by the legislative, executive, or judicial instrument granting its powers.

Democracy.   A system of government in which the people have ultimate political authority.

Depression.   A severe or long-lasting recession.

Diversity of citizenship.   Requirement that a federal court can only hear a case arising from a dispute between citizens of two different states where the amount in dispute is over $75,000, or a dispute between a U.S. citizen and a foreign government or foreign citizen.

Domestic policy.   Focuses on developing programs for the sustainment and improvement of a country's citizens, businesses, environment, and infrastructure.

Double jeopardy.   Stipulation in the Fifth Amendment of the U.S. Constitution that a person may not be tried in a court of law for the same crime twice.

Due process clause.   The constitutional guarantee established in the Fifth and Fourteenth Amendments of the U.S. Constitution that prohibits the government from depriving citizens of life, liberty, or property.

Economic political and security aid.   U.S. foreign assistance in the form of support for U.S. interests in international economic, political or security programs, mostly through the Economic Support Fund.

Economic regulation.   Government management and influence of the economy by setting controls over prices, regulating industries, and preventing companies from forming monopolies that purposely keep other businesses out of a market.

Electoral College.   A group of electors who are selected by the voters in each state to officially elect the president and vice president. The number of electors in each state is equal to the number of that state's representatives in both chambers of Congress.

Enabling legislation.   A law enacted by the legislature to establish an administrative agency, specifying the name, purpose, composition, and powers of the agency being created.

Engrossed bill.   Final version of proposed legislation passed by one chamber of Congress.

Enrolled bill.   Legislation that has been passed in identical form by both houses of Congress, signed by their presiding officers, and sent to the president for signature.

Enumerated powers.   A list of specific responsibilities found in Article I, Section 8, of the U.S. Constitution, which enumerate the authority granted to the U.S. Congress. Congress may exercise only those powers granted to it by the Constitution, limited by the Bill of Rights and the other protections found in the constitutional text.

Equal protection clause.   Portion of the Fourteenth Amendment to the U.S. Constitution that prohibits discrimination by state government institutions. The clause grants all people "equal protection of the laws," which means that the states must apply the law equally and cannot give preference to one person or class of persons over another.

Establishment clause.   Part of the First Amendment of the U.S. Constitution that forbids the government from establishing religion.

Excise taxes.   Government levies on such products as alcohol, tobacco, crude oil, windfall profit, telephone, ozone-depleting chemicals or products, and transportation fuels.

Executive agreement.   Agreement between the president of the United States and the government of another country that does not require congressional approval and is only in effect during the term of office of the initiating president.

Executive order.   Formal policy issued by the president to provide direction to executive branch agencies and officers on specific matters.

Executive powers.   The authority granted to the president under Article II of the U.S. Constitution.

Executive privilege.   Assertion that U.S. presidents have inherent Constitutional powers derived by their position as head of the executive branch to make decisions necessary to accomplish the duties of that office, and to maintain checks and balances over the legislative and judicial branches.

Expressed powers.   Federal government powers or authority specifically provided by the U.S. Constitution or congressional laws.

Faith-based organization.   Community, civic, or charitable organization established and operated based on religious principles.

Federal jurisdiction.   Requirement that the federal courts can only hear cases involving a violation of the U.S. Constitution, a suit arising from an act of Congress or an executive branch decision, a dispute under a treaty, controversies between states, or a dispute between the United States and another foreign government.

Federalism.   Political philosophy that the national government shares sovereign power with the state governments.

Federalists.   Political group started by Alexander Hamilton that supported the adoption of the U.S. Constitution and the creation of a strong central government.

Filibustering.   Tactic to delay the passage of a bill into a law by a Congressman or Congresswoman engaging in extensive debate and using all available time.

First reading.   Mechanism by which a bill is introduced to a chamber of Congress. Typically, a draft of a bill is read, assigned a tracking number, and immediately assigned to a committee. It is usually amended by committee between the first and second readings.

Fiscal year.   A twelve-month period established for bookkeeping and accounting purposes. The U.S. government's fiscal year runs from October 1 through September 30 of the following year.

Fiscal policy.   Government policies that influence the economy by adjusting government spending and the federal tax system.

Five-minute rule.   Rule in the House of Representatives that prevents filibustering by only allowing a House member five minutes to explain proposed amendments to a bill.

Foreign policy.   The official relationship a country's government establishes with other nations, both allies and enemies, and the stance it takes on issues involving foreign nations, groups, or individuals.

Forma pauperis.   Waiving of the court fee normally required in federal court.

Free exercise clause.   Part of the First Amendment of the U.S. Constitution that guarantees citizens the right to practice the religion of their choice.

Full faith and credit clause.   Stipulation in Article IV of the U.S. Constitution that states are required to abide by public acts, records, and rulings in judicial proceedings of other states.

Functions.   Subcategories of spending in the U.S. federal budget (see also **Superfunctions**).

General election.   A regularly scheduled election to elect the president, vice president, and senators in Congress. In the United States general elections are held in even-numbered years (every four years) on the first Tuesday after the first Monday in November.

General schedule.   Designation for government jobs that are classified as white-collar, i.e., professional.

Geneva Conventions.   Treaties that outline how nations are to engage during times of war, specifically in the humanitarian treatment of prisoners of war and civilians not actively engaged in a battle.

Germaneness rule.   Rule in the House of Representatives that prevents a House member from making amendments to bills on a subject or issue that is different from those already contained in the bill.

Gerrymandering.   The attempted, deliberate action of one political party to influence the redistricting process to create districts that will include most of its party members.

Giving aid and comfort.   The act of assisting enemies of the United States to harm the United States or its citizens or providing enemies such things as shelter and food, as prohibited by Article III of the U.S. Constitution.

Government corporations.   Corporations that conduct government activities and have similarities to commercial businesses.

Government-sponsored enterprises.   Types of government corporations Congress creates to offer affordable lending programs and other financial services to specific sectors of the economy, such as farmers, students, homeowners, and insolvent savings and loan institutions.

Grassroots.   Local or community level support, action, or involvement.

Gross Domestic Product (GDP).   The market value of all goods and services produced in a nation each year.

Gross National Product (GNP).   Dollar value of all goods and services produced in a nation in any given year.

Homeland Security presidential directives.   Presidential executive orders that deal with issues involving the security of the United States.

House Journal.   The official record of the proceedings of each legislative day in the House of Representatives.

Humanitarian aid.   U.S. foreign assistance to nations to support economic and social recovery.

Ideologue.   An individual who holds very strong political opinions.

Ideology.   A set of beliefs about human nature, social inequality, and government institutions that forms the basis of a political or economic system.

Immigration.   The legal or illegal relocation of a person from one nation to another.

Impeachment.   A formal criminal proceeding against a public official for misconduct or wrongdoing while in office.

Implied powers.   Powers of the federal government that are implied by the expressed powers in the U.S. Constitution.

Independent agencies.   Agencies within the executive and legislative branches that operate outside of the executive branch departments or Congress.

Independent regulatory commissions.   Established by Congress to operate outside the three branches to set policy, and regulate public and private activities that fall under the delegated authority of each commission.

Inflation.   Increase in the average price of goods and services in an economy over a period of time.

Inherent powers.   Federal government powers not expressly granted (i.e., specifically stated) in the U.S. Constitution but that are required to ensure the nation's integrity and survival as a political entity.

Institutional interest groups.   Interest groups representing formal organizations, such as businesses, foundations, or universities.

Interest group.   Group comprised of members with collective concerns formed to influence the government to support their issues through legislation and official policy.

Intergovernmental lobby.   A special interest group formed by governors, mayors, highway commissioners, or other public officials for the purpose of obtaining federal funds for state governments.

Interstate commerce.   Trade between two or more states.

Iron triangle.   A three-way alliance among legislators, bureaucrats, and interest groups to establish or preserve policies that benefit their respective interests.

Invoking cloture.   Process in the Senate that ends the debate on a bill by a motion from at least sixteen senators and carried by three-fifths of the Senate.

Item veto.   The presidential disapproval of a specific part, or item, of a bill.

Joint Committee.   A congressional committee composed of members from the House of Representatives and the Senate.

Joint Resolution.   Legislative proposal that addresses similar or identical issues of concern in both chambers of Congress.

Judicial review.   The Supreme Court's power to review all acts and decisions of the executive and legislative branches, and invalidate any that the Court rules are in conflict with the U.S. Constitution.

Law.   Legislation that has been approved by both chambers of Congress and signed by the president, or passed by a two-thirds majority of the members of Congress if the president vetoed the proposed law.

Legal standing.   Requirement that a person bringing a case to court has been directly affected by the opposing party in the case.

Liberal.   Political ideology defined as being in favor of citizens being free to act on their personal views with little or no infringement on those rights by the government.

Liberty.   The freedom of individuals to believe, express, and act freely according to their personal beliefs as long as doing so does not infringe upon the rights of others.

Lobby.   Attempts by organizations and individuals to influence the passage of legislation, influence government decision making, or the election of a candidate.

Lobbyist.   Experts hired by interest groups to make direct contact with elected officials in attempts to influence (or lobby support for) the passage of legislation that will benefit interest group members or the general public.

Loopholes.   Unintentional or intentional vague statements, or specific conditional statements in laws that allow those being regulated to take actions that are contrary to the terms, conditions, or legislative intention of the law.

Madison model.   The model of government devised by James Madison in which the government is separated into three branches: executive, legislative, and judicial.

Magistrate.   Judge appointed by district court judges to perform special functions.

Major Non-NATO Ally (MNNA).   Special designation provided to nations the U.S establishes major alliances with that are not members of NATO.

Majority leader.   The political party leader selected by the party having the most members in the House of Representatives or in the Senate.

Majority vote in Congress.   A simple majority consists of more than half of the votes cast in each chamber of Congress. An absolute majority requires that more than half of all the members of the legislative body (including those absent and those present but not voting) must vote in favor of a proposition in order for it to be passed.

Malapportionment.   A condition that results when, based on population and representation, the voting power of the citizens in one district becomes more influential than the voting power of citizens in another district.

Markup session.   Congressional committee deliberation held after hearings on a bill to debate the pros and cons of passing the bill, and to make any necessary revisions to its wording.

Marshall Plan.   A plan providing for U.S. economic assistance to European nations following World War II to help those nations recover from the war; named after George C. Marshall, secretary of state from 1947 until 1949.

Mediation.   Process where a neutral third party meets with two disputing parties, and relays information from one party to the other in an attempt to reach a mutual agreement on a settlement.

Membership interest groups.   Interest groups comprised of and representing individual citizens versus a formal group such as an industry or collection of businesses.

Merit promotion.   Government personnel program in which civil servants compete for promotions based on their professional experience, seniority, on-the-job training, and professional training.

Military aid.   U.S. foreign assistance in the form of funds provided to U.S. allies and friendly nations to assist them in acquiring U.S. military equipment and training.

Military tribunal.   Type of military court established by the executive branch and used during times of war to try members of the enemy force.

Minority leader.   The political party leader selected by the party having the fewest members in the House of Representatives or the Senate.

Minority–majority district.   A congressional district whose boundaries are drawn to maximize the voting power of a minority group.

Mixed economy.   Economy, such as that of the United States, that is based on the interaction of both free enterprise and government management.

Moderate.   Political positions within a political spectrum ranging from liberal to conservative where a person's views are in the center of the spectrum.

Monetary policy.   Government policies to influence the economy where the Federal Reserve adjusts the government's buying and selling of U.S. government securities, the money supply, or credit and interest rates.

Monroe Doctrine.   A U.S. policy announced in 1823 by President James Monroe that the United States would not tolerate foreign interventions in the western hemisphere, and in return the United States would stay out of European affairs.

Motion to recommit.   A vote in Congress after debating a bill to send the bill back to a committee for further review before considering it again.

Multilateral aid.   U.S. foreign assistance in combination with funds from partnering nations given to an international agency such as the World Bank or the United Nations International Children's Fund (UNICEF) to support needy countries.

National security directives.   Presidential executive orders that deal with issues of national security or national defense.

Naturalization.   Process by which an immigrant, or alien, becomes a U.S. citizen.

Necessary and Proper clause.   Article I, Section 8, of the U.S. Constitution that grants Congress the authority and responsibility to make laws necessary to carry out its constitutional powers.

New Deal.   A program instituted by President Franklin D. Roosevelt's administration in 1933 to help the nation recover from the Great Depression.

Nondelegation doctrine.   Principle that Congress cannot delegate its law-making duties outlined in Article I, Section 8, of the U.S. Constitution to any other person or body, nor can it delegate authority it does not have.

Off-budget.   Portion of the U.S. federal budget that includes revenues and spending to Social Security trust funds (the Old-Age and Survivors Insurance Trust Fund and the Disability Insurance Trust Fund) and the transactions of the Postal Service.

Omnibus bill.   Several bills packaged into one legislative package.

On-budget.   All budgetary accounts in the U.S. federal budget that are not designated as off-budget.

Open primary.   A primary in which a voter can vote for a presidential candidate regardless of that voter's political party affiliation.

Order.   Decision reached by an administrative law judge that outlines the ruling in an administrative case and reason(s) for the judge's decision.

Outsourcing.   Private contracting of government work that has historically been performed by government employees.

Partisan politics.   Political actions or decisions that are influenced by political party ideologies.

Party platform.   An outline of the goals and principles for major programs and policies a political party deems necessary to serve the people. See also **Plank**s, below.

Party ticket.   A list of a political party's candidates for various offices.

Patronage.   A practice of rewarding loyal or active members of, or contributors to, a political party with government jobs or contracts.

Performance standards.   Threshold levels of employee performance required to be rated as unsuccessful, successful, or exceptional in the performance of their duties.

Permanent Normal Trade Relations.   Designated status the US government may give to countries the U.S. does free trade with.

Petition for an extraordinary writ.   Demand by the Supreme Court to try a specific case because exceptional circumstances exist whereby the Supreme Court feels that only it can adequately review the case.

Petition for a writ of certiorari.   Formal request for the Supreme Court to review the decision of a lower court (most are denied by the Supreme Court).

Planks.   Categories of issues contained in the party platform of political parties.

Pocket veto.   The president's killing of a bill by not sending it back to Congress before the end of a congressional session.

Political Action Committee (PAC).   Defined by the Federal Election Commission as an organization that receives or makes political contributions in excess of $1,000 during a calendar year for the purpose of influencing a federal election.

Political culture.   The set of ideas, values, and attitudes about the government and the political process held by the members of a community or nation.

Political party.   Organization composed of individuals with common ideas and ideologies joining together to use their collective power and influence to sway the government to make decisions in favor of their positions on specific issues.

Politics.   The process of making decisions in the government.

Poll tax.   A fee charged voters; historically used in the United States to prevent African Americans from voting.

Poll watcher.   An individual appointed by a political party or candidate to monitor a polling place to make sure that elections are run fair.

Position description.   Document that outlines the duties, responsibilities, and areas of accountability for a position held by a civil servant.

Precedent.   The application of the rulings and decisions reached in previous courts cases on the same or similar issue in the ruling of a current court case.

President pro tempore.   The senior member of the political party with the most members in the Senate who presides over the Senate in the absence of the vice president of the United States.

Press secretary.   A member of the White House staff who holds press conferences for reporters and makes a public statement for the president.

Primary.   A political party election held in a state where members of that party select the presidential candidate they will support at the national party convention.

Procedural law.   Body of law that outlines how an agency will enforce the provisions of statutory law.

Proclamations.   Presidential executive orders that are generally issued as ceremonial announcements.

Private bill.   Congressional bill that addresses an individual, small group, or specific segment of the population.

Private interest groups.   Interest groups formed to influence government legislation and policy affecting their members or others with similar interests. Also called *special interest groups*.

Public bill.   Congressional bill that affects the general public.

Public interest groups.   Interest groups that form to influence government legislation and policy over issues affecting the general public.

Quorum call.   Tally of Congress members present during a congressional session to ensure a majority of members are present to vote on an issue or bill.

Reapportionment.   The process of realigning or reapportioning the seats in the U.S. House of Representatives among the fifty states.

Recession.   Decline in a nation's output for two consecutive quarters, measured by the Gross Domestic Product (GDP).

Redistricting.   Revising the geographic areas of each district where citizens elect members of the U.S. House of Representatives, state congressional members, local councils, and school board members.

Request for certification.   Request from a lower court for the Supreme Court to provide assistance and insight on specific issues surrounding a case.

Rider.   Amendment attached to a popular bill, or one with a good chance of being passed, in an attempt to assure passage of the amendment.

Roll call.   Tally of the members of the House of Representative or the Senate that are present during a congressional session.

Rule of four.   Supreme Court requirement that an affirmative vote by at least four of the nine Justices is required to grant a case a hearing.

Rule making.   The process agencies follow in establishing, revising, or eliminating rules and regulations.

Rules committee.   A standing committee in the House of Representatives that provides special rules governing how particular bills will be considered and debated by members of the House.

Second reading.   Reading of a bill before the full House of Representatives or Senate after it has been returned from a committee (see also **First reading**).

Segregation.   The intentional denial of equal access to facilities or accommodations because of an individual's race, color, religion, or national origin.

Separate but equal doctrine.   A Supreme Court ruling that the Equal Protection Clause of the Fourteenth Amendment of the U.S. Constitution did not forbid racial segregation as long as facilities and accommodations provided to different racial groups were equal.

Separation of powers.   The division of authorities and duties of the U.S. government into three sectors or branches: the executive, the judicial, and legislative.

Simple resolution.   Legislative proposal that does not require the president's approval and addresses matters affecting operations in either the House of Representatives or the Senate, or are issued to express official positions of either chamber.

Slip law.   The final version of a passed bill issued until the end of a congressional session, after which it becomes an official law.

Social regulation.   Government management and influence of the economy by setting rules and standards for companies to protect employees, citizens, and the environment.

Soft money.   Political campaign donations from individuals, corporations, and unions not donated directly to a candidate but rather to a candidate's political party and which have an impact on elections.

Special committees.   Temporary committees established in either the House of Representatives or the Senate to deal with special or emergency issues.

Stagflation.   Economic period of growing inflation, stagnant (slow or no) economic growth, rising unemployment, and that leads to an eventual recession.

Standing committees.   Permanent committees in the House of Representatives and the Senate that have oversight over specific areas of legislation.

Statute.   A written law passed by Congress and signed by the president stipulating policy.

Statute of limitations.   The maximum amount of time allowed for a case to be brought to court, depending upon the type of case.

Straw polls.   Unofficial surveys of randomly selected people in a state's population conducted to gauge the level of support for political candidates before a caucus or primary takes place.

Substantive law.   Administrative law resulting from a congressional statute creating an agency that outlines it duties and specifically outlines what the agency was developed to enforce.

Suffrage.   The civil right to vote.

Superfunctions.   Major categories of spending in the U.S. federal budget.

Supremacy clause.   Article VI of the U.S. Constitution that stipulates the Constitution, and associated laws and treaties passed by the federal government, must be upheld by all legislative, executive, and judicial officers.

Taxation without representation.   The practice of a governmental body levying taxes against a portion of its citizens who have no voice in the government's legislative body.

Temporary bill.   Bill introduced in Congress for the passage of new legislation that will only be in effect for a specific period of time.

Terrorism.   The random use of staged violence at infrequent intervals to achieve political, economic, social, or religious goals.

Third reading.   Stage of a legislative process in which a bill is read with all amendments and given final approval by a legislative body.

Three-fifths compromise.   A compromise reached during the Constitutional Convention in which it was agreed that three-fifths of all slaves could be counted for the apportionment of the members House of Representatives and for the distribution of taxes.

Trade agreement.   Treaty or other binding accord between two or more countries on what and how goods and/or services will be traded.

Trade organizations.   Associations formed by members of a particular industry to develop standards and goals for that industry.

Treasury bills.   Short-term government securities that mature (i.e., reach full value) one year after their date of issue.

Treasury notes.   Government securities that mature (i.e., reach full value) between one and ten years after their date of issue.

Treaty.   Binding and documented agreement between the governments of one or more countries over a particular issue(s).

Two-thirds vote.   Minimum number of votes required of members in the House of Representatives and the Senate to override a presidential veto vote.

United States Code.   Federal repository of laws passed by Congress, with titles organized by subjects.

Veto.   Presidential action to refuse to sign a proposed law that has already been approved by both chambers of Congress.

Veto power.   A Constitutional power that enables the president to reject a bill and return it to Congress with reasons for the rejection.

Wage grade.   Designation for government jobs that are considered blue-collar.

War Powers Resolution.   Grants power to the president to commit troops up to ninety days in response to a specific military threat.

Weapons of mass destruction.   Nuclear, chemical, and biological weapons that can inflict massive casualties on the civilian population.

Whip.   A member of Congress who assists the majority or minority leader in the House of Representatives or Senate in managing the party's legislative policies.

World policeman.   Title the United States has gained due to the nation's involvement in so many international conflicts and the internal affairs of other nations.

Writ of mandamus.   Judicial remedy whereby a court can order a government body or inferior court to follow a law and take or cease action.

Write-in candidate.   A candidate whose name is not printed on the ballot during an election but written on the ballot by a voter.

Xenophobia.   Fear and hatred of foreigners.

Appendix C

How to Read Legal and Statutory Citations

Throughout this book, citations are provided to federal statutes, federal codes, and federal court cases. The following examples explain how to interpret these citations.

Federal Statute in *Statutes at Large*

Example: Civil Rights Act of 1964, P.L. 88-353, 78 Stat. 241 (1964)
Explanation:

Civil Rights Act of 1964	Name of the Act
P.L. 88-353	Public Law number
78	Volume of *Statutes at Large* in which the statute can be found
Stat.	Title of the book (*Statutes at Large*)
241	Page number in book
1964	Year enacted

Federal Statute in the *United States Code*

Example: 5 U.S.C. 2301
Explanation: Title 5, Section 2301 of the *United States Code*

Regulation in the *Code of Federal Regulations*

Example: 5 CFR Part 2635
Explanation: Title 5 located in the *Code of Federal Regulations*, Section 2635

COURT CASES

Supreme Court Case

Example: *Roe v. Wade*, 410 U.S. 113 (1973)
Explanation:

Roe v. Wade	Name of the case
Roe	Plaintiff
Wade	Defendant
410	Volume of *United States Reports* in which the case can be found
U.S.	Title of the book (*United States Reports*)
133	Page number case begins on
1973	Year case was decided

District Court Case

Example: United States v. Microsoft, 87 F. Supp 2d 30 (D.D.C. 2000)
Explanation:

United States v. Microsoft	Name of the case
United States	Plaintiff
Microsoft	Defendant
87	Volume number
F. Supp	Title of the book (*Federal Supplement*)
2d	The reporter, or series (here, the 2d, which commenced in 1998)
30	Page number the case begins on
D.D.C.	Court (here, the U.S. District Court for the District of Columbia)
2000	Year the case was decided

STATUTES

Session Law

Example: Civil Rights Act of 1964, P.L. 88-353, 78 Stat. 241 (1964)
Explanation:

Civil Rights Act of 1964	Popular name of the law
P.L. 88-353	Public law number
78	Volume number
Stat.	Title of the book (*Statutes at Large*)
241	Page number
1964	Year enacted

Codes

Example: Civil Rights Act of 1964, 42 U.S.C. §1971 et seq. (1988)
Explanation:

Civil Rights Act of 1964	Popular name of the act
42	Title or chapter number
U.S.C	Title of the book (*United States Code*)
1971 et seq.	Session number or part number
1988	Year of completion

Appendix D

LIST OF RELEVANT WEB SITES

U.S. Government official web page   www.usa.gov
The White House   www.whitehouse.gov

EXECUTIVE BRANCH DEPARTMENTS

Department of Agriculture	www.usda.gov
Department of Commerce	www.commerce.gov
Department of Defense	www.defenselink.gov
Department of Education	www.ed.gov
Department of Energy	www.energy.gov
Department of Health and Human Services	www.os.dhhs.gov
Department of Homeland Security	www.dhs.gov
Department of Housing and Urban Development	www.hud.gov
Department of the Interior	www.doi.gov
Department of Justice	www.usdoj.gov
Department of Labor	www.dol.gov
Department of State	www.state.gov
Department of Transportation	www.dot.gov
Department of the Treasury	www.ustreas.gov
Department of Veterans Affairs	www.va.gov

CONGRESSIONAL SITES

U.S. Congress. House of Representatives	www.house.org
U.S. Congress. Senate	www.senate.gov

THE SUPREME COURT

The Supreme Court   www.supremecourtus.gov

STATE GOVERNMENTS

U.S. state governments and territories   www.usa.gov/Agencies/
State_and_Territories.shtml

state and local government on the net   www.statelocalgov.net

MAJOR POLITICAL PARTIES

Democratic National Committee   www.democrats.org
Republican National Committee   www.rnc.org

UNITED STATE GOVERNMENT AGENCIES

Advisory Council on Historic Preservation (ACHP)	www.achp.gov
African Development Foundation	www.adf.gov
Agency for International Development (USAID)	www.info.usaid.gov
American Battle Monuments Commission	www.abmc.gov
AMTRAK	www.amtrak.com
Appalachian Regional Commission	www.arc.gov
Architectural and Transportation Barriers Compliance Board	www.access-board.gov
Ballistic Missile Defense Organization	www.mda.mil
Bureau of Alcohol, Tobacco, Firearms, and Explosives	www.atf.treas.gov
Bureau of Arms Control	www.state.gov/www/global/arms/bureauac.html
Bureau of Engraving & Printing	www.bep.treas.gov
Bureau of Labor Statistics	www.bls.gov
Bureau of the Census	www.census.gov
Bureau of Transportation Statistics	www.bts.gov
Centers for Medicare and Medicaid Services	cms.hhs.gov
Central Intelligence Agency (CIA)	www.cia.gov
Chemical Safety and Hazard Investigations Board (USCSB)	www.chemsafety.gov
Commission on Civil Rights	www.usccr.gov
Commodity Futures Trading Commission (CFTC)	www.cftc.gov
Consumer Product Safety Commission (CPSC)	www.cpsc.gov
Corporation For National Service (CNS)	www.cns.gov
Defense Advanced Research Projects Agency	www.darpa.mil
Defense Information Systems Agency	www.disa.mil
Defense Intelligence Agency	www.dia.mil
Defense Logistics Agency	www.supply.dla.mil
Defense Nuclear Facilities Safety Board	www.dnfsb.gov
Defense Security Service	www.dss.mil
Defense Threat Reduction Agency	www.dtra.mil
Drug Enforcement Administration	www.usdoj.gov/dea

Environmental Protection Agency (EPA)	www.epa.gov
Equal Employment Opportunity Commission	www.eeoc.gov
Export-Import Bank of the U.S.	www.exim.gov
Farm Credit Administration (FCA)	www.fca.gov
Federal Accounting Standards Advisory Board	www.fasab.gov
Federal Aviation Administration	www.faa.gov
Federal Bureau of Investigation	www.fbi.gov
Federal Communications Commission (FCC)	www.fcc.gov
Federal Deposit Insurance Corporation (FDIC)	www.fdic.gov
Federal Election Commission (FEC)	www.fec.gov
Federal Emergency Management Agency (FEMA)	www.fema.gov
Federal Energy Regulatory Commission	www.ferc.fed.us
Federal Highway Administration	www.fhwa.dot.gov
Federal Housing Finance Board (FHFB)	www.fhfb.gov
Federal Labor Relations Authority	www.flra.gov
Federal Maritime Commission	www.fmc.gov
Federal Mediation & Conciliation Service	www.fmcs.gov
Federal Mine Safety & Health Review Commission	www.fmshrc.gov
Federal Railroad Administration	www.fra.dot.gov
Federal Reserve System	www.federalreserve.gov
Federal Retirement Thrift Investment Board	www.frtib.gov
Federal Trade Commission (FTC)	www.ftc.gov
Food & Drug Administration	www.fda.gov
Government Accountability Office	www.gao.gov
General Services Administration (GSA)	www.gsa.gov
Ginnie Mae	www.ginniemae.gov
Institute of Museum and Library Services	www.imls.gov
Inter-American Development Bank	www.iadb.org
Inter-American Foundation	www.iaf.gov
Internal Revenue Service	www.irs.ustreas.gov
International Bank for Reconstruction & Development	www.worldbank.org
International Labor Organization	www.us.ilo.org
International Monetary Fund	www.imf.org
International Trade Commission (USITC)	www.usitc.gov
Legal Services Corporation	www.lsc.gov
Medicare Payment Advisory Commission	www.medpac.gov
Merit Systems Protection Board	www.mspb.gov
National Aeronautics and Space Administration (NASA)	www.nasa.gov
National Archives and Records Administration (NARA)	www.nara.gov
National Bioethics Advisory Commission	www.bioethics.gov
National Capital Planning Commission	www.ncpc.gov
National Commission on Libraries and Information Science (NCLIS)	www.nclis.gov
National Council on Disability (NCD)	www.ncd.gov
National Credit Union Administration	www.ncua.gov
National Endowment for the Arts	arts.endow.gov
National Endowment for the Humanities	www.neh.gov
National Highway Traffic Safety Administration	www.nhtsa.dot.gov
National Geospatial-Intelligence Agency	www.nga.mil

National Institute of Justice	www.ojp.usdoj.gov/nij
National Institute of Mental Health	www.nimh.nih.gov
National Institute of Standards & Technology	www.nist.gov
National Institutes of Health	www.nih.gov
National Labor Relations Board	www.nlrb.gov
National Mediation Board	www.nmb.gov
National Oceanic & Atmospheric Administration	www.noaa.gov
National Park Service	www.nps.gov
National Science Foundation (NSF)	www.nsf.gov
National Security Agency (NSA)	www.nsa.gov
National Technology Transfer Center (NTTC)	www.nttc.edu
National Telecommunications Information Administration	www.ntia.doc.gov
National Transportation Safety Board	www.ntsb.gov
Neighborhood Reinvestment Corporation	www.nw.org
Nuclear Regulatory Commission (NRC)	www.nrc.gov
Occupational Safety and Health Review Commission	www.oshrc.gov
Office of Federal Housing Enterprise Oversight	www.ofheo.gov
Office of Government Ethics	www.usoge.gov
Office of Personnel Management (OPM)	www.opm.gov
Office of Special Counsel	www.osc.gov
Office of Thrift Supervision	www.ots.treas.gov
Organization for Economic Cooperation & Development	www.oecdwash.org
Organization of American States	www.oas.org
Overseas Private Investment Corp.	www.opic.gov
Pan American Health Organization	www.paho.org
Patent & Trademark Office	www.uspto.gov
Peace Corps	www.peacecorps.gov
Pension Benefit Guaranty Corporation (PBGC)	www.pbgc.gov
Postal Regulatory Commission	www.prc.gov
Railroad Retirement Board (RRB)	www.rrb.gov
Securities Exchange Commission (SEC)	www.sec.gov
Securities Investor Protection Corp.	www.sipc.org
Selective Service System (SSS)	www.sss.gov
Small Business Administration (SBA)	www.sba.gov
Smithsonian Institution	www.si.edu
Social Security Administration (SSA)	www.ssa.gov
Substance Abuse & Mental Health Services Administration	www.samhsa.gov
Surface Transportation Board	www.stb.dot.gov
Tennessee Valley Authority	www.tva.gov
Trade and Development Agency	www.tda.gov
United Nations Information Center	www.unicwash.org
United States Code	www.gpoaccess.gov/uscode
United States Holocaust Memorial Council	www.ushmm.org
United States Postal Service (USPS)	www.usps.gov
U.S. Citizenship and Immigration Services	www.uscis.gov/portal/site/uscis

U.S. Customs Service	www.customs.gov
U.S. Fish and Wildlife Service	www.fws.gov
U.S. Forest Service	www.fs.fed.us
U.S. Government Printing Office	www.gpo.gov
U.S. Institute of Peace	www.usip.org
U.S. Marshals Service	www.usdoj.gov/marshals/
U.S. Office of Government Ethics (USOGE)	www.usoge.gov
U.S. Treasury	www.treas.gov
Voice of America (VOA)	www.voa.gov
Walter Reed Army Medical Center	www.wramc.amedd.army.mil
White House Fellows	www.whitehousefellows.gov
White House Commission on Remembrance	www.remember.gov
Women's History Commission	www.gsa.gov/staff/pa/whc.htm

Appendix E

The Declaration of Independence

In Congress, July 4, 1776,

THE UNANIMOUS DECLARATION OF THE THIRTEEN UNITED STATES OF AMERICA

When in the Course of human events, it becomes necessary for one people to dissolve the political bands which have connected them with another, and to assume, among the Powers of the earth, the separate and equal station to which the Laws of Nature and of Nature's God entitle them, a decent respect to the opinions of mankind requires that they should declare the causes which impel them to the separation.

We hold these truths to be self-evident, that all men are created equal, that they are endowed by their Creator with certain unalienable Rights, that among these are Life, Liberty, and the pursuit of Happiness. That, to secure these rights, Governments are instituted among Men, deriving their just Powers from the consent of the governed. That, whenever any Form of Government becomes destructive of these ends, it is the Right of the People to alter or to abolish it, and to institute new Government, laying its foundation on such Principles and organizing its Powers in such form, as to them shall seem most likely to effect their Safety and Happiness. Prudence, indeed, will dictate that Governments long established should not be changed for light and transient causes; and, accordingly, all experience hath shown, that mankind are more disposed to suffer, while evils are sufferable, than to right themselves by abolishing the forms to which they are accustomed. But, when a long train of abuses and usurpations, pursuing invariably the same Object, evinces a design to reduce them under absolute Despotism, it is their right, it is their duty, to throw off such Government, and to provide new Guards for their future security. Such has been the patient sufferance of these Colonies; and such is now the necessity which constrains them to alter their former Systems of Government. The history of the present King of Great Britain is a history of repeated injuries and usurpations, all having in direct object the establishment of an absolute Tyranny over these States. To prove this, let Facts be submitted to a candid world.

He has refused his Assent to Laws the most wholesome and necessary for the public good.

He has forbidden his Governors to pass Laws of immediate and pressing importance, unless suspended in their operation till his Assent should be obtained; and when so suspended, he has utterly neglected to attend to them.

He has refused to pass other Laws for the accommodation of large districts of People, unless those People would relinquish the right of Representation in the legislature; a right inestimable to them and formidable to tyrants only.

He has called together legislative bodies at places unusual, uncomfortable, and distant from the depository of their Public Records, for the sole purpose of fatiguing them into compliance with his measures.

He has dissolved Representative Houses repeatedly, for opposing, with manly firmness, his invasions on the rights of the People.

He has refused for a long time, after such dissolutions, to cause others to be elected; whereby the Legislative Powers, incapable of Annihilation, have returned to the People at large for their exercise; the State remaining in the mean time exposed to all the dangers of invasion from without, and convulsions within.

He has endeavoured to prevent the Population of these States; for that purpose obstructing the Laws of Naturalization of Foreigners; refusing to pass others to encourage their migrations hither, and raising the conditions of new Appropriations of Lands.

He has obstructed the Administration of Justice, by refusing his Assent to Laws for establishing Judiciary Powers.

He has made Judges dependent on his Will alone, for the tenure of their offices, and the amount and payment of their salaries.

He has erected a multitude of New Offices, and sent hither swarms of Officers to harass our People, and eat out their substance.

He has kept among us, in times of Peace, Standing Armies without the Consent of our legislatures.

He has affected to render the Military independent of and superior to the Civil Power.

He has combined with others to subject us to a jurisdiction foreign to our constitution, and unacknowledged by our laws; giving his Assent to their Acts of pretended Legislation:

For quartering large bodies of armed troops among us:
For protecting them, by a mock Trial, from Punishment for any Murders which they should commit on the Inhabitants of these States:

For cutting off our Trade with all parts of the world:

For imposing Taxes on us without our Consent:

For depriving us, in many cases, of the benefits of Trial by Jury:

For transporting us beyond Seas to be tried for pretended offences:

For abolishing the free System of English Laws in a neighbouring Province, establishing therein an Arbitrary government, and enlarging its Boundaries so as to render it at once an example and fit instrument for introducing the same absolute rule into these Colonies:

For taking away our Charters, abolishing our most valuable Laws, and altering fundamentally the Forms of our Governments:

For suspending our own Legislatures, and declaring themselves invested with Power to legislate for us in all cases whatsoever.

He has abdicated Government here, by declaring us out of his protection, and waging War against us.

He has plundered our seas, ravaged our Coasts, burnt our towns, and destroyed the Lives of our People.

He is at this time transporting large Armies of foreign Mercenaries to compleat the works of death, desolation and tyranny, already begun with circumstances of Cruelty and perfidy scarcely paralleled in the most barbarous ages, and totally unworthy the Head of a civilized nation.

He has constrained our fellow Citizens, taken Captive on the high Seas to bear Arms against their Country, to become the executioners of their friends and Brethren, or to fall themselves by their Hands.

He has excited domestic insurrections amongst us, and has endeavoured to bring on the inhabitants of our frontiers, the merciless Indian Savages, whose known rule of warfare, is an undistinguished destruction of all ages, sexes and conditions.

In every stage of these Oppressions, We have Petitioned for Redress in the most humble terms: Our repeated Petitions have been answered only by repeated injury. A Prince, whose character is thus marked by every act which may define a Tyrant, is unfit to be the ruler of a free People.

Nor have We been wanting in attentions to our British brethren. We have warned them from time to time of attempts by their legislature to extend an unwarrantable jurisdiction over us. We have reminded them of the circumstances of our emigration and settlement here. We have appealed to their native justice and magnanimity, and we have conjured them by the ties of our common kindred, to disavow these usurpations, which would inevitably interrupt our connections and correspondence. They too have been deaf to the voice of justice and of consanguinity. We must, therefore, acquiesce in the necessity, which denounces our Separation, and hold them, as we hold the rest of mankind, Enemies in War, in Peace Friends.

We, therefore, the Representatives of the *united States of America*, in GENERAL CONGRESS assembled, appealing to the Supreme Judge of the World for the rectitude of our intentions, DO, in the Name, and by Authority of the good People of these Colonies, solemnly PUBLISH and DECLARE, That these United Colonies are, and of Right, ought to be *free and Independent States*; that they are Absolved from all Allegiance to the British Crown, and that all political connection between them and the State of Great Britain, is and ought to be totally dissolved; and that, as FREE and INDEPENDENT STATES, they have full Power to levy War, conclude Peace, contract Alliances, establish Commerce, and to do all other Acts and Things which INDEPENDENT STATES may of right do. AND for the support of this Declaration, with a firm reliance on the protection of divine Providence, we mutually pledge to each other our Lives, our Fortunes and our sacred Honor.

JOHN HANCOCK, President

Attested, CHARLES THOMSON, Secretary

New Hampshire: JOSIAH BARTLETT, WILLIAM WHIPPLE, MATTHEW THORNTON

Massachusetts-Bay: SAMUEL ADAMS, JOHN ADAMS, ROBERT TREAT PAINE, ELBRIDGE GERRY

Rhode Island: STEPHEN HOPKINS, WILLIAM ELLERY

Connecticut: ROGER SHERMAN, SAMUEL HUNTINGTON, WILLIAM WILLIAMS, OLIVER WOLCOTT

Georgia: BUTTON GWINNETT, LYMAN HALL, GEO. WALTON

Maryland: SAMUEL CHASE, WILLIAM PACA, THOMAS STONE, CHARLES CARROLL OF CARROLLTON

Virginia: GEORGE WYTHE, RICHARD HENRY LEE, THOMAS JEFFERSON, BENJAMIN HARRISON, THOMAS NELSON, JR., FRANCIS LIGHTFOOT LEE, CARTER BRAXTON.

New York: WILLIAM FLOYD, PHILIP LIVINGSTON, FRANCIS LEWIS, LEWIS MORRIS

Pennsylvania: ROBERT MORRIS, BENJAMIN RUSH, BENJAMIN FRANKLIN, JOHN MORTON, GEORGE CLYMER, JAMES SMITH, GEORGE TAYLOR, JAMES WILSON, GEORGE ROSS

Delaware: CAESAR RODNEY, GEORGE READ, THOMAS M'KEAN

North Carolina: WILLIAM HOOPER, JOSEPH HEWES, JOHN PENN

South Carolina: EDWARD RUTLEDGE, THOMAS HEYWARD, JR., THOMAS LYNCH, JR., ARTHUR MIDDLETON

New Jersey: RICHARD STOCKTON, JOHN WITHERSPOON, FRANCIS HOPKINS, JOHN HART, ABRAHAM CLARK

Appendix F

THE CONSTITUTION OF THE UNITED STATES

PREAMBLE

We the People of the United States, in Order to form a more perfect Union, establish Justice, insure domestic Tranquility, provide for the common defence, promote the general Welfare, and secure the Blessings of Liberty to ourselves and our Posterity, do ordain and establish this Constitution for the United States of America.

ARTICLE I. THE LEGISLATIVE BRANCH

Section 1. The Legislature

All legislative Powers herein granted shall be vested in a Congress of the United States, which shall consist of a Senate and House of Representatives.

Section 2. The House

The House of Representatives shall be composed of Members chosen every second Year by the People of the several States, and the Electors in each State shall have the Qualifications requisite for Electors of the most numerous Branch of the State Legislature.

No Person shall be a Representative who shall not have attained to the Age of twenty five Years, and been seven Years a Citizen of the United States, and who shall not, when elected, be an Inhabitant of that State in which he shall be chosen.

Representatives and direct Taxes shall be apportioned among the several States which may be included within this Union, according to their respective Numbers, which shall be determined by adding to the whole Number of free Persons, including those bound to Service for a Term of Years, and excluding Indians not taxed, three fifths of all other Persons. The actual Enumeration shall be made within three Years after the first Meeting of the Congress of the United States, and within every subsequent Term of ten Years, in such Manner as they shall by Law direct. The Number of Representatives shall not exceed one for every thirty Thousand, but each State shall have at Least one Representative; and until such enumeration shall be made, the State of New Hampshire shall be entitled to chuse three, Massachusetts eight, Rhode Island and Providence Plantations one, Connecticut five, New York six, New Jersey four, Pennsylvania eight, Delaware one, Maryland six, Virginia ten, North Carolina five, South Carolina five and Georgia three.

When vacancies happen in the Representation from any State, the Executive Authority thereof shall issue Writs of Election to fill such Vacancies.

The House of Representatives shall chuse their Speaker and other Officers; and shall have the sole Power of Impeachment.

Section 3. The Senate

The Senate of the United States shall be composed of two Senators from each State, chosen by the Legislature thereof, for six Years; and each Senator shall have one Vote.

Immediately after they shall be assembled in Consequence of the first Election, they shall be divided as equally as may be into three Classes. The Seats of the Senators of the first Class shall be vacated at the Expiration of the second Year, of the second Class at the Expiration of the fourth Year, and of the third Class at the Expiration of the sixth Year, so that one third may be chosen every second Year; and if Vacancies happen by Resignation, or otherwise, during the Recess of the Legislature of any State, the Executive thereof may make temporary Appointments until the next Meeting of the Legislature, which shall then fill such Vacancies.

No person shall be a Senator who shall not have attained to the Age of thirty Years, and been nine Years a Citizen of the United States, and who shall not, when elected, be an Inhabitant of that State for which he shall be chosen.

The Vice President of the United States shall be President of the Senate, but shall have no Vote, unless they be equally divided.

The Senate shall chuse their other Officers, and also a President pro tempore, in the absence of the Vice President, or when he shall exercise the Office of President of the United States.

The Senate shall have the sole Power to try all Impeachments. When sitting for that Purpose, they shall be on Oath or Affirmation. When the President of the United States is tried, the Chief Justice shall preside: And no Person shall be convicted without the Concurrence of two thirds of the Members present.

Judgment in Cases of Impeachment shall not extend further than to removal from Office, and disqualification to hold and enjoy any Office of honor, Trust or Profit under the United States: but the Party convicted shall nevertheless be liable and subject to Indictment, Trial, Judgment and Punishment, according to Law.

Section 4. Elections, Meetings

The Times, Places and Manner of holding Elections for Senators and Representatives, shall be prescribed in each State by the Legislature thereof; but the Congress may at any time by Law make or alter such Regulations, except as to the Place of Chusing Senators.

The Congress shall assemble at least once in every Year, and such Meeting shall be on the first Monday in December, unless they shall by Law appoint a different Day.

Section 5. Membership, Rules, Journals, Adjournment

Each House shall be the Judge of the Elections, Returns and Qualifications of its own Members, and a Majority of each shall constitute a Quorum to do Business; but a smaller number may adjourn from day to day, and may be authorized to compel the Attendance of absent Members, in such Manner, and under such Penalties as each House may provide.

Each House may determine the Rules of its Proceedings, punish its Members for disorderly Behavior, and, with the Concurrence of two-thirds, expel a Member.

Each House shall keep a Journal of its Proceedings, and from time to time publish the same, excepting such Parts as may in their Judgment require Secrecy; and the Yeas and Nays of the Members of either House on any question shall, at the Desire of one fifth of those Present, be entered on the Journal.

Neither House, during the Session of Congress, shall, without the Consent of the other, adjourn for more than three days, nor to any other Place than that in which the two Houses shall be sitting.

Section 6. Compensation

The Senators and Representatives shall receive a Compensation for their Services, to be ascertained by Law, and paid out of the Treasury of the United States. They shall in all Cases, except Treason, Felony and Breach of the Peace, be privileged from Arrest during their Attendance at the Session of their respective Houses, and in going to and returning from the same; and for any Speech or Debate in either House, they shall not be questioned in any other Place.

No Senator or Representative shall, during the Time for which he was elected, be appointed to any civil Office under the Authority of the United States which shall have been created, or the Emoluments whereof shall have been increased during such time; and no Person holding any Office under the United States, shall be a Member of either House during his Continuance in Office.

Section 7. Revenue Bills, Legislative Process, Presidential Veto

All bills for raising Revenue shall originate in the House of Representatives; but the Senate may propose or concur with Amendments as on other Bills.

Every Bill which shall have passed the House of Representatives and the Senate, shall, before it become a Law, be presented to the President of the United States; If he approve he shall sign

it, but if not he shall return it, with his Objections to that House in which it shall have originated, who shall enter the Objections at large on their Journal, and proceed to reconsider it. If
after such Reconsideration two thirds of that House shall agree to pass the Bill, it shall be sent,
together with the Objections, to the other House, by which it shall likewise be reconsidered,
and if approved by two thirds of that House, it shall become a Law. But in all such Cases the
Votes of both Houses shall be determined by Yeas and Nays, and the Names of the Persons
voting for and against the Bill shall be entered on the Journal of each House respectively. If any
Bill shall not be returned by the President within ten Days (Sundays excepted) after it shall have
been presented to him, the Same shall be a Law, in like Manner as if he had signed it, unless
the Congress by their Adjournment prevent its Return, in which Case it shall not be a Law.

Every Order, Resolution, or Vote to which the Concurrence of the Senate and House of Representatives may be necessary (except on a question of Adjournment) shall be presented to the
President of the United States; and before the Same shall take Effect, shall be approved by him,
or being disapproved by him, shall be repassed by two thirds of the Senate and House of
Representatives, according to the Rules and Limitations prescribed in the Case of a Bill.

Section 8. Powers of Congress

The Congress shall have Power To lay and collect Taxes, Duties, Imposts and Excises, to pay the
Debts and provide for the common Defence and general Welfare of the United States; but all
Duties, Imposts and Excises shall be uniform throughout the United States;

To borrow money on the credit of the United States;

To regulate Commerce with foreign Nations, and among the several States, and with the Indian
Tribes;

To establish an uniform Rule of Naturalization, and uniform Laws on the subject of Bankruptcies
throughout the United States;

To coin Money, regulate the Value thereof, and of foreign Coin, and fix the Standard of Weights
and Measures;

To provide for the Punishment of counterfeiting the Securities and current Coin of the United
States;

To establish Post Offices and Post Roads;

To promote the Progress of Science and useful Arts, by securing for limited Times to Authors
and Inventors the exclusive Right to their respective Writings and Discoveries;

To constitute Tribunals inferior to the supreme Court;

To define and punish Piracies and Felonies committed on the high Seas, and Offenses against
the Law of Nations;

To declare War, grant Letters of Marque and Reprisal, and make Rules concerning Captures on
Land and Water;

To raise and support Armies, but no Appropriation of Money to that Use shall be for a longer Term than two Years;

To provide and maintain a Navy;

To make Rules for the Government and Regulation of the land and naval Forces;

To provide for calling forth the Militia to execute the Laws of the Union, suppress Insurrections and repel Invasions;

To provide for organizing, arming, and disciplining the Militia, and for governing such Part of them as may be employed in the Service of the United States, reserving to the States respectively, the Appointment of the Officers, and the Authority of training the Militia according to the discipline prescribed by Congress;

To exercise exclusive Legislation in all Cases whatsoever, over such District (not exceeding ten Miles square) as may, by Cession of particular States, and the acceptance of Congress, become the Seat of the Government of the United States, and to exercise like Authority over all Places purchased by the Consent of the Legislature of the State in which the Same shall be, for the Erection of Forts, Magazines, Arsenals, dock-Yards, and other needful Buildings; And

To make all Laws which shall be necessary and proper for carrying into Execution the foregoing Powers, and all other Powers vested by this Constitution in the Government of the United States, or in any Department or Officer thereof.

Section 9. Limits on Congress

The Migration or Importation of such Persons as any of the States now existing shall think proper to admit, shall not be prohibited by the Congress prior to the Year one thousand eight hundred and eight, but a tax or duty may be imposed on such Importation, not exceeding ten dollars for each Person.

The privilege of the Writ of Habeas Corpus shall not be suspended, unless when in Cases of Rebellion or Invasion the public Safety may require it.

No Bill of Attainder or ex post facto Law shall be passed.

No capitation, or other direct, Tax shall be laid, unless in Proportion to the Census or Enumeration herein before directed to be taken.

No Tax or Duty shall be laid on Articles exported from any State.

No Preference shall be given by any Regulation of Commerce or Revenue to the Ports of one State over those of another: nor shall Vessels bound to, or from, one State, be obliged to enter, clear, or pay Duties in another.

No Money shall be drawn from the Treasury, but in Consequence of Appropriations made by Law; and a regular Statement and Account of the Receipts and Expenditures of all public Money shall be published from time to time.

No Title of Nobility shall be granted by the United States: And no Person holding any Office of Profit or Trust under them, shall, without the Consent of the Congress, accept of any present, Emolument, Office, or Title, of any kind whatever, from any King, Prince or foreign State.

Section 10. Powers Prohibited of States

No State shall enter into any Treaty, Alliance, or Confederation; grant Letters of Marque and Reprisal; coin Money; emit Bills of Credit; make any Thing but gold and silver Coin a Tender in Payment of Debts; pass any Bill of Attainder, ex post facto Law, or Law impairing the Obligation of Contracts, or grant any Title of Nobility.

No State shall, without the Consent of the Congress, lay any Imposts or Duties on Imports or Exports, except what may be absolutely necessary for executing it's inspection Laws: and the net Produce of all Duties and Imposts, laid by any State on Imports or Exports, shall be for the Use of the Treasury of the United States; and all such Laws shall be subject to the Revision and Controul of the Congress.

No State shall, without the Consent of Congress, lay any duty of Tonnage, keep Troops, or Ships of War in time of Peace, enter into any Agreement or Compact with another State, or with a foreign Power, or engage in War, unless actually invaded, or in such imminent Danger as will not admit of delay.

ARTICLE. II. THE EXECUTIVE BRANCH

Section 1. The President

The executive Power shall be vested in a President of the United States of America. He shall hold his Office during the Term of four Years, and, together with the Vice-President chosen for the same Term, be elected, as follows:

Each State shall appoint, in such Manner as the Legislature thereof may direct, a Number of Electors, equal to the whole Number of Senators and Representatives to which the State may be entitled in the Congress: but no Senator or Representative, or Person holding an Office of Trust or Profit under the United States, shall be appointed an Elector.

The Electors shall meet in their respective States, and vote by Ballot for two persons, of whom one at least shall not lie an Inhabitant of the same State with themselves. And they shall make a List of all the Persons voted for, and of the Number of Votes for each; which List they shall sign and certify, and transmit sealed to the Seat of the Government of the United States, directed to the President of the Senate. The President of the Senate shall, in the Presence of the Senate and House of Representatives, open all the Certificates, and the Votes shall then be counted. The Person having the greatest Number of Votes shall be the President, if such Number be a Majority of the whole Number of Electors appointed; and if there be more than one who have such Majority, and have an equal Number of Votes, then the House of Representatives shall immediately chuse by Ballot one of them for President; and if no Person have a Majority, then from the five highest on the List the said House shall in like Manner chuse the President. But in chusing the President, the Votes shall be taken by States, the Representation from each State having one Vote; a quorum for this Purpose shall consist of a Member or Members from two-thirds of the States, and a Majority of all the States shall be necessary to a Choice. In every Case, after the Choice of the President, the Person having the greatest Number of Votes of the Electors shall be the Vice President. But if there should remain two or more who have equal Votes, the Senate shall chuse from them by Ballot the Vice-President.

The Congress may determine the Time of chusing the Electors, and the Day on which they shall give their Votes; which Day shall be the same throughout the United States.

No person except a natural born Citizen, or a Citizen of the United States, at the time of the Adoption of this Constitution, shall be eligible to the Office of President; neither shall any Person be eligible to that Office who shall not have attained to the Age of thirty-five Years, and been fourteen Years a Resident within the United States.

In Case of the Removal of the President from Office, or of his Death, Resignation, or Inability to discharge the Powers and Duties of the said Office, the same shall devolve on the Vice President, and the Congress may by Law provide for the Case of Removal, Death, Resignation or Inability, both of the President and Vice President, declaring what Officer shall then act as President, and such Officer shall act accordingly, until the Disability be removed, or a President shall be elected.

The President shall, at stated Times, receive for his Services, a Compensation, which shall neither be increased nor diminished during the Period for which he shall have been elected, and he shall not receive within that Period any other Emolument from the United States, or any of them.

Before he enter on the Execution of his Office, he shall take the following Oath or Affirmation:

"I do solemnly swear (or affirm) that I will faithfully execute the Office of President of the United States, and will to the best of my Ability, preserve, protect and defend the Constitution of the United States."

Section 2. Civilian Power over Military, Cabinet, Pardon Power, Appointments

The President shall be Commander in Chief of the Army and Navy of the United States, and of the Militia of the several States, when called into the actual Service of the United States; he may require the Opinion, in writing, of the principal Officer in each of the executive Departments, upon any subject relating to the Duties of their respective Offices, and he shall have Power to Grant Reprieves and Pardons for Offenses against the United States, except in Cases of Impeachment.

He shall have Power, by and with the Advice and Consent of the Senate, to make Treaties, provided two thirds of the Senators present concur; and he shall nominate, and by and with the Advice and Consent of the Senate, shall appoint Ambassadors, other public Ministers and Consuls, Judges of the supreme Court, and all other Officers of the United States, whose Appointments are not herein otherwise provided for, and which shall be established by Law: but the Congress may by Law vest the Appointment of such inferior Officers, as they think proper, in the President alone, in the Courts of Law, or in the Heads of Departments.

The President shall have Power to fill up all Vacancies that may happen during the Recess of the Senate, by granting Commissions which shall expire at the End of their next Session.

Section 3. State of the Union, Convening Congress

He shall from time to time give to the Congress Information of the State of the Union, and recommend to their Consideration such Measures as he shall judge necessary and expedient; he may, on extraordinary Occasions, convene both Houses, or either of them, and in Case of Disagreement between them, with Respect to the Time of Adjournment, he may adjourn them to such Time as he shall think proper; he shall receive Ambassadors and other public Ministers; he shall take Care that the Laws be faithfully executed, and shall Commission all the Officers of the United States.

Section 4. Disqualification

The President, Vice President and all civil Officers of the United States, shall be removed from Office on Impeachment for, and Conviction of, Treason, Bribery, or other high Crimes and Misdemeanors.

ARTICLE III. THE JUDICIAL BRANCH

Section 1. Judicial powers

The judicial Power of the United States, shall be vested in one supreme Court, and in such inferior Courts as the Congress may from time to time ordain and establish. The Judges, both of the supreme and inferior Courts, shall hold their Offices during good Behavior, and shall, at stated Times, receive for their Services a Compensation which shall not be diminished during their Continuance in Office.

Section 2. Trial by Jury, Original Jurisdiction, Jury Trials

The judicial Power shall extend to all Cases, in Law and Equity, arising under this Constitution, the Laws of the United States, and Treaties made, or which shall be made, under their Authority; to all Cases affecting Ambassadors, other public Ministers and Consuls; to all Cases of admiralty and maritime Jurisdiction; to Controversies to which the United States shall be a Party; to Controversies between two or more States; between a State and Citizens of another State; between Citizens of different States; between Citizens of the same State claiming Lands under Grants of different States, and between a State, or the Citizens thereof, and foreign States, Citizens or Subjects.

In all Cases affecting Ambassadors, other public Ministers and Consuls, and those in which a State shall be Party, the supreme Court shall have original Jurisdiction. In all the other Cases before mentioned, the supreme Court shall have appellate Jurisdiction, both as to Law and Fact, with such Exceptions, and under such Regulations as the Congress shall make.

The Trial of all Crimes, except in Cases of Impeachment, shall be by Jury; and such Trial shall be held in the State where the said Crimes shall have been committed; but when not committed within any State, the Trial shall be at such Place or Places as the Congress may by Law have directed.

Section 3. Treason

Treason against the United States, shall consist only in levying War against them, or in adhering to their Enemies, giving them Aid and Comfort. No Person shall be convicted of Treason unless on the Testimony of two Witnesses to the same overt Act, or on Confession in open Court.

The Congress shall have power to declare the Punishment of Treason, but no Attainder of Treason shall work Corruption of Blood, or Forfeiture except during the Life of the Person attainted.

ARTICLE. IV. THE STATES

Section 1. Each State to Honor all others

Full Faith and Credit shall be given in each State to the public Acts, Records, and judicial Proceedings of every other State. And the Congress may by general Laws prescribe the Manner in which such Acts, Records and Proceedings shall be proved, and the Effect thereof.

Section 2. State citizens, Extradition

The Citizens of each State shall be entitled to all Privileges and Immunities of Citizens in the several States.

A Person charged in any State with Treason, Felony, or other Crime, who shall flee from Justice, and be found in another State, shall on demand of the executive Authority of the State from which he fled, be delivered up, to be removed to the State having Jurisdiction of the Crime.

No Person held to Service or Labour in one State, under the Laws thereof, escaping into another, shall, in Consequence of any Law or Regulation therein, be discharged from such Service or Labour, But shall be delivered up on Claim of the Party to whom such Service or Labour may be due.

Section 3. New States

New States may be admitted by the Congress into this Union; but no new States shall be formed or erected within the Jurisdiction of any other State; nor any State be formed by the Junction of two or more States, or parts of States, without the Consent of the Legislatures of the States concerned as well as of the Congress.

The Congress shall have Power to dispose of and make all needful Rules and Regulations respecting the Territory or other Property belonging to the United States; and nothing in this Constitution shall be so construed as to Prejudice any Claims of the United States, or of any particular State.

Section 4. Republican government

The United States shall guarantee to every State in this Union a Republican Form of Government, and shall protect each of them against Invasion; and on Application of the Legislature, or of the Executive (when the Legislature cannot be convened) against domestic Violence.

ARTICLE. V. AMENDMENT

The Congress, whenever two thirds of both Houses shall deem it necessary, shall propose Amendments to this Constitution, or, on the Application of the Legislatures of two thirds of the several States, shall call a Convention for proposing Amendments, which, in either Case, shall be valid to all Intents and Purposes, as part of this Constitution, when ratified by the Legislatures of three fourths of the several States, or by Conventions in three fourths thereof, as the one or the other Mode of Ratification may be proposed by the Congress; Provided that no Amendment which may be made prior to the Year One thousand eight hundred and eight shall in any Manner affect the first and fourth Clauses in the Ninth Section of the first Article; and that no State, without its Consent, shall be deprived of its equal Suffrage in the Senate.

ARTICLE. VI. DEBTS, SUPREMACY, OATHS

All Debts contracted and Engagements entered into, before the Adoption of this Constitution, shall be as valid against the United States under this Constitution, as under the Confederation.

This Constitution, and the Laws of the United States which shall be made in Pursuance thereof; and all Treaties made, or which shall be made, under the Authority of the United States, shall be the supreme Law of the Land; and the Judges in every State shall be bound thereby, any Thing in the Constitution or Laws of any State to the Contrary notwithstanding.

The Senators and Representatives before mentioned, and the Members of the several State Legislatures, and all executive and judicial Officers, both of the United States and of the several States, shall be bound by Oath or Affirmation, to support this Constitution; but no religious Test shall ever be required as a Qualification to any Office or public Trust under the United States.

ARTICLE. VII. RATIFICATION

The Ratification of the Conventions of nine States, shall be sufficient for the Establishment of this Constitution between the States so ratifying the Same.

Done in Convention by the Unanimous Consent of the States present the Seventeenth Day of September in the Year of our Lord one thousand seven hundred and Eighty seven and of the Independence of the United States of America the Twelfth. In Witness whereof We have hereunto subscribed our Names.

George Washington—President and deputy from Virginia

New Hampshire—John Langdon, Nicholas Gilman

Massachusetts—Nathaniel Gorham, Rufus King

Connecticut—Wm Saml. Johnson, Roger Sherman

New York—Alexander Hamilton

New Jersey—Wil Livingston, David Brearley, Wm Paterson, Jona. Dayton

Pensylvania—B Franklin, Thomas Mifflin, Robt Morris, Geo. Clymer, Thos FitzSimons, Jared Ingersoll, James Wilson, Gouv Morris

Delaware—Geo. Read, Gunning Bedford jun, John Dickinson, Richard Bassett, Jaco. Broom

Maryland—James McHenry, Dan of St Tho Jenifer, Danl Carroll

Virginia—John Blair, James Madison Jr.

North Carolina—Wm Blount, Richd Dobbs Spaight, Hu Williamson

South Carolina—J. Rutledge, Charles Cotesworth Pinckney, Charles Pinckney, Pierce Butler

Georgia—William Few, Abr Baldwin

Attest: William Jackson, Secretary

THE AMENDMENTS

Amendment 1. Freedom of Religion, Press, Expression.

Congress shall make no law respecting an establishment of religion, or prohibiting the free exercise thereof; or abridging the freedom of speech, or of the press; or the right of the people peaceably to assemble, and to petition the Government for a redress of grievances.

Amendment 2. Right to Bear Arms.

A well regulated Militia, being necessary to the security of a free State, the right of the people to keep and bear Arms, shall not be infringed.

Amendment 3. Quartering of Soldiers.

No Soldier shall, in time of peace be quartered in any house, without the consent of the Owner, nor in time of war, but in a manner to be prescribed by law.

Amendment 4. Search and Seizure.

The right of the people to be secure in their persons, houses, papers, and effects, against unreasonable searches and seizures, shall not be violated, and no Warrants shall issue, but upon probable cause, supported by Oath or affirmation, and particularly describing the place to be searched, and the persons or things to be seized.

Amendment 5. Trial and Punishment, Compensation for Takings.

No person shall be held to answer for a capital, or otherwise infamous crime, unless on a presentment or indictment of a Grand Jury, except in cases arising in the land or naval forces, or in the Militia, when in actual service in time of War or public danger; nor shall any person be subject for the same offense to be twice put in jeopardy of life or limb; nor shall be compelled in any criminal case to be a witness against himself, nor be deprived of life, liberty, or property, without due process of law; nor shall private property be taken for public use, without just compensation.

Amendment 6. Right to Speedy Trial, Confrontation of Witnesses.

In all criminal prosecutions, the accused shall enjoy the right to a speedy and public trial, by an impartial jury of the State and district wherein the crime shall have been committed, which district shall have been previously ascertained by law, and to be informed of the nature and cause of the accusation; to be confronted with the witnesses against him; to have compulsory process for obtaining witnesses in his favor, and to have the Assistance of Counsel for his defence.

Amendment 7. Trial by Jury in Civil Cases.

In Suits at common law, where the value in controversy shall exceed twenty dollars, the right of trial by jury shall be preserved, and no fact tried by a jury, shall be otherwise re-examined in any Court of the United States, than according to the rules of the common law.

Amendment 8. Cruel and Unusual Punishment.

Excessive bail shall not be required, nor excessive fines imposed, nor cruel and unusual punishments inflicted.

Amendment 9. Construction of Constitution.

The enumeration in the Constitution, of certain rights, shall not be construed to deny or disparage others retained by the people.

Amendment 10. Powers of the States and People.

The powers not delegated to the United States by the Constitution, nor prohibited by it to the States, are reserved to the States respectively, or to the people.

Amendment 11. Judicial Limits.

The Judicial power of the United States shall not be construed to extend to any suit in law or equity, commenced or prosecuted against one of the United States by Citizens of another State, or by Citizens or Subjects of any Foreign State.

Amendment 12. Choosing the President, Vice-President.

The Electors shall meet in their respective states, and vote by ballot for President and Vice-President, one of whom, at least, shall not be an inhabitant of the same state with themselves; they shall name in their ballots the person voted for as President, and in distinct ballots the person voted for as Vice-President, and they shall make distinct lists of all persons voted for as

President, and of all persons voted for as Vice-President and of the number of votes for each, which lists they shall sign and certify, and transmit sealed to the seat of the government of the United States, directed to the President of the Senate;

The President of the Senate shall, in the presence of the Senate and House of Representatives, open all the certificates and the votes shall then be counted;

The person having the greatest Number of votes for President, shall be the President, if such number be a majority of the whole number of Electors appointed; and if no person have such majority, then from the persons having the highest numbers not exceeding three on the list of those voted for as President, the House of Representatives shall choose immediately, by ballot, the President. But in choosing the President, the votes shall be taken by states, the representation from each state having one vote; a quorum for this purpose shall consist of a member or members from two-thirds of the states, and a majority of all the states shall be necessary to a choice. And if the House of Representatives shall not choose a President whenever the right of choice shall devolve upon them, before the fourth day of March next following, then the Vice-President shall act as President, as in the case of the death or other constitutional disability of the President.

The person having the greatest number of votes as Vice-President, shall be the Vice-President, if such number be a majority of the whole number of Electors appointed, and if no person have a majority, then from the two highest numbers on the list, the Senate shall choose the Vice-President; a quorum for the purpose shall consist of two-thirds of the whole number of Senators, and a majority of the whole number shall be necessary to a choice. But no person constitutionally ineligible to the office of President shall be eligible to that of Vice-President of the United States.

Amendment 13. Slavery Abolished.

1. Neither slavery nor involuntary servitude, except as a punishment for crime whereof the party shall have been duly convicted, shall exist within the United States, or any place subject to their jurisdiction.

2. Congress shall have power to enforce this article by appropriate legislation.

Amendment 14. Citizenship Rights.

1. All persons born or naturalized in the United States, and subject to the jurisdiction thereof, are citizens of the United States and of the State wherein they reside. No State shall make or enforce any law which shall abridge the privileges or immunities of citizens of the United States; nor shall any State deprive any person of life, liberty, or property, without due process of law; nor deny to any person within its jurisdiction the equal protection of the laws.

2. Representatives shall be apportioned among the several States according to their respective numbers, counting the whole number of persons in each State, excluding Indians not taxed. But when the right to vote at any election for the choice of electors for President and Vice-President of the United States, Representatives in Congress, the Executive and Judicial officers of a State, or the members of the Legislature thereof, is denied to any of the male inhabitants of such State, being twenty-one years of age, and citizens of the United States, or in any way

abridged, except for participation in rebellion, or other crime, the basis of representation therein shall be reduced in the proportion which the number of such male citizens shall bear to the whole number of male citizens twenty-one years of age in such State.

3. No person shall be a Senator or Representative in Congress, or elector of President and Vice-President, or hold any office, civil or military, under the United States, or under any State, who, having previously taken an oath, as a member of Congress, or as an officer of the United States, or as a member of any State legislature, or as an executive or judicial officer of any State, to support the Constitution of the United States, shall have engaged in insurrection or rebellion against the same, or given aid or comfort to the enemies thereof. But Congress may by a vote of two-thirds of each House, remove such disability.

4. The validity of the public debt of the United States, authorized by law, including debts incurred for payment of pensions and bounties for services in suppressing insurrection or rebellion, shall not be questioned. But neither the United States nor any State shall assume or pay any debt or obligation incurred in aid of insurrection or rebellion against the United States, or any claim for the loss or emancipation of any slave; but all such debts, obligations and claims shall be held illegal and void.

5. The Congress shall have power to enforce, by appropriate legislation, the provisions of this article.

Amendment 15. Race No Bar to Vote.

1. The right of citizens of the United States to vote shall not be denied or abridged by the United States or by any State on account of race, color, or previous condition of servitude.

2. The Congress shall have power to enforce this article by appropriate legislation.

Amendment 16. Status of Income Tax Clarified.

The Congress shall have power to lay and collect taxes on incomes, from whatever source derived, without apportionment among the several States, and without regard to any census or enumeration.

Amendment 17. Senators Elected by Popular Vote.

The Senate of the United States shall be composed of two Senators from each State, elected by the people thereof, for six years; and each Senator shall have one vote. The electors in each State shall have the qualifications requisite for electors of the most numerous branch of the State legislatures.

When vacancies happen in the representation of any State in the Senate, the executive authority of such State shall issue writs of election to fill such vacancies: Provided, That the legislature of any State may empower the executive thereof to make temporary appointments until the people fill the vacancies by election as the legislature may direct.

This amendment shall not be so construed as to affect the election or term of any Senator chosen before it becomes valid as part of the Constitution.

Amendment 18. Liquor Abolished.

1. After one year from the ratification of this article the manufacture, sale, or transportation of intoxicating liquors within, the importation thereof into, or the exportation thereof from the United States and all territory subject to the jurisdiction thereof for beverage purposes is hereby prohibited.

2. The Congress and the several States shall have concurrent power to enforce this article by appropriate legislation.

3. This article shall be inoperative unless it shall have been ratified as an amendment to the Constitution by the legislatures of the several States, as provided in the Constitution, within seven years from the date of the submission hereof to the States by the Congress.

Amendment 19. Women's Suffrage.

The right of citizens of the United States to vote shall not be denied or abridged by the United States or by any State on account of sex.

Congress shall have power to enforce this article by appropriate legislation.

Amendment 20. Presidential, Congressional Terms.

1. The terms of the President and Vice President shall end at noon on the 20th day of January, and the terms of Senators and Representatives at noon on the 3d day of January, of the years in which such terms would have ended if this article had not been ratified; and the terms of their successors shall then begin.

2. The Congress shall assemble at least once in every year, and such meeting shall begin at noon on the 3d day of January, unless they shall by law appoint a different day.

3. If, at the time fixed for the beginning of the term of the President, the President elect shall have died, the Vice President elect shall become President. If a President shall not have been chosen before the time fixed for the beginning of his term, or if the President elect shall have failed to qualify, then the Vice President elect shall act as President until a President shall have qualified; and the Congress may by law provide for the case wherein neither a President elect nor a Vice President elect shall have qualified, declaring who shall then act as President, or the manner in which one who is to act shall be selected, and such person shall act accordingly until a President or Vice President shall have qualified.

4. The Congress may by law provide for the case of the death of any of the persons from whom the House of Representatives may choose a President whenever the right of choice shall have devolved upon them, and for the case of the death of any of the persons from whom the Senate may choose a Vice President whenever the right of choice shall have devolved upon them.

5. Sections 1 and 2 shall take effect on the 15th day of October following the ratification of this article.

6. This article shall be inoperative unless it shall have been ratified as an amendment to the Constitution by the legislatures of three-fourths of the several States within seven years from the date of its submission.

Amendment 21. Amendment 18 Repealed.

1. The eighteenth article of amendment to the Constitution of the United States is hereby repealed.

2. The transportation or importation into any State, Territory, or possession of the United States for delivery or use therein of intoxicating liquors, in violation of the laws thereof, is hereby prohibited.

3. The article shall be inoperative unless it shall have been ratified as an amendment to the Constitution by conventions in the several States, as provided in the Constitution, within seven years from the date of the submission hereof to the States by the Congress.

Amendment 22. Presidential Term Limits.

1. No person shall be elected to the office of the President more than twice, and no person who has held the office of President, or acted as President, for more than two years of a term to which some other person was elected President shall be elected to the office of the President more than once. But this Article shall not apply to any person holding the office of President, when this Article was proposed by the Congress, and shall not prevent any person who may be holding the office of President, or acting as President, during the term within which this Article becomes operative from holding the office of President or acting as President during the remainder of such term.

2. This article shall be inoperative unless it shall have been ratified as an amendment to the Constitution by the legislatures of three-fourths of the several States within seven years from the date of its submission to the States by the Congress.

Amendment 23. Presidential Vote for District of Columbia.

1. The District constituting the seat of Government of the United States shall appoint in such manner as the Congress may direct: A number of electors of President and Vice President equal to the whole number of Senators and Representatives in Congress to which the District would be entitled if it were a State, but in no event more than the least populous State; they shall be in addition to those appointed by the States, but they shall be considered, for the purposes of the election of President and Vice President, to be electors appointed by a State; and they shall meet in the District and perform such duties as provided by the twelfth article of amendment.

2. The Congress shall have power to enforce this article by appropriate legislation.

Amendment 24. Poll Tax Barred.

1. The right of citizens of the United States to vote in any primary or other election for President or Vice President, for electors for President or Vice President, or for Senator or Representative

in Congress, shall not be denied or abridged by the United States or any State by reason of failure to pay any poll tax or other tax.

2. The Congress shall have power to enforce this article by appropriate legislation.

Amendment 25. Presidential Disability and Succession.

1. In case of the removal of the President from office or of his death or resignation, the Vice President shall become President.

2. Whenever there is a vacancy in the office of the Vice President, the President shall nominate a Vice President who shall take office upon confirmation by a majority vote of both Houses of Congress.

3. Whenever the President transmits to the President pro tempore of the Senate and the Speaker of the House of Representatives his written declaration that he is unable to discharge the powers and duties of his office, and until he transmits to them a written declaration to the contrary, such powers and duties shall be discharged by the Vice President as Acting President.

4. Whenever the Vice President and a majority of either the principal officers of the executive departments or of such other body as Congress may by law provide, transmit to the President pro tempore of the Senate and the Speaker of the House of Representatives their written declaration that the President is unable to discharge the powers and duties of his office, the Vice President shall immediately assume the powers and duties of the office as Acting President.

Thereafter, when the President transmits to the President pro tempore of the Senate and the Speaker of the House of Representatives his written declaration that no inability exists, he shall resume the powers and duties of his office unless the Vice President and a majority of either the principal officers of the executive department or of such other body as Congress may by law provide, transmit within four days to the President pro tempore of the Senate and the Speaker of the House of Representatives their written declaration that the President is unable to discharge the powers and duties of his office. Thereupon Congress shall decide the issue, assembling within forty eight hours for that purpose if not in session. If the Congress, within twenty one days after receipt of the latter written declaration, or, if Congress is not in session, within twenty one days after Congress is required to assemble, determines by two thirds vote of both Houses that the President is unable to discharge the powers and duties of his office, the Vice President shall continue to discharge the same as Acting President; otherwise, the President shall resume the powers and duties of his office.

Amendment 26. Voting Age Set to 18 Years.

1. The right of citizens of the United States, who are eighteen years of age or older, to vote shall not be denied or abridged by the United States or by any State on account of age.

2. The Congress shall have power to enforce this article by appropriate legislation.

Amendment 27. Limiting Congressional Pay Increases.

No law, varying the compensation for the services of the Senators and Representatives, shall take effect, until an election of Representatives shall have intervened.

Appendix G

THE PRESIDENTS OF THE UNITED STATES OF AMERICA

No.	President	Political party	No. of times elected to office	Years in office	Age at inauguration	Vice President (for each term of office)
1	George Washington	None	2	1789–1797	57	John Adams John Adams
2	John Adams	Federalist	1	1797–1801	61	Thomas Jefferson
3	Thomas Jefferson	Democratic-Republican	2	1801–1809	57	Aaron Burr George Clinton
4	James Madison	Democratic-Republican	2	1809–1817	57	George Clinton Elbridge Gerry
5	James Monroe	Democratic-Republican	2	1817–1825	58	Daniel D. Tompkins
6	John Quincy Adams	Democratic-Republican	1	1825–1829	57	John C. Calhoun
7	Andrew Jackson	Democrat	2	1829–1837	61	John C. Calhoun Martin Van Buren
8	Martin Van Buren	Democrat	1	1837–1841	54	Richard M. Johnson
9	William Henry Harrison	Whig	1	1841–1841	68	John Tyler
10	John Tyler	Whig	1	1841–1845	51	None
11	James Knox Polk	Democrat	1	1845–1849	49	George M. Dallas
12	Zachary Taylor	Whig	1	1849–1850	64	Millard Fillmore
13	Millard Fillmore	Whig	1	1850–1853	50	None

(*Continued*)

No.	President	Political party	No. of times elected to office	Years in office	Age at inauguration	Vice President (for each term of office)
14	Franklin Pierce	Democrat	1	1853–1857	48	William R.D. King
15	James Buchanan	Democrat	1	1857–1861	65	John C. Breckinridge
16	Abraham Lincoln	Republican	2	1861–1865	52	Hannibal Hamlin Andrew Johnson
17	Andrew Johnson	Democrat	1	1865–1869	56	None
18	Ulysses Simpson Grant	Republican	2	1869–1877	46	Schuyler Colfax Henry Wilson
19	Rutherford Birchard Hayes	Republican	1	1877–1881	54	William A. Wheeler
20	James Abram Garfield	Republican	1	1881–1881	49	Chester A. Arthur
21	Chester Alan Arthur	Republican	1	1881–1885	51	None
22	Grover Cleveland	Democratic	1	1885–1889	47	Thomas A. Hendricks
23	Benjamin Harrison	Republican	1	1889–1893	55	Levi P. Morton
24	Grover Cleveland	Democratic	1	1893–1897	55	Adlai E. Stevenson
25	William McKinley	Republican	2	1897–1901	54	Garret A. Hobart Theodore Roosevelt
26	Theodore Roosevelt	Republican	2	1901–1909	42	Charles W. Fairbanks
27	William Howard Taft	Republican	1	1909–1913	51	James S. Sherman
28	Woodrow Wilson	Democrat	2	1913–1921	56	Thomas R. Marshall
29	Warren Gamaliel Harding	Republican	1	1921–1923	55	Calvin Coolidge
30	Calvin Coolidge	Republican	2	1923–1929	51	Charles G. Dawes
31	Herbert Clark Hoover	Republican	1	1929–1933	54	Charles Curtis
32	Franklin Delano Roosevelt	Democrat	4	1933–1945	51	John N. Garner Henry A. Wallace Harry S. Truman

(*Continued*)

No.	President	Political party	No. of times elected to office	Years in office	Age at inauguration	Vice President (for each term of office)
33	Harry S. Truman	Democrat	2	1945–1953	60	Alben W. Barkley
34	Dwight David Eisenhower	Republican	2	1953–1961	62	Richard M. Nixon
35	John Fitzgerald Kennedy	Democrat	1	1961–1963	43	Lyndon B. Johnson
36	Lyndon Baines Johnson	Democrat	2	1963–1969	55	None Hubert H. Humphrey
37	Richard Milhous Nixon	Republican	2	1969–1974	56	Spiro T. Agnew Gerald R. Ford
38	Gerald Rudolph Ford	Republican	1	1974–1977	61	Nelson A. Rockefeller
39	Jimmy Earl Carter, Jr.	Democrat	1	1977–1981	52	Walter F. Mondale
40	Ronald Wilson Reagan	Republican	2	1981–1989	69	George H.W. Bush
41	George Herbert Walker Bush	Republican	1	1989–1993	64	J. Danforth Quayle
42	William Jefferson Clinton	Democrat	2	1993–2001	46	Albert A. Gore Jr.
43	George Walker Bush	Republican	2	2001–2009	54	Richard B. Cheney

Appendix H

Organizational Chart of the United States Senate for the 110th Congress

U.S. Constitution

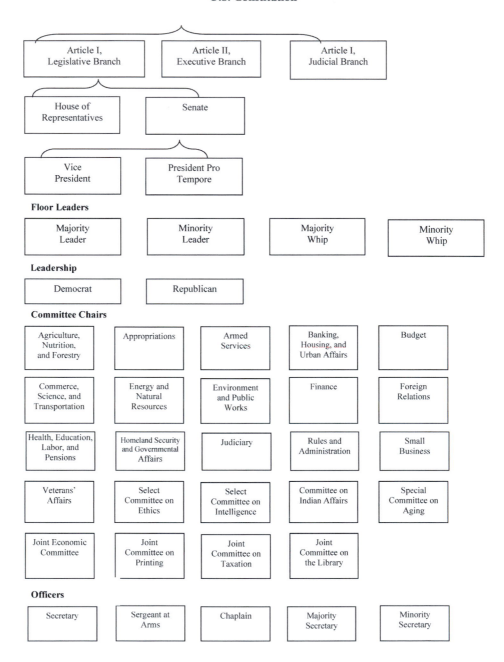

Floor Leaders

Leadership

Committee Chairs

Officers

Appendix I

INDEPENDENT AGENCIES, COMMISSIONS, BOARDS, AND GOVERNMENT CORPORATIONS

INDEPENDENT AGENCIES, COMMISSIONS, AND BOARDS

Central Intelligence Agency (CIA)
Commodity Futures Trading Commission (CFTC)
Consumer Product Safety Commission (CPSC)
Court Services and Offender Supervision Agency for the District of Columbia (CSOSA)
Defense Nuclear Facilities Safety Board (DNFSB)
Election Assistance Commission (EAC)
Environmental Protection Agency (EPA)
Equal Employment Opportunity Commission (EEOC)
Farm Credit Administration (FCA)
Federal Communications Commission (FCC)
Federal Election Commission (FEC)
Federal Housing Finance Board (FHFB)
Federal Labor Relations Authority (FLRA)
Federal Maritime Commission (FMC)
Federal Mediation and Conciliation Service (FMCS)
Federal Mine Safety and Health Review Commission (FMSHRC)
Federal Reserve System
Federal Trade Commission (FTC)
General Service Administration (GSA)
Institute of Museum and Library Services (IMLS)
International Broadcasting Bureau (IBB)
Merit Systems Protection Board (MSPB)
National Aeronautics and Space Administration (NASA)
National Archives and Records Administration (NARA)
National Capital Planning Commission (NCPC)
National Council on Disability (NCD)

National Endowment for the Arts (NEA)
National Endowment for the Humanities (NEH)
National Labor Relations Board (NLRB)
National Mediation Board (NMB)
National Science Foundation (NSF)
National Transportation Safety Board (NTSB)
Nuclear Regulatory Commission (NRC)
Office of Compliance
Office of the National Counterintelligence Executive (NCIX)
Peace Corps
Postal Rate Commission
Selective Service System
U.S. Agency for International Development (USAID)
U.S. Commission on Civil Rights (USCCR)
U.S. Occupational Safety and Health Review Commission (OSHRC)
U.S. Office of Government Ethics (OGE)
U.S. Office of Personnel Management (OPM)
U.S. Office of Special Counsel (OSC)
U.S. Railroad Retirement Board (RRB)
U.S. Securities and Exchange Commission (SEC)
U.S. Small Business Administration (SBA)
U.S. Social Security Administration (SSA)
U.S. Trade and Development Agency (USTDA)
United States International Trade Commission (USITC)

GOVERNMENT CORPORATIONS

AMTRAK (National Railroad Passenger Corporation)
Commodity Credit Corporation (CCC)
Corporation for National and Community Service
Corporation for Public Broadcasting (CPB)
Export-Import Bank of the United States (Ex-Im)
Federal Deposit Insurance Corporation (FDIC)
Federal Retirement Thrift Investment Board (FRTIB)
Inter-American Foundation (IAF)
Legal Services Corporation (LSC)
National Credit Union Administration (NCUA)
National Endowment for Democracy (NED)
Overseas Private Investment Corporation (OPIC)
Pension Benefit Guaranty Corporation (PBGC)
Tennessee Valley Authority (TVA)
U.S. African Development Foundation (USADF)
United States Postal Service (USPS)

Appendix J

PATRIOTIC AND CHARITABLE NONPROFIT ORGANIZATIONS

Agricultural Hall of Fame
Air Force Sergeants Association
American Academy of Arts and Letters
American Chemical Society
American Council of Learned Societies
American Ex-Prisoners of War
American GI Forum of the United States
American Gold Star Mothers, Incorporated
American Historical Association
American Hospital of Paris
The American Legion
The American National Theater and Academy
The American Society of International Law
American Symphony Orchestra League
American War Mothers
AMVETS (American Veterans)
Army and Navy Union of the United States of America
Aviation Hall of Fame
Big Brothers—Big Sisters of America
Blinded Veterans Association
Blue Star Mothers of America, Inc.
Board for Fundamental Education
Boy Scouts of America
Boys & Girls Clubs of America
Catholic War Veterans of the United States of America, Incorporated
Civil Air Patrol
Congressional Medal of Honor Society of the United States of America
Corporation for the Promotion of Rifle Practice and Firearms Safety

Daughter of Union Veterans of the Civil War 1861–1865
Disabled American Veterans
82nd Airborne Division Association, Incorporated
Fleet Reserve Association
Former Members of Congress
The Foundation of the Federal Bar Association
Frederick Douglas Memorial and Historical Association
Future Farmers of America
General Federation of Women's Club
Girl Scouts of the United States of America
Gold Star Wives of America
Italian American War Veterans of the United States
Jewish War Veterans of the United States of America, Incorporated
Ladies of the Grand Army of the Republic
Legion of Valor of the United States of America, Incorporated
Little League Baseball, Incorporated
Marine Corps League
The Military Chaplain's Association of the United States of America
Military Order of the Purple Heart of the United States of America, Incorporated
Military Order of the World Wars
National Academy of Public Administration
National Academy of Sciences
National Conference of State Societies, Washington, District of Columbia
National Conference on Citizenship
National Council on Radiation Protection and Measurements
National Education Association of the United States
National Fallen Firefighters Foundation
National Federation of Music Clubs
National Film Preservation Foundation
National Fund for Medical Education
National Mining Hall of Fame and Museum
National Music Council
National Recording Preservation Foundation
National Safety Council
Help America Vote Foundation
National Ski Patrol System, Incorporated
National Society, Daughters of the American Colonists
National Society of the Daughters of the American Revolution
National Society of the Sons of the American Revolution
National Tropical Botanical Garden
National Woman's Relief Corps, Auxiliary to the Grand Army of the Republic
The National Yoemen F
Naval Sea Cadets Corps
Navy Club of the United States of America
Navy Wives Clubs of America
Non Commissioned Officers Association of the United States of America, Incorporated
Paralyzed Veterans of America
Pearl Harbor Survivors Association
Polish Legion of American Veterans, U.S.A.

Reserve Officers Association of the United States
Retired Enlisted Association, Incorporated
Society of American Florists and Ornamental Horticulturists
Sons of Union Veterans of the Civil War
Theodore Roosevelt Association
369th Veterans Association
United Service Organizations, Incorporated
United States Capitol Historical Society
United States Olympic Committee
United States Submarine Veterans of World War II
Veterans of Foreign Wars of the United States
Veterans of World War I of the United States of America, Incorporated
Vietnam Veterans of America, Inc.
Women's Army Corps Veterans Association

Source: 36 U.S.C., Subtitle II, Part B

Appendix K

U.S. Supreme Court Chief Justices and Associate Justices Since 1900

Name	Years of service	State appointed from	Appointing president	Age appointed	Political affiliation
Chief Justices of the Supreme Court					
Melville Weston Fuller	1888–1910	Illinois	Grover Cleveland	55	Democrat
Edward Douglass White	1910–1921	Louisiana	William H. Taft	65	Democrat
William Howard Taft	1921–1930	Connecticut	Warren G. Harding	64	Republican
Charles Evan Hughes	1930–1941	New York	Herbert C. Hoover	68	Republican
Harlan Fiske Stone	1941–1946	New York	Franklin D. Roosevelt	69	Republican
Frederick Moore Vinson	1946–1953	Kentucky	Harry S. Truman	56	Democrat
Earl Warren	1953–1969	California	Dwight D. Eisenhower	62	Republican
Warren Earl Burger	1969–1986	Virginia	Richard M. Nixon	62	Republican
William Hubbs Rehnquist	1986–2005	Virginia	Ronald W. Reagan	62	Republican
John G. Roberts, Jr.	2005–	Maryland	George W. Bush	50	Republican
Associate Justices of the Supreme Court					
John Marshall Harlan	1877–1911	Kentucky	Rutherford B. Hayes	61	Republican

(*Continued*)

Name	Years of service	State appointed from	Appointing president	Age appointed	Political affiliation
Horace Gray	1882–1902	Massachusetts	Chester A. Arthur	54	Republican
David Josiah Brewer	1890–1910	Kansas	Benjamin Harrison	53	Republican
Henry Billings Brown	1891–1906	Michigan	Benjamin Harrison	55	Republican
George Shiras Jr.	1892–1903	Pennsylvania	Benjamin Harrison	61	Republican
Edward Douglas White	1894–1910	Louisiana	Grover Cleveland	49	Democrat
Rufus Wheeler Peckham	1896–1909	New York	Grover Cleveland	58	Democrat
Joseph McKenna	1898–1925	California	William McKinley	55	Republican
Oliver Wendell Holmes Jr.	1902–1932	Massachusetts	Theodore Roosevelt	61	Republican
William Rufus Day	1903–1922	Ohio	Theodore Roosevelt	54	Republican
William Henry Moody	1906–1910	Massachusetts	Theodore Roosevelt	53	Republican
Horace Harmon Lurton	1910–1914	Tennessee	William H. Taft	66	Democrat
Charles Evans Hughes	1910–1916	New York	William H. Taft	48	Republican
Willis Van Devanter	1911–1937	Wyoming	William H. Taft	52	Republican
Joseph Rucker Lamar	1911–1916	Georgia	William H. Taft	54	Democrat
Mahlon Pitney	1912–1922	New Jersey	William H. Taft	54	Republican
James Clark McReynolds	1914–1941	Tennessee	Woodrow Wilson	52	Democrat
Louis Dembitz Brandeis	1916–1939	Massachusetts	Woodrow Wilson	60	Democrat
John Hessin Clarke	1916–1922	Ohio	Woodrow Wilson	59	Democrat
George Sutherland	1922–1938	Utah	Warren G. Harding	60	Republican
Pierce Butler	1923–1939	Minnesota	Warren G. Harding	57	Democrat
Edward Terry Sanford	1923–1930	Tennessee	Warren G. Harding	58	Republican
Harlan Fiske Stone	1925–1941	New York	Calvin Coolidge	53	Republican
Owen Josephus Roberts	1930–1945	Pennsylvania	Herbert C. Hoover	55	Republican
Benjamin Nathan Cardozo	1932–1938	New York	Herbert C. Hoover	62	Democrat

(Continued)

Name	Years of service	State appointed from	Appointing president	Age appointed	Political affiliation
Hugo Lafeyette Black	1937–1971	Alabama	Franklin D. Roosevelt	51	Democrat
Stanley Forman Reed	1938–1957	Kentucky	Franklin D. Roosevelt	54	Democrat
Felix Frankfurter	1939–1962	Massachusetts	Franklin D. Roosevelt	57	Independent
William Orville Douglas	1939–1975	Connecticut	Franklin D. Roosevelt	41	Democrat
Frank Murphy	1940–1949	Michigan	Franklin D. Roosevelt	50	Democrat
James Francis Byrnes	1941–1942	South Carolina	Franklin D. Roosevelt	62	Democrat
Robert Hough-wout Jackson	1941–1954	New York	Franklin D. Roosevelt	49	Democrat
Wiley Blount Rutledge	1943–1949	Iowa	Franklin D. Roosevelt	49	Democrat
Harold Hitz Burton	1945–1958	Ohio	Harry S. Truman	57	Republican
Thomas Campbell Clark	1949–1967	Texas	Harry S. Truman	50	Democrat
Sherman Minton	1949–1956	Indiana	Harry S. Truman	59	Democrat
John Marshall Harlan	1955–1971	New York	Dwight D. Eisenhower	56	Republican
William J. Brennan Jr.	1956–1990	New Jersey	Dwight D. Eisenhower	50	Democrat
Charles Evans Whittaker	1957–1962	Missouri	Dwight D. Eisenhower	56	Republican
Potter Stewart	1958–1981	Ohio	Dwight D. Eisenhower	43	Republican
Byron Raymond White	1962–1993	Colorado	John F. Kennedy	45	Democrat
Arthur Joseph Goldberg	1962–1965	Illinois	John F. Kennedy	54	Democrat
Abe Fortas	1965–1969	Tennessee	Lyndon B. Johnson	55	Democrat
Thurgood Marshall	1967–1991	New York	Lyndon B. Johnson	59	Democrat
Harry A. Blackmun	1970–1994	Minnesota	Richard M. Nixon	62	Republican
Lew F. Powell, Jr.	1972–1987	Virginia	Richard M. Nixon	65	Democrat
William H. Rehnquist	1972–1986	Arizona	Richard M. Nixon	48	Republican
John Paul Stevens	1975–	Illinois	Gerald R. Ford	55	Republican
Sandra Day O'Connor	1981–2006	Arizona	Ronald W. Reagan	51	Republican
Antonin Scalia	1986–	Virginia	Ronald W. Reagan	50	Republican

(*Continued*)

Name	Years of service	State appointed from	Appointing president	Age appointed	Political affiliation
Anthony M. Kennedy	1988–	California	Ronald W. Reagan	52	Republican
David Hackett Souter	1990–	New Hampshire	George H.W. Bush	51	Republican
Clarence Thomas	1991–	Georgia	George H.W. Bush	43	Republican
Ruth Bader Ginsburg	1993–	New York	Bill Clinton	60	Democrat
Stephen G. Breyer	1994–	Massachusetts	Bill Clinton	56	Democrat
Samuel Anthony Alito Jr.	2006–	New Jersey	George W. Bush	55	Republican

Source: Elder Witt, *Guide to the U.S. Supreme Court,* 2nd ed. (Washington, DC: CQ Press, 1990).

Appendix L

MEMBER STATES OF THE UNITED NATIONS

The following is the alphabetical list of the 192 Member States of the United Nations with the date on which they joined.

Afghanistan (19 November 1946)
Albania (14 December 1955)
Algeria (8 October 1962)
Andorra (28 July 1993)
Angola (1 December 1976)
Antigua and Barbuda (11 November 1981)
Argentina (24 October 1945)
Armenia (2 March 1992)
Australia (1 November 1945)
Austria (14 December 1955)
Azerbaijan (2 March 1992)
Bahamas (18 September 1973)
Bahrain (21 September 1971)
Bangladesh (17 September 1974)
Barbados (9 December 1966)
Belarus (24 October 1945)
Belgium (27 December 1945)
Belize (25 September 1981)
Benin (20 September 1960)
Bhutan (21 September 1971)
Bolivia (14 November 1945)
Bosnia and Herzegovina (22 May 1992)
Botswana (17 October 1966)
Brazil (24 October 1945)
Brunei Darussalam (21 September 1984)
Bulgaria (14 December 1955)
Burkina Faso (20 September 1960)

Burundi (18 September 1962)
Cambodia (14 December 1955)
Cameroon (20 September 1960)
Canada (9 November 1945)
Cape Verde (16 September 1975)
Central African Republic (20 September 1960)
Chad (20 September 1960)
Chile (24 October 1945)
China (24 October 1945)
Colombia (5 November 1945)
Comoros (12 November 1975)
Congo, Republic of the (20 September 1960)
Costa Rica (2 November 1945)
Cote d'Ivoire (20 September 1960)
Croatia (22 May 1992)
Cuba (24 October 1945)
Cyprus (20 September 1960)
Czech Republic (19 January 1993)
Democratic People's Republic of Korea (17 September 1991)
Democratic Republic of the Congo (20 September 1960)
Denmark (24 October 1945)
Djibouti (20 September 1977)
Dominica (18 December 1978)
Dominican Republic (24 October 1945)
Ecuador (21 December 1945)
Egypt (24 October 1945)
El Salvador (24 October 1945)
Equatorial Guinea (12 November 1968)
Eritrea (28 May 1993)
Estonia (17 September 1991)
Ethiopia (13 November 1945)
Fiji (13 October 1970)
Finland (14 December 1955)
France (24 October 1945)
Gabon (20 September 1960)
Gambia (21 September 1965)
Georgia (31 July 1992)
Germany (18 September 1973)
Ghana (8 March 1957)
Greece (25 October 1945)
Grenada (17 September 1974)
Guatemala (21 November 1945)
Guinea (12 December 1958)
Guinea-Bissau (17 September 1974)
Guyana (20 September 1966)
Haiti (24 October 1945)
Honduras (17 December 1945)
Hungary (14 December 1955)
Iceland (19 November 1946)

India (30 October 1945)
Indonesia (28 September 1950)
Iran, Islamic Republic of (24 October 1945)
Iraq (21 December 1945)
Ireland (14 December 1955)
Israel (11 May 1949)
Italy (14 December 1955)
Jamaica (18 September 1962)
Japan (18 December 1956)
Jordan (14 December 1955)
Kazakhstan (2 March 1992)
Kenya (16 December 1963)
Kiribati (14 September 1999)
Kuwait (14 May 1963)
Kyrgyzstan (2 March 1992)
Lao People's Democratic Republic (14 December 1955)
Latvia (17 September 1991)
Lebanon (24 October 1945)
Lesotho (17 October 1966)
Liberia (2 November 1945)
Libyan Arab Jamahiriya (14 December 1955)
Liechtenstein (18 September 1990)
Lithuania (17 September 1991)
Luxembourg (24 October 1945)
Madagascar (20 September 1960)
Malawi (1 December 1964)
Malaysia (17 September 1957)
Maldives (21 September 1965)
Mali (28 September 1960)
Malta (1 December 1964)
Marshall Islands (17 September 1991)
Mauritania (27 October 1961)
Mauritius (24 April 1968)
Mexico (7 November 1945)
Micronesia, Federated States of (17 September 1991)
Moldova (2 March 1992)
Monaco (28 May 1993)
Mongolia (27 October 1961)
Montenegro (28 June 2006)
Morocco (12 November 1956)
Mozambique (16 September 1975)
Myanmar (19 April 1948)
Namibia (23 April 1990)
Nauru (14 September 1999)
Nepal (14 December 1955)
Netherlands (10 December 1945)
New Zealand (24 October 1945)
Nicaragua (24 October 1945)
Niger (20 September 1960)

Nigeria (7 October 1960)
Norway (27 November 1945)
Oman (7 October 1971)
Pakistan (30 September 1947)
Palau (15 December 1994)
Panama (13 November 1945)
Papua New Guinea (10 October 1975)
Paraguay (24 October 1945)
Peru (31 October 1945)
Philippines (24 October 1945)
Poland (24 October 1945)
Portugal (14 December 1955)
Qatar (21 September 1971)
Republic of Korea (17 September 1991)
Romania (14 December 1955)
Russian Federation (24 October 1945)
Rwanda (18 September 1962)
Saint Kitts and Nevis (23 September 1983)
Saint Lucia (18 September 1979)
Saint Vincent and the Grenadines (16 September 1980)
Samoa (15 December 1976)
San Marino (2 March 1992)
Sao Tome and Principe (16 September 1975)
Saudi Arabia (24 October 1945)
Senegal (28 September 1960)
Serbia (1 November 2000)
Seychelles (21 September 1976)
Sierra Leone (27 September 1961)
Singapore (21 September 1965)
Slovakia (19 January 1993)
Slovenia (22 May 1992)
Solomon Islands (19 September 1978)
Somalia (20 September 1960)
South Africa (7 November 1945)
Spain (14 December 1955)
Sri Lanka (14 December 1955)
Sudan (12 November 1956)
Suriname (4 December 1975)
Swaziland (24 September 1968)
Sweden (19 November 1946)
Switzerland (10 September 2002)
Syrian Arab Republic (24 October 1945)
Tajikistan (2 March 1992)
Thailand (16 December 1946)
The former Yugoslav Republic of Macedonia (8 April 1993)
Timor-Leste (27 September 2002)
Togo (20 September 1960)
Tonga (14 September 1999)
Trinidad and Tobago (18 September 1962)

Tunisia (12 November 1956)
Turkey (24 October 1945)
Turkmenistan (2 March 1992)
Tuvalu (5 September 2000)
Uganda (25 October 1962)
Ukraine (24 October 1945)
United Arab Emirates (9 December 1971)
United Kingdom of Great Britain and Northern Ireland (24 October 1945)
United Republic of Tanzania (14 December 1961)
United States of America (24 October 1945)
Uruguay (18 December 1945)
Uzbekistan (2 March 1992)
Vanuatu (15 September 1981)
Venezuela, Bolivarian Republic of (15 November 1945)
Viet Nam (20 September 1977)
Yemen (30 September 1947)
Zambia (1 December 1964)
Zimbabwe (25 August 1980)

Appendix M

MEMBERS OF THE WORLD TRADE ORGANIZATION

The following are the 151 members of the World Trade Organization (WTO) as of July 27, 2007 (with their dates of membership).

Albania (8 September 2000)
Angola (23 November 1996)
Antigua and Barbuda (1 January 1995)
Argentina (1 January 1995)
Armenia (5 February 2003)
Australia (1 January 1995)
Austria (1 January 1995)
Bahrain, Kingdom of (1 January 1995)
Bangladesh (1 January 1995)
Barbados (1 January 1995)
Belgium (1 January 1995)
Belize (1 January 1995)
Benin (22 February 1996)
Bolivia (12 September 1995)
Botswana (31 May 1995)
Brazil (1 January 1995)
Brunei Darussalam (1 January 1995)
Bulgaria (1 December 1996)
Burkina Faso (3 June 1995)
Burundi (23 July 1995)
Cambodia (13 October 2004)
Cameroon (13 December 1995)
Canada (1 January 1995)
Central African Republic (31 May 1995)
Chad (19 October 1996)
Chile (1 January 1995)
China (11 December 2001)

Colombia (30 April 1995)
Congo (27 March 1997)
Costa Rica (1 January 1995)
Cote d'Ivoire (1 January 1995)
Croatia (30 November 2000)
Cuba (20 April 1995)
Cyprus (30 July 1995)
Czech Republic (1 January 1995)
Democratic Republic of the Congo (1 January 1997)
Denmark (1 January 1995)
Djibouti (31 May 1995)
Dominica (1 January 1995)
Dominican Republican (9 March 1995)
Ecuador (21 January 1996)
Egypt (30 June 1995)
El Salvador (7 May 1995)
Estonia (13November 1999)
European Communities (1 January 1995)
Fiji (14 January 1996)
Finland (1 January 1995)
Former Yugoslav Republic of Macedonia (FYROM) (4 April 2003)
France (1 January 1995)
Gabon (1 January 1995)
The Gambia (23 October 1996)
Georgia (14 June 2000)
Germany (1 January 1995)
Ghana (1 January 1995)
Greece (1 January 1995)
Grenada (22 February 1996)
Guatemala (21 July 1995)
Guinea (25 October 1995)
Guinea Bissau (31 May 1995
Guyana (1 January 1995)
Haiti (30 January 1996)
Honduras (1 January 1995)
Hong Kong, China (1 January 1995)
Hungary (1 January 1995)
Iceland (1 January 1995)
India (1 January 1995)
Indonesia (1 January 1995)
Ireland (1 January 1995)
Israel (21 April 19950
Italy (1 January 1995)
Jamaica (9 March 1995)
Japan (1 January 1995)
Jordan (11 April 2000)
Kenya (1 January 1995)
Korea, Republic of (1 January 1995)
Kuwait (1 January 1995)

Kyrgyz Republic (20 December 1988)
Latvia (10 February 1999)
Lesotho (31 May 1995)
Liechtenstein (1 September 1995)
Lithuania (31 May 2001)
Luxembourg (1 January 1995)
Macao, China (1 January 1995)
Madagascar (17 November 1995)
Malawi (31 May 1995)
Malaysia (1 January 1995)
Maldives (31 May 1995)
Mali (31 May 1995)
Malta (1 January 1995)
Mauritania (31 May 1995)
Mauritius (1 January 1995)
Mexico (1 January 1995)
Moldova (26 July 2001)
Mongolia (29 January 1997)
Morocco (1 January 1995)
Mozambique (26 August 1995)
Myanmar (1 January 1995)
Namibia (1 January 1995)
Nepal (23 April 2004)
Netherlands (1 January 1995)
New Zealand (1 January 1995)
Nicaragua (3 September 1995)
Niger (13 December 1996)
Nigeria (1 January 1995)
Norway (1 January 1995)
Oman (9 November 2000)
Pakistan (1 January 1995)
Panama (6 September 1997)
Papua New Guinea (9 June 1996)
Paraguay (1 January 1995)
Peru (1 January 1995)
Philippines (1 January 1995)
Poland (1 July 1995)
Portugal (1 January 1995)
Qatar (13 January 1996)
Romania (1 January 1995)
Rwanda (22 May 1996)
Saint Kitts and Nevis (21 February 1996)
Saint Lucia (1 January 1995)
Saint Vincent & the Grenadines (1 January 1995)
Saudi Arabia (11 December 2005)
Senegal (1 January 1995)
Sierra Leone (23 July 1995)
Singapore (1 January 1995)
Slovak Republic (1 January 1995)

Slovenia (30 July 1995)
Solomon Islands (26 July 1996)
South Africa (1 January 1995)
Spain (1 January 1995)
Sri Lanka (1 January 1995)
Suriname (1 January 1995)
Swaziland (1 January 1995)
Sweden (1 January 1995)
Switzerland (1 July 1995)
Chinese Taipei (1 January 2002)
Tanzania (1 January 1995)
Thailand (1 January 1995)
Togo (31 May 1995)
Tonga (27 July 2007)
Trinidad and Tobago (1 March 1995)
Tunisia (29 March 1995)
Turkey (26 March 1995)
Uganda (1 January 1995)
United Arab Emirates (10 April 1996)
United Kingdom (1 January 1995)
United States of America (1 January 1995)
Uruguay (1 January 1995)
Venezuela (Bolivarian Republic of) (1 January 1995)
Vietnam (11 January 2007)
Zambia (1 January 1995)
Zimbabwe (5 March 1995)

Appendix N

UNITED STATES EMBASSIES

Afghanistan
Albania
Algeria
Angola
Argentina
Armenia
Australia
Austria
Azerbaijan
Bahamas
Bahrain
Bangladesh
Barbados
Belarus
Belgium
Belize
Benin
Bolivia
Bosnia and Herzegovina
Botswana
Brazil
Brunei
Bulgaria
Burkina Faso
Burundi
Cambodia
Cameroon
Canada
Cape Verde
Central African Republic
Chad
Chile

China
Colombia
Congo (Democrat Republic)
Congo (Republic)
Costa Rica
Cote d'Ivoire
Croatia
Cyprus
Czech Republic
Denmark
Djibouti
Dominican Republic
East Timor
Ecuador
Egypt
El Salvador
Equatorial Guinea
Eritrea
Estonia
Ethiopia
Fiji
Finland
France
Gabon
Gambia
Georgia
Germany
Ghana
Greece
Grenada
Guatemala
Guinea

Guyana
Haiti
Holy See (Vatican City)
Honduras
Hungary
Iceland
India
Indonesia
Iraq
Ireland
Israel
Italy
Jamaica
Japan
Jordan
Kazakhstan
Kenya
Korea
Kuwait
Kyrgyzstan
Laos
Latvia
Lebanon
Lesotho
Liberia
Lithuania
Luxembourg
Macedonia
Madagascar
Malawi
Malaysia
Mali

Malta
Marshall Islands
Mauritania
Mauritius
Mexico
Micronesia
Moldova
Mongolia
Montenegro
Morocco
Mozambique
Myanmar
Namibia
Nepal
Netherlands
New Zealand
Nicaragua
Niger
Nigeria
Norway
Oman
Pakistan
Palau
Panama

Papua New Guinea
Paraguay
Peru
Philippines
Poland
Portugal
Qatar
Romania
Russia
Rwanda
Samoa
Saudi Arabia
Senegal
Serbia
Sierra Leone
Singapore
Slovakia
Slovenia
South Africa
Spain
Sri Lanka
Sudan
Suriname
Swaziland

Sweden
Switzerland
Syria
Tajikistan
Tanzania
Thailand
Togo
Trinidad and Tobago
Tunisia
Turkey
Turkmenistan
Uganda
Ukraine
United Arab Emirates
United Kingdom
Uruguay
Uzbekistan
Venezuela
Vietnam
Yemen
Zambia
Zimbabwe

BIBLIOGRAPHY

Abrasom, Paul, and David Rohde. 2003. *Change and Continuity in the 2000 and 2002 Elections.* Washington, DC: CQ Press.

Biersack, Bob, Ian Stirton, Kelly Huff, and George Smaragdis. 2006. *PAC Financial Activity Increases.* Washington, DC: Federal Election Commission. Retrieved September 1, 2007, from http://www.fec.gov/press/press2006/20060828pac/20060830pac.html

Board of Governors of the Federal Reserve System. 2005. *The Federal Reserve System: Purposes and Functions.* Washington, DC: U.S. Federal Reserve System. Available at: http://www .federalreserve.gov/pf/pdf/pf_1.pdf

Board of Governors of the Federal Reserve System. 2007. *Report on Foreign Portfolio Holdings of U.S. Securities as of June 30, 2006.* New York: Federal Reserve Bank of New York, Department of the Treasury.

Bureau of Alcohol, Tobacco, Firearms, and Explosives. 2007. *About ATF.* Washinton, DC: U.S. Department of Justice. Retrieved August 1, 2007, from http://www.atf.treas.gov/ related.htm

Burton, Michael, and Daniel Shea. 2002. *Campaign Mode: Strategy, Leadership, and Successful Elections.* Lanham, MD: Rowman & Littlefield.

Central Intelligence Agency. 2007. *About CIA.* Washington. DC: Central Intelligence Agency Office of Public Affairs. Retrieved December 24, 2007, from http://www.careers.state .gov/officer/index.html

Cheeseman, Henry R. 2007. *Business Law: Legal Environment, Online Commerce, Business Ethics, and International Issue,* 6th ed. Upper Saddle River, NJ: Pearson Prentice Hall.

Collier, Christopher and James Collier. 1986. *Decisions in Philadelphia: The Constitution Convention of 1787.* New York: Random House.

Comiskey, Michael. 2004. *The Judging of Supreme Court Nominees.* Lawrence: University of Kansas Press.

Committee on Rules. 2008. *Summary of the Byrd Rule.* Washingtn, DC: U.S. House of Representatives. Retrieved January 4, 2008, from http://www.rules.house.gov/Archives/ byrd_rule.htm

Congressional Research Service. 2001. *Treaties and Other International Agreements: The Role of the United States Senate.* Wasihngton, DC: Library of Congress, Congressional Research Service.

Corrado, Anthony, Thomas Mann, Daniel Ortiz, and Trevor Potter. 2005. *The New Campaign Finance Sourcebook.* Washington, DC: Brookings Institute.

Coven, Martha, and Richard Kogan. 2007. *Introduction to the Federal Budget Process.* Washington, DC: Center for Budget and Policy Priorities.

Dahl, Robert. 2002. *How Democratic Is the American Constitution.* New Haven, CT: Yale University Press.

The Democratic National Committee. 2008. *The Democratic Party: What We Stand For.* Washington, DC: Democratic National Committee. Retrieved January 31, 2008, from http://www.democrats.org/a/party/stand.html

DiClerico, Robert E. (Ed.). 2000. *Campaigns and Elections in America.* Upper Saddle River, NJ: Prentice Hall.

Dodd, Lawrence, and Bruce Oppenheimer (Eds.). 2004. *Congress Reconsidered.* Washington, DC: CQ Press.

Ellis, Joseph. 2002. *Founding Brothers: The Revolutionary Generation.* New York: Knopf.

Environmental Protection Agency. 2007. *About EPA: What We Do.* Washington, DC: Environmental Protection Agency. Retrieved November 26, 2007, from http://www.epa.gov/epahome/aboutepa.htm

"Executive Orders Disposition Tables Index." 2008. Available at http://www.archives.gov/federal-register/executive-orders/disposition.html

Farazmand, Ali. 1997. *Modern Systems of Government: Exploring the Role of Bureaucrats and Politicians.* Sage Publications: Thousand Oaks, California.

Federal Bureau of Investigation. 2003. *Federal Bureau of Investigation Strategic Plan, 2004–2009.* Washington, DC: U.S. Department of Justice.

Federal Election Commission. 2007a. *Campaign Finance Reports and Data.* Washington, DC: Federal Election Commission. Retrieved April 15, 2007, from http://www.fec.gov/disclosure.shtml

Federal Election Commission. 2007b. *Presidential Election Campaign Fund (PECF).* Washington, DC: Federal Election Commission. Retrieved September 21, 2007, from http://www.fec.gov/press/bkgnd/fund.shtml

Financial Management Service. 2007 (September). *Treasury Bulletin.* Washington, DC: U.S. Department of the Treasury. Available at http://www.fms.treas.gov/bulletin/index.html

Food Safety and Inspection Service. 2007. *About FSIS.* Washington, DC: U.S. Department of Agriculture. Retrieved July 26, 2007, from http://www.fsis.usda.gov/About_FSIS/Agency_History/index.asp

Friedman, Milton and Walter W. Heller. 1969. *Monetary versus Fiscal Policy.* New York: Norton.

Goff, Michael. 2004. *The Money Primary: The New Politics of the Early Presidential Nomination Process.* Lanham, MD: Rowman & Littlefield.

Gould, Lewis. 2005. *The Most Exclusive Club: A History of the Modern United States Senate.* New York: Basic Books.

Graham, John D. 2001 (September 20). *Memorandum for the President's Management Council: Presidential Review of Agency Rulemaking by OIRA.* Washington, DC: Office of Management and Budget.

Greenberg, Ellen. 1997. *The Supreme Court Explained.* New York: Norton.

Greider, William. 1987. *Secrets of the Temple: How the Federal Reserve Runs the Country.* New York: Simon & Schuster.

Hamilton , Lee. 2004. *How Congress Works and Why You Should Care.* Bloomington: Indiana University Press.

Harrington, Michael. 1994. *The Other America.* New York: MacMillan.

Heniff, Bill Jr. 2003. *The Congressional Budget Process Timetable.* Washington, DC: The Library of Congress, Congressional Research Service.

House Committee on International Relations and Senate Committee on Foreign Relations. 2003. *Legislation on Foreign Relations Through 2002*, Vols. 1A and 1B. Washington, DC: U.S. Government Printing Office.

House Committee on Standards of Official Conduct. 1992. *Ethics Manual for Members, Officers, and Employees of the U.S. House of Representatives* (53-077). Washington, DC: U.S. Government Printing Office.

Internal Revenue Service. 2007a. *2006 Federal Tax Rate Schedules*. Washington, DC: U.S. Department of the Treasury. Retrieved December 1, 2007, from http://www.irs.gov/formspubs/article/0,,id=150856,00.html.

Internal Revenue Service. 2007b. *The Agency, its Mission and Statutory Authority*. Washington, DC: U.S. Department of the Treasury. Retrieved November 23, 2007, from http://www.irs.gov/irs/article/0,,id=98141,00.html.

Johnson, Paul. 1997. *A History of the American People*. New York: Harper Collins.

Judicial Conference of the United States: Committee on Codes of Conduct. 2006. *Ethics Essentials: A Primer for New Judges on Conflicts, Outside Activities, and Other Potential Pitfalls*. Washington, DC: Office of General Counsel, Administrative Office of the United States Courts.

Justice, S. Craig, and Maureen Burton. 1988. *Economics*. New York: Harper and Row.

Keck, Thomas. 2004. *The Most Activist Supreme Court in History*. Chicago: University of Chicago Press.

Keith, Robert. 2004. *The Budget Reconciliation Process: The Senate's "Byrd Rule."* Washington, DC: The Library of Congress, Congressional Research Service.

Kelman, Steven. 1987. *Making Public Policy: A Hopeful View of American Government*. New York: Basic Books.

Litwak, Robert. 2000. *Rogue States and U.S. Foreign Policy*. Washington, DC: Woodrow Wilson Center Press and John Hopkins University Press.

Madison, James. 1787 (November 22). The utility of the union as a safeguard against domestic faction and insurrection. *The Federalist*, No. 10.

Margesson, Rhoda. 2006. *International Crisis and Disasters: U.S. Humanitarian Assistance, Budget Trends, and Issues for Congress*. Washington, DC: Library of Congress, Congressional Research Service.

Matlin, Mary, and James Carville. 1994. *All's Fair in Love, War, and Running for President*. New York: Random House and Simon & Schuster.

Mecham, Leondas Ralph. 2003. *Understanding the Federal Courts*. Washington, DC: Office of Judges Programs, Administrative Office of the U.S. Courts.

Mosley, Raymond A., and John W. Carlin. 2002. *The United States Government Manual 2002/2003*. Washington, DC: Office of the Federal Register, National Archives and Records Administration.

Nincic, Miroslav. 2005. *Renegades Regimes: Confronting Deviant Behavior in World Politics*. New York: Columbia University Press.

Office of the Federal Register. 2002. *The United States Government Manual, 2002–2003*. Washington, DC: National Archives and Records Administration.

Office of Management and Budget. 2007a. *Historical Tables, Budget of the United States Government, Fiscal Year 2008*. Superintendent of Documents, Washington, DC: U.S. Government Printing Office. Retrieved December 30, 2007, from http://origin.www.gpoaccess.gov/usbudget/fy08/pdf/hist.pdf

Office of Management and Budget. 2007b. *OMB's Mission*. Washington, DC: The White House. Retrieved December 27, 2007, from http://www.whitehouse.gov/omb/organization/role.html

Office of the Under Secretary of Defense. Comptroller. 2003. *Operation and Maintenance Overview, April 2003: FY 2004 Budget Estimates*. Washington, DC: Department of Defense.

Oleszek, Walter. 2004. *Congressional Procedures and the Policy Process*. Washington, DC: CQ Press.

Olson, William J., P.C., Attorneys at Law. 1999 (October 27). William J. Olson, testimony to the Committee on Rules, Subcommittee on Legislative and Budget Process, The Impact of Executive Orders on the Legislative Process: Executive Lawmaking? Available at http://www.cato.org/testimony/ct-wo102799.html

"Party History." 2008. Available at http://www.democrats.org/a/party/history.html

Polsby, Nelson and Aaron Wildavsky. 2000. *Presidential Elections*. New York: Scribner's.

Press and Information Office of the Federal Government. 2008. *G8 – Challenges and achievements*. G8: Heiligendamm, Germany. Retrieved January 18, 2008, from http://www.g-8.de/Webs/G8/EN/Homepage/home.html

Ragone, Nick. 2004. *The Everything American Government Book*. Avon, MA: Adams Media.

Rakove, Jack. 1996. *Original Meanings: Politics and Ideas in the Making of the Constitution*. New York: Vintage Press.

"The Republican Party—GOP History." 2008. Available at http:///www.gop.com./About/AboutRead.aspx?Guid=a747a888-0ae6-4441-94f4-2a3ab561f872

Rothkopf, David. 2005. *Running the World: The Inside Story of the National Security Council and the Architects of American Power*. New York: Public Affairs Press.

Rubin, Irene S. 2000. *The Politics of Public Budgeting*. New York: Chatham House.

Saturno, James V. 2004. *The Congressional Budget Process: A Brief Overview*. Washington, DC: The Library of Congress, Congressional Research Service.

Savage, James. 1988. *Balanced Budgets and American Politics*. Ithaca, NY: Cornell University Press.

Scheb, John M., and John M. Scheb, II. 2005. *Law and the Administrative Process*. Belmont, CA: Thomas Wadsworth.

Simon, James. 2002. *What Kind of Nation: Thomas Jefferson, John Marshall, and the Epic Struggle to Create a United States*. New York: Simon & Schuster.

Stanton, Elizabeth Cady. 1889. *A History of Woman Suffrage*. Rochester, NY: Fowler and Wells.

Tarnoff, Curt, and Larry Nowels. 2005. *Foreign Aid: An Introductory Overview of U.S. Programs and Policy* (Order Code 98-916). Washington, DC: The Library of Congress, Congressional Research Service.

Tarr, G. Alan. 2006. *Judicial Process and Judicial Policymaking*, 4th ed. Belmont, CA: Thomson Wadsworth.

United Nations. 1945. *Charter of the United Nations*. New York: United Nations.

United Nations Security Council. 2007. *Functions and Powers*. New York: United Nations. Retrieved December 25, 2007, from http://www.un.org/Docs/sc/unsc_functions.html

United States Agency for International Development. 2002. *Foreign Aid in the National Interest: Promoting Freedom, Security, and Opportunity*. Washington, DC: United States Agency for International Development.

"United States Code: Main Page." 2008. Available at http://www.gpoaccess.gov/uscode

U.S. Census Bureau. 2000. *Census 2000 Apportionment Data Released*. Washington, DC: U.S. Department of Commerce, December 8. Retrieved April 29, 2007, from http://www.census.gov/population/cen2000/tab01.pdf

U.S. Census Bureau. 2007. *Foreign Trade Statistics*. Washington, DC: U.S. Census Bureau. Retrieved September 27, 2007, from http://www.census.gov/foreign-trade/statistics/highlights/top/top0612.html

U.S. Commission on Civil Rights. 2007. *Mission*. Washington, DC: U.S. Commission on Civil Rights. Retrieved July 4, 2007, from http://www.usccr.gov/

U.S. Department of State, Publication 1983. *Peace and War: United States Foreign Policy, 1931–1941* (Washington, D.C.: U.S. Government Printing Office, 1943, pp 265–271.

U.S. Department of State. 2001 (November 13). Detention, Treatment, and Trial of Certain Non-Citizens in the War Against Terrorism. Washington, DC: White House Press Release, Office of the Spokesman. Available at http://www.state.gov.coalition/cr/prs/6077/htm

U.S. Department of State. 2007a. *Careers Representing America*. Washington, DC: Department of State. Retrieved December 24, 2007, from http://www.careers.state.gov/officer/index.html

U.S. Department of State. 2007b. *Mission Statement*. Washington, DC: Department of State. Retrieved September 1, 2007, from http://www.state.gov/s/d/rm/rls/dosstrat/2004/23503.htm

U.S. Equal Employment Opportunity Commission. 2003. *Federal Laws Prohibiting Job Discrimination: Questions and Answers*. Washington, DC: U.S. Equal Employment Opportunity Commission.

U.S. Equal Employment Opportunity Commission. 2004. *Discriminatory Practices*. Washington, DC: EEOC. Retrieved April 1, 2007, from http://www.eeoc.gov/abouteeo/overview_practices.html

U.S. Food and Drug Administration. 2007. *History of the FDA*. Washington, DC: U.S. Department of Health and Human Services. Retrieved July 21, 2007, from http://www.fda.gov/oc/history/historyoffda/default.htm

U.S. Office of Personnel Management. 2006 (September 30). *Profile of Federal Civilian Non-Postal Employees*. Washington, DC: U.S. Office of Personnel Management. Retrieved July 4, 2007, from http://www.opm.gov/feddata/html/prof0906.asp

U.S. Office of Personnel Management. 2007. *Employment and Trends*. Retrieved April 14, 2007, from http://www.opm.gov/feddata/html/2007/january/table2.asp

U.S. Senate Select Committee on Ethics. 2003. *Senate Ethics Manual: 2003 Edition*. Washington, DC: U.S. Government Printing Office.

U.S. Supreme Court. 2008. Bound Volumes. Available at http://www.supremecourtus.gov/opinions/boundvolumes/html

Weber, Max. 1946. *Essays in Sociology*. New York: Oxford University Press.

Whitaker, L. Paige. 2007. *Congressional Redistricting: The Constitutionality of Creating an At-Large District* (Order Code RS22628). Washington, DC: Library of Congress, Congressional Research Service.

The White House. 2002. *The National Security Strategy of the United States of America*. Washington, DC: The White House.

The White House. 2008. *The Executive Office of the President*. Washingtn, DC: The White House. Retrieved January 30, 2008, from http://www.whitehouse.gov/government/eop.html

White House Office of Faith-Based and Community Initiatives. 2003. *Guidance to Faith-Based and Community Organizations on Partnering with the Federal Government*. Washington, DC: White House Office of Faith-Based and Community Initiatives.

White House Office of the Press Secretary. 1996 (October 2). *Statement by the President*. Washington, DC: The White House Office.

Witt, Elder. 1990. *Guide to the U.S. Supreme Court*, 2nd ed. Wasihngton, DC: CQ Press.

Woolley, John T., and Peters, Gerhard, *The American Presidency Project* [online]. Santa Barbara, CA: University of California (hosted), Gerhard Peters (database). Retrieved May 28, 2007, from http://www.presidency.ucsb.edu/ws/?pid=14927

Woolley, John T., and Peters, Gerhard, *The American Presidency Project* [online]. Santa Barbara, CA: University of California (hosted), Gerhard Peters (database). Retrieved May 28, 2007, from http://www.presidency.ucsb.edu/ws/?pid=8545

World Bank. 2007. *World Development Indicators Database, World Bank, 1 July 2007.* Washington, DC: The World Bank. Retrieved December 15, 2007, from http://siteresources .worldbank.org/DATASTATISTICS/Resources/GDP.pdf

WTO Information and Media Relations Division. 2007. *The World Trade Organization.* Geneva: World Trade Organization.

Zelizer, Julian. 2004. *On Capitol Hill: The Struggle to Reform Congress and Its Consequences, 1948–2000.* Cambridge: Cambridge University Press.

LEGAL CASES CITED

A.L.A. Schecter Poultry Corp. v. United States, 295 U.S. 495 (1935).
Allegheny County v. Greater Pittsburgh ACLU, 492 U.S. 573 (1989).
Baker v. Carr, 369 U.S. 186 (1962).
Brown v. Board of Education of Topeka, 347 U.S. 483 (1954).
Buckley v. Valeo, 424 U.S. 1 (1976).
California Democratic Party v. Jones, 530 U.S. 567 (2000).
Chamber of Commerce of the United States, et al, v. Reich, 74 F.3d 1322 (D.C. Cir. 1996).
Charles River Bridge v. Warren Bridge, 36 U.S. 420 (1837).
City of Richmond v. Croson, 488 U.S. 469 (1989).
Dred Scott v. Sandford, 60 U.S. 393 (1857).
Edwards v. Aquillard, 482 U.S. 578 (1987).
Engel v. Vitale, 370 U.S. 421 (1962).
Fletcher v. Peck, 10 U.S. 87 (1810).
Gregg v. Georgia, 428 U.S. 153 (1976).
Grutter v. *Bollinger*, 539 U.S. 306 (2003).
Ledbetter v. Goodyear Tire & Rubber Co, 550 U.S.___ (2007).
Loving v. Virginia, 388 U.S. 1 (1967).
Marbury v. Madison, 5 U.S. 137 (1803).
Miller v. California, 413 U.S. 15 (1973).
Miranda v. Arizona, 384 U.S. 436 (1966).
Mistretta v. United States, 488 U.S. 361 (1989).
Munn v. Illinois, 94 U.S. 113 (1877).
Oncale v. Sundowner Offshore Services, Incorporated, 523 U.S. 75 (1998).
Plessy v. Ferguson, 163 U.S. 537 (1896).
Pollock v. Farmers' Lock & Trust Co., 157 U.S. 429 (1895).
Regents of the University of California v. Bakke, 438 U.S. 265 (1978).
Roe v. Wade, 410 U.S. 113 (1973).
Roth v. United States, 354 U.S. 476 (1957).
Standard Oil Co. of New Jersey v. United States, 221 U.S. 1 (1911).
Stone v. Graham, 449 U.S. 39 (1980).
Torcaso v. Watkins, 367 U.S. 488 (1961).
United States v. Microsoft, 87 F. Supp 2d 30 (D.D.C. 2000).
United States v. Nixon, 418 U.S. 683 (1974).
Utah et al. v. Evans, Secretary of Commerce, 536 U.S. 452 (2002).
Youngstown Sheet and Tube Co. v. Sawyer, 343 U.S. 579 (1952).

Index

About the Authors

GLENN L. STARKS has more than 15 years of experience in government procurement, most recently in his current position as Strategic Material Sourcing Program Manager, Defense Logistics Agency, and prior to that as Chief of Planning and Requirements, Defense Supply Center Richmond. He has written extensively on public administration and American politics and holds a doctorate in Public Policy and Administration from Virginia Commonwealth University's L. Douglas Wilder School of Government and Public Affairs. He has taught graduate courses at Georgia Southern University in Organizational Behavior, Managing Small Cities and Counties, and Public Law and Administration.

F. ERIK BROOKS is an Associate Professor of Political Science at Georgia Southern University. He holds a doctorate in Public Policy and Administration from Virginia Commonwealth University's L. Douglas Wilder School of Government and Public Affairs. He has written extensively on public administration, American politics, and African American history. He has taught undergraduate courses in American Government, Foundations of the Contemporary World, the United States Presidency, African-American Politics, Southern Politics, and the Civil Rights Movement. He has taught graduate courses in Public Administration, Public Personnel, Organization Behavior, Nonprofit Management, Intergovernmental Relations, Diversity, and Ethics.